URBAN SPACE

ROB KRIER

URBAN SPACE

(STADTRAUM)

Foreword by Colin Rowe

In memory of Camillo Sitte
Written for students of architecture
Dedicated to my brother Leon
My deepest gratitude to Gudrun for her criticism, corrections and patience

First published in the USA in 1979 by
RIZZOLI INTERNATIONAL PUBLICATIONS, INC.
712 Fifth Avenue/New York 10019

First published in German in 1975
Translated by Christine Czechowski and George Black

Printed and bound in Great Britain

CONTENTS

FOREWORD
by Colin Rowe

In the jungle-like politics of architectural self advertisement it has become a misfortune of the late Emil Kaufman's great achievement, inadvertently and considerably after his death, to have sponsored a highly edited and, often, somewhat mindless version of neo-classicism. Was it *Von Ledoux bis Le Corbusier* or was it *Three Revolutionary Architects* which gave the cue? And it was probably the latter, with its so desirable connotations of dynamic and anti-academic insurrection. For, when the architectural Boy Scout camps of the 1920s (La Sarraz and all the rest) could be seen as equipped with a respectable, and still revolutionary, pedigree, then the possibilities of annexation became endless. For, then, it became possible to be interested in the late eighteenth century without seeming to be desperately old hat, and for a series of hero figures to be observed. And so, and after certain strange leaps of the mind, Ledoux-Boullée was followed by the constellation of Saint Simon, Comte and Fourier and then, after the whole panoply of the French socialist tradition became exposed, by Karl Marx and the so curious notion that a William Morris society might be constructed out of French neo-classical components; and one might abbreviate the possible process of argument by which all this may have come about:

With the nitty-gritty of the Welfare State and the appalling bureaucratic details of pseudo-Capitalist administration we will have nothing to do; instead, we will simplify, abstract and project to the degree of extravagance a highly restricted, private and not very hospitable version of what the good society might be assumed to be; we will give a nod to Kaufmann; we will give three muted cheers for the Stalinallée; we will adore the manifesto pieces of Boullée; we will (mostly) refuse to observe the built work of Soane; instead, and if necessary, we will unroll a few hundred yards of neutral Adolf Loos facade, build a lot of little towers and stand around on top of them a quantity of Ledoux villas, wave quietly but not too exuberantly to Louis Kahn (congratulations on the Trenton Bath House), insinuate a reference to the metaphysic of Giorgio de Chirico, display a conversance with Leonidov, become highly enthusiastic about the more evocative aspects of Art Deco, exhibit the intimidation of curtains waving in the wind, and, then, gently warm up the ensuing goulash in the *pastoso* of Morandi.

But, if here is displayed the solution (with all its atavistic seductions) fresh from Milano-Venezia, one might also be prompted to ask whether its Marxism is not a little too romantic and its presumptions a little too premature. Apropos of the so-called New York Five and their alleged intellectualistic involutions, Aldo Giurgola spoke of *the discreet charm of the bourgeoisie;* and about this other context of gestures, postures, antics which has just been abruptly summarized, where social conscience, social agony and high fashion are almost inextricably interrelated, just what is there that needs to be said? That, although the stage set is almost completely changed from that of a few years ago, the form of words which the players use is, in some way, distressingly familiar?

For, the idea that 'art stopped short at the cultivated court of the Empress Josephine' has, in one form or another, been around for a considerable time; and, recently, though in a different framework of values, it has been given fresh currency. But, of course, even in 1881, W. S. Gilbert's endearing, philistine and distinctly inadequate satire of the miscellaneous aesthetes who populate the pages of *Patience* disclosed a quasi-critical orientation which was in no way new.

Something went wrong in 1714, or 1750, or 1789, or 1804, with the beginning of the Georgian era or at its end, with the death of Queen Anne or the accession of Queen Victoria, with Andrew Jackson, with Ulysses S. Grant, with the discovery of Pompeii, with the emergence of the Roman Empire, with the collapse of the Roman Empire, with the decline of the Middle Ages, with the appearance of Brunelleschi, or Michelangelo, or Inigo Jones, or Borromini. One can rearrange the dates, rename the style phases, reidentify the personalities which decorate this scenario but the basic structure of what, after all, must still be historical myth will remain surprisingly consistent and intact. At some moment in time there occurred a cessation of meaningful artistic production and a catastrophic decline in all sense of value. Standards of craftsmanship were abruptly terminated. Collective endeavour declined. Society became atomised and the individual alienated. Disassociation of sensibility ensued and tragic schism between feeling and thinking was the inevitable result. But, now, *nous avons changé tout cela.* For we, the protagonists of the new, have scrutinized and discriminated. We know the evil, we have the remedy, ours is the prescription; and, as for you, just you take a good look and a good listen.

Such, in its time, was one of the primary messages of modern architecture – a primary message of Walter Gropius, Sigfried Giedion, Le Corbusier and Nikolaus Pevsner. Only believe in this: and if you will but do so, the world will become re-integrated, the joys of craftsmanship restored and the wounds of society healed. But if, contributing to the litany of this myth, there have been many of the would-be self-consciously critical names of recent Western civilisation, it must still remain a particularly savage irony that modern architecture's most favored polemic has now been enlisted against modern architecture itself. For the locus of the historical rift valley is now shifted; the bad date is now 1923 – or thereabouts; the bad gestures/propositions are those of CIAM; and the really evil guys (the Pied Pipers who lead the children in the wrong direction and finally deposited them in a Carpathian wilderness, *terribly* dangerous and *ever* so far from home) are rapidly coming to be the bearers of just those names which, only the other day, seemed to be so firmly respectable and so highly established among the commemorators of architectural progress.

So, perhaps, we now inhabit a somewhat desperate Transylvanian landscape of the mind, lugubriously furnished with the wreckage of reputations and the debris of good intentions. Hamelin town is far away ('in Brunswick near famous Hanover City'); but, having been brought to our present destitution by the most charming of music, the most interesting of leaders, the most curious of subterranean routes, we can only feel disquieted, abused, disturbed and, being unable to forget the Hansel and Gretel toy town from out of which we were seduced, we can now only suspect the instrument of our temptation – the notion of an impeccable and 'scientific' solution through instant 'total' design – was itself no more than a species of late Biedermayer ornamental gingerbread. For, apparently, nobody – ever – was really very good, and nothing – ever – was really very true and, in the twentieth century, even those few who almost approached goodness, almost embodied truth, were invariably debauched by the flagrant influence of a local grandee – a capitalist Dracula, monstrous, sadic and perverse – who distorted the message and rendered its results utterly vain.

Or, at least, something like this seems to be among the many inherently inconsistent diagnoses of modern architecture's impending collapse; and, up to a point, this diagnosis is almost believable. But, it is surely not so much the credibility as it is the wholly conventional character of such argument which deserves attention. For, if in their implication that most of the cities of the world have been approximately wrecked via the agency of modern architecture the proponents of *architettura razionale* can only be entirely correct, then should it not seem strange that the style of argument, even the vocabulary of argument, in which these judgements are delivered – bourgeois angst, apocalyptic threat, incipient world transforming event, holistic deliverance – is representative of a critical strategy of which modern architecture should have made us only too sceptical? For, again, the decorations of the stage infer something significantly *avant garde*, while the libretto of the opera comes over as a standardized and entirely to be anticipated plot. To repeat: the bad date is now 1923, the good date is now 1974, or '75, or '76; and it is the persistence of an old argument, transferred from context to visual context and still presented as novelty which is here the profoundly disquieting factor. For what we are here presented with is something professing to be radical chic, elegant *fa figura*, social concern; and if, in terms of the visuals, what we receive is an engaging archaeology of the future, then, in terms of the verbals, the situation is much the same. *The verbals are antique;* and the problem of the symbiosis of antiquity and the would-be way-out, though not insuperable, is certainly considerable. For *avant garde* protestation (hey, look at our acrobatics!) and the eternal creakings of old verbal machinery are, in the end, not the best of all possible bedfellows; and, simply, the combination is less than respectably athletic.

Until recently when modern architecture, in spite of its longevity, was still, universally, proclaimed as 'new', almost any architect under the age of sixty (with appropriate achievements to his credit) was likely to be saluted and advertised as 'young' and the question 'But just how old does one have to be in order to become a young architect (?)' was scarcely ever propounded. For the legend of uncorrupted, incorruptible architectural youth (youth synonymous with the only quest worthwhile – the ongoing quest for the new and the agile) persisted as one of the most fundamental of fictions; and, indeed, the collusion between Peter Pan, Jugendstil, the Boy Scouts and the early Fascist '*giovinezza, giovinezza*' is likely to remain among the more observable phenomena of early twentieth century culture – perhaps part of the inevitable heritage of the *art nouveau.*

So it was an important idea – and a dangerous one; and, like many important – and dangerous – ideas, it has become fossilized and survives as no more than unexamined and tedious tradition: let us rather be potential than productive; let us be dynamic rather than introspective; let us prefer animation to reflection; let us condemn the unjust sophistications and special moral codes of established society; since Rousseau's noble savage (primordial energy uncontaminated by culture) is almost the same as Peter Pan (who is almost the same as the statue of Eros in Piccadilly Circus) then, in order to make *tabula rasa,* in order to disclose a *primitive* house and to engender a *future* society – redeemed, and of renewed aboriginal purity – let us proceed to mock, to injure and to destroy the existing.

Now the fiesta of destruction (one imagines broken bottles on a New Year's Eve in Naples) which has continued since the Enlightenment surely deserves to be applauded. For the most part it has been exhilarating; also it has resulted in previously undreamed of blessings; and as one attempts to imagine the condition of provincial society, *circa* 1770, in almost any small city in the world, then one can only say: Thank God for the ventilations which, over the last two hundred years, have been made!

But, at least for the impatient, the route of what might be conceived to be progress has still taken an extremely long time; and, of course, one of the major road blocks to emancipation has now become the fantasies which the architect entertains about himself, fantasies now little more than the platitudes of criticism, but, still, fantasies which, in their own day – now a very good many years ago – were conceived of as permanent, indeed dazzling, illuminations which were for ever to make visible the surface of a glorious *autostrada* leading to a crystalline social condition of limpid authenticity.

'And I John saw the Holy City, New Jerusalem, coming down from God out of heaven, . . . and the City lieth foursquare, and the length is as large as the breadth: . . . and the City was pure gold like unto clear glass . . . and the street of the City was *pure gold*, as it were transparent glass . . . and the City had no need of the sun, neither of the moon to shine in it: for the glory of God did lighten it, . . . and there shall in no wise enter into it anything that defileth, neither whatsoever worketh abomination or *maketh* a lie: but they which are are written in the Lamb's Book of Life.'

The vision of Final Judgement and Deliverance, of the Great Hallelujah, when equipped with a technological gloss, is, of course, immensely like in kind to the vision of the *ville radieuse* to be later experienced by Le Corbusier; and, if this later vision, of a world redeemed by architecture, is now severely discredited, it is still not too unreasonable to suggest that some eschatological framework of this kind still survives as the psychological underpinning of much currently fashionable architectural polemic – and particularly that of Italian origin. For this is a polemic which, professing to be coolly critical, is still, more often than not, evidently inflamed by notions of that glaring turbulent upsurge which will for ever release us from the stinking limitations of bourgeois culture and effectively initiate the millennial establishment.

And this (though, to a degree, charming and of a period) is surely something of a pity. For, if the advocates of *architettura razionale* (who are in great danger of flooding the market and inspiring a counter-wave of disgust) are able to make a highly apt critique of modern architecture's urbanistic failure and if this is of immense value, it does not automatically follow that *all* the physical achievements of modern architecture are to be condemned and that we are entirely obliged to return to a simplified and innocent world, *à la Laugier*, a species of ante-diluvian (and Marxist) *belle époque*, reminiscent more of Knossos than New York, in which strangely deserted piazzas, seemingly prepared for not yet to be anticipated rituals, in the meantime support a somewhat scanty population of mildly desperate hippies.

Indeed, it may be a rather curious commentary upon a contemporary failure of nerve that a merely abbreviated reconstitution of the nineteenth-century city, enticingly equipped with surrealistic overtones, is now so widely received as the most pregnant and potential of disclosures. For, though such a reconstitution is, in many ways, what is required, there are still inhibitions to be felt about the tricking out of Beaux-Arts plans with neo-primitive facades ('a poor thing but Minoan', as Sir Arthur Evans almost certainly did *not* say about his Cretan restorations) and there are still reserves of feeling (oddly Futurist and strangely technophile?) which will operate to prevent any such, immediate, dispensation.

So much could seem to be a highly negative series of remarks with which to open an introduction to the English edition of Rob Krier's *Stadtraum;* but they are not intended so to be interpreted. An implicit theme of Krier's book is a *rappel à l'Ordre.* It is an evident critique of 'planning', highway engineering, the urbanistic propositions of CIAM, of science fiction cities, populist do-it-yourself and townscape; and, if as such it is a book which one can only receive with sympathy and happiness, then the purpose of all the foregoing rather protracted observations is to suggest, not apropos of Rob Krier but apropos of the context to which, ostensibly, he has been assigned – the context of *architettura razionale* post-modernism and all the rest – that a recall to order need not directly involve the flushing out of both the baby and this bathwater, that we do not only revolve but also evolve, that if a reasonable object of criticism is certainly the cutting of modern architecture down to size, then it is slightly preposterous to attempt any such undertaking while still assenting to a particular mystique – the mystique of the critical date, of *Giovinezza*, of the *Zeitgeist*, of building as a version of physics, etc., etc.

Indeed, to attempt a critique of the modern movement, damning its physical embodiments while still concerned with the endorsement of its psychological virulence, one must finally say is a procedure so extravagantly half-witted as to defeat comprehension. At which stage, and mercifully, the time is now come to reverse the argument. We are confronted with a book, equipped with lots of visuals and not really too many words; but, if some of the visuals and some of the words display an affiliation, the book both impresses and invites and there are many specific things to be said about it. So like what to say?

That Rob Krier somehow doesn't fit, that he cannot rapidly be relegated to a category, might quite well be a first observation. For, if one can sense in this book a romantically Marxist and Italian connection and, if by many of its readers it will be placed in something very like the context of ideas which has already been noticed, this can then seem to be only a very small part of the whole. For Krier has produced a highly eclectic book which is evidently charged with conviction and a highly radical book which is eminently conservative in its tone. It is, perhaps, not a very highly self-conscious book. Its author is, maybe, a little too sure of his principles and a little too unconcerned in protecting himself against flank attacks, possibly a little more equivocal than he is aware. He dedicates his performance, rather surprisingly, to Sitte; he seems to owe a great deal to Stübben; he certainly owes very much to the urbanistic contributions of Matthias Ungers; his graphics oscillate between late nineteenth-century Old Fashioned and strip cartoon Pop; but, clearly, this is a book which has been put together with a controlled indignation and it is the quality of Rob Krier's quiet indignation, issuing in an exhaustive encyclopaedia of urban spaces, which one feels compelled and happy to salute.

For it is the destruction of Stuttgart which is, intrinsically, the anguished theme of this book; and it is the contemplation of this destruction – the juxtaposition of what *was*, what *is*, and what *might be* – which leads and obliges Krier to make spatial proposals, for the renewal of both practice and society. And in these terms, patently, Stuttgart is not simply Stuttgart. It is by no means a one time small *residenzstadt* lying in a fold of big hills and successively wiped out by heavy industry, allied bombs, planning blight, and simple silliness. Rather it is the type of any and every city of the world, destroyed by strange abstract agencies, the faceless, obtuse (and plausible) creatures of government and university. And how to argue with, how to inhibit the population of those bureaucracies which, supposing its judgement to be scientific, convinced of its intelligence and responsibility, unaware of how much its working theorems are derived from the wild men of forty to fifty years ago, is mostly unable to perceive either the reason or the necessity for argument?

Now it is an enormous merit of *Urban Space* that Krier neither considers, refuses, nor disdains, the possibility of discourse with such persons. He simply ignores it. He does not muddy or confuse his proposals with qualifications addressed to the incorrigible. He prefers that evidence should be submitted to the eye (with the assumption that the eye communicates with the other senses?). He has little use for the stimulants of the ear and the extensive deliveries of the mouth. He is essentially laconic. And, since the incorrigible of today are apt to become the docile sheep of tomorrow, almost certainly, by ignoring argument with them, Krier has produced a text book for 'planners' of the year 2000.

His techniques are subdued. He implies no critical neutrality (nor even its possibility). He has, really, very little to say about either 'science' or 'history'. (Though a victim of neither.) His approaches are completely the opposite of the rabble rousing strategies to be associated with the protagonists of modern architecture. Instead he comes on as a person of *détente*. Indeed, mostly he operates with apparent naivety (well just why not?) *and* great decisiveness. For, if this is clearly not a populist book (almost certainly it proposes a liberal Communist society conceived as almost acceptable to the former Kings of Wurttemberg) it is still a book concerned with an order which many innocent individuals of South German and Catholic upbringing might well be expected to understand.

So much, again, as belonging to its merits; but now it might be possible to speak of a neo-antique content which may, sometimes, be a little disturbing. And particularly this is evident in Krier's proposals for the vicinity of the Schloss, pp. 142–153, where one might be reminded of Mamie Eisenhower's alleged statement that things are no more like what they used to be than they ever were before. Here Krier publishes, p. 151, Von Thouret's solution of 1800, the condition as of 1972, then the city's proposals, then his own; and it is of interest to bring his own proposals into comparison with Sitte's suggestions for the Vienna Ring, p. 50. For are Sitte's suggestions significantly superior to the situation which he felt obliged to condemn? Are there not just *too* many forecourts? Is there not a *too* exaggerated preoccupation with space at the expense of object? And is not something like this also true of Krier's operations in the Charlottenplatz and the Schlossplatz? He is over-reacting, of course, to the present condition of these spaces; but, in his anxiety to provide them with adequate structure, in his anxiety to exceed the condition of 1800 – a highly interesting balance of space and object, order and accident, in which non-contiguous buildings are allowed to experience each other's magnetism – it might be felt that, to some extent, he recapitulates the anomalies of Sitte's proposals for Vienna.

But, if this is to go too far, to complicate by a conscientious excess of zeal, in another area of interest, that related to the texture of solids, it can also seem that Krier is reluctant to go far enough. And one refers to a condition of void-solid relationship which seems to derive from an undue preoccupation with intersecting movement systems and linear models and which is apt to leave what are alleged to be streets unsupported by a sufficient back-up of density.

This is a type of recurrent solution (particularly well illustrated on pp. 24–25) which is clearly propounded as normative but which is apt to instigate doubts as to what might really be the preferred route by which the observer/user would traverse these configurations. Would he or she, indeed, follow the somewhat relentless lines of the streets? Or would he or she be far more predisposed to hop from Palais Royal to Palais Royal, negotiating what is presented as the prime movement system with a combination of mild frustration and patience? For there is here a considerable problem as to what is public and what is private, what is major and what is secondary; and, if public spaces are said to occur at the intersections of prime movement, then there may be some scepticism as to whether these spaces could ever become animated when so extremely adjacent to an alternative and apparently much more charming route of travel. And this issue might be focused by proposing a Place Vendome and then proposing, in its immediate vicinity, the presence of no less than four Palais Royals, by making this proposal and then asking the question: *What*, in the process, has happened to the Place Vendome and *what, what* has happened to the Palais Royal?

This, no doubt, is an aspect of the problem of which is front and which is back, which part of the building belongs to the world of indisputably private idiosyncrasy and which possesses the proudly proclaimed status of the irrefutably public event, which side is random happening and which side is grandly generalized set piece? And this seems to be a question, involving the profitable intercourse between order and confusion, dress and undress, which Krier seems to be reluctant to entertain. But, if with Krier nearly everything has *only* a public facade (meaning nearly everything is equipped with the profusion of *two* equally representative vertical surfaces), if there is very little idea of one building surface being smooth, cursive and continuous and the other being bumpy, syncopated and staccato (the empirical constitution of the traditional city), there are many other instances – Le Corbusier's *maisons à redents*, Jellicoe's Motopia and Stirling's Runcorn – which might be considered as exactly illustrating the inherent difficulty of performing one of the most necessary of operations, *the discrimination of back and front*.

So Krier (like Le Corbusier and many others) largely fails to understand the *res privata*; but, if with him, the public front is an invariable, his solutions also have a decency all of their own. For, fundamentally, his book is an unashamed panegyric upon public fronts (he illustrates them by means of a somewhat enigmatic anthology of what appear to be Stuttgart high bourgeois houses of – give or take a few years – circa 1900); and, if Le Corbusier as an architect was, at bottom, very like this (so much of his architecture was a eulogium of public fronts, most of his urbanism was ostensibly the reverse), with regard to this issue *Krier comes through clean*.

He is not interested in factories and he is clearly infatuated by palaces. He would not propose a factory as an appropriate model for a student residence (Pavillon Suisse); but if, in these terms, he might be thinking of a Prince-Archbishop of Salzburg (building nice buildings but awfully cruel to Mozart), then he invariably sheers away from any such idea. Because, though the Kings of Württemberg and the Archbishops of Salzburg are evidently a large part of his ideal apparatus, then, equally evident is his great anxiety to check *all that* – the residue of the Holy Roman Empire, the panoply of the Almanach de Gotha – against the more 'rational' and philanthropic findings of a sensitive social democracy.

Reactions to this book can easily be ambivalent. In this book there are no Metabolists, no Kenzo Tange, no Futurists, no Technos, no Archigram, little trace of surrender to the romantic manifestations of scientism. Krier is enormously good at trees in the French style – and don't we need it? Krier is unaware of the virtues of congestion, a little too quietly ordered, too Apollonian, insufficiently Dionysiac. Isn't it all a bit like Albert Speer, relieved of his imperial mission and making far more intelligent demonstrations in the Germany of Metternich? Many of his minor spaces are elegant and excellent (Östereichischer Platz, pp. 123–31, Rotebühl Platz, pp. 118–9); but are not the outer suburban proposals a little too predictable and linear.

Such is a casual collection of American reactions to *Urban Space;* and they are mostly the reaction of students at Cornell, of persons familiar with the issues and, at the same time, agitated by them. But they are, probably, slightly more profound, sympathetic and elaborate reactions than are likely to be found elsewhere. For instance, in the cultural amnesia of the Germanic lands it would be greatly interesting to know how *Stadtraum* has been received; and, in the United Kingdom one might also, prospectively, wonder. But then how is this book likely to be received in the great North American theatre of ideas which is so turbulent, so classical in its ultimate bias and so eternally irrational?

To some persons, both in England and the Germanic lands, the question of North America will appear redundant. We have our liberalism, we have our conservatism, we have our quasi-Marxist postures: and just *what* else is there to talk about? But it is the great merit of this book to have transcended such noisy and smelly barriers, to be rooted in south Germany but to be addressing itself to a situation which knows no frontiers. For Rob Krier has here done a major thing. He has destroyed the *Zeilenbau* and restored the perimeter block. As a result of Krier, we reject Hilberseimer and return to think about the Karl Marx Hof in Vienna; and, if the Karl Marx Hof is scarcely what we are anxious to see, if we might want to qualify it, then this must be all to the good. For Rob Krier's book is remarkably unassuming and, in spite of obviously Marxian overtones, it prescribes solutions which are applicable anywhere and everywhere – including North America.

It is a book published in Germany in 1975 and the projects which it exhibits date back to 1971–72. So during much of this time something has faded – though not much; and, therefore, about this book one would finally like to say (as about much else) that, if only abstractions could be relaxed, more empirical material allowed to enter and a further generalisation to take place, then how happy one would be. And, no doubt how happy would be Robert Krier.

But the afterview is not very much allowed; and, meanwhile, imagine Krier's possible afterviews, what has here been done is constructive, suggestive and tremendously important.

CHAPTER 1

TYPOLOGICAL AND MORPHOLOGICAL ELEMENTS OF

THE CONCEPT OF URBAN SPACE

CHAPTER 1

TYPOLOGICAL AND MORPHOLOGICAL ELEMENTS OF THE CONCEPT OF URBAN SPACE

INTRODUCTION

The basic premise underlying this chapter is my conviction that in our modern cities we have lost sight of the traditional understanding of urban space. The cause of this loss is familiar to all city dwellers who are aware of their environment and sensitive enough to compare the town planning achievements of the present and the past and who have the strength of character to pronounce sentence on the way things have gone. This assertion alone is of no great service to town planning research. What has to be clearly defined is what should be understood by the term urban space and what meaning it holds within the urban structure, so that we can go on to examine whether the concept of urban space retains some validity in contemporary town planning and on what grounds. 'Space' in this context is a hotly disputed concept. It is not my intention here to generate a new definition but rather to bring its original meaning back into currency.

DEFINITION OF THE CONCEPT 'URBAN SPACE'

If we wish to clarify the concept of urban space without imposing aesthetic criteria, we are compelled to designate all types of space between buildings in towns and other localities as urban space.

This space is geometrically bounded by a variety of elevations. It is only the clear legibility of its geometrical characteristics and aesthetic qualities which allows us consciously to perceive external space as urban space.

The polarity of internal-external space is constantly in evidence in this chapter, since both obey very similar laws not only in function but also in form. Internal space, shielded from weather and environment is an effective symbol of privacy; external space is seen as open, unobstructed space for movement in the open air, with public, semi-public and private zones.

The basic concepts underlying the aesthetic characteristics of urban space will be expounded below and systematically classified by type. In the process, an attempt will be made to draw a clear distinction between precise aesthetic and confused emotional factors. Every aesthetic analysis runs the risk of foundering on subjective questions of taste. As I have been able to observe from numerous discussions on this topic, visual and sensory habits, which vary from one individual to the next, are augmented by a vast number of socio-political and cultural attitudes, which are taken to represent aesthetic truths. Accepted styles in art history – for example, baroque town plans, revolutionary architecture etc – are both useful and necessary.

However my observations indicate that they are almost always identified with the social structure prevailing at the time in question. Certainly it can scarcely be proved that, because of the wishes of the ruling classes and their artists, the stylistic canons of the period in European art history between 1600 and 1730 appeared almost to be determined by fate. Of course for the historian every period of history forms a unit with its own internal logic, which cannot be fragmented and interchanged with elements of other periods at will.

The creative person, such as the artist, may use a completely different method of approach. The decisions he makes in deploying his aesthetic skills are not always based on assumptions which can be unequivocally explained. His artistic 'libido' is of enormous importance here. The cultural contribution of an age develops on the basis of a highly complex pattern of related phenomena, which must subsequently be the subject of laborious research on the part of historians. This example throws us right into a complex problem which appears the same in whichever period of history we consider. We must discuss this example exhaustively before we start constructing our rational system. Each period in art history develops gradually out of the assimilated functional and formal elements which precede it. The more conscious a society is of its history, the more effortlessly and thoroughly it handles historical elements of style. This truism is important in as far as it legitimises the artist's relationship with the universally accepted wealth of formal vocabulary of all preceding ages – this is as applicable in the 20th as in the 17th century.

I do not wish to rally support for eclecticism, but simply to warn against an all too naive understanding of history, which has been guilty of such misjudgements as representing urban architecture amongst the Romans as markedly inferior to that of the Greeks, which from an historical point of view is simply not true. The same mistake persists today, as can be seen from attitude to the architecture of the 19th century.

Our age has a remarkably distorted sense of history, which can only be characterised as irrational. Le Corbusier's apparent battle against the 'Académie' was not so much a revolt against an exhausted, ageing school as the assumption of a pioneering stand in which he adopted its ideals and imbued them with a new and vigorous content.

This so-called 'pioneering act' was a pretended break with history, but in reality was an artistic falsehood. The facts were these: he abandoned the tradition current until then that art supported by the ruling classes enjoyed the stamp of legitimacy and, being at an advanced stage of development, materially shaped the periods which followed. It was a revolt at one remove, so to speak, for the 'Académie' lived on, and indeed came itself to share the same confused historical sense as the followers of the revolution.

I am speaking here about the modern age in general, and not about its exponents of genius who tower above the 'image of the age'. Rather than be indebted to elitist currents in art, the generation around the turn of the century sought new models. They found them in part in the folk art of other ages and continents, which had hitherto attracted little attention.

There began an unprecedented flurry of discovery of anonymous painting, sculpture, architecture, song and music of those peoples who were considered underdeveloped, and their contribution to culture was for the first time properly valued without regard to their stage of civilisation. Other artists sought their creative material in the realm of pure theory and worked with the basic elements of visual form and its potential for transformation (the 'abstracts'). Yet others found their material in social criticism and the denunciation of social injustice and carried out their mission using formally simple methods (the 'expressionists'). The break with the elitist artistic tradition was identical to the artist's struggle for emancipation from his patron – the ruling class and its cultural dictatorship – which had been brewing even before the French revolution.

The example of the baroque town layout has already been mentioned, and the question raised of the identity of form, content and meaning. We must be more exact in asking:

1 Was the resulting form the free expression of the creative artist?

2 Alternatively, were the artistic wishes of the employing class imposed on the artist, and was he forced to adopt their notions of form?

3 Do contemporaneous periods exist, which on the basis of different cultural traditions in different countries or continents where similar social conditions prevail, produce the same artistic solutions?

4 Alternatively, are there non-contemporaneous periods which led to fundamentally different artistic solutions, each being a stage in the development of the same cultural tradition in the same country under the same conditioning social factors?

In this series of permutations, the following factors are relevant: aesthetics, artist, patron, social environment, leeway given to artistic expression, formal restrictions imposed by the patron, formal restrictions imposed by the social environment, fashion, management, level of development, technology and its potential applications, general cultural conditions, scientific knowledge, enlightenment, nature, landscape, climate etc. We can conclude with a fair degree of certainty that none of these interrelated factors can be considered in isolation.

With this brief outline of the problem, we should just add a word of caution about an over-simplistic undiscriminating outlook. It is certainly worth trying to establish why certain kinds of urban space were created in the 17th century which we now identify with that period. And it would be even more interesting to examine the real reasons why 20th century town planning has been impoverished and reduced to the lowest common denominator.

The following classification does not make any value judgements. It enumerates the basic forms which constitute urban space, with a limited number of possible variations and combinations. The aesthetic quality of each element of urban space is characterised by the structural interrelation of detail. I shall attempt to discern this quality wherever we are dealing with physical features of a spatial nature. The two basic elements are the street and the square. In the category of 'interior space' we would be talking about the corridor and the room. The geometrical characteristics of both spatial forms are the same. They are differentiated only by the

1

dimensions of the walls which bound them and by the patterns of function and circulation which characterise them.

THE SQUARE

In all probability the square was the first way man discovered of using urban space. It is produced by the grouping of houses around an open space. This arrangement afforded a high degree of control of the inner space, as well as facilitating a ready defence against external aggression by minimising the external surface area liable to attack. This kind of courtyard frequently came to bear a symbolic value and was therefore chosen as the model for the construction of numerous holy places (Agora, Forum, cloister, mosque courtyard). With the invention of houses built around a central courtyard or atrium this spatial pattern became a model for the future. Here rooms were arranged around a central courtyard like single housing units around a square.

THE STREET

The street is a product of the spread of a settlement once houses have been built on all available space around its central square. It provides a framework for the distribution of land and gives access to individual plots. It has a more pronouncedly functional character than the square, which by virtue of its size is a more attractive place to pass the time than the street, in whose confines one is involuntarily caught up in the bustle of traffic. Its architectural backdrop is only perceived in passing. The street layouts which we have inherited in our towns were devised for quite different functional purposes. They were planned to the scale of the human being, the horse and the carriage. The street is unsuitable for the flow of motorised traffic, whilst remaining appropriate to human circulation and activity. It rarely operates as an autonomous isolated space, as for example in the case of villages built along a single street. It is mainly to be perceived as part of a network. Our historic towns have made us familiar with the inexhaustible diversity of spatial relationships produced by such a complex layout.

2

TYPICAL FUNCTIONS OF URBAN SPACES

The activities of a town take place in public and private spheres. The behavioural patterns of people are similar in both. So, the result is that the way in which public space has been organised has in all periods exercised a powerful influence on the design of private houses.

We might almost infer the existence of a kind of social ritual, which produces a perfect match between individual and collective. What concerns us above all here are those activities which take place in the town in the open air: i.e. actions which a person performs outside the familiar territory of his own home and for which he utilises public space, as for example travelling to work, shopping, selling goods, recreation, leisure activities, sporting events, deliveries etc. Although the asphalt carpet which serves as a channel for the movement of cars is still called a

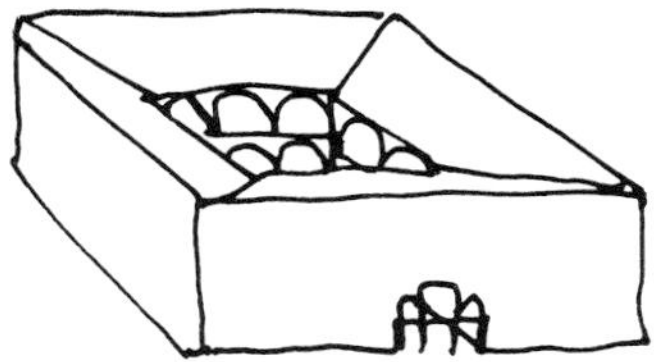

3 House

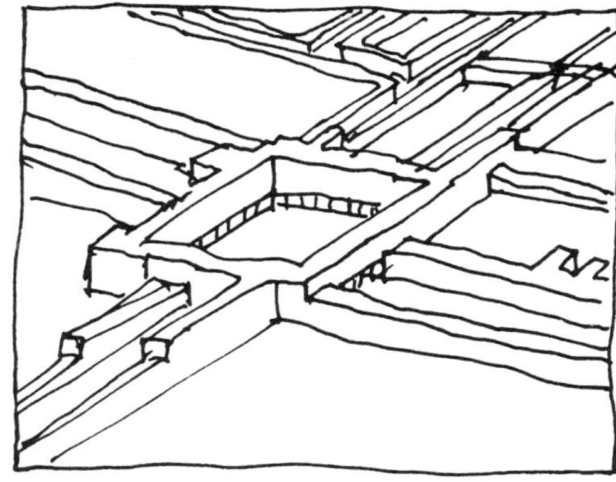

4 Urban structure

'street', it retains no connection with the original significance of the term. Certainly the motorised transportation of people and goods is one of the primary functions of the town, but it requires no scenery in the space around it. It is different in the case of the movement of pedestrians or public transport vehicles which move at a moderate speed, like carriages. Today we have boulevard situations which apparently draw their life from the *défilé* of flashy cars and pavement cafes are visited despite the fact that the air is polluted by exhaust fumes. Looking at planning schemes of the turn of the century one can appreciate that in cosmopolitan cities such as Paris, Rome or Berlin, the air was polluted in a different way: by horse manure, stinking sewage and uncollected refuse. A problem of urban hygiene, as old as the town itself, with the only difference that people can be poisoned by carbon monoxide but scarcely by horse manure.

On medical grounds we can no longer

5 The square as intersection of two roads, fixed point of orientation, meeting place.

indulge in this kind of boulevard romanticism. While the automobile in its present form continues to occupy streets, it excludes all other users.

Let us give a brief outline here of the characteristic functions of the space defined by the square and the street:

THE SQUARE

This spatial model is admirably suited to residential use. In the private sphere it corresponds to the inner courtyard or atrium. The courtyard house is the oldest type of town house. In spite of its undisputed advantages, the courtyard house has now become discredited. It is all too easily subject to ideological misinterpretation, and people are afraid that this design may imply enforced conformity to a communal lifestyle or a particular philosophy.

A certain unease about one's neighbours has undoubtedly led to the suppression of this building type. Yet in the same way as communal living has gained in popularity for a minority of young people with the disappearance of the extended family, the concept of neighbourhood and its accompanying building types will most certainly be readopted in the near future.

In the public sphere, the square has undergone the same development. Market places, parade grounds, ceremonial squares, squares in front of churches and townhalls etc, all relics of the Middle Ages, have been robbed of their original functions and their symbolic content and in many places are only kept up through the activities of conservationists.

The loss of symbolism in architecture was described and lamented by Giedion in *Space, Time, Architecture*. The literary torch which he carried for Le Corbusier in the 30s, and for Jorn Utzon in the 60s, expressed his hope that this loss would perhaps be compensated by a powerful impetus towards artistic expression. He hoped for the same thing from new construction techniques. I have already stressed the importance of the poetic content and aesthetic quality of space and buildings. It is not my wish to introduce into this discussion the concept of symbolism, with all its ethical and religious overtones; and I would also like to warn against the arbitrary confusion of aesthetic and symbolic categories. If I maintain that the Louvre, instead of being a museum, might equally well be housing, a castle, an office building etc, let me make it clear that I am speaking of space or building type, not of external detailing or historical and socio-political factors which led to this structural solution. The aesthetic value of the different spatial types is as independent of short-lived functional concerns as it is of symbolic interpretations which may vary from one age to the next.

Another example to clarify this argument:

The multi-storeyed courtyard house, from the Middle Ages up to modern times, was the building type which acted as the starting point for the castle, the renaissance and baroque palace etc. The Berlin tenements of the 19th century are also courtyard houses, but nowhere near being palaces. Anyone familiar with the architecture of Palladio should draw the right conclusion from this. The lavish use of materials certainly does not play the decisive role here. If that were the case, Palladio would long since have fallen into oblivion. So, even in the 20th century, I can construct a building with an inner courtyard without remotely aiming to imitate the palace architecture of the 16th century and the social class which produced it. There is no reason why the building types used by extinct dynasties to design their residences and show their material wealth should not serve as a model for housing today.

(I must add here that my critique of the ways of seeing such architectural forms applies mainly to the German cultural scene. By and large a frighteningly vague sense of history predominates in this country.)

The early Christians were not afraid to adopt the building type of Roman judicial and commercial buildings, the basilica, as the prototype of their religious monuments. Le Corbusier took his rows of 'redents' from baroque castles.

No contemporary public squares have been laid out which could be compared with urban squares like the Grande Place in Brussels, the Place Stanislas in Nancy, the Piazza del Campo in Siena, the Place Vendome and the Place des Vosges in Paris, the Plaza Mayor in Madrid, the Plaza Real in Barcelona etc. This spatial type awaits rediscovery. This can only occur firstly when it can be endowed with meaningful functions, and secondly is planned in the right place with the appropriate approaches within the overall town layout.

What are the functions which are appropriate to the square?

Commercial activities certainly, such as the market, but above all activities of a cultural nature. The establishment of public administrative offices, community halls, youth centres, libraries, theatres and concert halls, cafes, bars etc. Where possible in the case of central squares, these should be functions which generate activity twenty-four hours a day. Residential use should not be excluded in any of these cases.

6 The street as artery and means of orientation.

THE STREET

In purely residential areas streets are universally seen as areas for public circulation and recreation. The distances at which houses are set back from the street, as regulations demand in Germany today, are so excessive that attractive spatial situations can only be achieved by gimmickry. In most cases, there is ample space available for gardens in addition to the emergency access required for public service vehicles. This street space can only function when it is part of a system in which pedestrian access leads off the street. This system can be unsettled by the following planning errors:

1 If some houses and flats cannot be approached directly from the street but only from the rear. In this way the street is deprived of a vital activity. The result is a state of competition between internal and external urban space. This characterisation of space refers to the degree of public activity which takes place in each of these two areas.

2 If the garages and parking spaces are arranged in such a way that the flow of human traffic between car and house does not impinge upon the street space.

3 If the play spaces are squeezed out into isolated areas with the sole justification of preserving the intimacy of the residential zone. The same neurotic attitude towards neighbours is experienced in flats. The noise of cars outside the home is accepted, yet indoors children are prevented from playing noisily.

4 If no money can be invested in public open spaces, on such items as avenues of trees, paving and other such street furniture, given that the first priority is the visual appeal of space.

5 If the aesthetic quality of adjacent houses is neglected, if the facing frontages are out of harmony, if different sections of the street are inadequately demarcated or if the scale is unbalanced. These factors fulfil a precise cultural role in the functional coherence of the street and square. The need to meet the town's function of 'poetry of space' should be as self-evident as the need to meet any technical requirements. In a purely objective sense, it is just as basic.

Can you imagine people no longer

making music, painting, making pictures, dancing . . . ? Everybody would answer no to this. The role of architecture on the other hand is not apparently seen as so essential. 'Architecture is something tangible, useful, practical' as far as most people are concerned. In any case its role is still considered as the creation of cosiness indoors and of status symbols outdoors. Anything else is classed as icing on the cake, which one can perfectly well do without. I maintain that a stage in history when architecture is not granted its full significance shows a society in cultural crisis, the tragedy of which can scarcely be described in words. Contemporary music expresses it adequately.

The problems of the residential street touched on here apply equally to the commercial street. The separation of pedestrians and traffic carries with it the danger of the isolation of the pedestrian zone. Solutions must be carefully worked out which will keep the irritation of traffic noise and exhaust fumes away from the pedestrian, without completely distancing one zone from the other. This means an overlapping of these functions, to be achieved with considerable investment in the technological sphere, a price which the motorised society must be prepared to pay. This problem will remain much the same even when the well-known technical shortcomings and acknowledged design failings of the individual car have been ironed out. The number of cars, and their speed, remains a source of anxiety. With the way things are going at the moment, there seems little hope of either factor being corrected. On the contrary, nobody today can predict what catastrophic dimensions these problems will assume and what solutions will be needed to overcome them.

It is completely absurd to labour under the misapprehension that one day the growing need to adopt new modes of transport will leave our countryside littered with gigantic and obsolete monuments of civil engineering.

In fact, one is inclined to think that, considering the level of investment in the car and all that goes with it, a fundamental change is no longer feasible in the long term.

All this illustrates the enormous conflict of interests between investments for the demands of machine/car and investments for living creature/man; it also indicates that there is a price to be paid for the restoration of urban space, if our society is to continue to value life in its cities.

Back to the problem of the commercial street which has already been outlined. It must be fashioned differently from the purely residential street. It must be relatively narrow. The passer-by must be able to cast an eye over all the goods on display in the shops opposite without perpetually having to cross from one side of the street to the other. At least, this is what the shopper and certainly the tradesman would like to see. Another spatial configuration of the shopping street is provided by the old town centre of Berne, in which pedestrians can examine the goods on display protected by arcades from the inclemency of the weather. This type of shopping street has retained its charm and also its functional efficiency up to the present day. The pedestrian is relatively untroubled by the road, which lies on a lower level. This street space can serve as an example to us.

The same can be said of the glass-roofed arcades or passages which originated in the 19th century. Strangely enough, they have fallen out of favour today. From the point of view of ventilation it was obviously disadvantageous then to lead the street frontage into a passageway. With today's fully air-conditioned commercial and office buildings, however, this building type could come back into fashion. Protection against the elements is a financially justifiable amenity for shopping streets in our latitudes. The arcaded street, developed by the Romans from the colonnades which surrounded the Greek Agora, has completely died out. The remains of such formal streets can still be found at Palmyra, Perge, Apameia, Sidon, Ephesus, Leptis Magna, Timgad etc.

The appearance of this type of street is a fascinating event in the history of town planning. With the increased prosperity of Roman rule, a need arose for the uniform and schematic plan of the Greek colonial town to be modified, with emphasis being placed on arterial roads within the homogeneous network of streets, and this was achieved by marking them with particularly splendid architectural features. They certainly had important functional connotations which today can no longer be clearly surmised. Whatever these connotations were, they had an obviously commercial as well as symbolic character, in contrast to the Agora and the Forum, which were reserved primarily for political and religious purposes. Weinbrenner, with his proposed scheme for the improvement of the Kaiserstrasse in Karlsruhe, attempted to revive this idea. The Konigsbau in Stuttgart designed by Leins could be a fragment of the arcaded street of Ephesus. The Romans were astoundingly imaginative in perfecting this type of street space. So, for example, changes in the direction of streets, dictated by existing features of the urban structure, were highlighted as cardinal points by having gateways built across them. In the Galeries St. Hubert in Brussels, this problem has been solved on the same principle. By this expedient, the street space is divided up into visually manageable sections, in contrast to the seemingly infinite perspective of the remaining network of streets. It

should equally be noted that in rare cases streets broaden out into squares directly without their articulation being marked by buildings. The street and the square were conceived as largely independent and autonomous spaces.

Such devices, used by Roman and Greek town planners to indicate spatial relationships, lapsed into oblivion with the decline of the Roman empire in Europe. Isolated building types such as the forum and the basilica were adopted unchanged in the Middle Ages, for example in monasteries. The forum was no longer employed as a public space. Not so in North Africa and the Near East, and to some extent in Spain, where these ancient types of urban space survived almost unchanged until the turn of the century using traditional construction methods.

TYPOLOGY OF URBAN SPACE

In formulating a typology of urban space, spatial forms and their derivatives may be divided into three main groups, according to the geometrical pattern of their ground plan: these groups derive from the square, the circle or the triangle.

 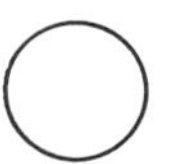 

Without doubt the scale of an urban space is also related to its geometrical qualities. Scale can only be mentioned in passing in this typology. I wish to try and deal with the significance of proportions in external space more comprehensively in a later chapter. They do not affect the arrangement of my typology.

7 One type of urban space on three different scales

MODULATION OF A GIVEN SPATIAL TYPE

The matrix drawn up below (Fig. 8) shows, reading from top to bottom: 1. The basic element; 2. The modification of the basic element resulting from the enlargement or reduction of the angles contained within it, where the external dimensions remain constant; 3. The angles remain constant and the length of two sides changes in the same proportion; 4. Angles and external dimensions are altered arbitrarily.

Reading from left to right, the matrix illustrates the following stages of modulation:

1. Angled space. This indicates a space which is a compound of two parts of the basic element with two parallel sides bent.

2. This shows only a segment of the basic element.

3. The basic element is added to.

4. The basic elements overlap or merge.

5. Under the heading 'distortion' are included spatial forms which are difficult or impossible to define. This category is intended to cover those shapes which can only with difficulty be traced back to their original geometric model. These shapes may also be described as species born out of chaos. Here the elevation of buildings may be distorted or concealed to such an extent that they can no longer be distinguished as clear demarcations of space – for example, a facade of mirror glass or one completely obscured by advertisements, so that a cuckoo-clock as big as a house stands next to an outsize ice-cream cone, or an advert for cigarettes or chewing gum stands in place of the usual pierced facade.

Even the dimensions of a space can have a distorting influence on its effect, to such an extent that it ceases to bear any relation to the original. The column headed 'distortion' has not been completed in this matrix, as these shapes cannot be diagrammatically expressed.

All these processes of change show regular and irregular configurations.

The basic elements can be modified by a great variety of building sections. I illustrate here 24 different types which substantially alter the features of urban space. See Fig. 9.

8

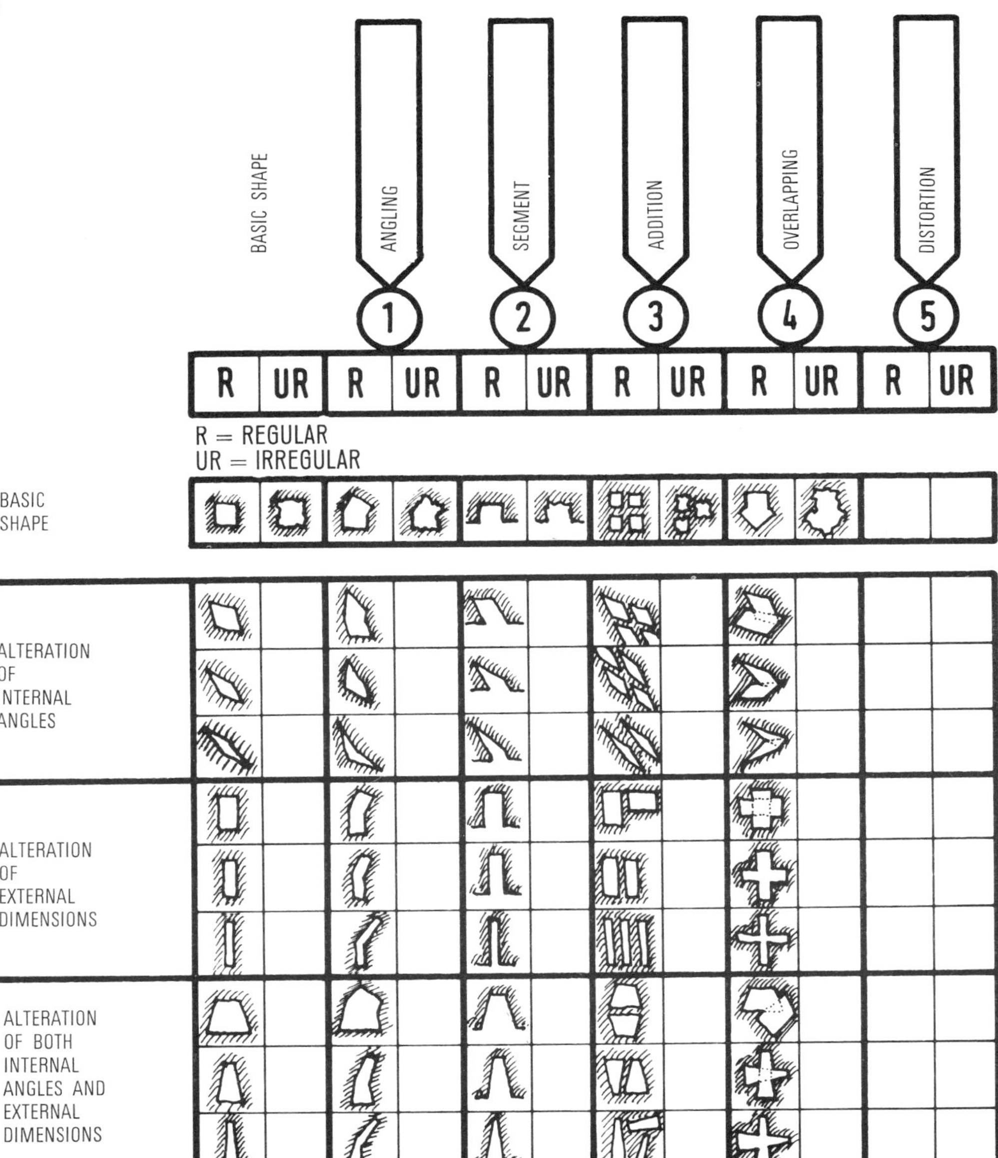

9

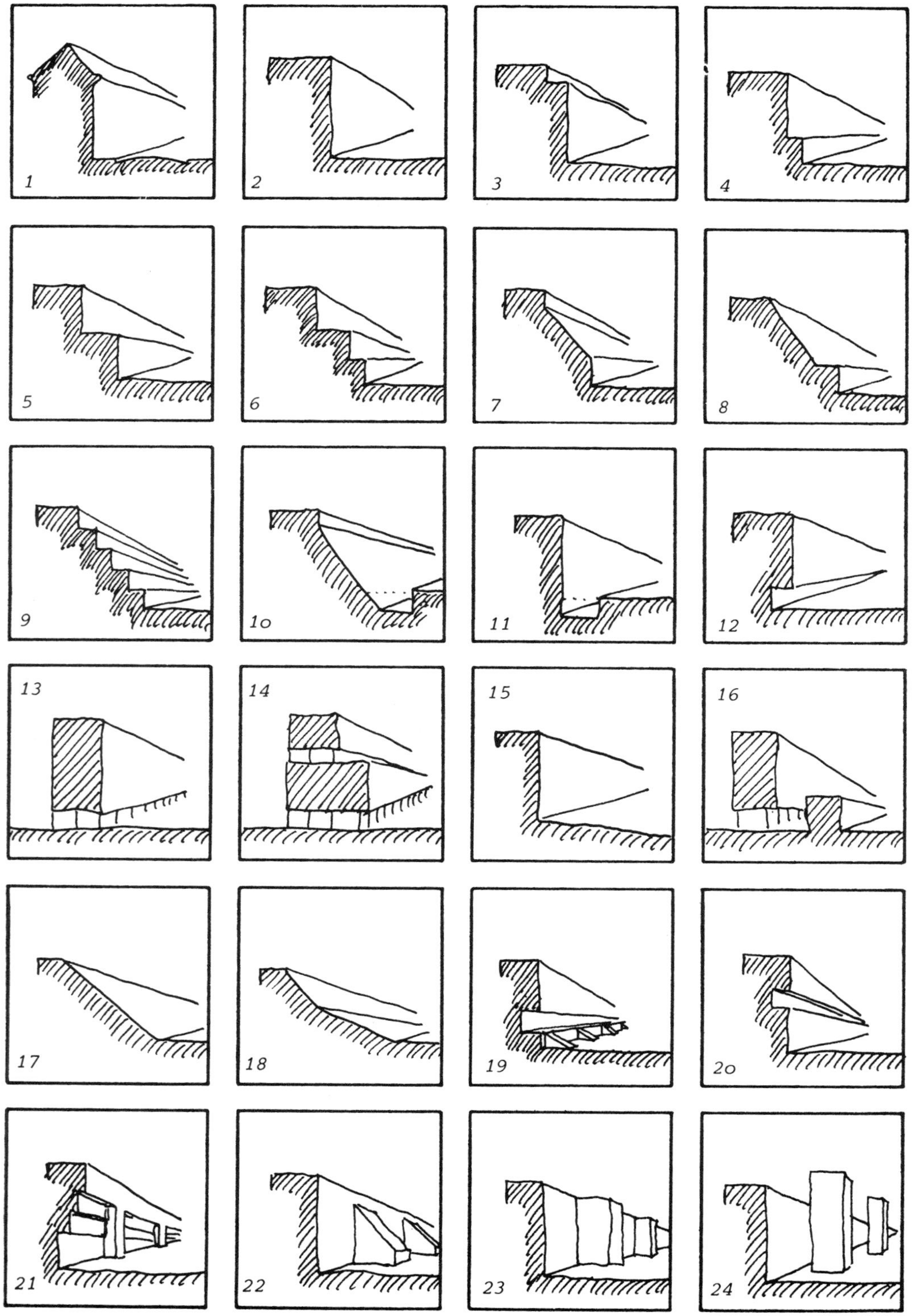

1 2 3 4 5 6 7 8 9 10 11 12 13 14 15 16 17 18 19 20 21 22 23 24

HOW BUILDING SECTIONS AFFECT URBAN SPACE

Notes on Fig. 9

1 Standard traditional section with pitched roof.
2 With flat roof.
3 With top floor set back. This device reduces the height of the building visible to the eye.
4 With a projection on pedestrian level in the form of an arcade or a solid structure. This device 'distances' the pedestrian from the real body of the building and creates a pleasing human scale. This type of section was applied with particular virtuosity by John Nash in his Park Crescent, London.
5 Half way up the building the section is reduced by half its depth; this allows for extensive floors on the lower level and flats with access balconies on the upper level.
6 Random terracing.
7 Sloping elevation with vertical lower and upper floors.
8 Sloping elevation with protruding ground floor.
9 Stepped section.
10 Sloping section with moat or free-standing ground floor.
11 Standard section with moat.
12 Building with ground floor arcades.
13 Building on pilotis.
14 Building on pilotis, with an intermediate floor similarly supported.
15 Sloping ground in front of building.
16 A free-standing low building placed in front of a higher one.
17/18 Buildings with a very shallow incline, as for example arenas.
19 Building with arcade above ground level and access to pedestrian level.
20 Building with access balcony.
21 Inverted stepped section.
22 Building with pitched projections.
23 Building with projections.
24 Building with free-standing towers.

Each of these building types can be given a facade appropriate to its function and method of construction.

The sketches reproduced here (Fig. 10) can only give some idea of the inexhaustible design possibilities. Each of these structures influences urban space in a particular way. It is beyond the scope of this work to describe the nature of this influence.

ELEVATIONS

Notes on sketches in Fig. 10:

Row 1 left to right:
Pierced facade: the lowest level is more generously glazed in each sketch, reducing the solid area to a simple load-bearing structure.

2 The glazed area within the load-bearing structure can be modified according to taste. The following three pictures show a reverse of the design process portrayed in 1. A solid base forces the glazed area upward.

3 The window type can be modified horizontally and vertically according to the imagination of the designer.

4 Faceless modular facade as a theoretical (abstract) way in which the building might be enclosed. The modular facade can be adapted to all variations in the shape of the building. Solid sections of the building can be combined with the grid.

5 Windowless buildings: windows are placed in niches etc. and the process starts again from the beginning.

6 Exploration of different geometries; a thematic interpretation of the elevation: lowest level = heavy; middle section = smooth with various perforations; upper part = light, transparent. (One of the sketches of squares shows a variation on this theme on three sides of a square.) Arcades placed in front of houses, different architectural styles juxtaposed.

10

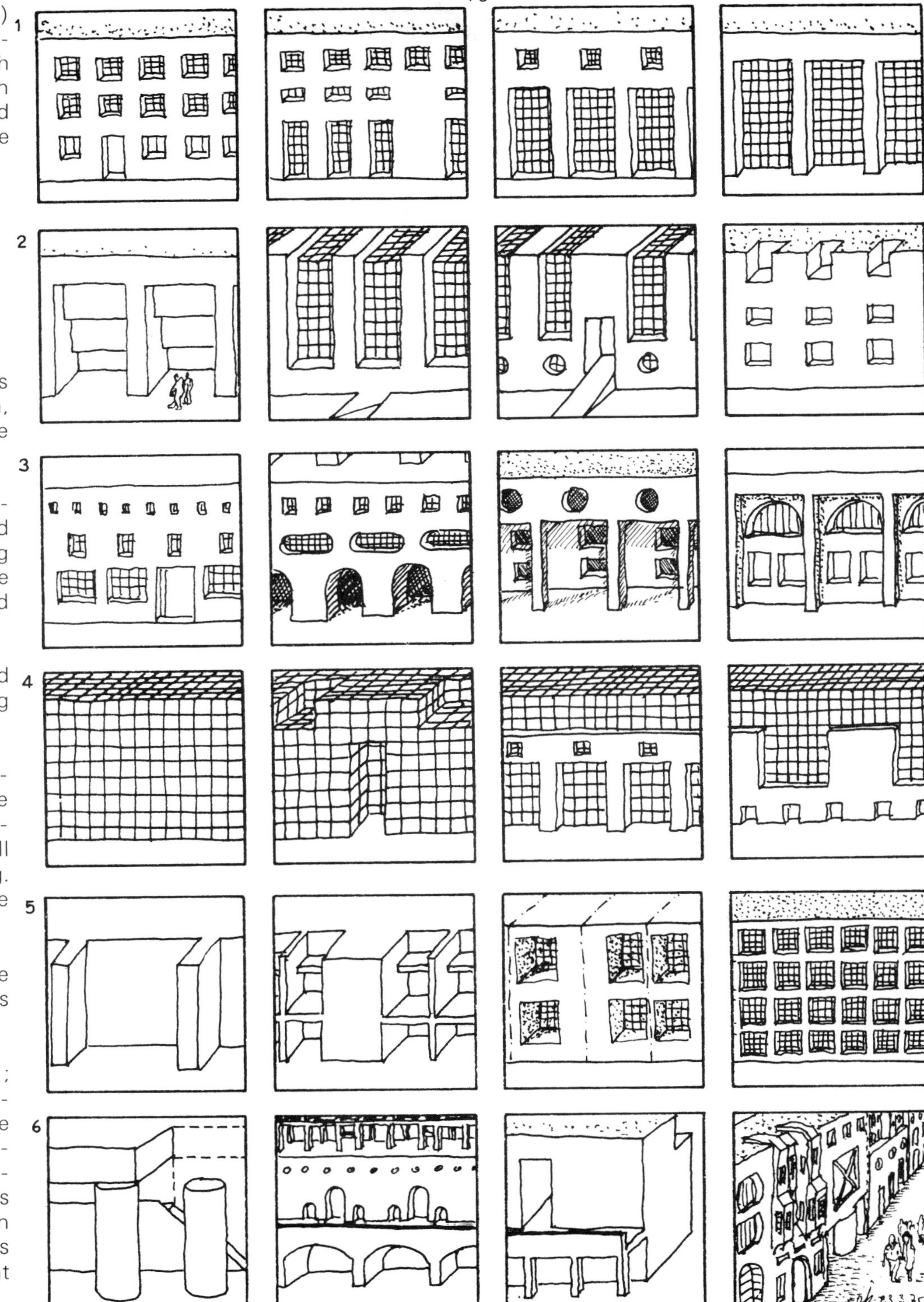

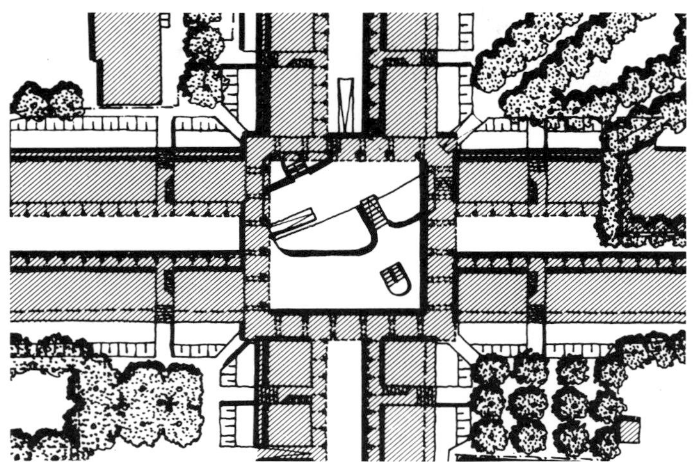

11 The square as intersection.

12 Arcade running round the square; high, narrow columns.

13 Lower arcade.

14 Low arcade, wide openings.

15 Combination of three different facades.

16 As 15, but overgrown with plants.

17 Relationship between single object and urban space.

18 Effect of materials.

19 Dialogue between old, new and green.

20 Green open space, trees with short and tall trunks.

21 Green open space with poplars.

22 Green open space, surrounded by different kinds of trees.

23

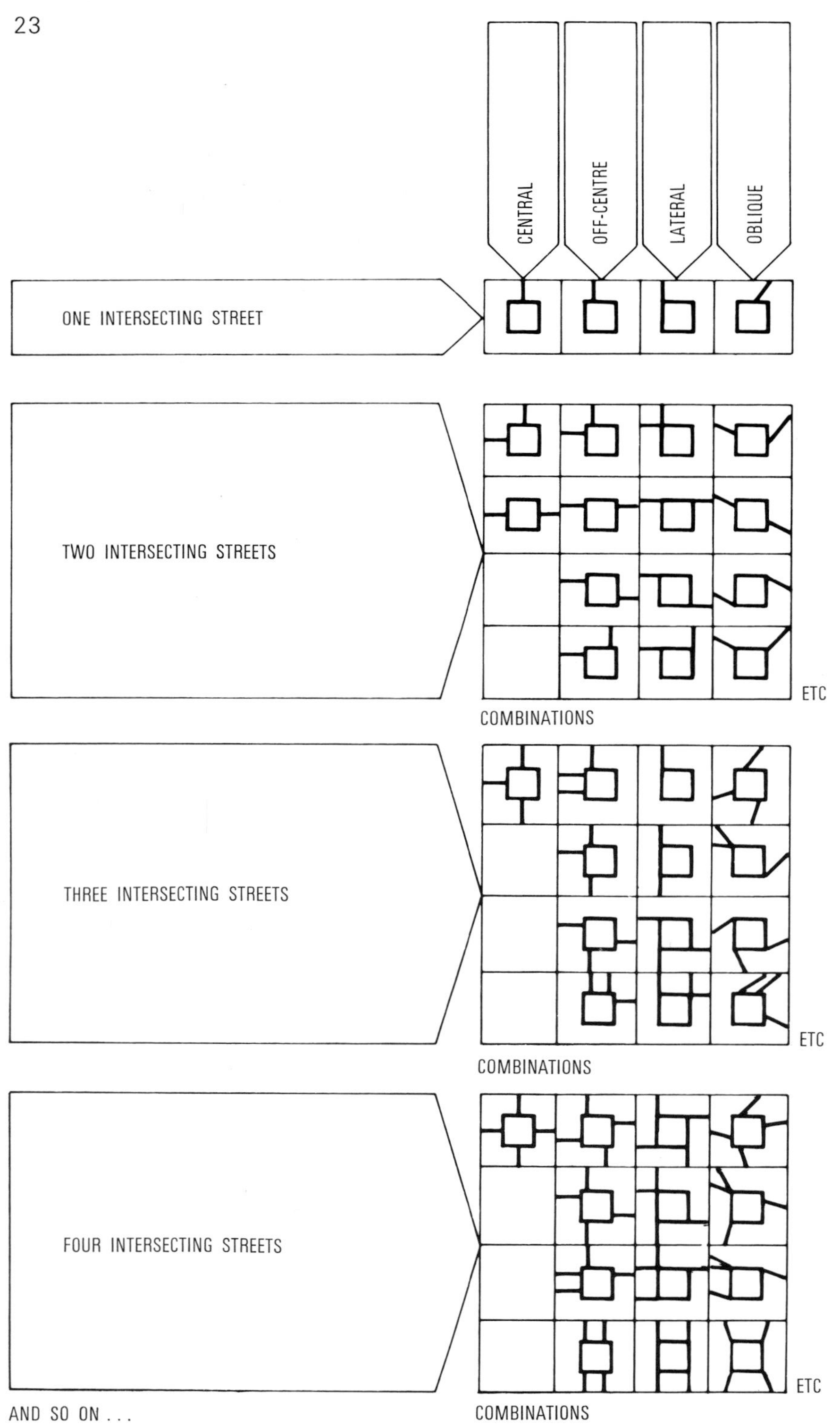

INTERSECTIONS OF STREET AND SQUARE

All spatial types examined up to now can be classified according to the types of street intersection laid out in the diagram opposite (Fig. 23). As an example here we have a set of permutations for up to four intersections at four possible points of entry. This chart should only be taken as an indication of the almost unlimited range of possible permutations of these spatial forms. To attempt a comprehensive display here would conflict with the aim of this typological outline.

The vertical columns of this diagram show the number of streets intersecting with an urban space. Horizontally, it shows four possible ways in which one or more streets may intersect with a square or street:

1 Centrally and at right angles to one side.

2 Off-centre and at right angles to one side.

3 Meeting a corner at right angles.

4 Oblique, at any angle and at any point of entry.

SPATIAL TYPES AND HOW THEY MAY BE COMBINED

We may summarise the morphological classification of urban spaces as follows:

The three basic shapes (square, circle

and triangle) are affected by the following modulating factors: angling; segmentation; addition; merging, overlapping or amalgamation of elements; and distortion.

These modulating factors can produce geometrically regular or irregular results on all spatial types.

At the same time, the large number of possible building sections influences the quality of the space at all these stages of modulation. All sections are fundamentally applicable to these spatial forms. In the accompanying sketches I have attempted to make clear as realistically as possible the effect of individual spatial types so that this typology can be more easily accessible and of practical use to the planner.

The terms 'closed' and 'open' may be applied to all spatial forms described up to now: i.e. spaces which are completely or partially surrounded by buildings.

Finally, many compound forms can be created at will from the three spatial types and their modulations. In the case of all spatial forms, the differentiation of scale plays a particularly important role, as does the effect of various architectural styles on the urban space.

Design exercises can be 'played' on the 'keyboard' I have just described. Apart from this 'formal' procedure, other factors also have their effect on space, and this effect is not insignificant. These factors are the rules governing building construction, which make architectural design possible in the first place, and above all else determine the use or function of a building, which is the essential prerequisite for architectural design. The logic of this procedure would therefore demand this sequence: function, construction and finally the resultant design.

24

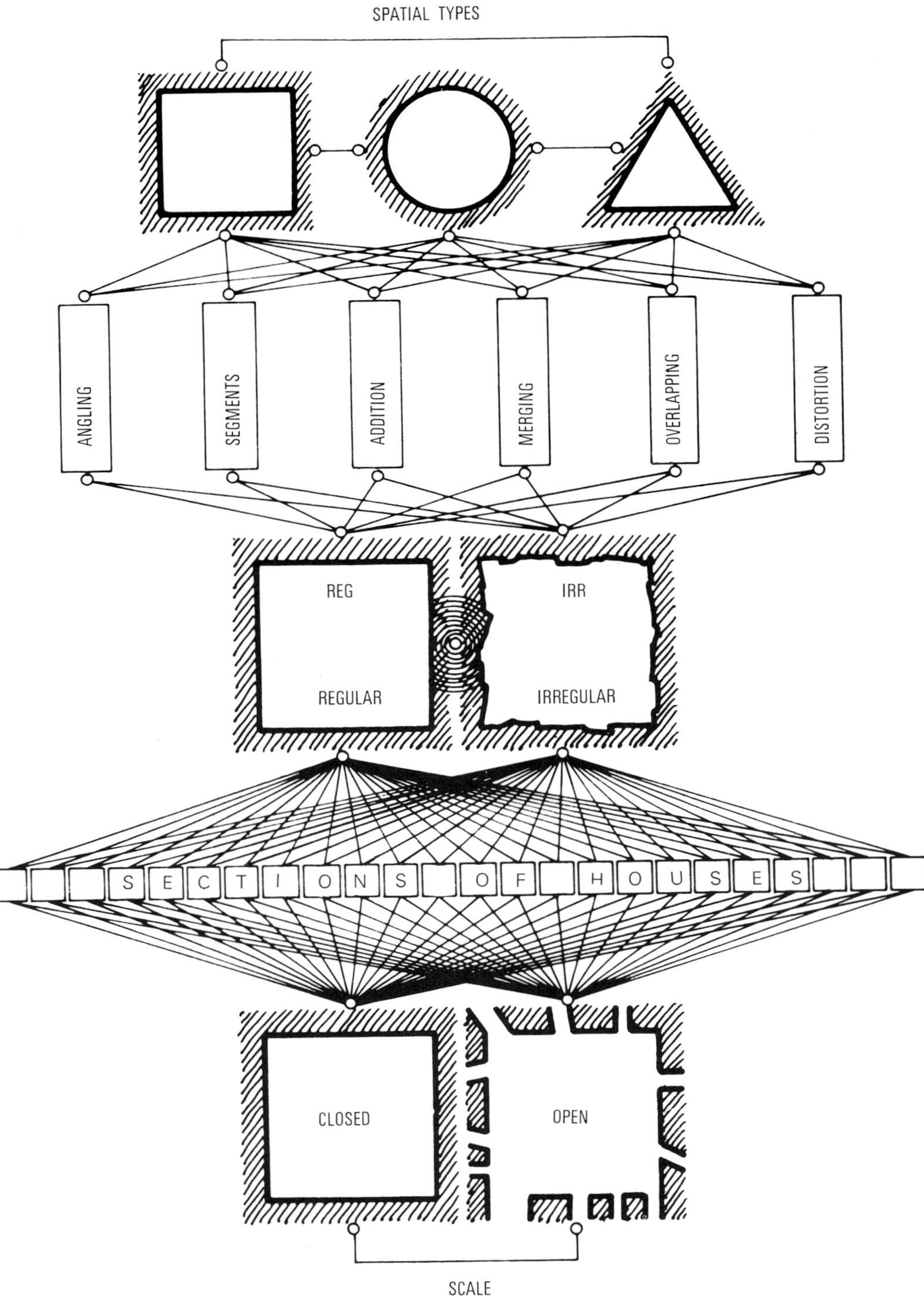

MORPHOLOGICAL SERIES OF URBAN SPACES

The series of spatial forms which I have sketched here is laid out simply according to the geometrical characteristics of the basic shape. It does not claim to be complete. It should indicate to the planner the wealth of spatial forms which is our town-planning heritage, and suggest what he can learn from these examples and apply to his own projects. In presenting this selection of drawings I would like to try and convince architectural theoreticians and historians that in future they must incorporate spatial considerations more exactly into their overall view of architecture and town planning. Such considerations have in fact been criminally neglected.

There is a widespread and naive view prevalent among art historians as well as the general public that this type of irregular or 'organic' architecture is more beautiful than a group of urban buildings planned synchronically. In reality, the facts of the matter are these :

25

26

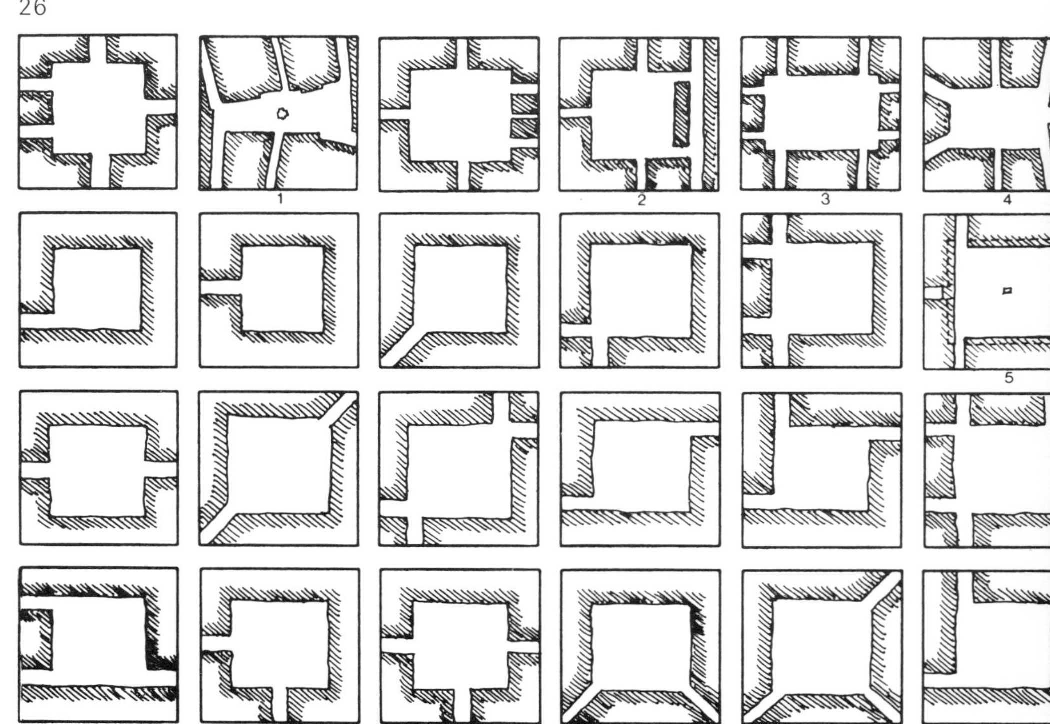

N.B. Sketches whose caption does not indicate a specific location are the product of the author's imagination.

25 Simple geometrical variations on a four sided square and examples of different types of street intersection. Anyone engaged on research or planning on the subject of 'urban space' will soon find that an almost inexhaustible range of possible forms exists, most clearly in evidence in our historic towns.

26/1 Vienna, Neuer Markt.
26/2 London, St. James' Square, 18th century.
26/3 London, Grosvenor Square, 18th century.
26/4 Turin, Corso Re d'Italia.
26/5 Paris, Place des Vosges.

27/1–20

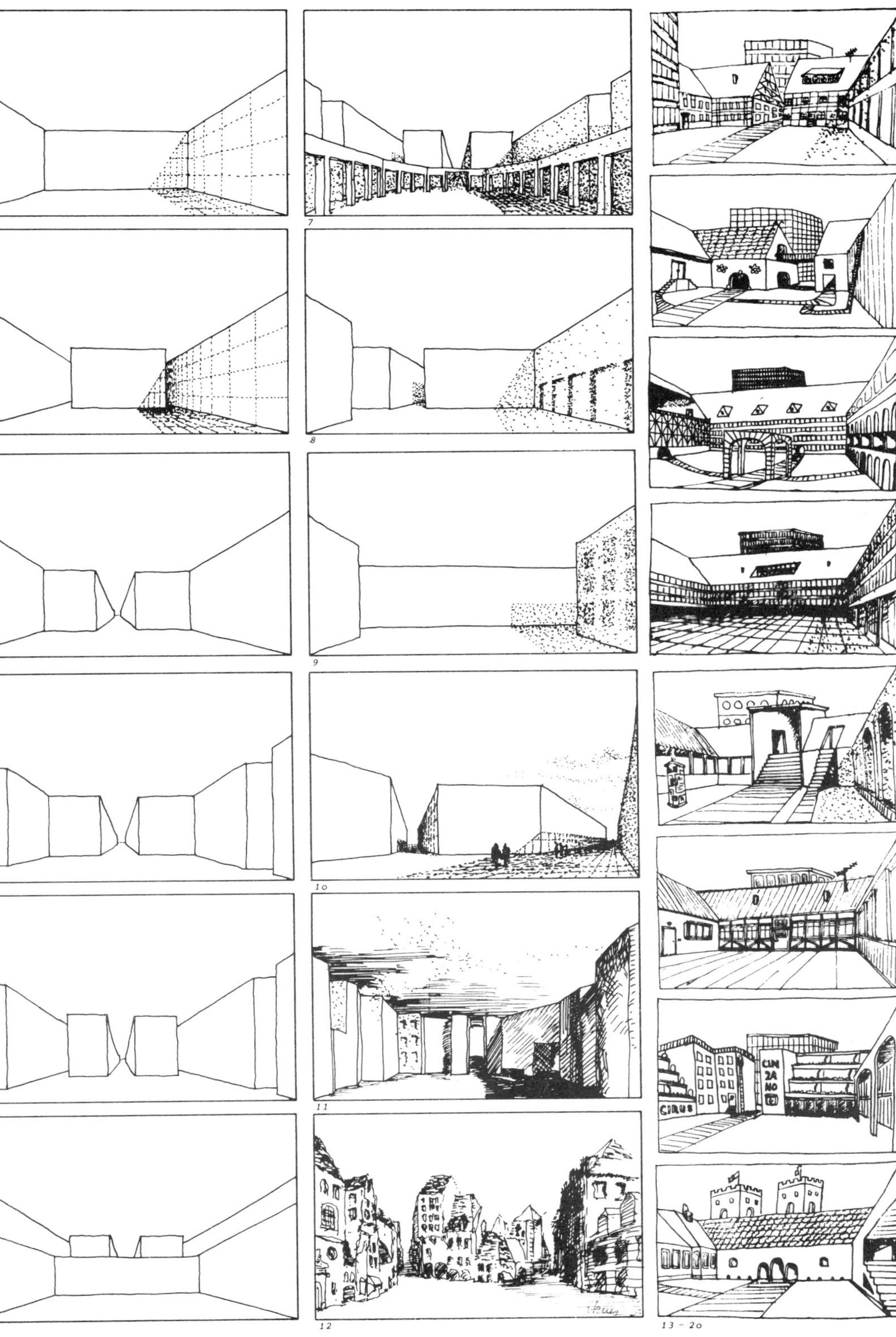

A clear, geometric urban spatial form calls for architecture of extreme delicacy and high quality. Any architectural error is immediately obvious and damages the overall impression. In the case of irregular forms, variety is the overriding characteristic. Defective architectural detailing is not so glaringly obvious, but is effectively buried.

The great popularity of mediaeval squares is rather more rooted in the fact that, first, they are squares of a type which no modern town could imitate, and second that they are surrounded by fine architecture. Our age cannot compete with the past in this area either.

27/1 Square enclosed on all sides.
27/2 Two parallel streets enter the square. A sense of spatial enclosure is now felt only in the centre of the square.
27/3 One street enters the square centrally. The sense of spatial enclosure can now be felt only at the edge of the square.
27/4, 5 Additional streets enter the square. The space gradually loses its clear geometrical outline.
27/6, 7 A projecting structure or colonnade restores the interrupted outline of the space.
27/8, 9 The sense of spatial enclosure is preserved.
27/10 Two streets meet the square radially. From this position its geometrical form can now only be perceived with difficulty.
27/11 Romantic square with irregular ground-plan and buildings of equal height.
27/12 Romantic square (in this case mediaeval) with irregular ground-plan and buildings of varying heights.

27/13–20
Sketches by W. Wallbrecht.

28/1–24

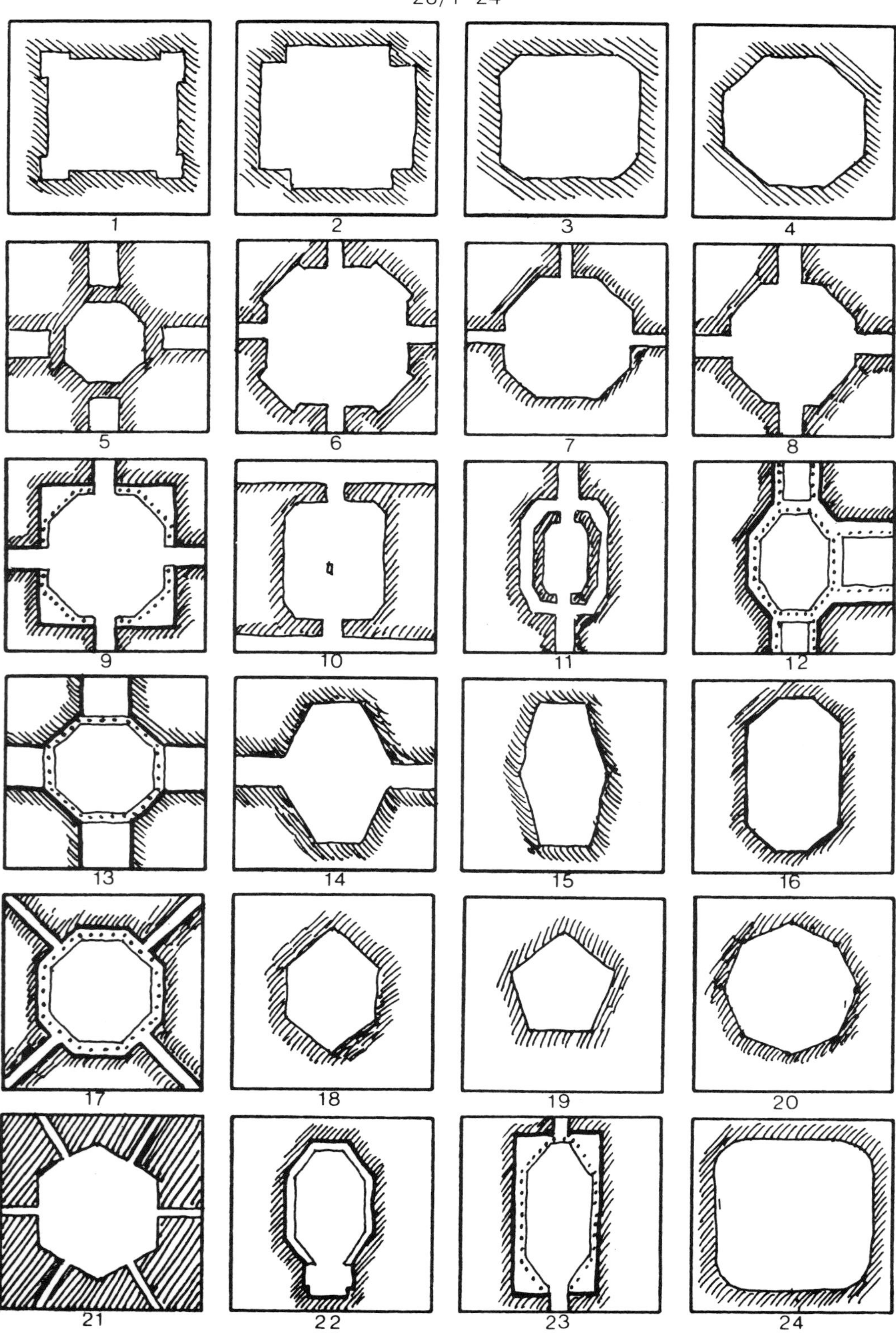

PLANS OF RECTANGULAR SQUARES WITH VARIATIONS

28/1–3 The corners of the square are modified in various ways.
28/4 This modification can produce an octagon.
28/5 Gerasa (Palestine; Roman Period). The Romans have marked the crossroads with a variety of architectural features. Here in Gerasa the corners of the houses face the crossroads at an angle of 45 degrees (see Barcelona) and the street space was blocked off from the crossroads by an archway.
28/6 Versailles, Place Dauphine; see also Copenhagen, Amalienborg.
28/7 Turin, San Lorenzo Nuovo, 1775. Architect Fr. Navone.
28/8 Geneva, on the ramparts, 1850.
28/10 Paris, Place Vendome, 1685-1697. Architect Mansart.
28/11 Leinfelden (Stuttgart), 1971. Architect Leon Krier.
28/12 Stuttgart, the Rotebühlplatz, 1973. Author's scheme.
28/21 Palmanova (Italy), 1593. Architect Giulio Savorgnan.

ORTHOGONAL PLANS FOR SQUARES

29/1 Livorno (Italy), Piazza V. Emanuele, 1605. Architect A. Pieron.
29/2 Montpazier (France), 1284.
29/3 San Giovanni Valdarno (Italy, Tuscany).
29/4 Turin (Italy), Piazza San Carlo, 18th century. Architect Carlo di Castellamonte.
29/5 London, Hanover Square, 18th century.
29/6 London, Golden Square, 18th century.
29/7 Catania (Italy), Piazza Dante, 1774. Architect Fr. Battaglia.
29/8 Catania (Italy), Piazza San Filippo.
29/9 Florence (Italy), Piazza Vittorio Emanuele.
29/10 Freudenstadt (Germany), 1599. Architect Schickardt.
29/11 Freudenstadt, main square with arcades.
29/12 Bordeaux (France), Place de la Bourse, 1733–1743. Architect J. Gabriel.
29/13 Reims (France), Place Royale, 1775. Architects Sufflot & Legendre.
29/14 Mannheim (Germany), Schlossplatz, 17th century. Plan after architect Coehorn.
29/15 Vienna (Austria), Piaristenplatz.
29/17 Stuttgart, Schlossplatz, 1750. After architect Retti.
29/18 Stuttgart, Hohe Carlsschule, 1740–1748. Architects Leger and Fischer.
29/19 Copenhagen (Denmark), Amalienborg, 1749. Architect Eighveid.
29/20 Ludwigsburg (Germany), Castle, 1795. Architect Frisoni.
29/21 Ludwigsburg (Germany), after 1715. Architects Nette and Frisoni.
29/22 Ludwigsburg (Germany), Marktplatz.
29/23 Le Corbusier's 'Redents', 1922.
29/24 Leinfelden (Stuttgart), Marktplatz, 1971. Author's scheme.

29/1—24

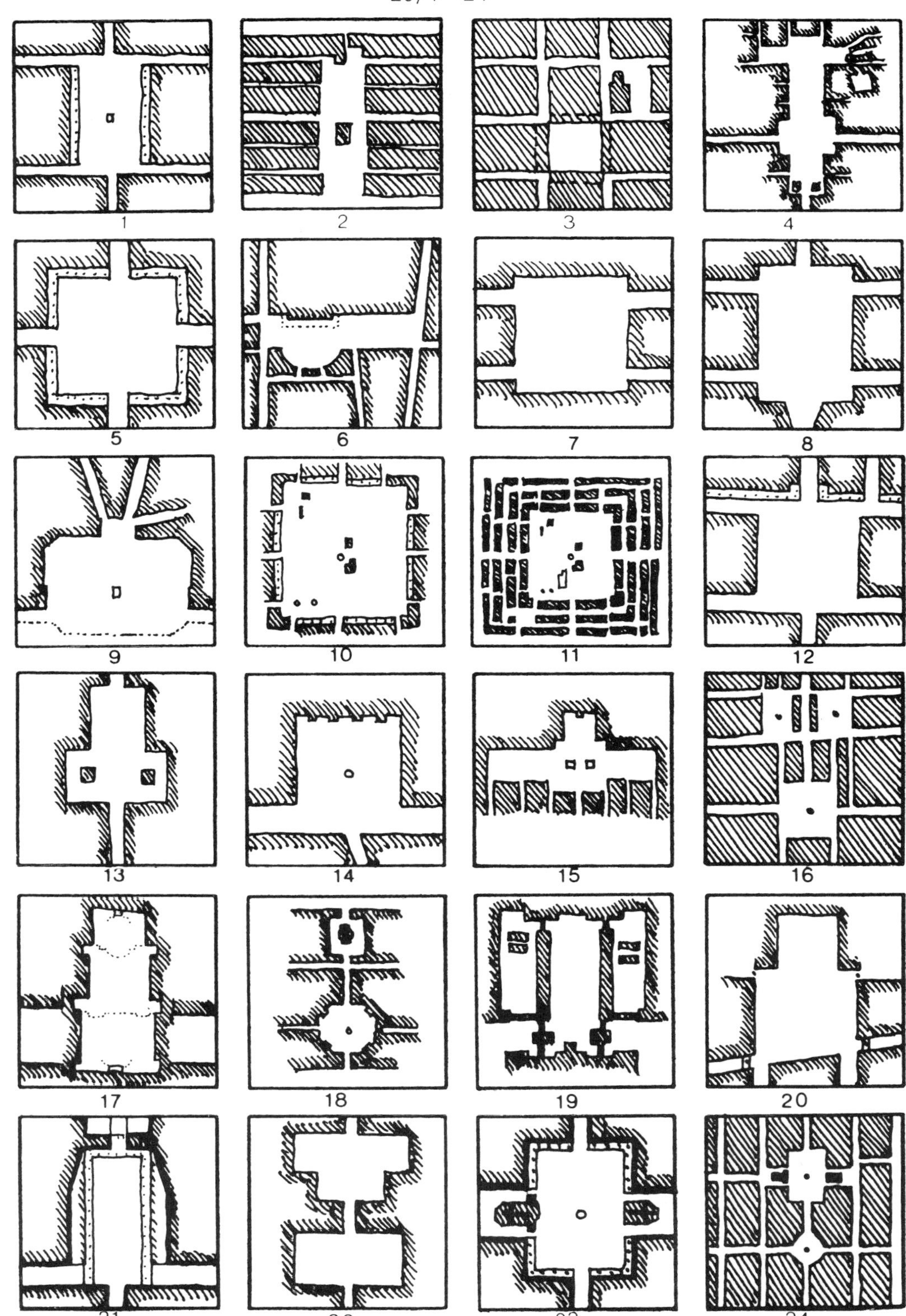

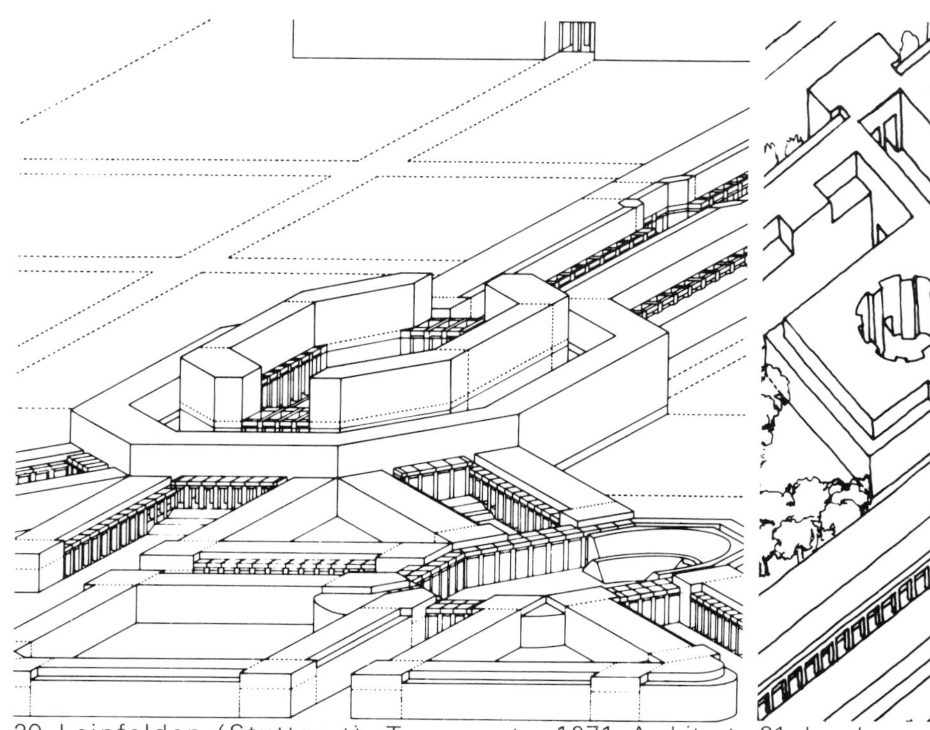
30 Leinfelden (Stuttgart), Town centre, 1971. Architect Leon Krier.

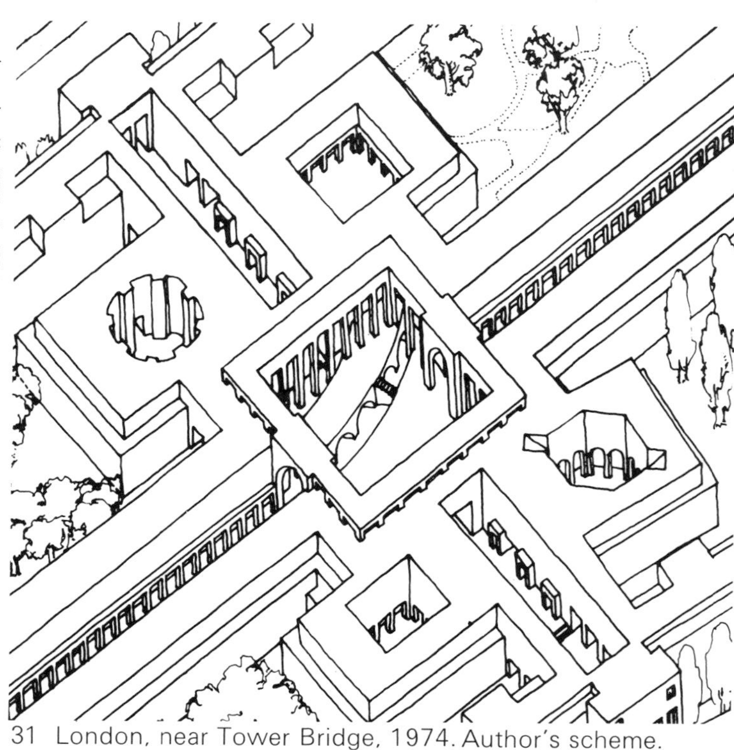
31 London, near Tower Bridge, 1974. Author's scheme.

32 Freiburg im Breisgau (Germany),1971. Author's scheme.

33 Freiburg im Breisgau, 1971 (alternative plan). Author's scheme.

34 Plaza Real, Barcelona, 1848.

35/1–24

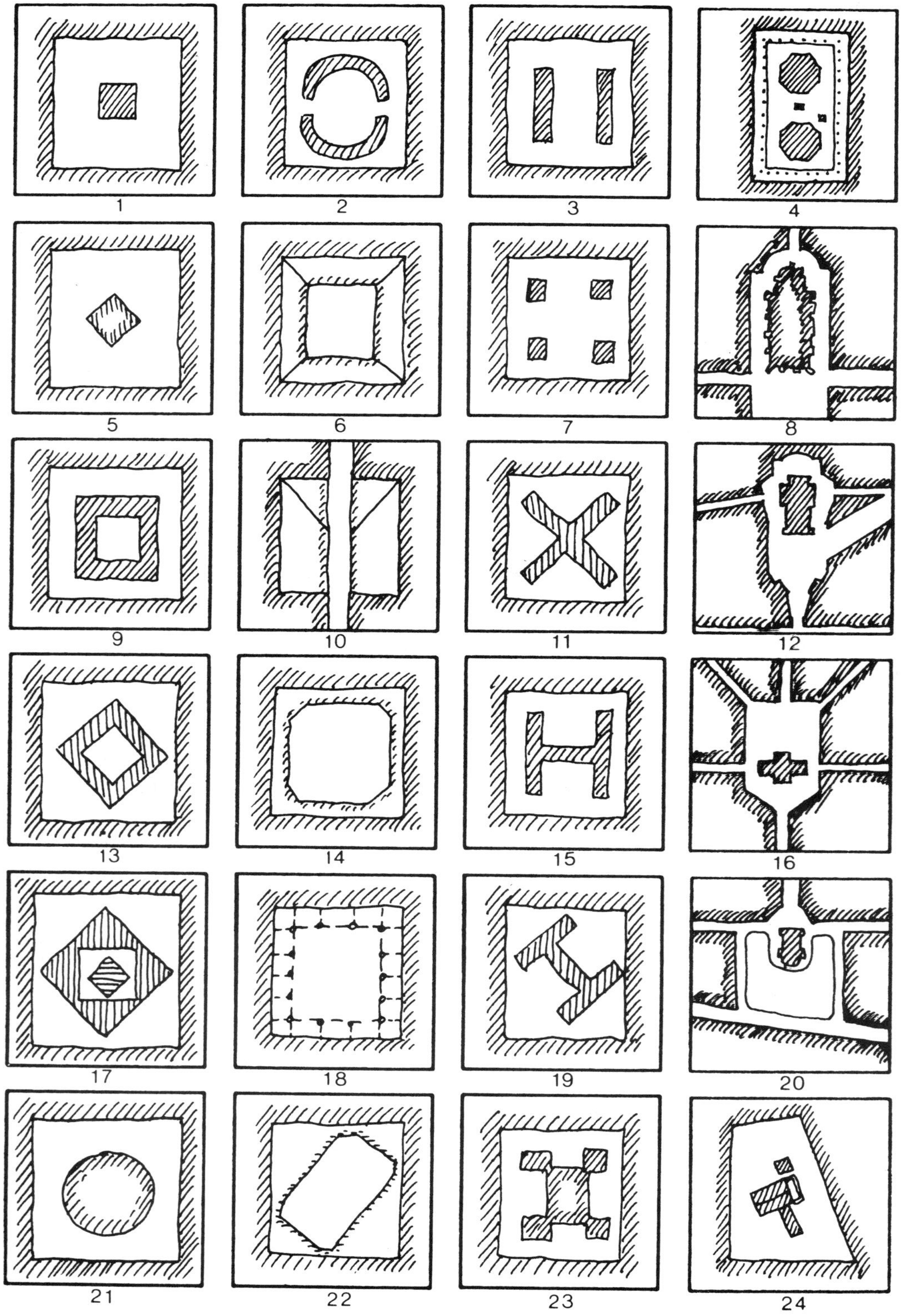

ORTHOGONAL PLANS FOR SQUARES WITH CENTRAL BUILDINGS

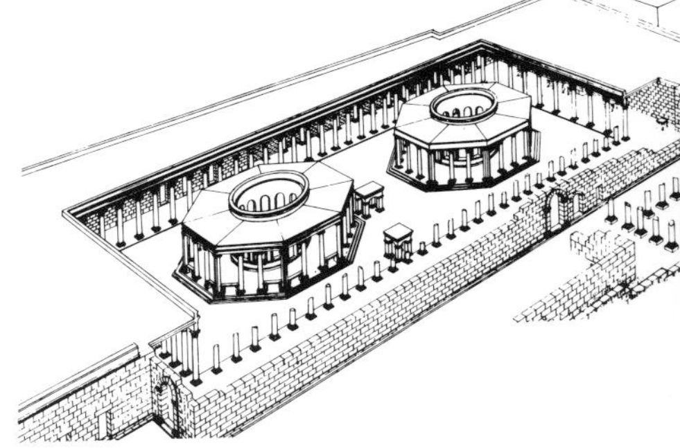

35/4 Leptis Magna (Libya), Roman period, Market square.

35/8 Wiesbaden (Germany), Luisenplatz.
35/12 Paris, Madeleine. Original plan.
35/16 After Gurlitt.
35/20 Stuttgart, Feuersee, 19th century.
35/24 Leptis Magna, Roman period.

36 Junction with markers. Leon Krier, 71.

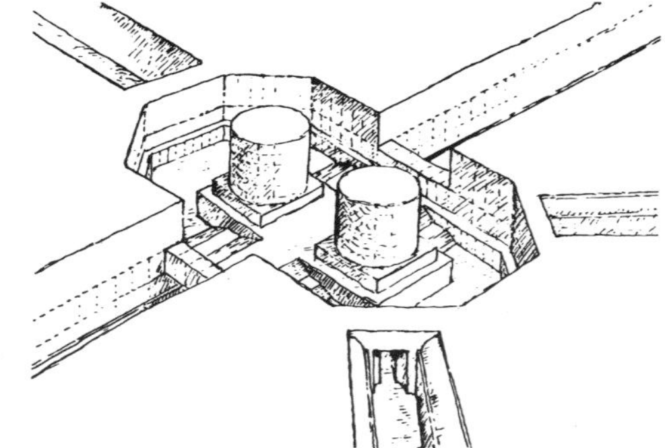

36/1 *below* Cambridge, architects Stirling and Gowan. 1958.

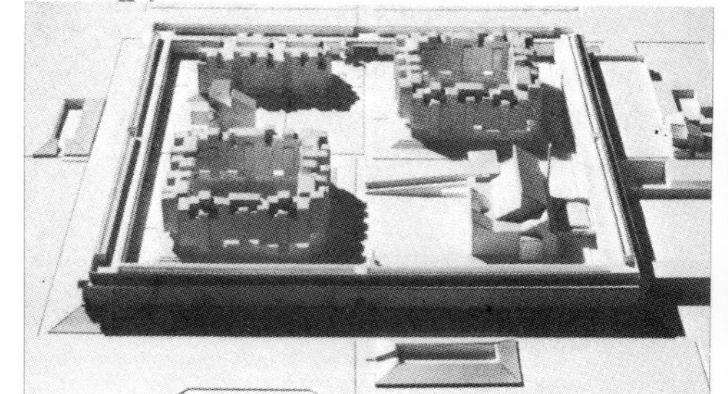

OPEN SQUARES WITH BUILDINGS INTRODUCED

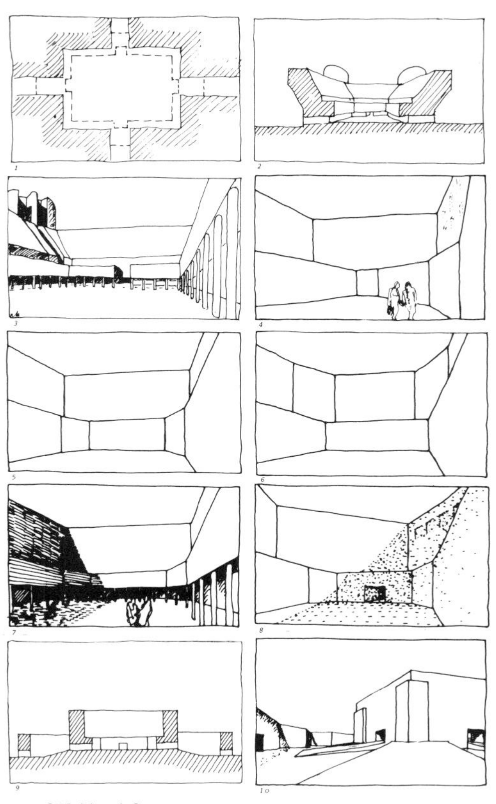

37/1–10

37/1, 2 and 35/6 Buildings around a square, and stepped back.
37/3 In addition, the corner is chamfered.
37/3 Arcade added.
37/4, 5, 7, 8 – 35/14 Rectangular square, arcade placed along side with angled corners.
37/6 Octagonal open space with rectangular arcade.
37/9, 10 see Fig. 38/23.

38/1 The square is open on one side.
38/2–5 An isolated building is placed in the open side.
38/5–24 Variations.

38/1–24

1 2 3 4

5 6 7 8

9 10 11 12

13 14 15 16

17 18 19 20

21 22 23 24

39

Streets as an aid to orientation. Squares at road intersections. Each house in the row has one side facing the paved street and one facing the public gardens.

40

The green area can be spatially articulated in the same way as architectural space. For landscaping and landscape architecture the same design principles apply as for town planning.

41/1–24

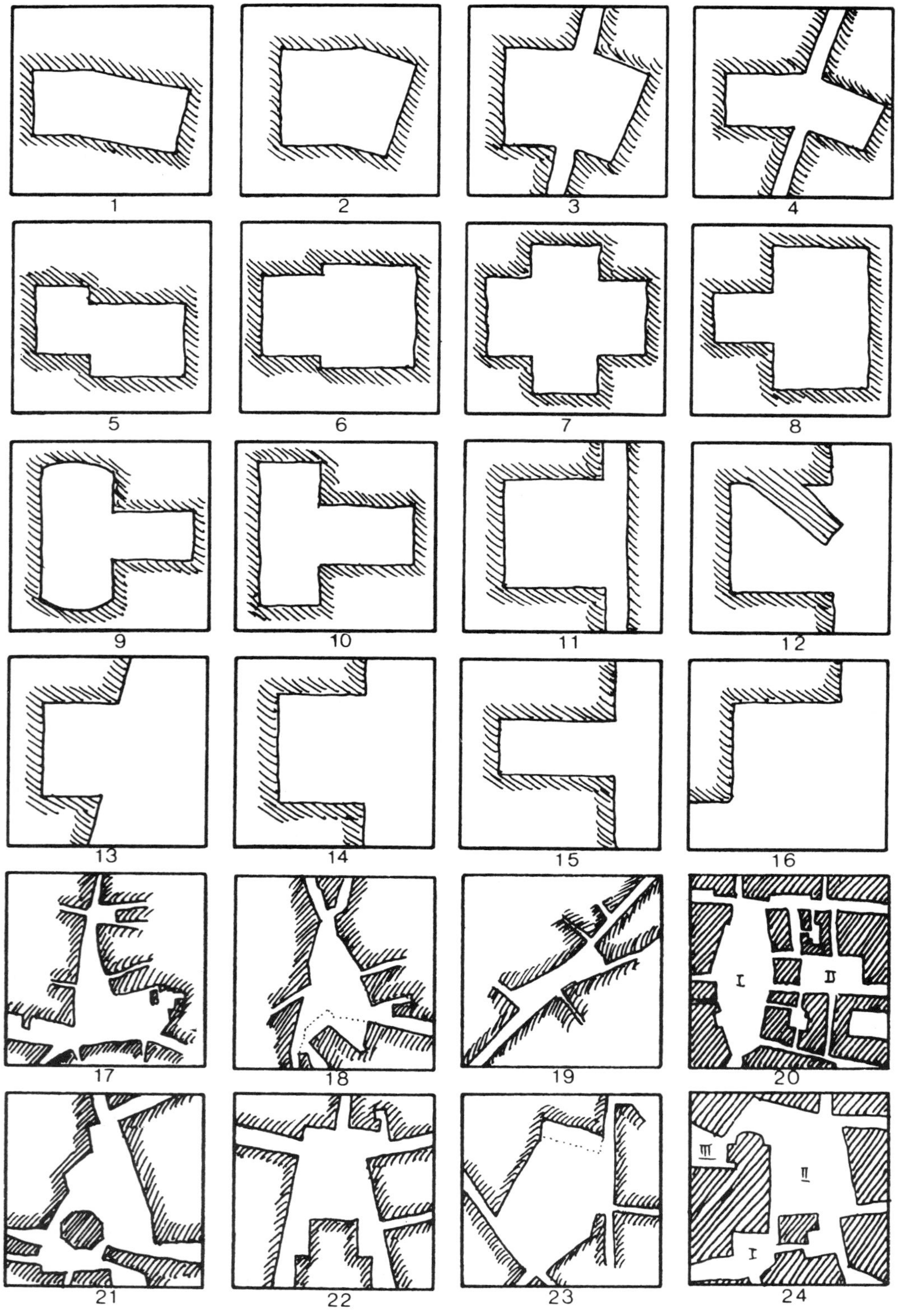

EXAMPLES OF SPACES WHICH ARE ANGLED, DIVIDED, ADDED TO AND SUPERIMPOSED

41/1, 2 A square is angled when two facing sides are not straight.
41/3, 4 The angle is articulated by an intersecting street.
41/5–7 Two geometrical figures are superimposed.
41/8–11 Two geometrical figures are joined.
41/12–16 Part of the space gives on to open country.
41/17–24 Examples of complex types of square.
41/17 St. Gall (Switzerland), early mediaeval.
41/18 Masso Maritimo (Italy), Piazza del Duomo.
41/19 Figline Valdarno (Italy, Tuscany).
41/20 Verona, 1. Piazza d'Erbe
2. Piazza dei Signori
41/21 Volterra (Italy), Piazza del Battistero.
41/22 Pienza (Italy), Piazza Pio II.
41/23 Florence, Piazza S. Maria Novella.
41/24 Modena, 1. Mercato delle Legna; 2. Piazza Grande; 3. Piazza della Torre.

42 Sketches of Nördlingen (Germany).

CIRCUSES

43 Lucca.

44 Siena.

45/1—24

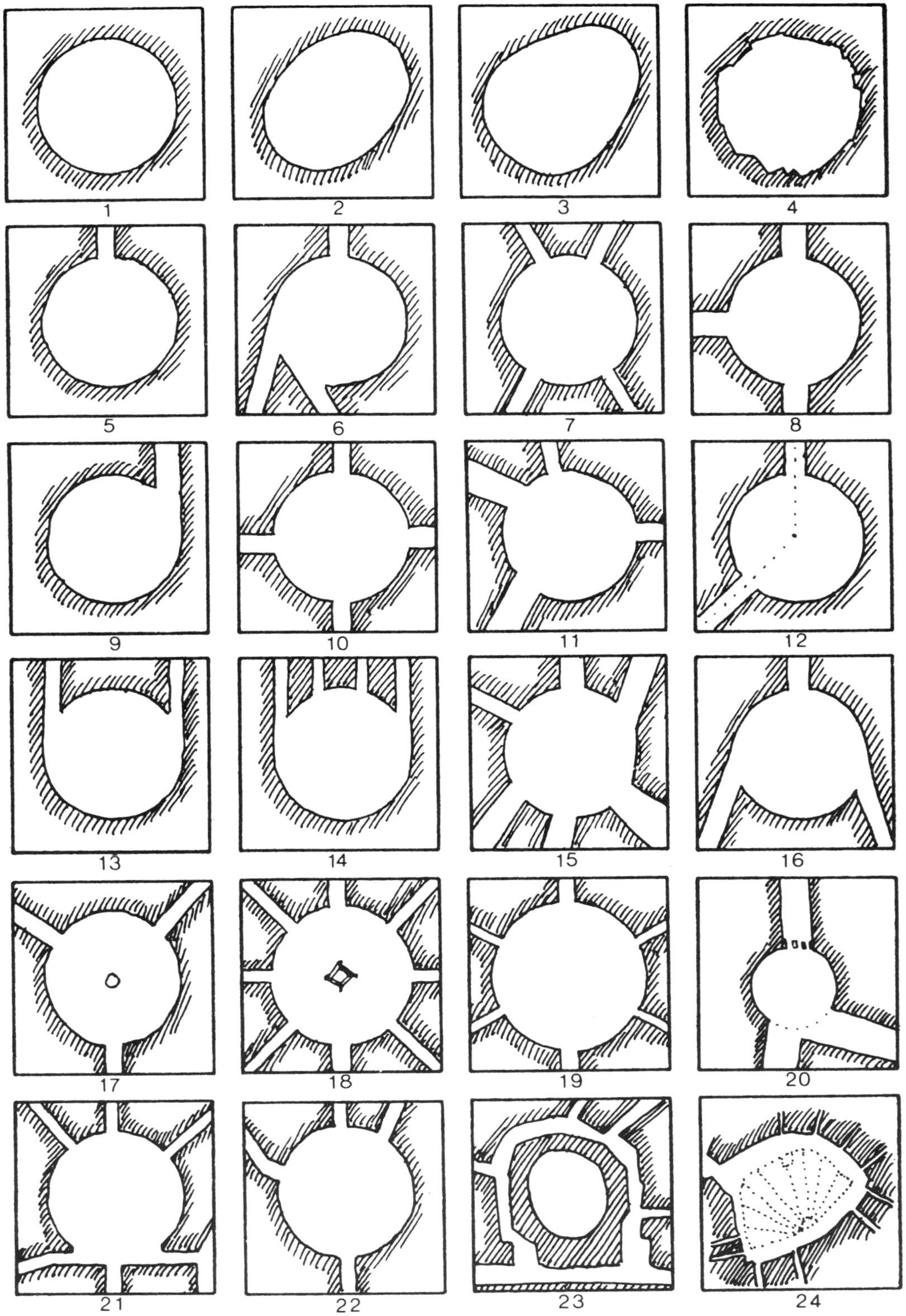

1 2 3 4

5 6 7 8

9 10 11 12

13 14 15 16

17 18 19 20

21 22 23 24

45/1–4 Regular or irregular circuses.
45/17 Bath (England), The Circus, 1754. Architect John Wood, father and son.
45/18 The Hague (Holland).
45/19 Kassel (Germany), Königsplatz, 18th century.
45/21 Paris, Place des Victoires, 1705. Architect Mansart.
45/22 Berlin (Germany), Belle-Alliance-Platz.
45/23 and 43 Lucca (Italy), Piazza del Mercato. This square was constructed on the site of the Roman amphitheatre (cf. Piazza Navona, Rome).
45/24 and 44 Siena (Italy), Piazza del Campo.

49/1–24

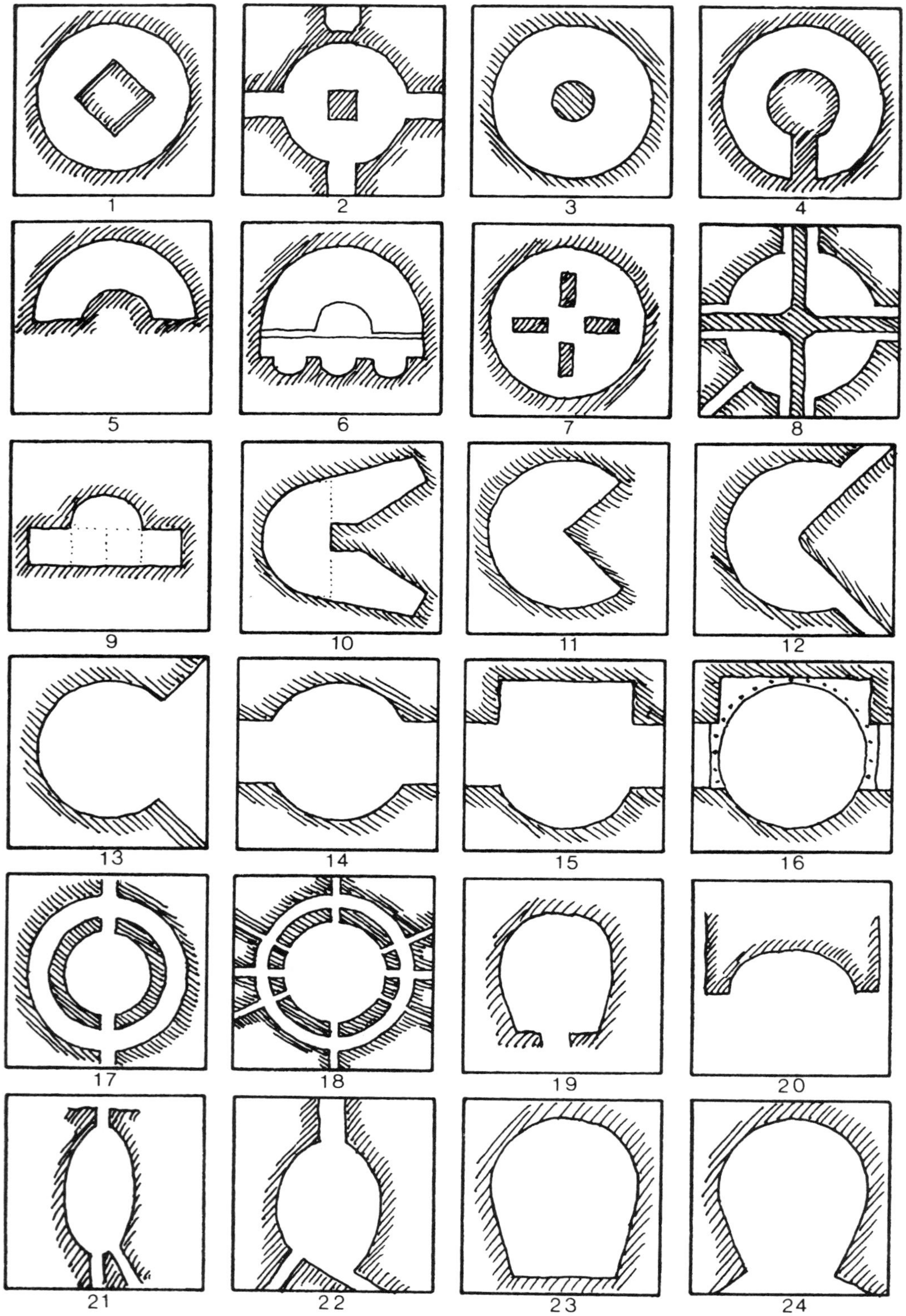

1 2 3 4

5 6 7 8

9 10 11 12

13 14 15 16

17 18 19 20

21 22 23 24

CIRCUSES CONTAINING BUILDINGS AND MODULATIONS OF THIS SPATIAL TYPE

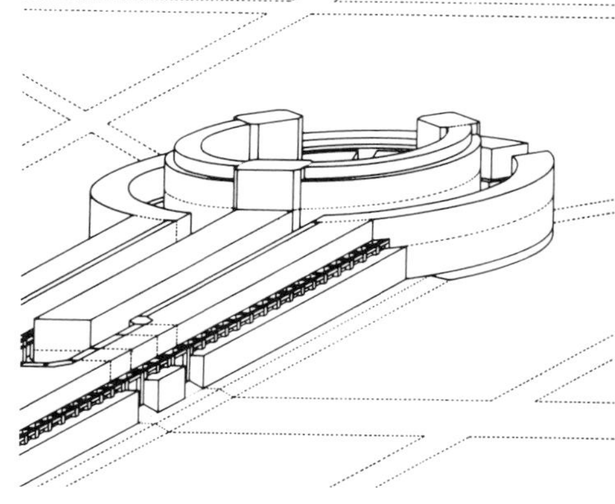

46 Leinfelden (Stuttgart), 1971 (scheme). Architect Leon Krier.

48 Author's scheme.

49/2 Gerasa (Palestine), Roman period.
49/6 Typical Roman theatre.
49/17 London, Regents Park, 1810. Architect John Nash.
49/18 Paris, Place Louis XV, 1750 (scheme). Architect M. Polard.
49/20 Bath (England). Architect John Wood.
49/21 Edinburgh (Scotland), 1766. Architect J. Brown.
49/22 Gerasa (Palestine), Roman period.

COMBINATIONS OF DIFFERENT TYPES OF CIRCUS

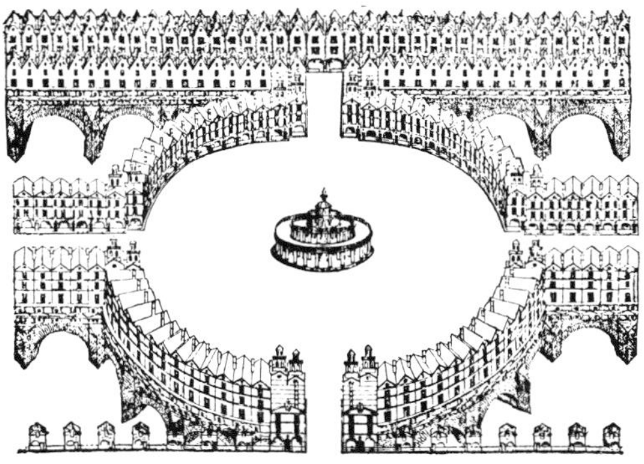

50 Paris (France), square on the Pont Neuf, 1510–1584. Architect Du Cerceau.

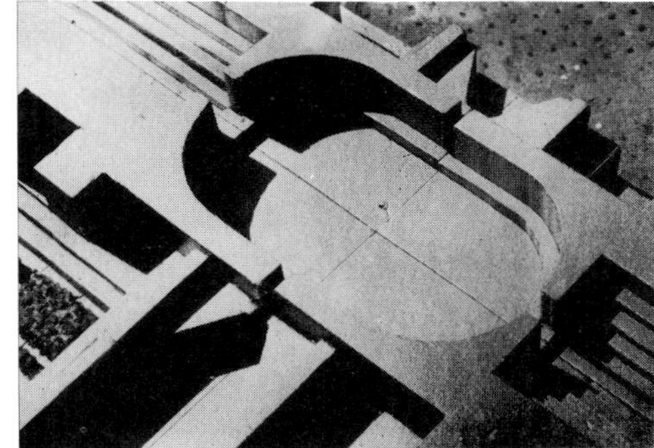

51 Author's scheme.

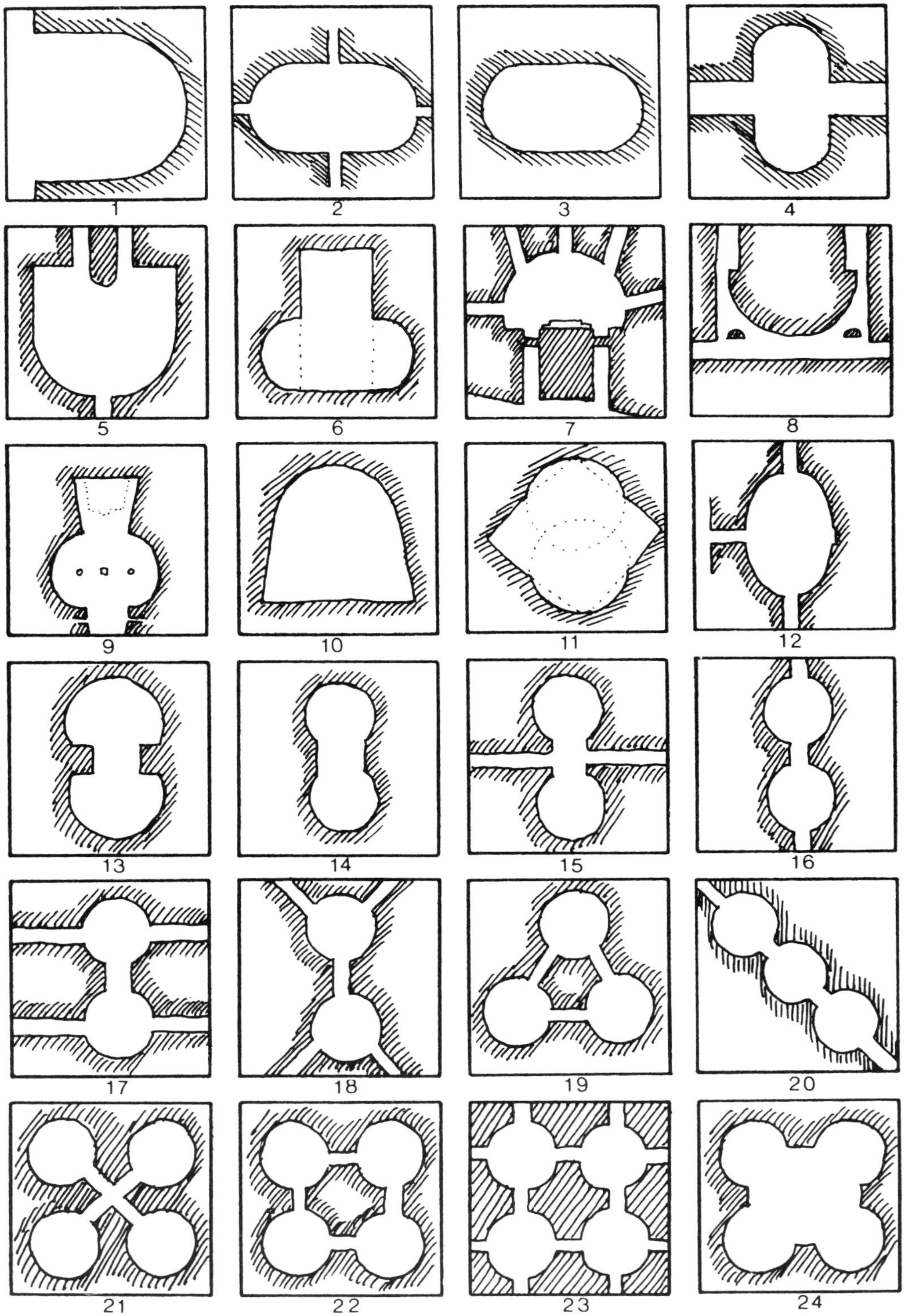

52/7 Paris (France), Place de l'Odéon, 1780.
52/8 Ostia (Italy), Roman Empire.
52/9 Rome (Italy), St. Peters, 1656. Architect Bernini.
52/12 London (England), Finsbury Circus.

A pedantic reader will notice that some spatial types in this morphological series are not in the correct place. I must admit that I did not have the patience necessary to reach this pinnacle of perfection. I nurse the silent hope that a dedicated expert will at some time apply himself to the task of compiling a perfect 'Encyclopaedia of Urban Spaces'. This is only a beginning, intended to whet the appetite for such a monstrous undertaking.

52/1–24

1 2 3 4 5 6 7 8 9 10 11 12 13 14 15 16 17 18 19 20 21 22 23 24

53 London (England), Park Crescent, 1812. Architect John Nash.

55/1–24

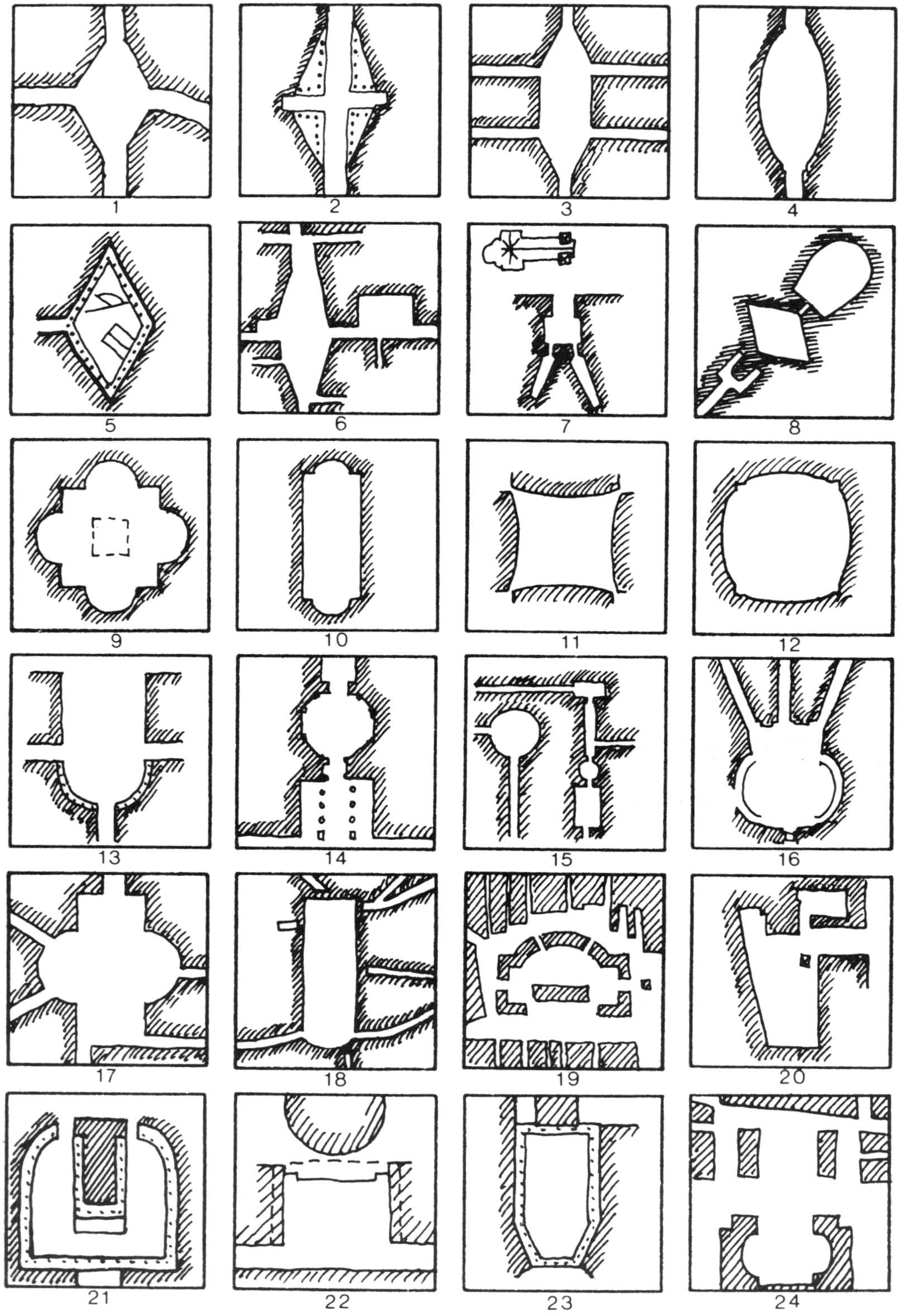

GEOMETRICALLY COMPLEX SYSTEMS

55/5, 7, 8 Stuttgart, Österreichischer Platz. Author's scheme.
55/10 Leptis Magna, Roman Empire.
55/13 London, Park Crescent, 1810. Architect John Nash.
55/16 Rome, Piazza del Populo, 1816 (proposed scheme). Architect G. Valadier.
55/18 Vigevano (Italy), Piazza Ducale, 15th century. Architect Bramante.
55/19 Turin (Italy), Mercato.
55/20 Venice (Italy), Piazza San Marco, 15th–16th centuries.
55/21 Rome, Temple of Trajan, Roman Empire.
55/22 Milan (Italy), square in front of San Carlo al Corso, 1857. Architect Carlo Amati.

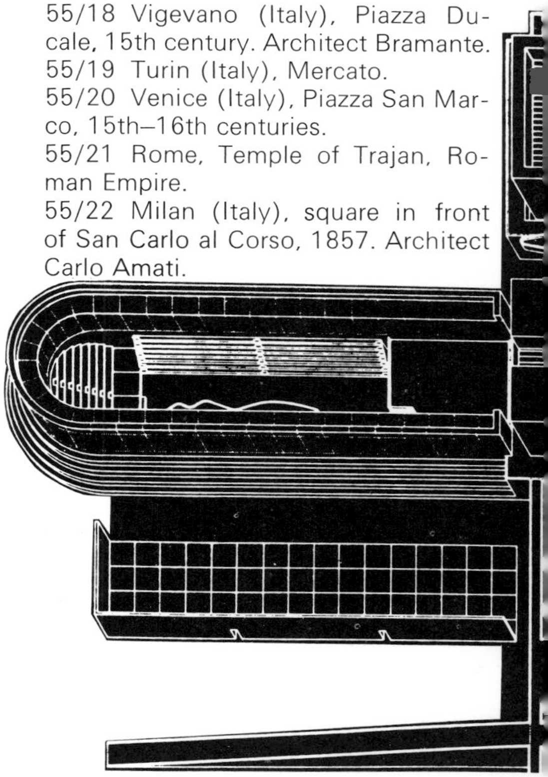

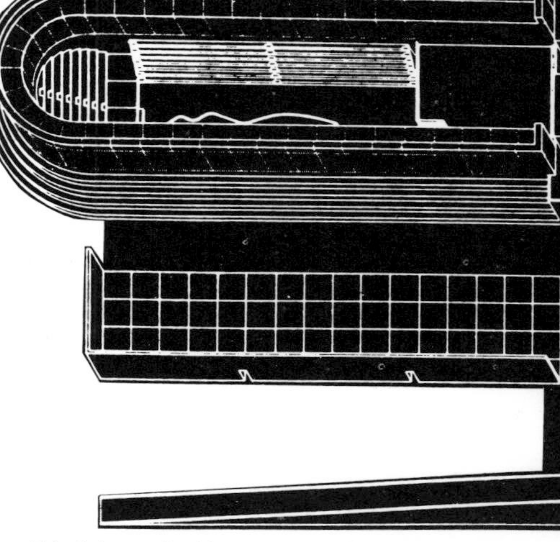

54 (above) Hannover, Sprengel Museum, 1972 (scheme). Architect Leon Krier.

55/23 Vienna, Atrium of the Votivkirche.
55/24 Vienna, Hofburg. Architect Gottfried Semper.
56/1 Rome, Piazza Navona.
56/3 Stuttgart, Königstrasse, 1782 (scheme). Architect R. F. H. Fischer.
56/5 Koblenz (Germany), Schlossplatz.
56/6 Stuttgart, Schlossplatz, 1782 (scheme). Architect R. F. H. Fischer.

GEOMETRICALLY COMPLEX SYSTEMS

56/7 Ludwigsburg (Germany), on the ramparts. Architect Frisoni.
56/8 The Hague (Holland). Architect Berlage.
56/9 Berlin–Charlottenburg, Königstrasse.
56/13 Nancy (France), Place Carrière and Place Stanislas, 1752. Architect Héré de Corny.
56/14 Ludwigsburg, Schlossplatz, 1709 (scheme). Architect J. F. Nette.
56/15 Ludwigsburg, Schlossplatz, 1713 (scheme). Architect Nette.
56/16 Edinburgh (Scotland), 1766. Architect James Brown.
56/18 Karlsruhe (Germany). Architect Weinbrenner.

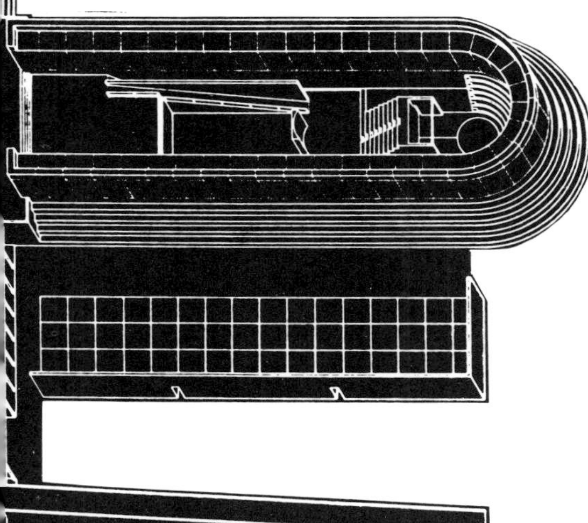

56/19 Rome, St. Peter's (scheme). Architect Fontana.
56/20 Rome, Piazza San Ignazio, 1727. Architect Raguzzini.
56/21 Stuttgart, Österreichischer Platz, 1810. Architect Thouret.
56/22 Stuttgart, Neues Schloss, 1750 (scheme). Architect Retti.
56/23 Stuttgart, Schloss Solitude, Hôtel Ducal, 1775. Architect C. V. Shell.
56/24 Stuttgart, Schloss Solitude, central area, 1764. Architects Guital, Weyhing, de la Guèpière.

56/1–24

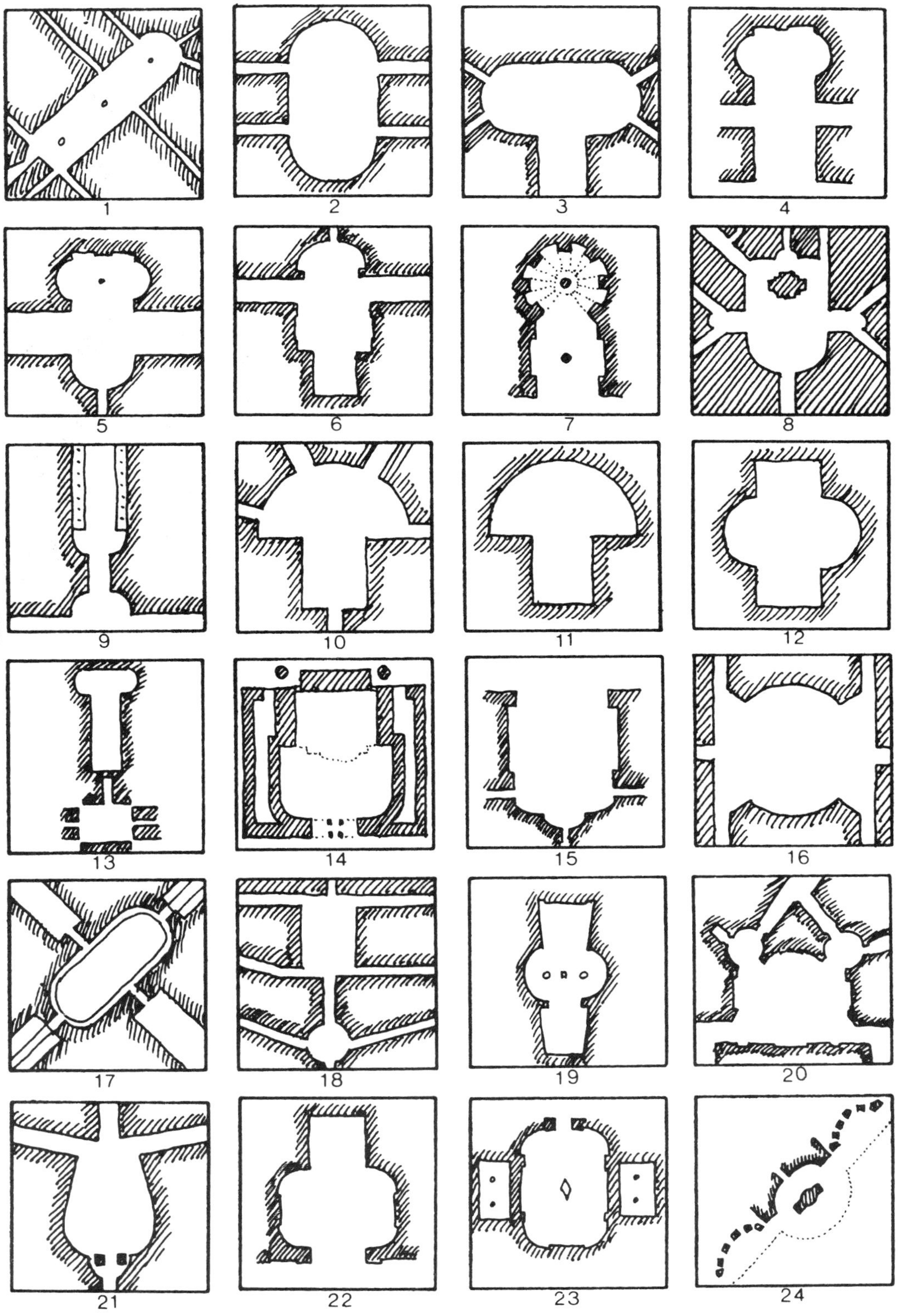

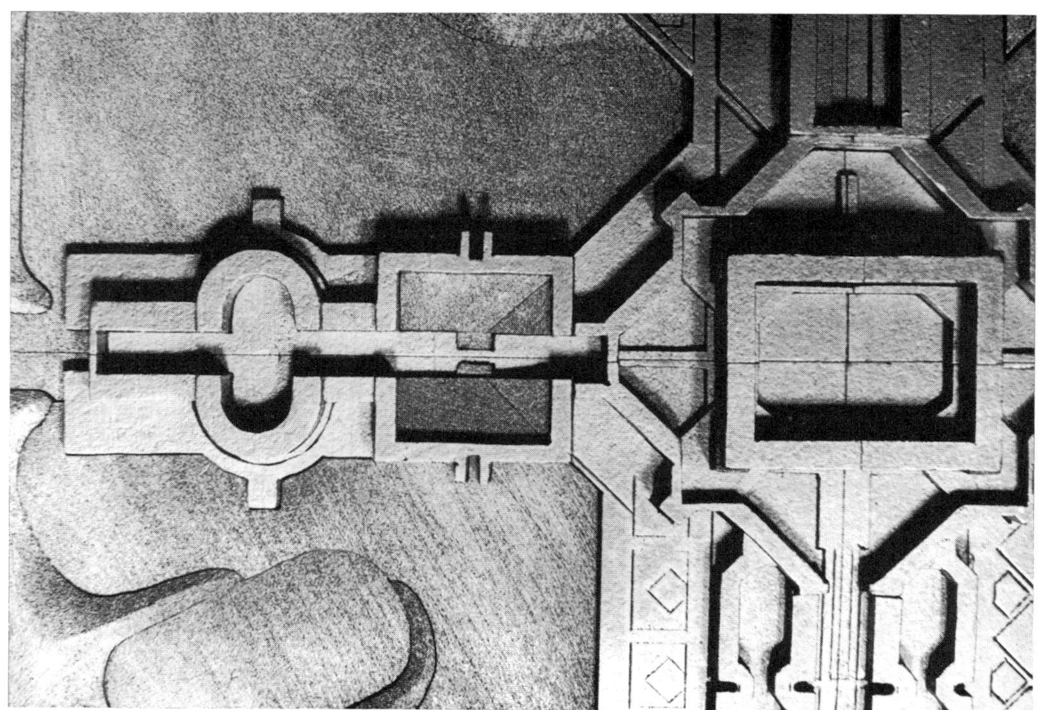

57 Design for town layout (author).

58 Stuttgart, Osterreichischer Platz (author's scheme).

59 Derby (England), 1970. Architects J. Stirling and Leon Krier.

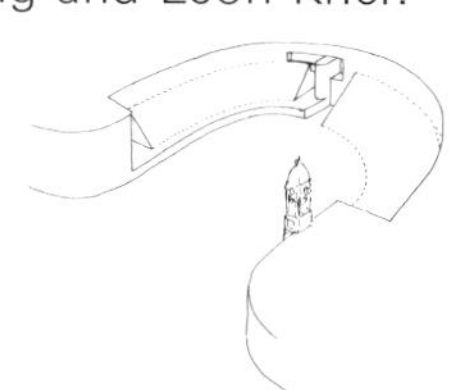

Town layout of Derby: before after.

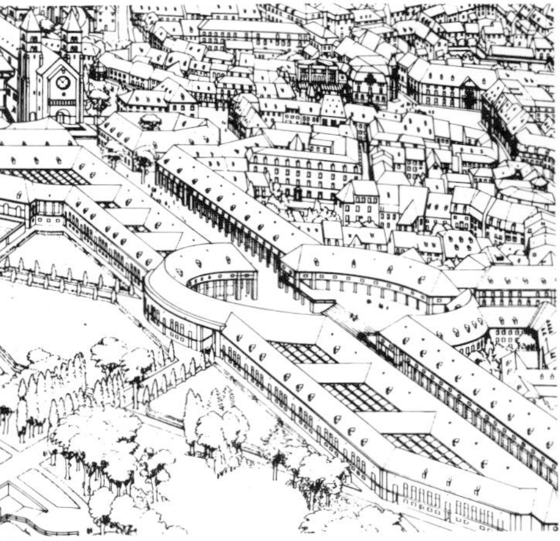

60 Echternach, 1969 (scheme). Leon Krier.

61 Piazza San Ignazio, Rome.

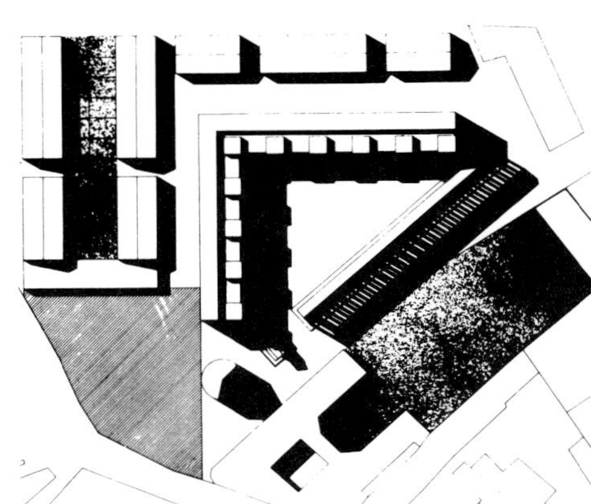

62 Square in Sannazzaro de Burgondi, 1967. Architect Aldo Rossi.

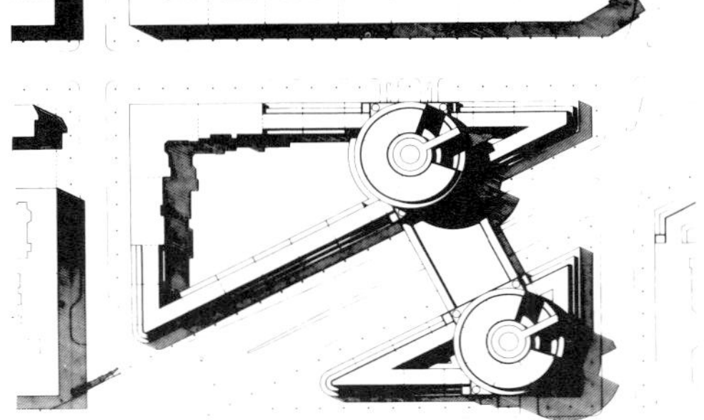

63 Berlin, 71. Scheme by Lewis–Ham–Towers. Architect Josef Paul Kleihues with Leon Krier.

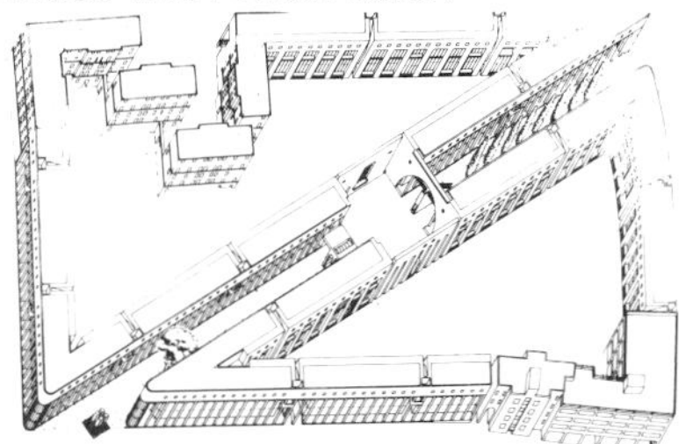

64 & 65 London, 74. Scheme by Leon Krier.

66 Triangular residential square, London 1974. Scheme by Leon Krier.

67 (see Fig. 65) Stuttgart, Charlottenplatz, 1973 (author).

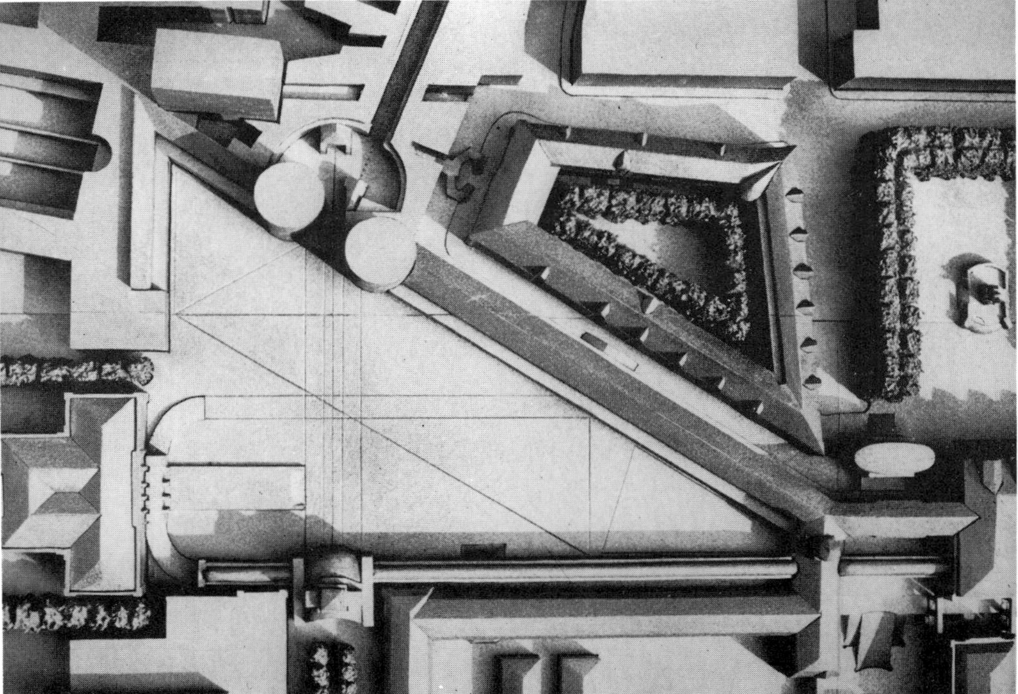

68/1–24

TRIANGULAR SQUARES AND THEIR DERIVATIVES

68/1 Paris, Place Dauphine.
68/2 Siena (Italy), Via d. Abbadia.
68/3 Siena, San Pietro alle Scale.
68/4 Siena, S. Maria de Provenzano.
68/5 Siena, San Virgilio.
68/7 Schwetzingen (Germany), Schlossgarten, 1750.
68/8 Monza (Italy).

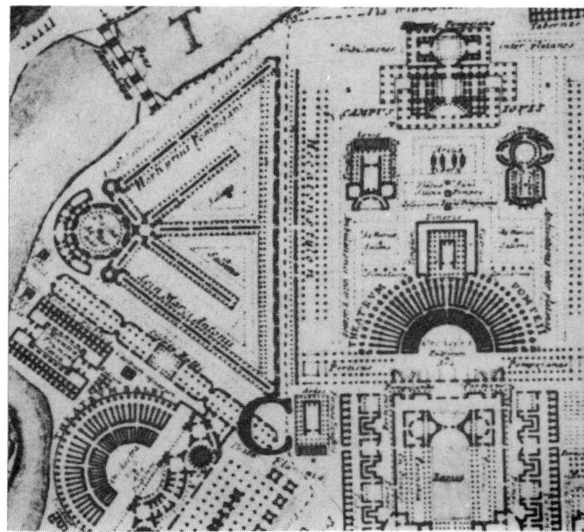

68/9 Karlsruhe (Germany), 1715.
68/10 Versailles (France), Place d'Armes. Architects Mansart and Le Vau.
68/11 Versailles, Écuries.
68/13 Vigevano (Italy), Palazzo Sforzesco.
68/14 St. Gall (Switzerland), Monastery.
68/15 Cracow (Poland).
68/16 Rome, Capitol. Architect Michelangelo.

LARGE-SCALE COMPOSITE PLANS

68/17, 18 Strasbourg (France). Designs by the architect Blondel, 1767.
68/19 Assos (Greece), Agora.
68/20 Paris, Louvre.
68/21 After Gurlitt.
68/22 San Gimignano (Italy), 1. Piazza del Duomo; 2. Piazza della Cisterna.
68/24 Turin (Italy).

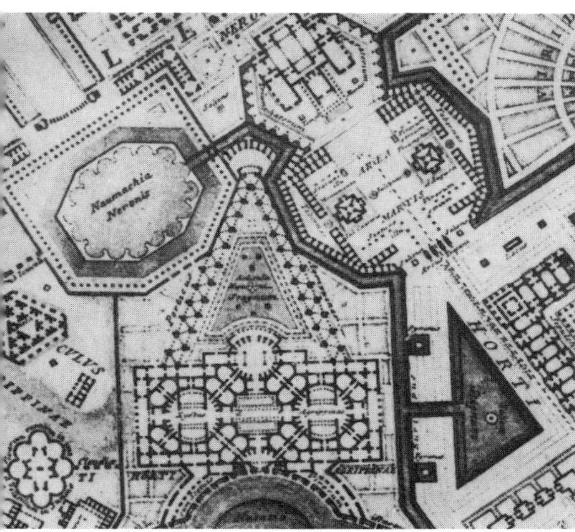

69 Section of Piranesi's proposed plan for the Campo Marti in Rome.

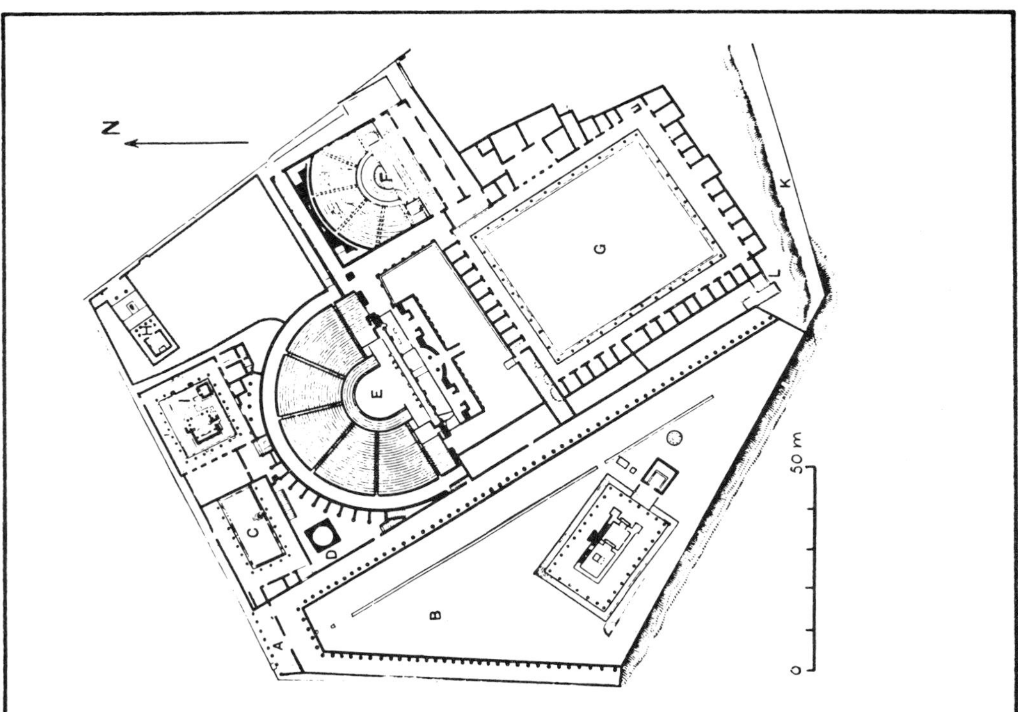

70

71

70 Pompeii, triangular forum, theatre and gladiatorial school.
71 Pompeii, comparative sketch of the same area, to clarify the spatial layout.

Regular triangular squares are extremely rare in the history of town-planning. On the other hand, there are many examples of mediaeval squares of an irregular and roughly triangular shape. These are usually formed by two roads forking.

72/1–6

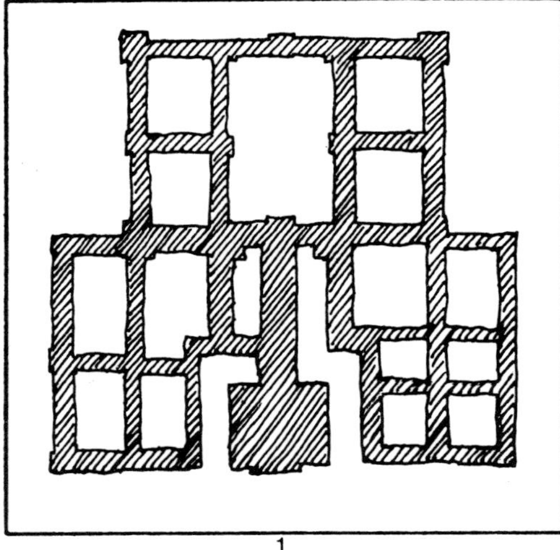
1

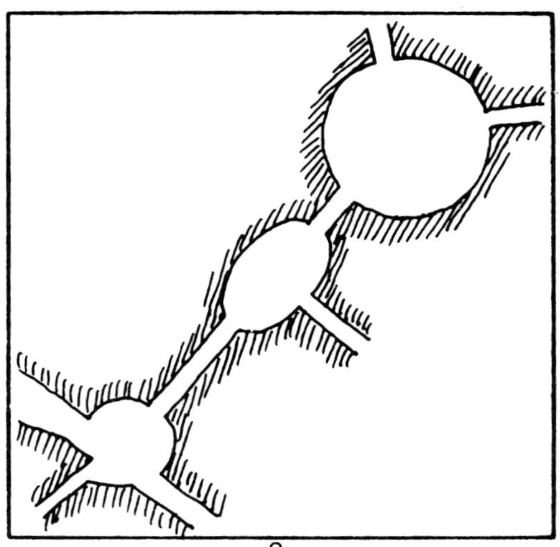
2

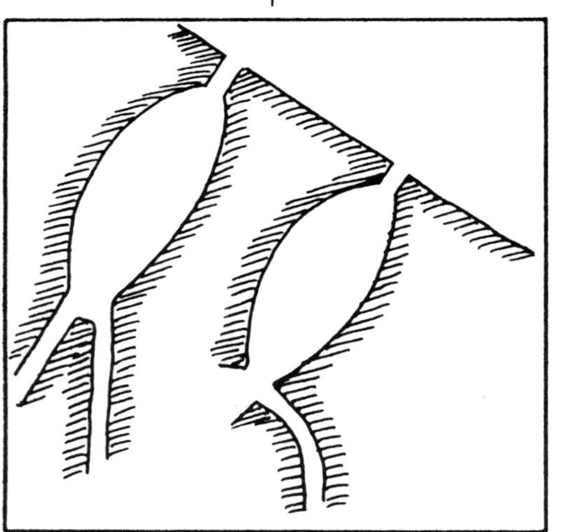
3

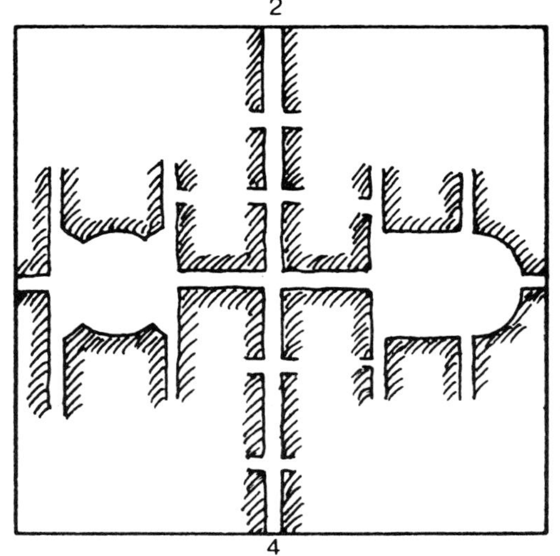
4

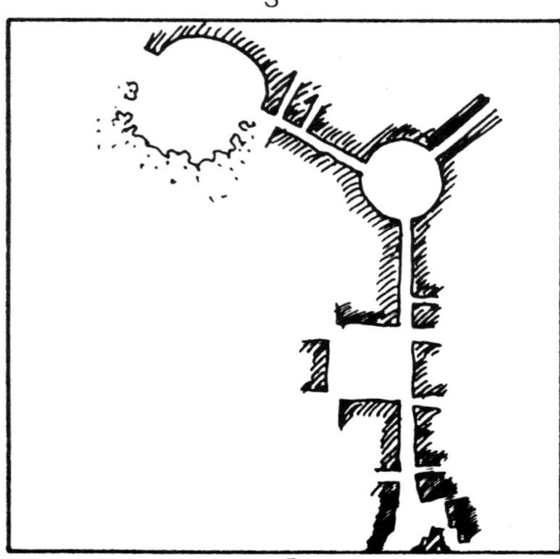
5

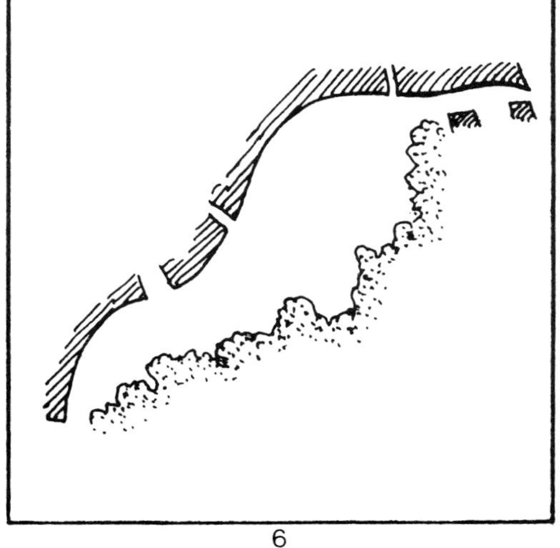
6

LARGE-SCALE COMPOSITE PLANS

72/1 Paris, Dome des Invalides, 1679–1706. Architects J. Hardouin and Mansart.
72/2, 3, 4 Edinburgh (Scotland), 1766. Architect James Brown.

73 Leningrad (U.S.S.R.), Mikhailovskaya (now Arts Square).

74 Leningrad, square in front of the Winter Palace. Architects B. Rastrelli and Carlo Rossi.

75 Naples (Italy), Piazza del Plebiscito, 1816–1846.

72/5 Bath (England), 1754–1775. Architects J. Wood sen. and jun.
72/6 Bath (England), Landsdown Crescent, 1794.

LARGE-SCALE COMPOSITE PLANS

76/4 Vienna (Austria), scheme for the alterations to the Rathausplatz. Architect Camillo Sitte.
76/5 Steyr (Austria).

See also Fig. 76/1. Architect Carlo Rossi.

See also Fig. 76/2.

See also Fig. 76/3.

76/6 Delhi, the Fort and Palace (after La Roche, Indian Architecture, 231). Note the imaginative treatment of a totally enclosed urban space.

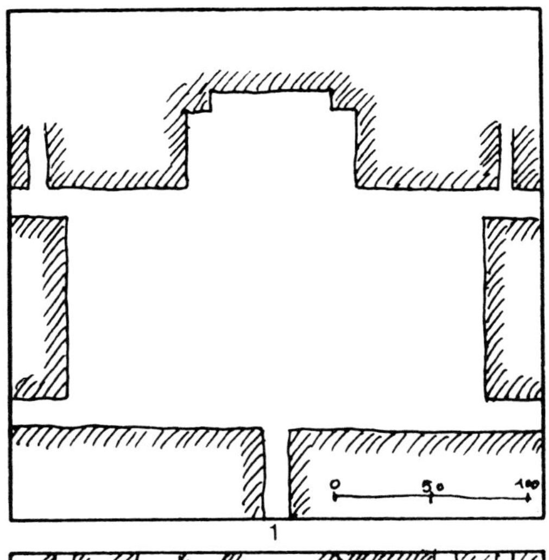

1

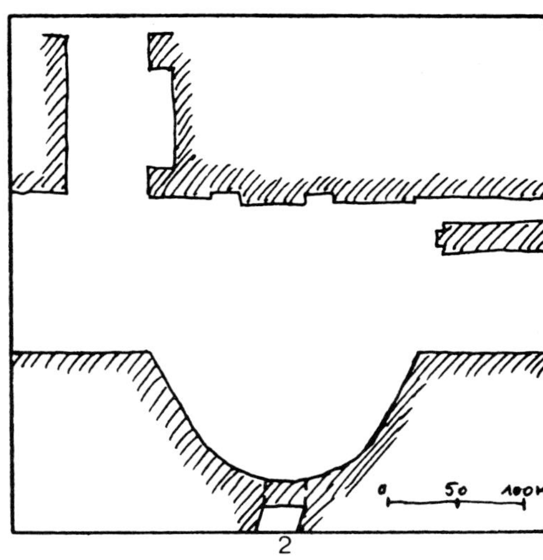

2

3

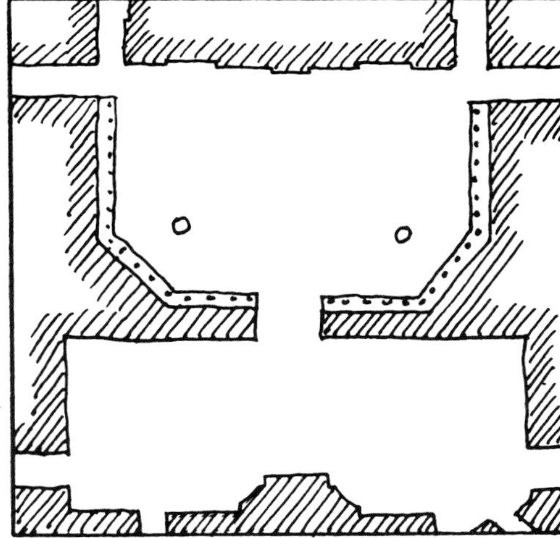

4

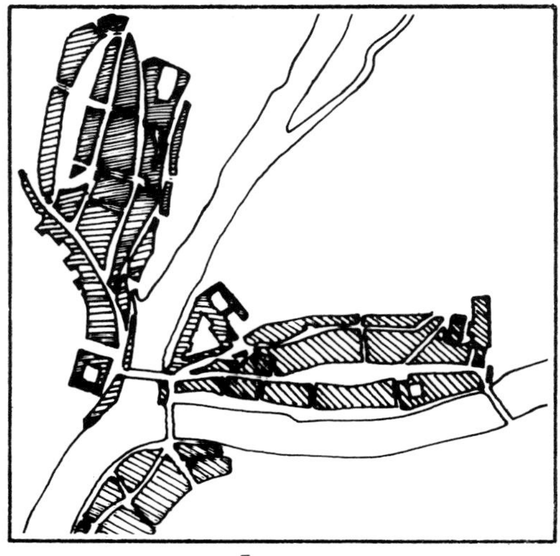

5

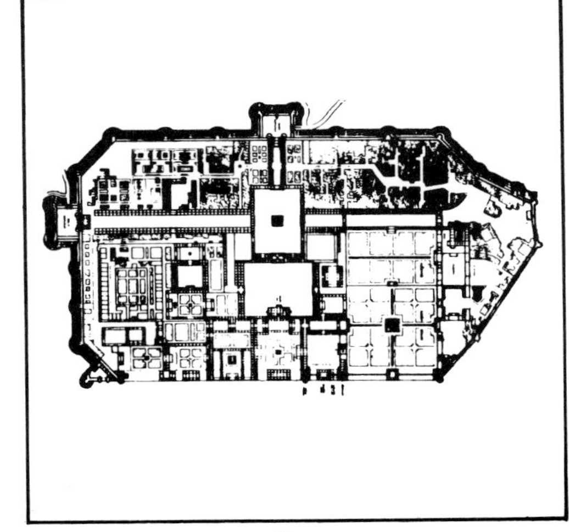

6

77/1–3

LARGE-SCALE COMPOSITE PLANS

77/1 Stupigni (Italy), 1730. Architect Filippo Juvara.
77/2 Leningrad, area containing the Alexander, Theatre and Cernysev squares, 1828–1832.
77/3 Turin (Italy), Piazza Vittorio Veneto, 1810. Architect G. Frizzi. Piazza della Gran Madre di Dio, 1818. Architect Bonsignore.

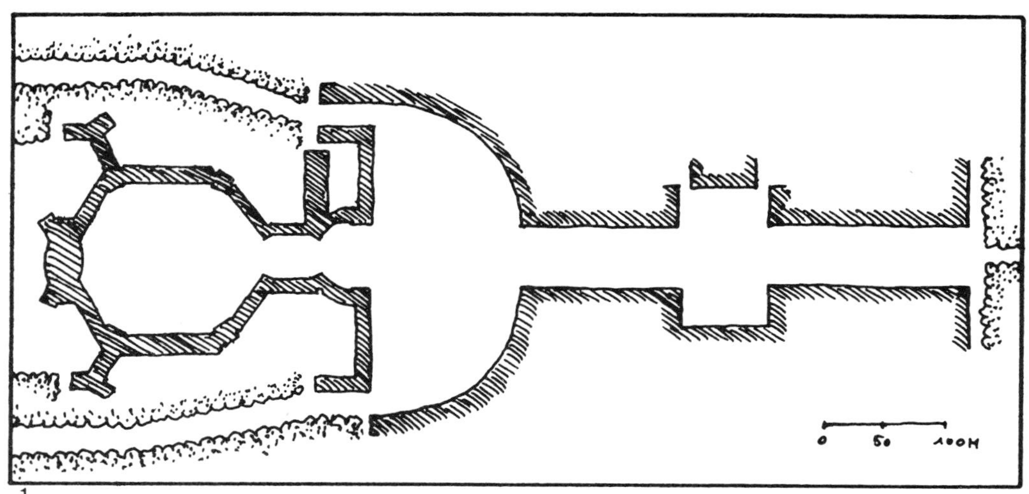

1

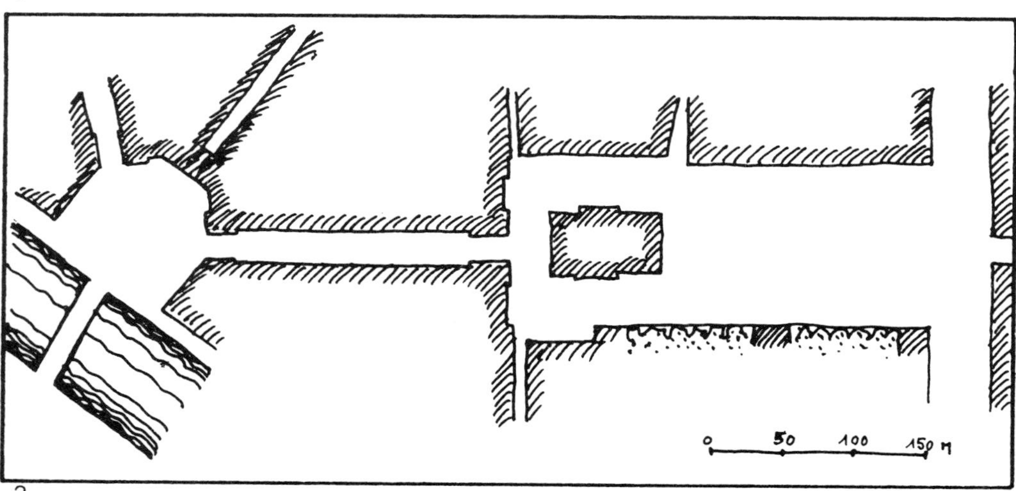

2

78 Reconstruction of the main street of Ephesus, 2nd century B.C.

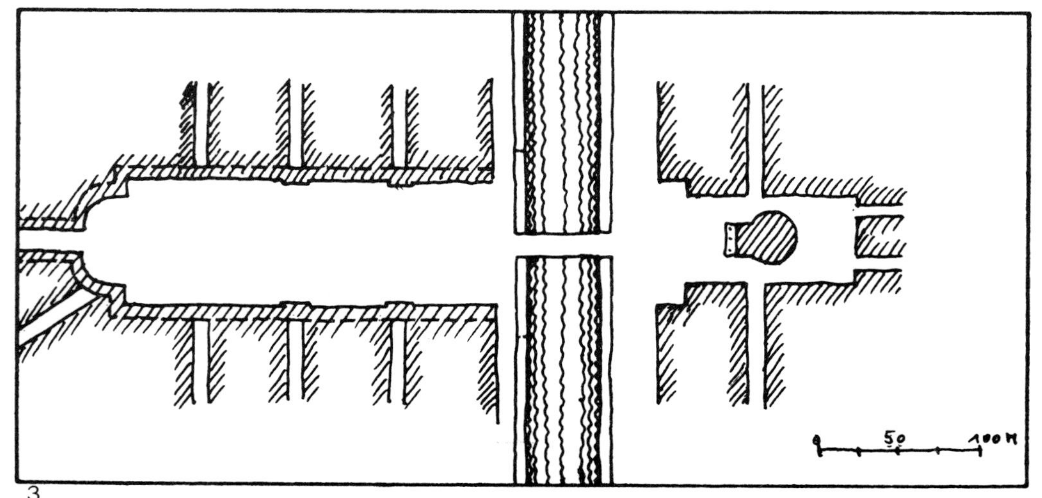

3

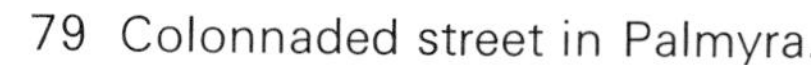

79 Colonnaded street in Palmyra.

LARGE-SCALE COMPOSITE PLANS

Let us take a look at the self-contained systems of street and square during the Roman period. The forums always lay adjacent to the streets: but the streets never actually ran through them. Even intersections in exposed spots were marked by the Romans with distinctive architectural features, as for example in Gerasa, Perge, Timgad, Leptis Magna or Palmyra. In the development of typical Roman urban architecture, an important part was played by the porticoed building borrowed from the Greeks. Originally, the Greek Agora was surrounded by one or more colonnades. In Assos, for example, and in Athens, there were two straight colonnades. In Knidos and Priene on the other hand, one straight and one U-shaped colonnade could sometimes be found opposite each other.

In his book *Grundformen der Europäischen Stadt*, Gantner shows the different stages of development of the Agoras in Milet as they progress from the open to the closed spatial system. The Agora in the lower town at Pergamon was an open space enclosed on all sides, and framed on three by colonnades. The Agora at Magnesia on the Mäander was similarly an enclosed rectangular site, but surrounded on all sides by a double colonnade. These last two Agoras were used as market places. The two Gymnasia at Priene were square open spaces, enclosed all round by a colonnade. The Romans developed these spatial types and the architecture which went with them to a perfect degree. Out of the colonnade grew the arcaded street, in evidence in almost all important Roman towns. The basilica was the next phase of development. This spatial type is a section of arcaded street, covered and enclosed.

80/1 Terracina (Italy), c. 1700.
80/2 Perge, Roman period.
80/3 Gerasa (Palestine), Roman period.

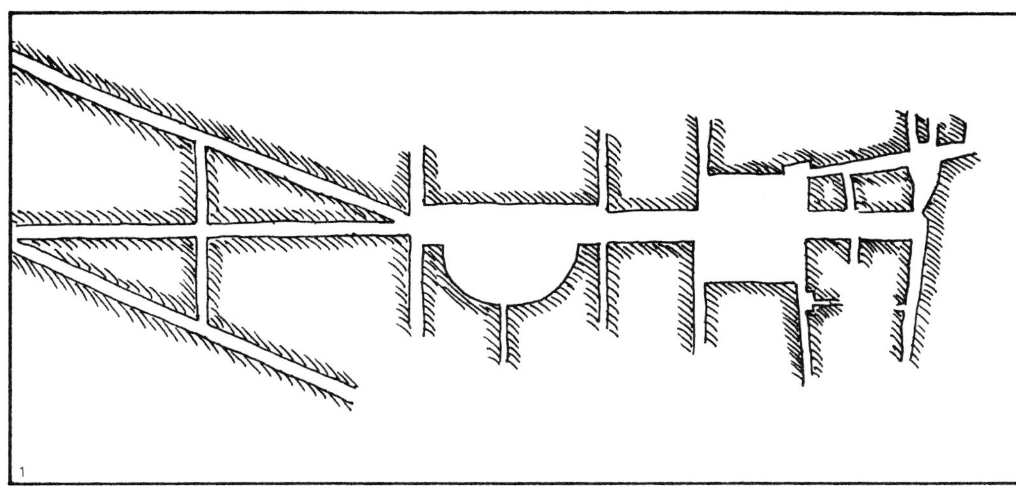
1

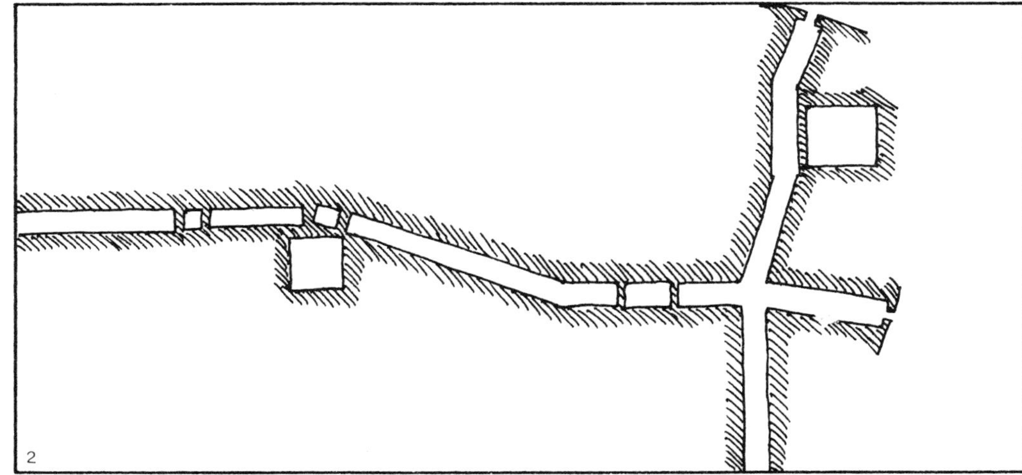
2

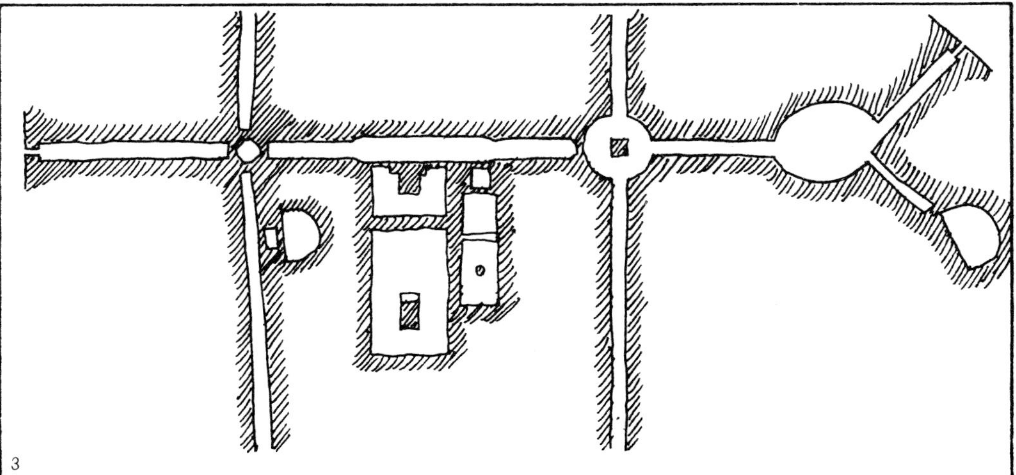
3

81/1 and 2

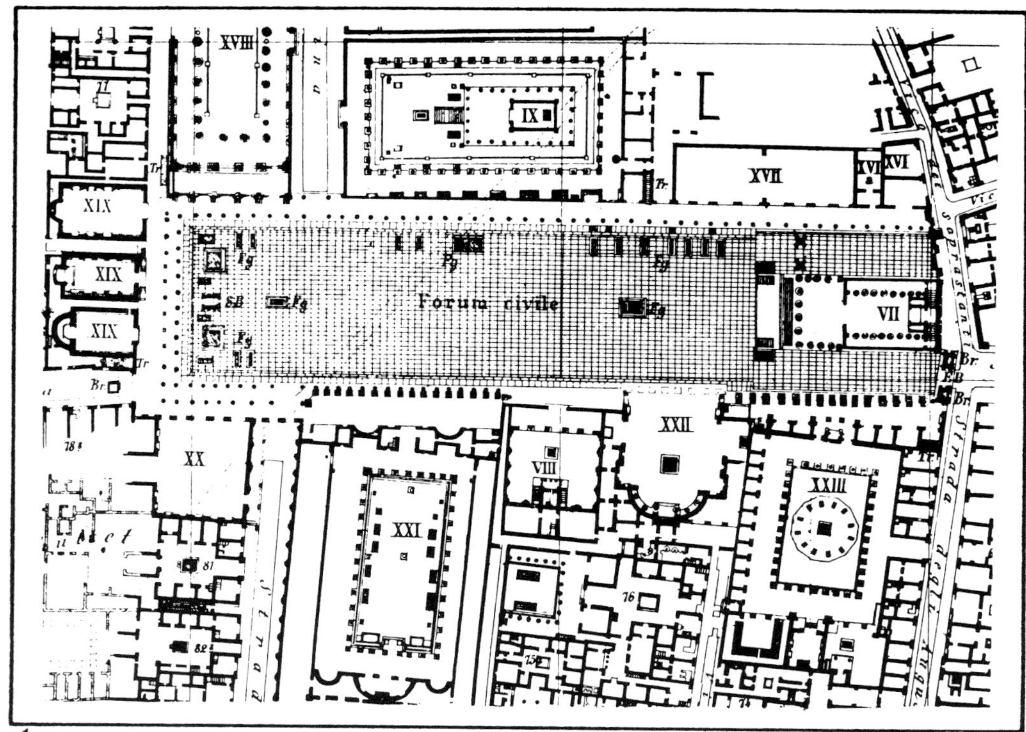

1

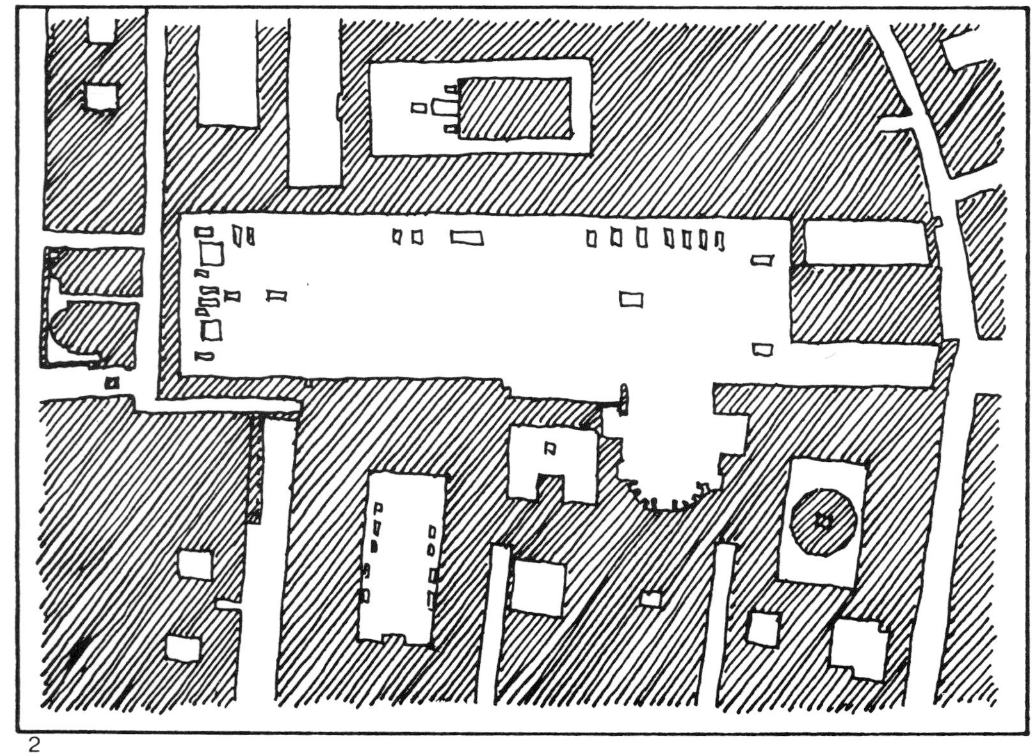

2

LARGE-SCALE COMPOSITE PLANS

81/1 Pompeii, Forum.
81/2 Pompeii, Forum: simplified sketch, bringing out clearly the layout of urban space. The streets which emerge on to the square are intercepted by the colonnades of the forum, so that the spatial effect of the enclosure of the square remains.

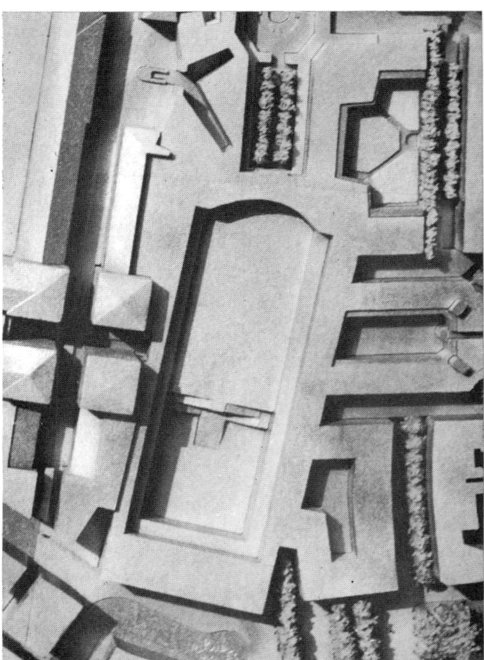

82 Stuttgart, Rotebühlstrasse, 1973 (author's scheme). Cf. Piazza Navona in Rome, Bramante's Piazza del Belvedere in the Vatican, and the Piazza del Duomo in Vigevano, also by Bramante.

83/1–3

LARGE-SCALE COMPOSITE PLANS

Coming from the old Forum, which was surrounded by a large variety of isolated buildings, you first enter directly the Forum of Caesar adjacent to the Curia. This was bordered by a colonnade. The temple, relatively spacious in relation to the square, occupies a good quarter of it. Next, you enter the Forum of Augustus. This was roughly twice as large as the first and its space was articulated in a fundamentally different way. The temple was not free-standing in the square, but was pushed back, which meant that it had no rear elevation. To heighten the perspective of the square, the single colonnade was taken almost to the front of the temple. Where the colonnades ended, semi-circular lateral niches were inserted, emphasising the transparency of the square. The rear

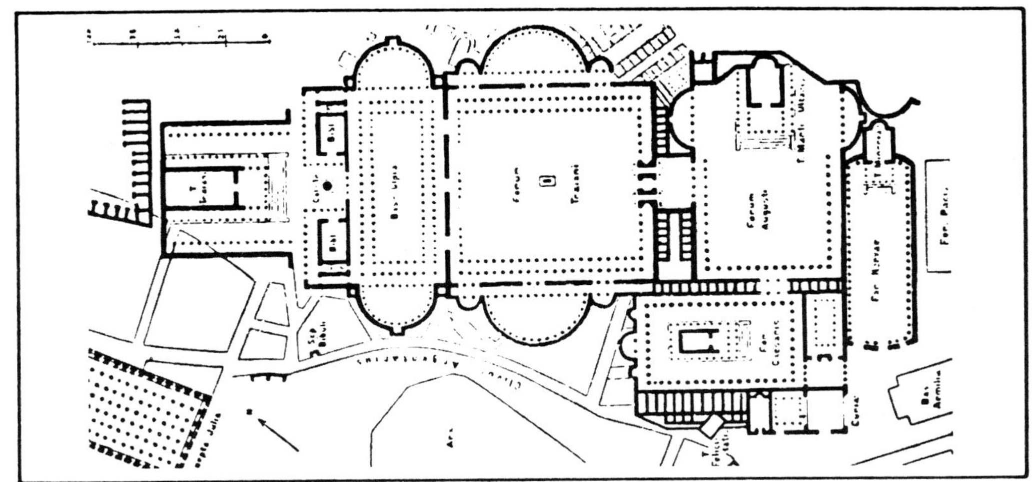

1

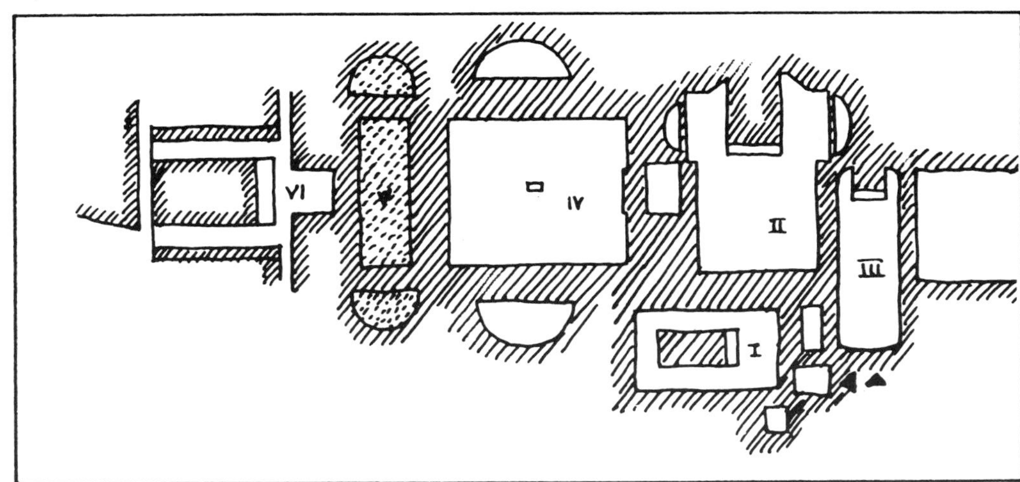

2

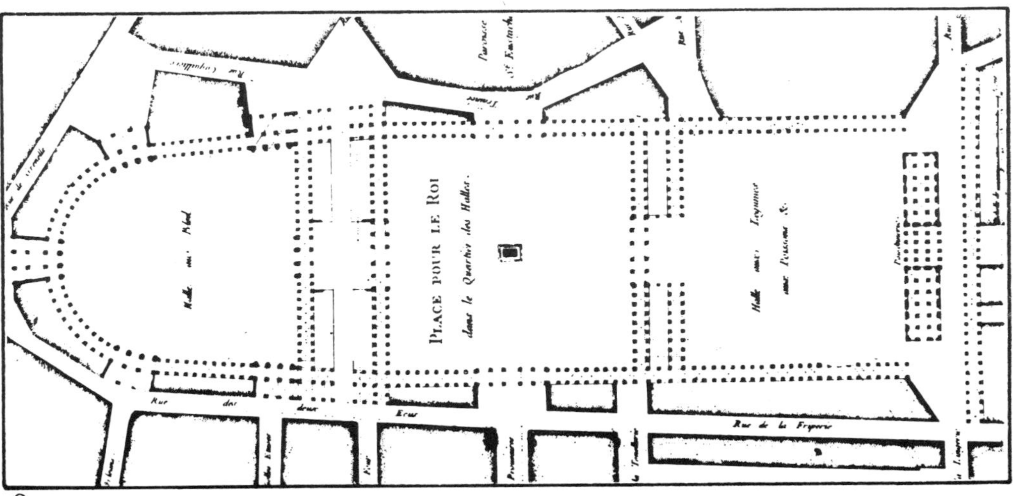

3

83/1 The Imperial Forum in Rome, completed under the emperor Trajan by the architect Apollodor of Damascus.

83/2 The spatial breakdown of the Forum complex : I have found so many different attempts to reconstruct this complex that it is difficult for someone who is not an architectural historian to opt for a convincing version. Whether mine is correct in every detail is not really relevant here. I only want to describe briefly the architectural and spatial features which broadly characterise this layout. It is important to say at the outset that – contrary to all expectations – the ceremonial layout is not flanked or approached by any formal avenues.

83/3 Second design by the architect Boffrand for a Place Louis XV in Paris (site of the recently demolished Les Halles). This scheme, c.1750, is obviously not comparable in its complexity to the Imperial Forum in Rome, but it has certainly been influenced by it.

84/1 and 2

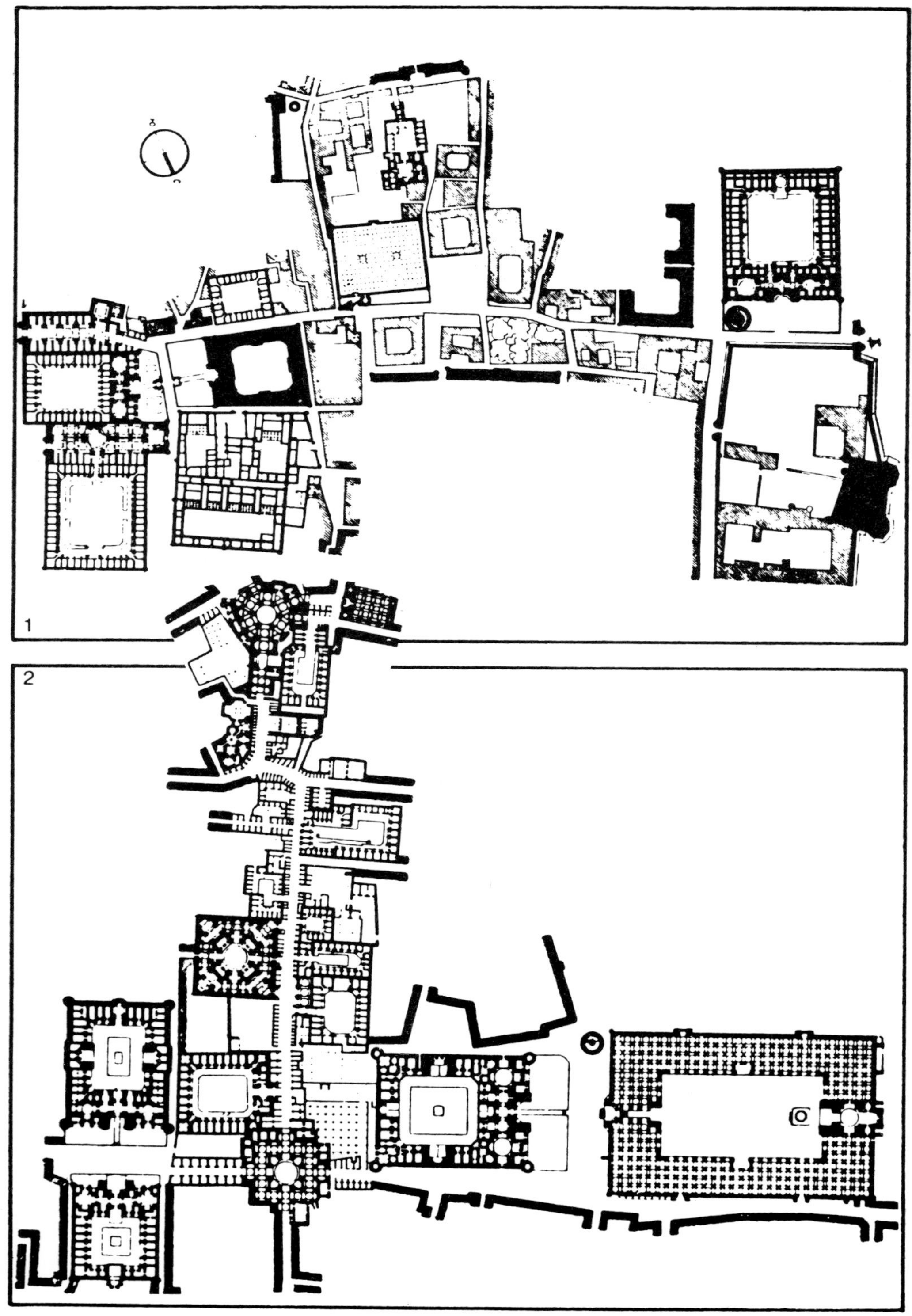

wall was angled towards the temple, theatrically exaggerating the depth of the space.

The Forum of Nerva, which flanked the first two, evinces the spatial impression described above in a different form, this time excessively so. The square was extremely elongated, and rounded off at its top end like a circus. The Temple of Minerva was squeezed out of the Forum altogether. All that remained in the square itself were the steps and the portico of the temple.

Moving on from the Forum of Augustus, you cross an Atrium into the Forum of Trajan, which measured approximately 90 x 110 metres. The entrance was adorned with a triumphal arch. From this point, the rest of the complex was laid out axially. It should be noted above all how the surrounding colonnades of the different forums were varied. In the latter, a single row of columns stood on each side of the triumphal arch, then to the left and right of the main axis a double colonnade, which created spatial depth by means of semi-circular apses. The facing wall of the square was unadorned except for the entrances to the adjacent Basilica Ulpia, which were decorated with columns. According to Paul Bigot's reconstruction, the central area and the two flanking colonnades were covered. The semi-circular apses at the top were left open. The result was two rows of columns on the longer axis of the basilica and three on its transverse axis.

Finally, after crossing a very narrow Atrium, in which Trajan's column

84/1 Chiwa (Usbekistan, U.S.S.R.), main streets. On the right, the east gate of the old town, on the left the west gate. Top left in the picture is the citadel.
84/2 Buchara (Usbekistan, U.S.S.R.), main crossroads of the old town.

LARGE-SCALE COMPOSITE FORMS

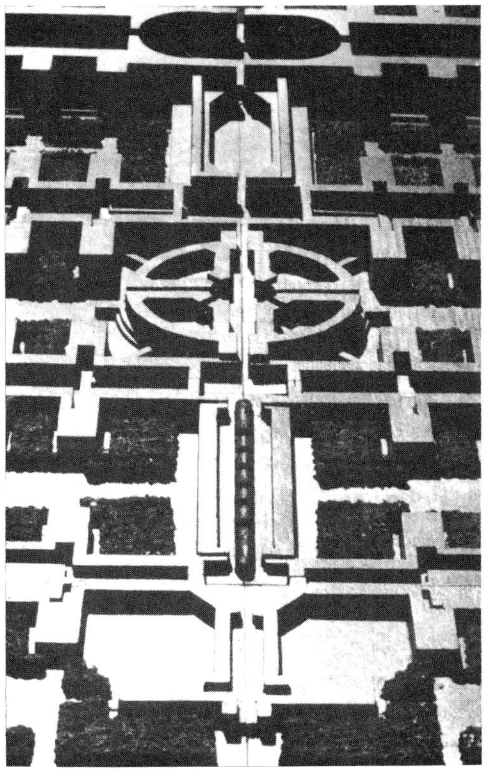

85 Author's scheme, in which particular attention is paid to the interplay of street and square.

stands, you reach the Temple of Trajan, built in an extraordinarily cramped site, so that on each side of the temple all we have is a space the width of a street. In the context of the whole compositional flow of the Imperial Forum complex, it is very easy to detect the intention behind this spatially constricted finale.

86/1 and 2

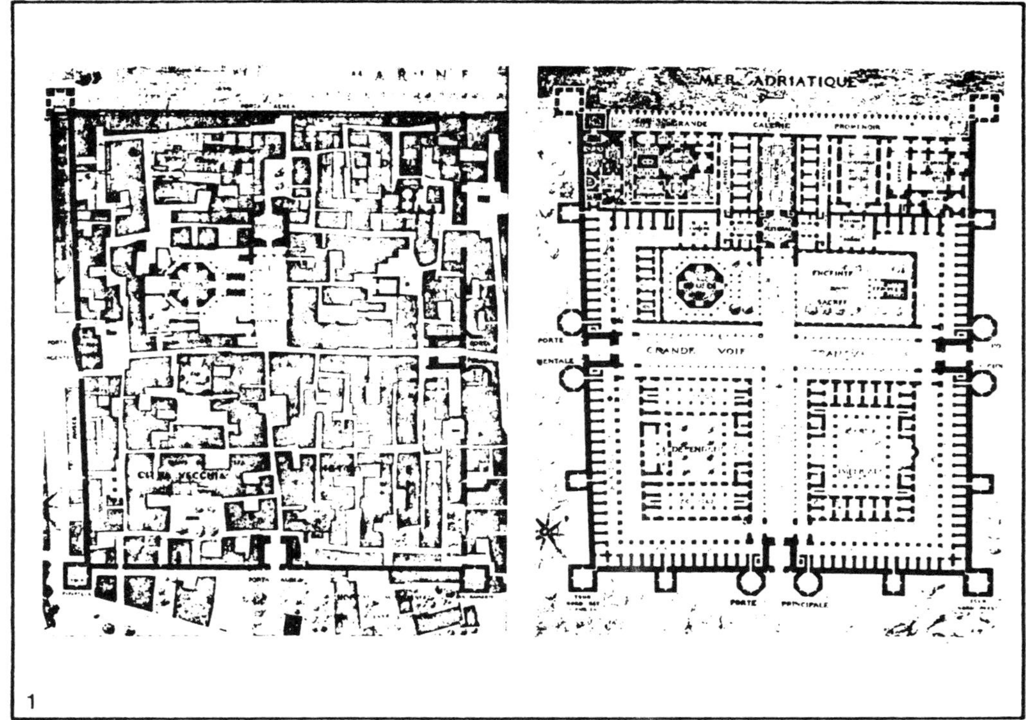

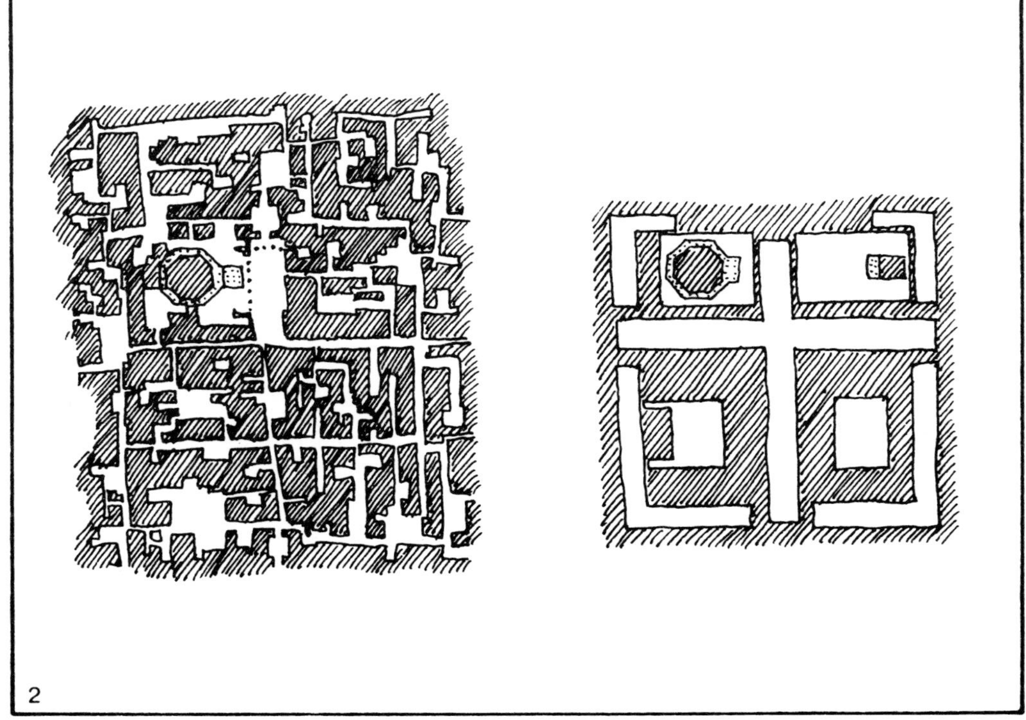

86/1 Spalato: on the right, the Palace of Diocletian, A.D. 300, as reconstructed by E. Hébrard (external dimensions 215 x 176 metres); on the left the town as it is today.
86/2 Comparison of the systems underlying the town plan.

87/1–6

1

2

3

4

5

6

STREET PLANS

This series of street plans can be infinitely expanded. Every town has a large number of extremely interesting street plans, which are uniquely linked to the place's history, its topography and its inhabitants.

87/1 Paris, Avenue Richelieu.
87/2 Naples (Italy), Corso Re d'Italia, 1888–1894.
87/3 Street plan, after Gurlitt.
87/4 Karlsruhe (Germany), Kaiserstrasse.
87/5 Paris, Rue de Tournon, 1780.
87/6 Rome, Circus Maximus. Looked at lengthwise, the elongated racecourse has the appearance of a street, and it is of course flanked by terracing.

88 Author's scheme, in which particular attention is paid to the interplay of street and square.

VARIATIONS AND INVENTIONS

For anyone who is creative or wishes to become so, these children's drawings can have a meaning which points far beyond the limits of the subject under discussion.

My seven year old daughter Caren didn't want to take second place to her daddy while he was busy assembling his collection. She has included people in her drawings, as if to remind her father that the whole abstract game-playing has no meaning without people. She is right, and I'm ashamed at so much 'useless messing around' . . . !

89

89–91 Streets with archway, fence and flags. Drawings by Caren.

90

91

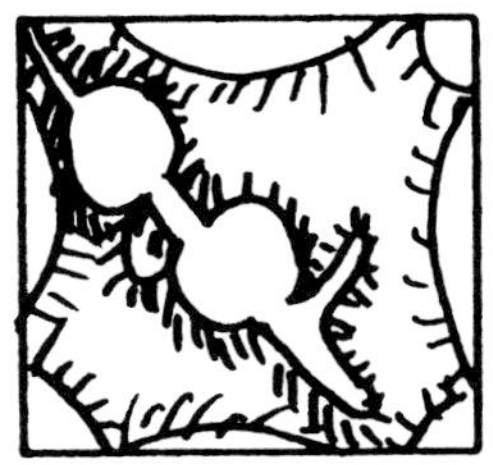
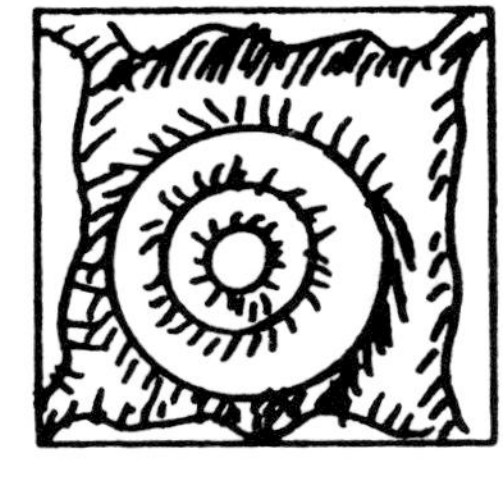
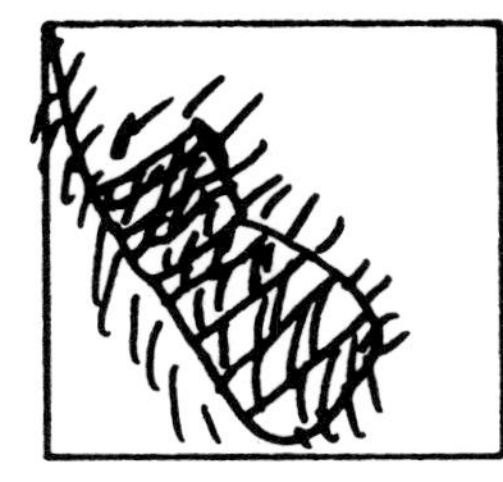
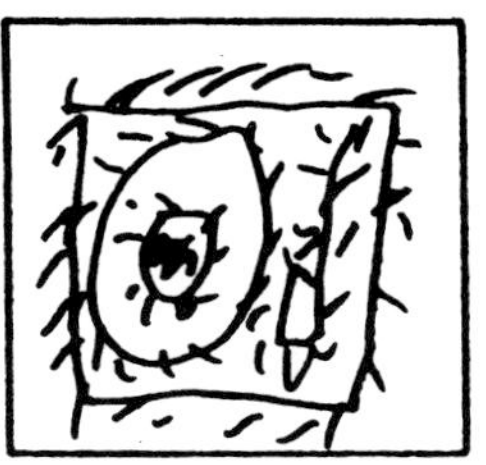

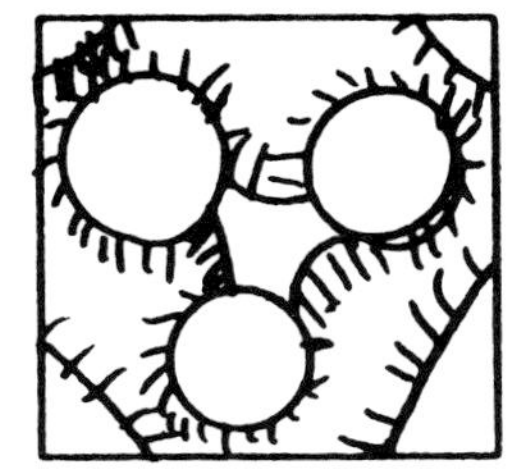
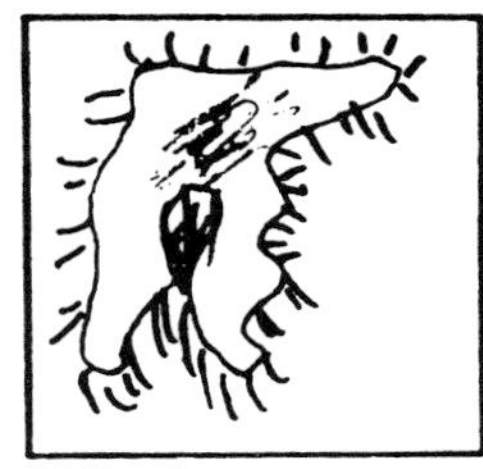

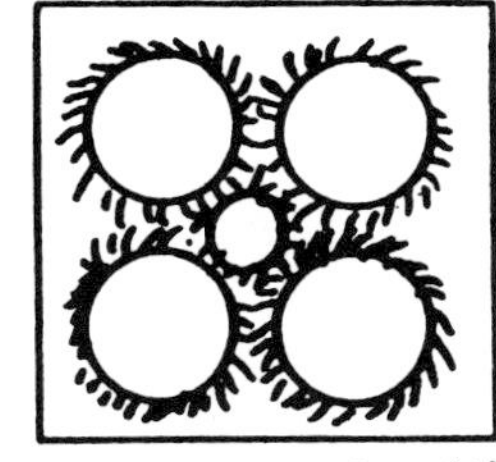
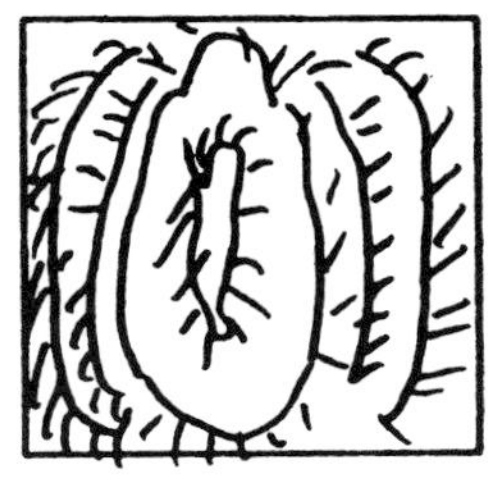
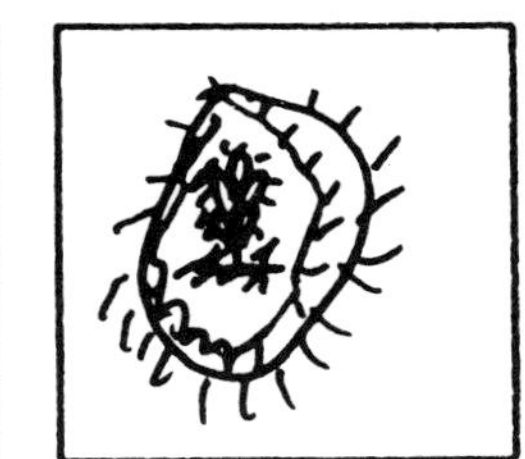

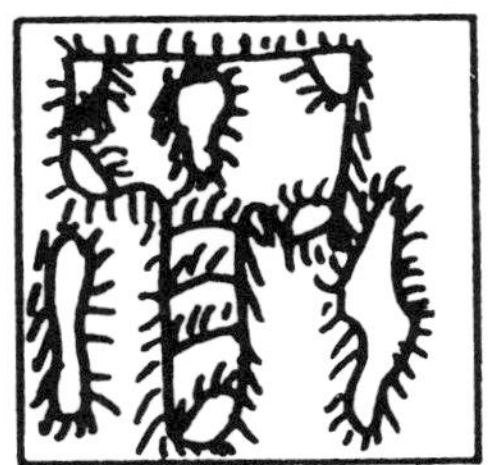
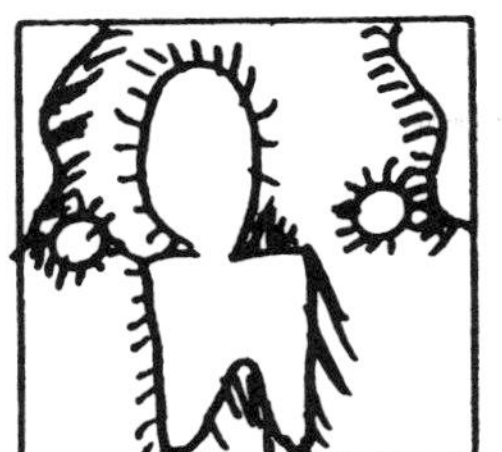

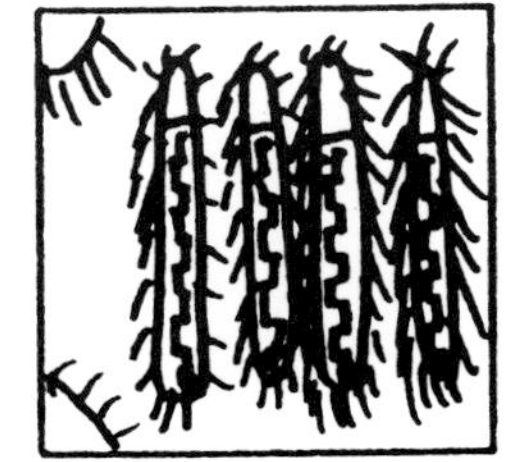

EPILOGUE TO THE CHAPTER: 'THEORY OF URBAN SPACE'

I hope to have shown by this wealth of material that my definition of the concept of urban space was arrived at after careful consideration. The fact that I had to rely so heavily on historical heritage only indicates that knowledge gained over the course of centuries carries a certain conviction which we cannot allow to go unnoticed. I have collected this material primarily for students, in the hope of encouraging them to delve more deeply into our architectural heritage. There are almost no further discoveries to be made in architecture. In our century the problems have merely changed their dimension. This is often so dramatic that one cannot warn too emphatically against hasty, untested solutions. As long as man needs two arms and two legs, the scale of his body must be the measure of size for all building. That concerns not only staircases and ceiling height, but also the design of public space in the urban context. In this respect, town planning in our century has been a miserable failure. To support this statement, I would like to follow with a chapter which describes the historical course which the destruction of urban space has followed.

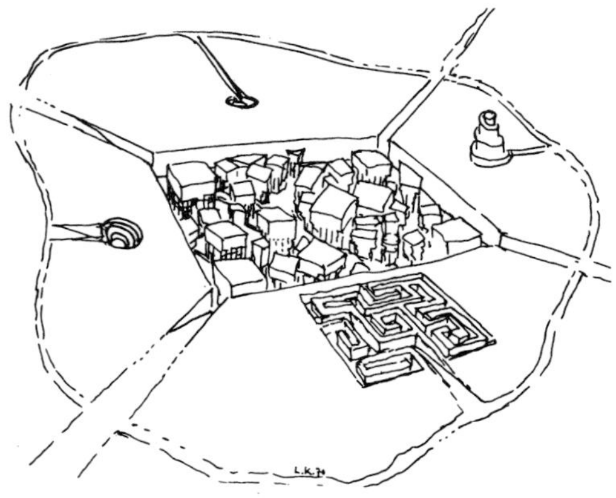

92 Drawing by Leon Krier.

CHAPTER 2

THE EROSION OF URBAN SPACE

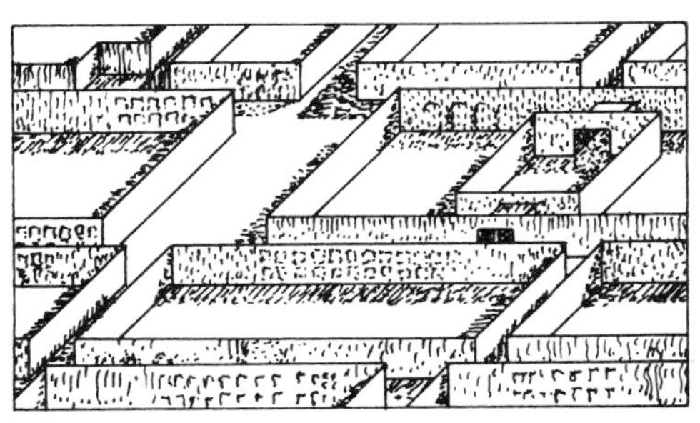
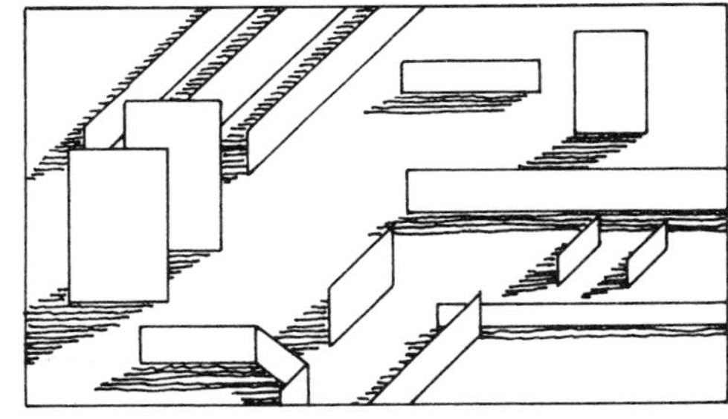

IN 20th CENTURY TOWN PLANNING

CHAPTER 2

THE EROSION OF URBAN SPACE IN 20th CENTURY TOWN PLANNING

HISTORICAL SUMMARY

The development after the French Revolution of new military technology and new tactical patterns for warfare ushered in an era in which all assumptions and empirical principles about town planning were fundamentally questioned. This was a break with tradition which is unique in cultural history, and for which neither architects nor lawyers and politicians

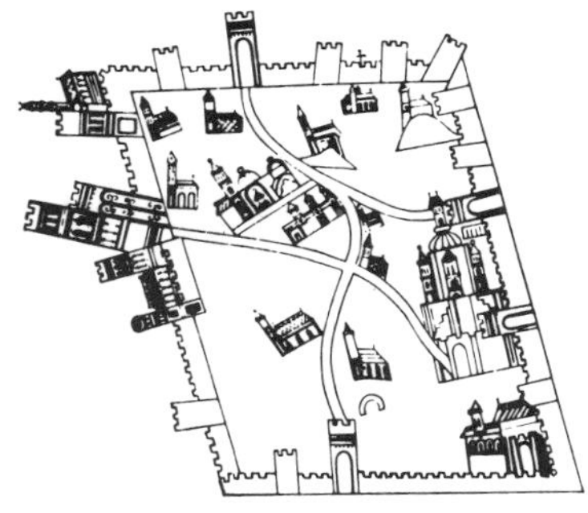

93 Jerusalem, plan by Cambrai.

were prepared. The defensive systems of towns no longer offered adequate protection against the new weaponry. Warfare had taken on fresh dimensions, and city walls, now no more than a futile shell around the old core of the town, were demolished. Until this time, defensive measures had played a well-defined role in town planning. They could be described as salient factors in planning, 'regulators' of urban space.

94 Vienna, early 19th century.

The absolute necessity of protection and security had imposed a total discipline on every aspect of the town: its construction, rebuilding and expansion. This holds true from the time of the earliest known human settlements. The decline of the city wall coincided with the onset of industrial development, which forced cities into unprecedented growth. The spread of cities over the surrounding countryside now went on unchecked. The first new residential areas were for the most part laid out regularly around the old town centre, according to the then familiar chessboard pattern, which was almost always used as the basis for new settlements.

Until about 1900 there was no significant variation in this method of town-planning. Four publications around this time attempted to use new ideas to challenge this type of development: Ebenezer Howard with his book *Garden Cities of Tomorrow*, Soria y Mata with his notion of the linear city (1882), Tony Garnier with his *Cité industrielle* (1904) and Camillo Sitte with *Stadtebau nach seinen kunstlerischen Grundsatzen*. Howard proposed a unit of 'reasonable size' as an alternative to unwieldy agglomerated centres. His study is based on sociological considerations and a concern for public health. Sitte criticised above all the artistic impoverishment of urban space.

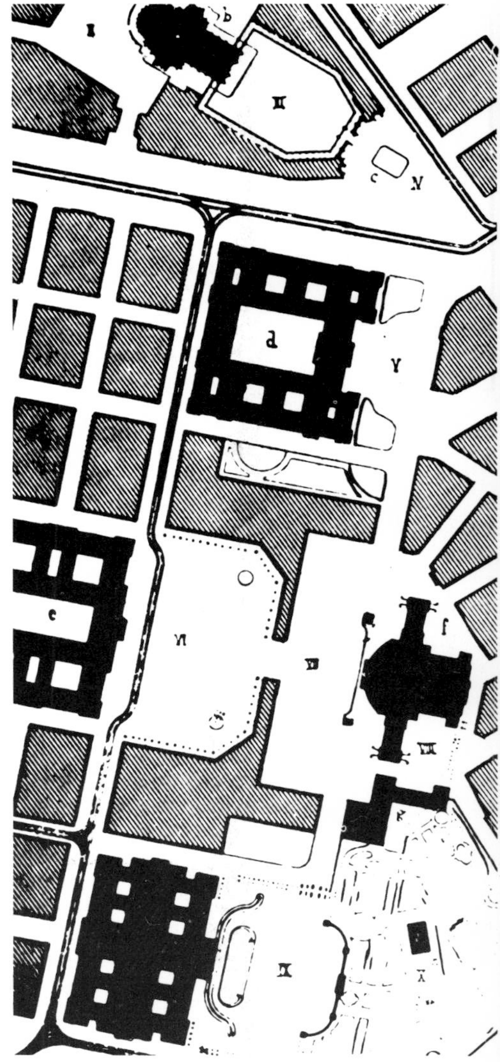

95 Camillo Sitte: proposed development of the Vienna Ring.

By this he meant the aesthetic repertoire of architectural resources used to shape urban space. These books excited a great deal of attention around the turn of the century, and in the years which followed were widely misinterpreted. The garden city: this term alone became a shibboleth and still serves today as a selling line for the most unethical commercial interests. The concept of the garden city had a quite unforeseen impact, because of

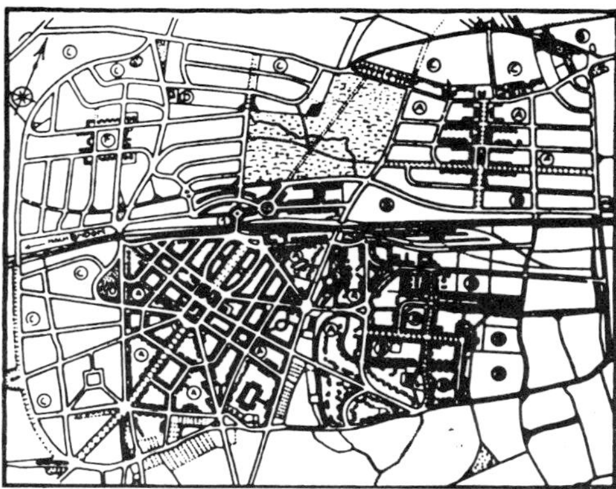

96 Letchworth Garden City: Unwin and Parker.

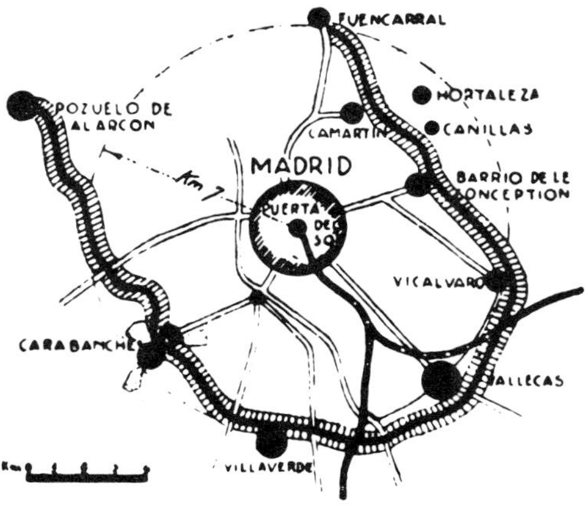

97 Proposals for the expansion of Madrid: Soria y Mata.

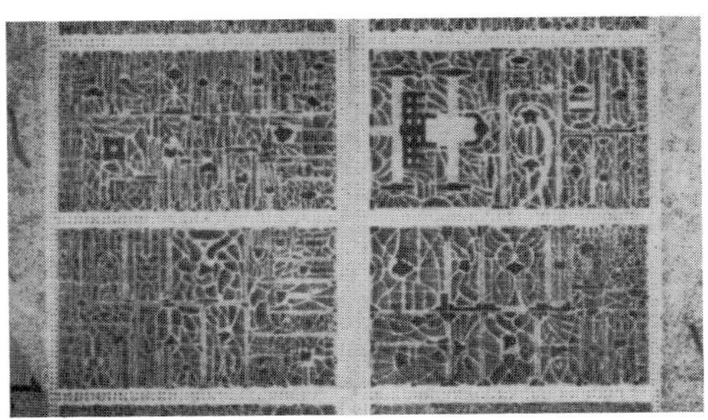

98 Detail of Soria y Mata's linear city.

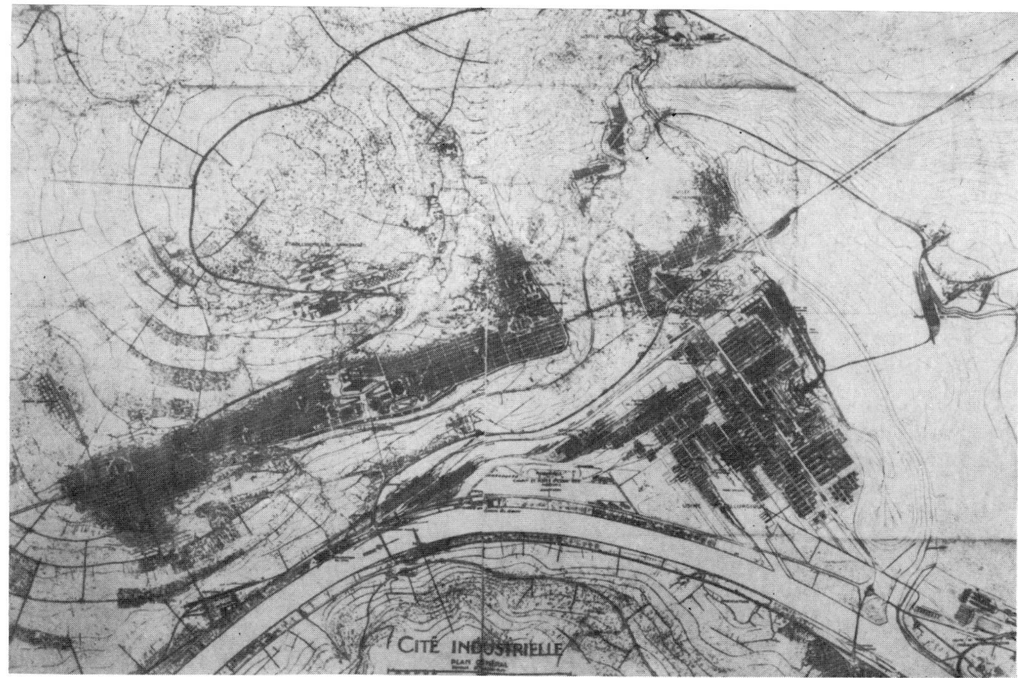

99 'Cité industrielle': Tony Garnier 1904.

the many ways in which the original idea was misinterpreted. It gave rise to a movement, which today is rudely dismissed as 'urban sprawl'. Nowhere in Howard's writings is the single-family house with garden put forward as the only possible house type for the garden city. His diagrams outline a self-sufficient community which on public health grounds provides for substantially greater areas of green space in the private and public zones than were usual at the time. Otherwise, Howard based his proposals on currently accepted ideas about urban space. Unwin and Parker's plans for Letchworth indicate this clearly. Sitte's aesthetic principles are forgotten. Today they appear obsolete, because Sitte derives his thesis from a knowledge of town-planning history. His architectural tools are those of the turn of the century. They could hardly be otherwise. But this does not apply to his proposals for the use of urban space. They have a validity which is independent of time and style.

100 and 101 Details of Tony Garnier's 'Cité industrielle'.

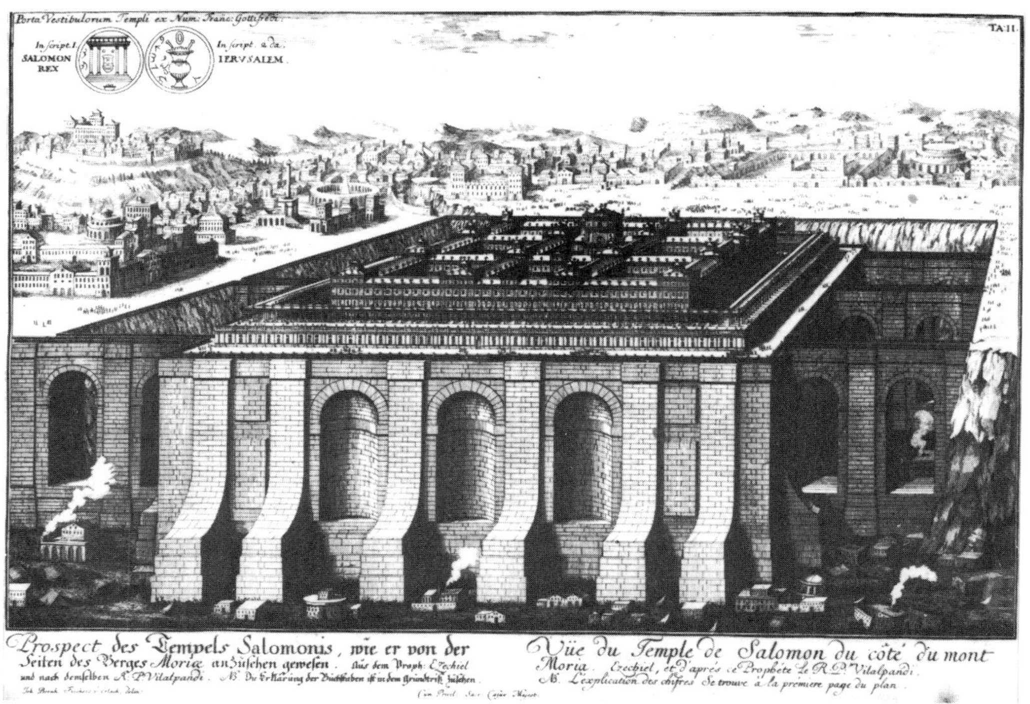

102 View of the Temple of Solomon, Jerusalem.

103 Spectacula Babylonica.

The plans of Soria y Mata and Garnier were a different matter. The streets of their ideal cities were laid out on the old grid system, but the buildings were placed in isolation from each other. Their proposals dissolved the traditional urban form and created in its place a villa landscape.

I would like to use an historical summary to show that this development, which would have a lasting influence on modern town-planning, was not without precedent. It was harking back to a substantial body of architectural theory, which clearly had its origin in the villa architecture of the 16th and 17th centuries. The detached villa – not without reason – is still considered the ideal type of dwelling. The problem is simply that no town can ever be constructed by continual addition of this type of house alone.

I have singled out the most striking phases of this development, and would first like to look at some drawings by J. B. Fischer von Erlach (1656–1723).

Fischer von Erlach made an idealised translation into graphic terms of the travel journals of his friends and acquaintances and then had his sketches elaborated as engravings. In so doing, he gave his imagination free rein and in many plates placed little value on the faithful reproduction of historical reality. What is particularly interesting in his various compositions is the depiction of a comprehensive typology of building forms. So for example in the engraving of the city of Jerusalem we can see a very clear range of different types of squares and courtyards, with their various modulations. It is also interesting to note the juxtaposition of a very rigidly laid out citadel complex and an urban structure which is quite free and apparently disjointed.

I cannot imagine that this kind of

representation of a town was simply a draughtsman's trick. It was the norm in isometric drawings to distort the basic outline of the town to some extent: that is, to depict streets as wider than they in fact were, in order that the architectural qualities of the buildings lining the streets should remain visible. This was not true of the standard town perspectives of Merian. I am assuming that Fischer von Erlach used this device to make clear his vision of the town. But I am convinced that his drawings were also in accordance with his conception of the ideal city, and in my view this must have corresponded to the idealised classical notion of architecture prevalent during the period.

What this signifies is this: 'The more precisely the three-dimensional quality of a building is expressed on each elevation, the more successful that building is.' This theory is old as architectural history itself. The finest monumental buildings are a result of it. In the case of urban architecture however, the theory cannot automatically be subscribed to: if it is, the town breaks down into individual buildings, as it did with Fischer von Erlach. At this point, I would like to give a brief summary of those theorems which determine patterns of urban building. In my comments on the Stuttgart schemes, they will be referred to frequently.

1 Each building in a town must be subordinate to the overall plan. That is, its scale, building type, architectural vocabulary must harmonise with the existing architectural fabric.

2 The existing conception of urban space must not be destroyed, but complemented by new building. If such a conception of urban space does not already exist, the new building must create it. As our morphological selection of urban spatial forms shows, the isolated building may very well

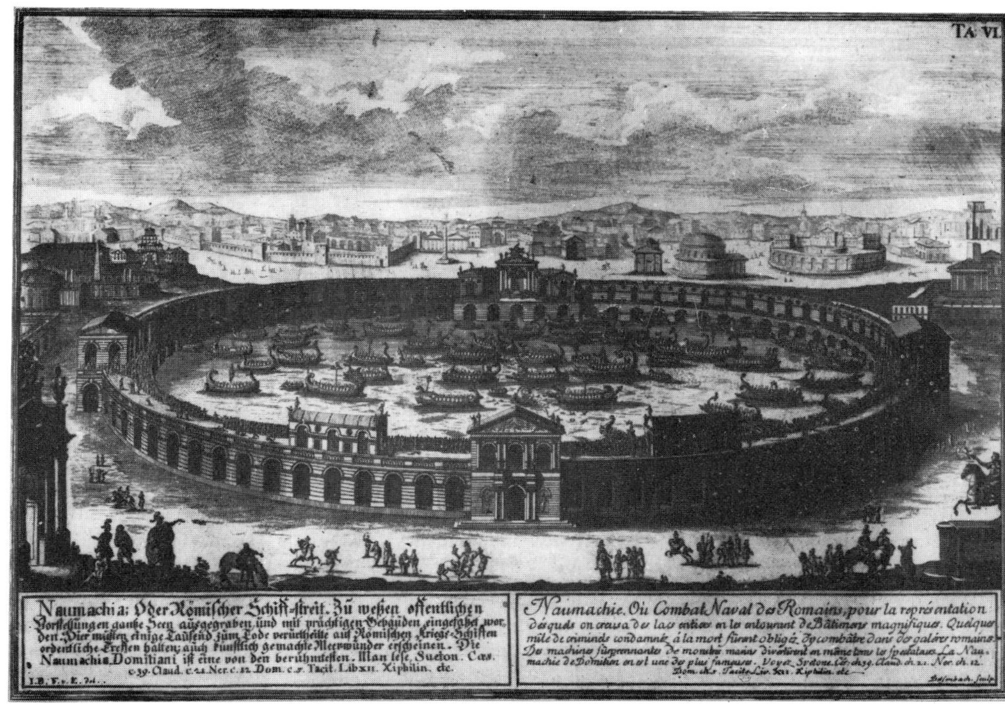

104 Naumachia.

105 Mecca.

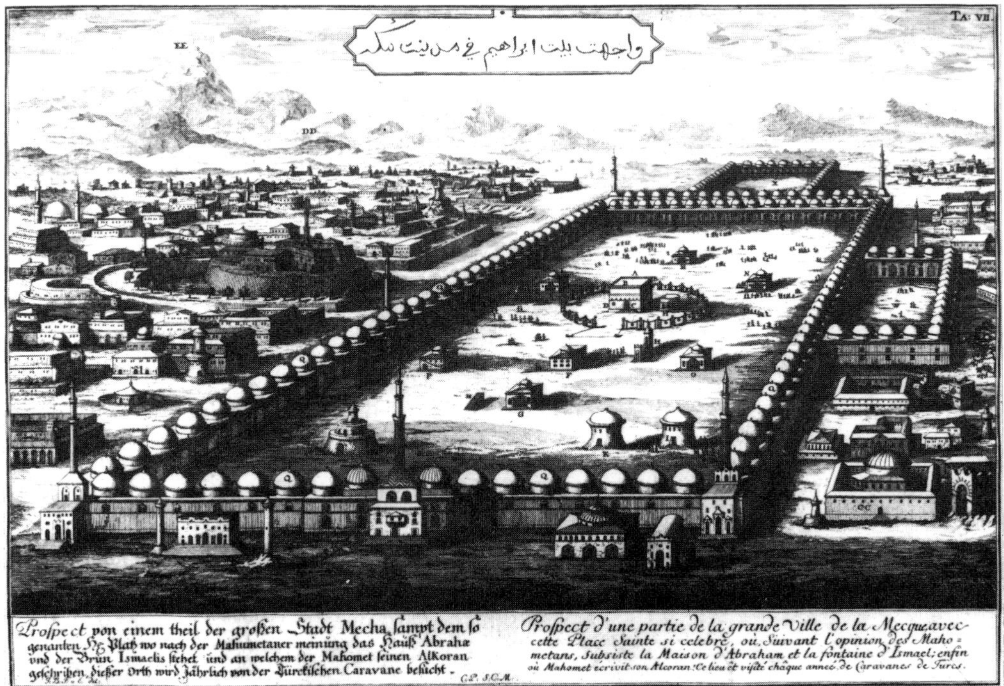

have a role to play in the urban framework. This role must of course be based on the function of the building and its corresponding form. It must, so to speak, tear no holes in the urban fabric, nor must it create any spatial vacuum around itself.

3 The terms 'regular' and 'irregular', in the context of urban fabric and building form, should not be postulated on any ideological grounds. If they were, their value would be debased. The introduction of the orthogonal town-plan in Greece is attributed to Hippodamus of Milet (5th century B.C.). This plan was subsequently widely imitated, especially in new urban settlements. During the same period, towns were being built on an irregular ground plan. History shows that architectural and spatial masterpieces were produced by both types. This observation is valid for all cultural periods.

One further remark could be added about the drawings of Fischer von Erlach: that he deliberately placed side by side isolated buildings and urban spaces of a very different character, in order to underline the diversity and richness of the urban morphology which he wished to depict.

I have no way of proving either these conjectures or the claim that Fischer von Erlach played a definite role in a historical development which saw the breakdown of traditional patterns of urban space.

Nevertheless, his drawings provide sufficient evidence to substantiate this hypothesis and consequently to rate him as one of the spiritual precursors of this development. In no sense does this challenge his reputation as a first-rate architect.

Individual building types, such as the colosseum, the circus, the baths and

106 J. B. Piranesi (1720–1778). Imaginary scheme for the Campo Martii in Rome, with a dedication to the English architect Robert Adam. This fantastic composition is a unique document in the history of architecture. With incredible inventiveness, Piranesi has created an idealised version of the Campo Martii, which of course has never looked like this. He spent his whole life studying Roman ruins with great passion and sketching plans for their reconstruction. With this six-part etching he added a kind of 'divertimento' to Roman town-planning.

many others, are interlocked like pieces of a jigsaw puzzle, without any recognisable town plan resulting. Most of the structures are placed in the landscape independently. See Fig. 106. This kind of ideal city then is in perfect accord with the visions of Fischer von Erlach.

This scheme is especially interesting for its almost inexhaustible range of architectural styles.

Of course the layout of the town was not produced by purely aesthetic reasons. It is not by chance that the town centre is a factory, a workplace. If one takes the trouble to decipher Ledoux's plans and read his explanatory notes, it becomes clear that this is not a plan for the glorification of capital and the employer class, and that the manager's house – whose hall was to be graced with an altar – is not designed as a symbol of oppression. Ledoux, a monarchist and Rousseauist, planned an ideal city for an ethically intact society which will never exist. Although he worked as an artist in Paris, and was highly respected there, he seems in this plan to negate the town as a spatial concept, in contrast to his contemporaries.

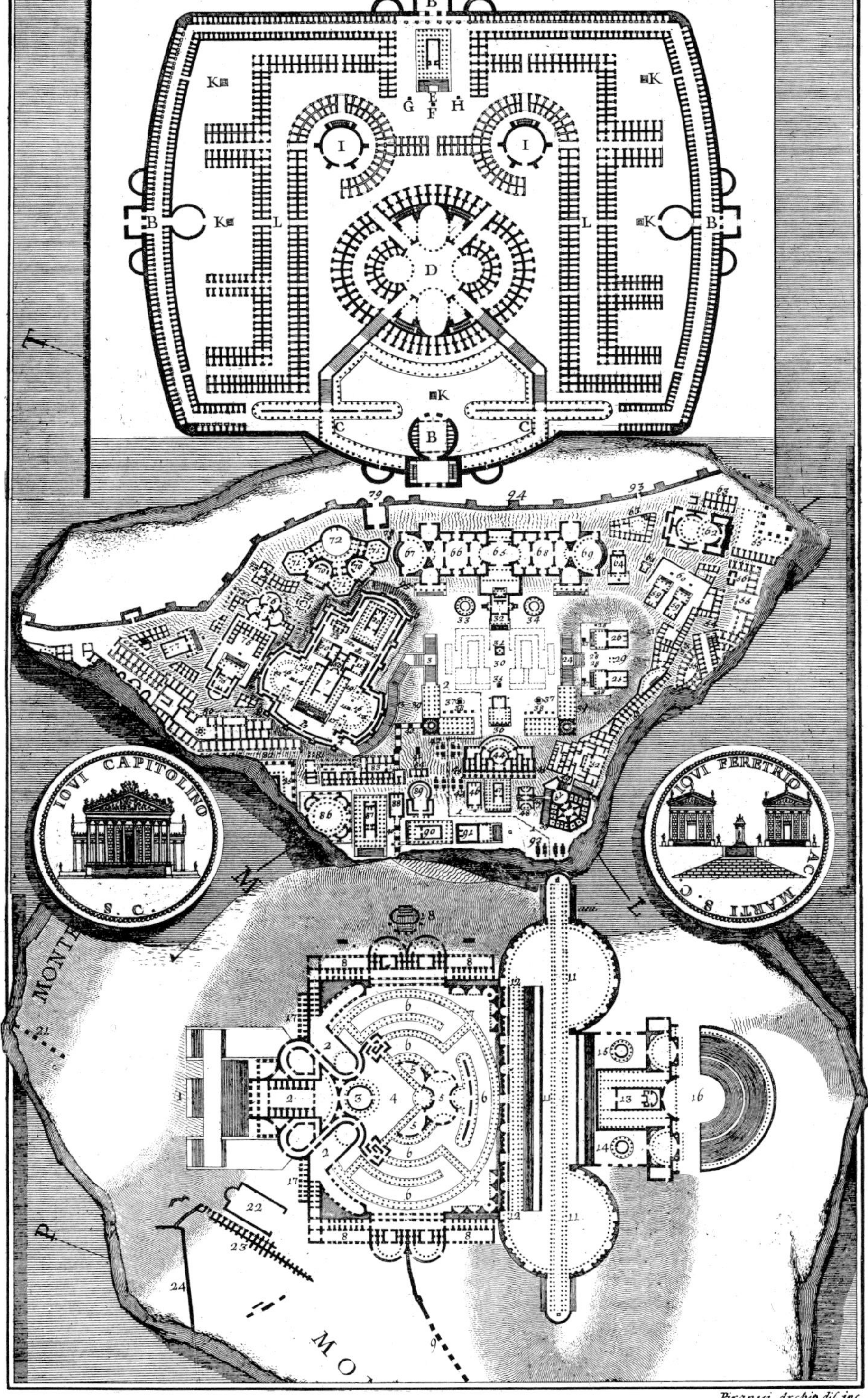

107 (Piranesi) from top to bottom . . . Porta di Aureliano, Capitol, Monte Palatino (author's collage).

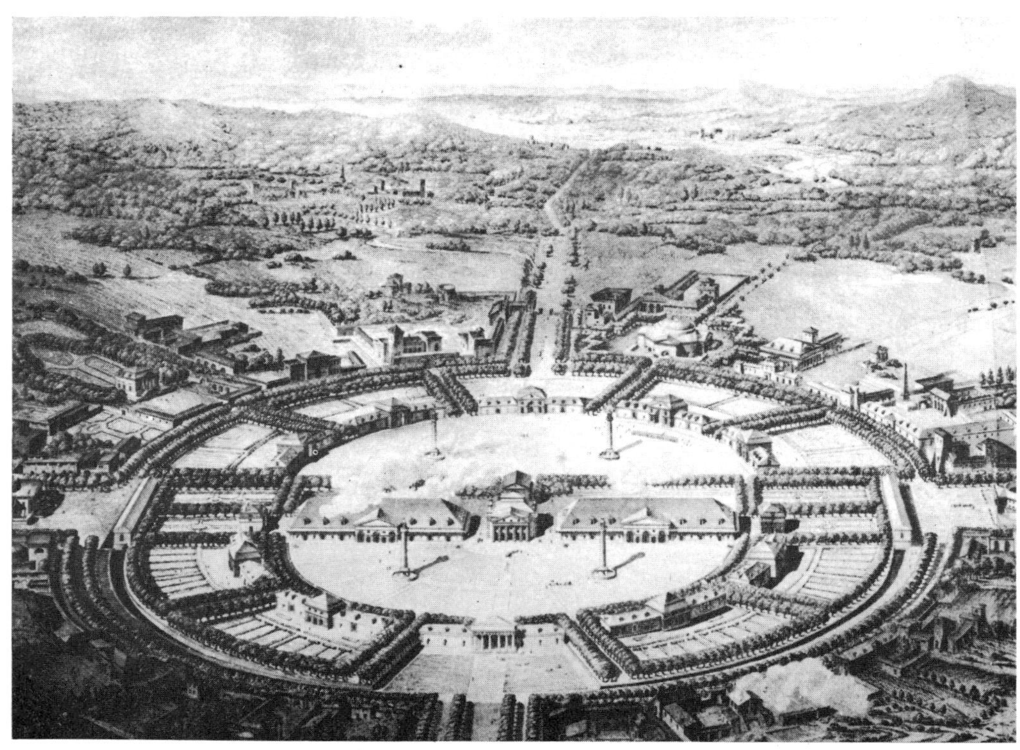

108 Claude Nicolas Ledoux (1736–1806). Imaginary scheme for the 'Ville de Chaux', today 'Salines de Chaux' in Arc-et-Senans.

109 The plan as built. According to Emil Kaufman, Ledoux has 'destroyed the unity of the Baroque town'. This is in fact true. Only the austere, street-like layout of tree-lined avenues recalls the plan of the Baroque town. The central semi-circular area of the finished plan is surrounded by isolated buildings. The spatial impression given by this magnificent complex is overwhelming in its seductive clarity. However, the town, laid out around its salt pits, disintegrates into a series of isolated buildings, which are set so far apart that it is no longer possible to have any coherent sense of urban space.

110 Etienne Louis Boullée (1728–1791). Scheme for a museum, 1783.
111–117 J. N. L. Durand (1760–1834), pupil of Boullée. From *Précis des leçons d'architecture données à l'école polytechnique*. Boullée and Durand's proposals for major building complexes. The pupil is rather more modest in his scale than the master. What is interesting for our considerations of urban space is first of all the fact that an attempt is being made to design a building from an internal plan outwards, preserving architectural balance between its elevations. Within the outer walls of these large buildings are courtyards of very differing types. This kind of formal composition goes directly back to the Roman baths. We have already come across similar complexes in Piranesi's work.

110

111

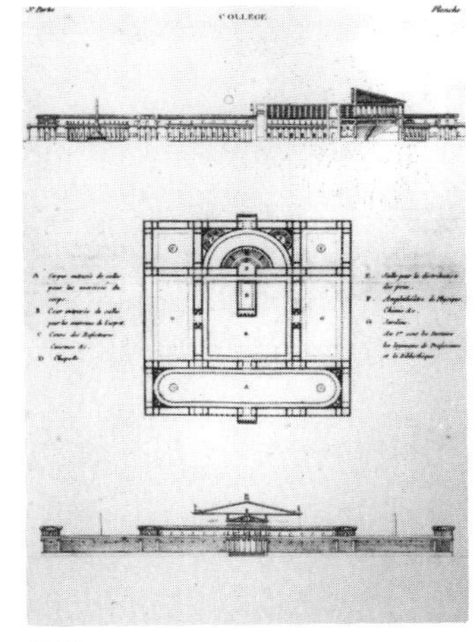

112

113

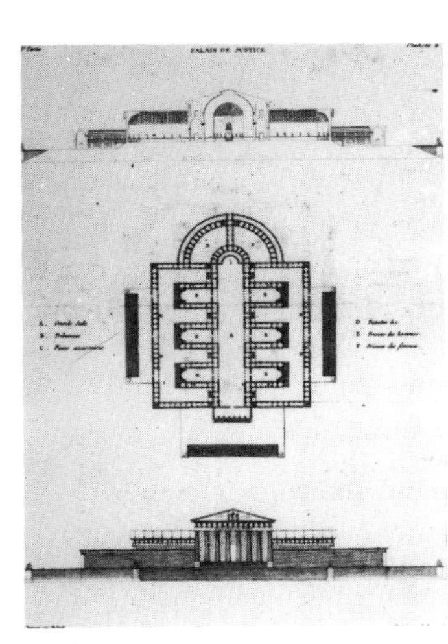

114

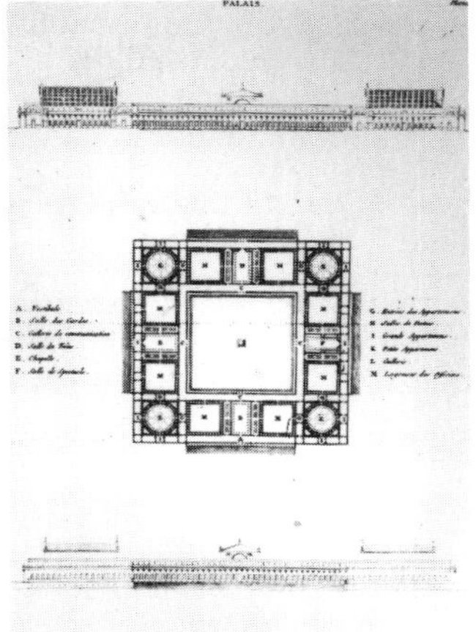

115

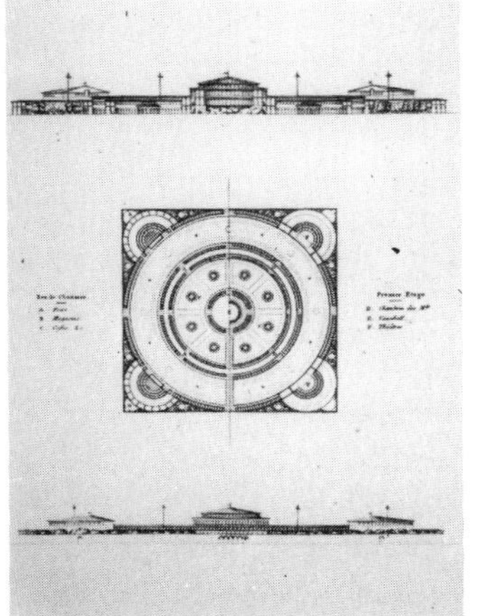

116

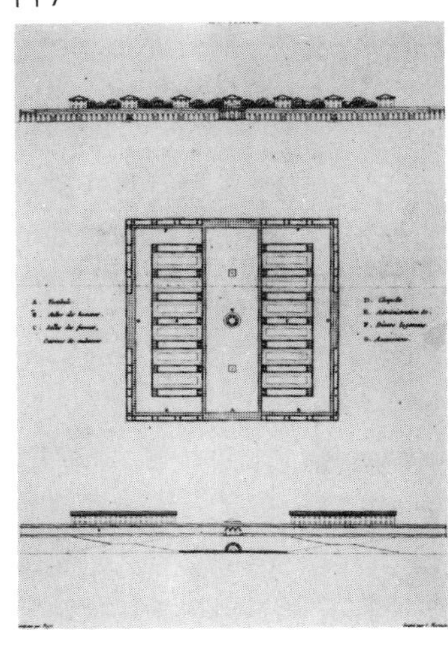

117

117 Illustrates a scheme for a hospital. Because of the danger of infection, the individual wards are not connected. Access is given simply by an arcade which links the wards. The whole building is enclosed by an arcaded outer wall. In these drawings we see for the first time the emergence of a model for terraced housing. This kind of hospital was introduced in England around 1715 and was to have a decisive influence on hospital construction in the 19th century. I am sure that these models also served as the prototype for typical 20th century row housing.

FACTORIES AND HOSPITALS IN THE 19TH CENTURY

118 Krupp factory in Essen, 1860.

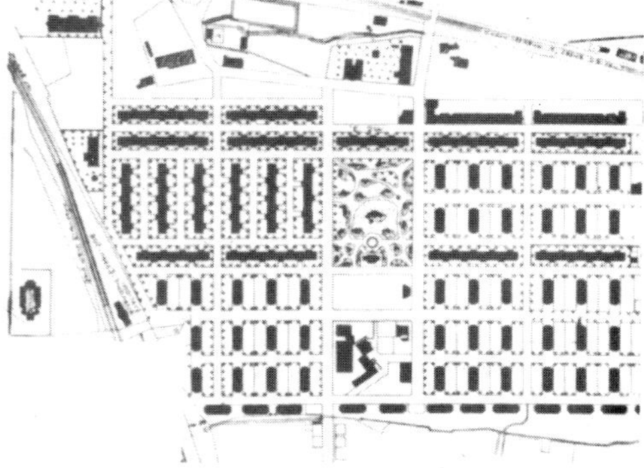

119 Kronenberg housing estate for Krupp factory workers in Essen, 1872, plan of site.

120–123 New hospitals of the type built in Germany in the second half of the 19th century.

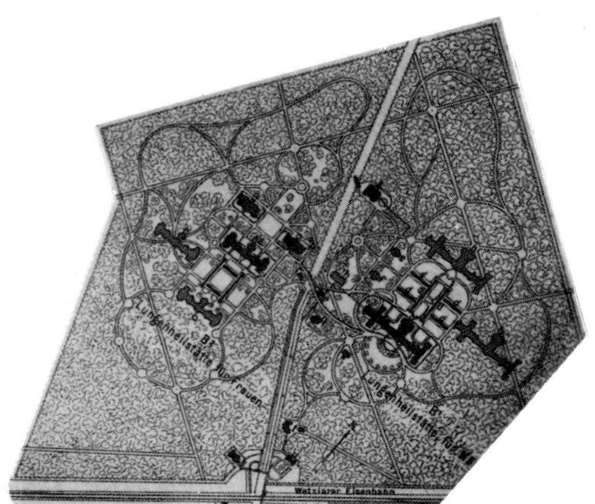

120 Sanatorium in Berlin–Beelitz, architects Schmieden and Böthke.

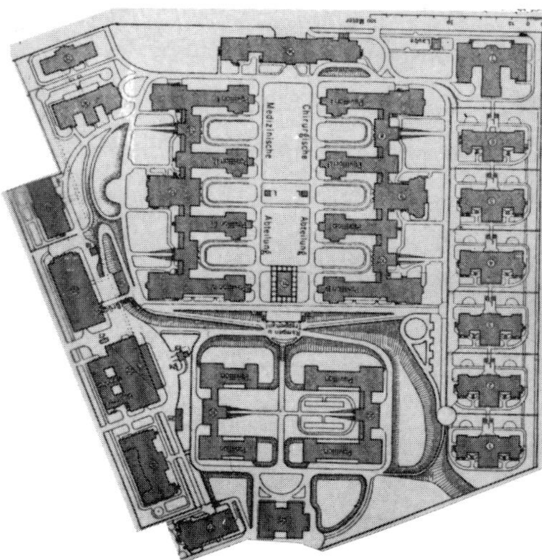

121 Municipal hospital in Berlin–Charlottenburg, architects Schmieden and Böthke.

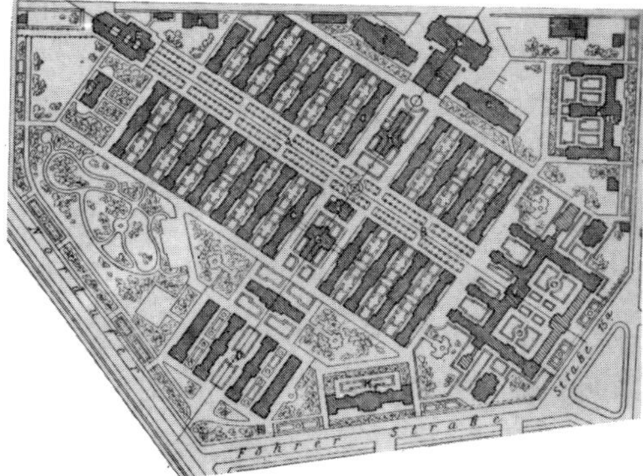

122 R. Virchow hospital in Berlin, architect L. Hoffman.

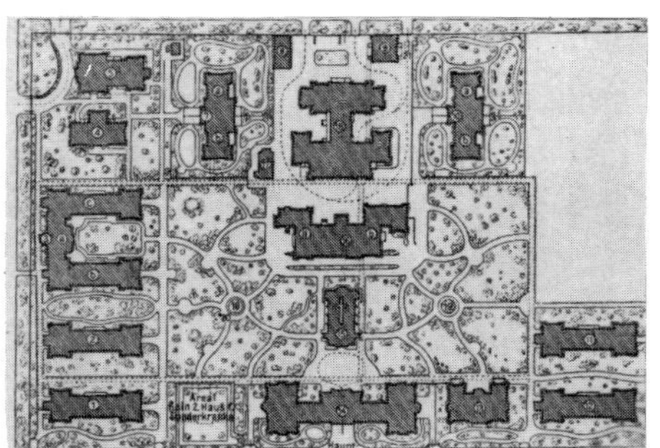

123 Municipal hospital in the Johannstadt, Dresden, architect Bräter.

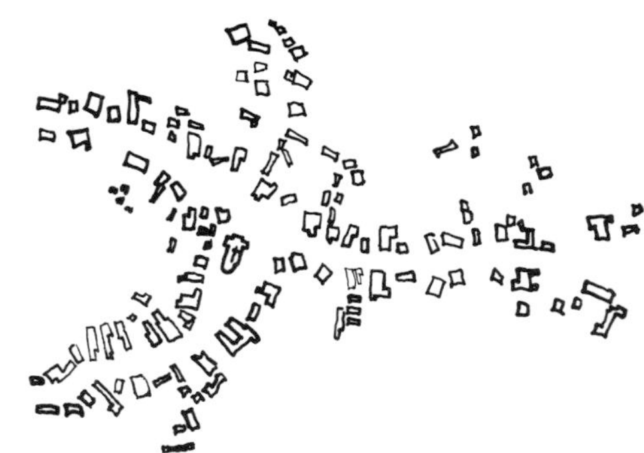

124 Standard type of unplanned rural village.

A comparable development in architectural typology took place simultaneously in industrial building (Fig. 118), hospital construction (Figs. 120–123) and residential building in the 19th century.

We have already described why hospital construction was in the forefront of this development. It is hardly surprising that the constantly growing factory complexes should have shaped themselves into a heterogeneous and fragmented architectural jigsaw puzzle. Building forms were exclusively conditioned by the interests of productive efficiency. When for example the AEG firm engaged an architect like Peter Behrens, they were motivated by the search for prestige, which would play a major role in promoting their outside commercial interests. Such cases were extremely rare. The laws of architecture and harmonious urban design were of little importance in industrial building. Nevertheless, in many respects industrial building had its own distinct influence on these two sets of laws. The achievements of 19th century industrial building in the fields of engineering and technology were to provide the essential impetus for modern architecture in the early 20th century. They were also to lead to numerous misconceived developments, such as the movements towards a purely functional or constructional orientation, which caused the impoverishment of present-day architecture. The influence of industrial building on urban planning was catastrophic. There was nothing in the internal functional logic of a factory which would necessarily lead to an aesthetic external appearance. Any pretence at beauty was restricted to the entrance area or the management and administrative buildings. The appearance of the works itself, in terms of its architecture and design, seemed to be of no consequence. Inhuman conditions were imposed on the worker. So the state of repression in society had its direct and all too visible result in the architecture of the workplace.

TERRACED BUILDING

125 Plan for expansion of South Amsterdam. In the foreground the area planned and executed by Berlage between 1902 and 1915, in the background the development plan proposed by the city planning department and Cornelis van Eesteren in 1934. The contrast between the two schemes is enormous. Berlage is still working within the 19th century tradition and uses the grid-system to create a rich variety of streets and squares. In the later plan terraced building is repeated on a vast scale, removing every basic point of orientation and in conflict with the ways in which people identify with their environment. There is no recognisable configuration of urban space.

126 and 127 Two diagrams from Walter Gropius' *Architektur*.

126 Evolution of the block built around a central courtyard into row housing.

127 Use of site area and daylighting improve in proportion to the number of storeys! Terraced building cannot be justified on these two very basic criteria.

128 Le Corbusier: the sketch shows the site and the site-area occupied by a 'Unité d'habitation' and for comparison a sketch of the site area taken up by a development of equal density consisting of single-family houses. The two

125

126 127 128

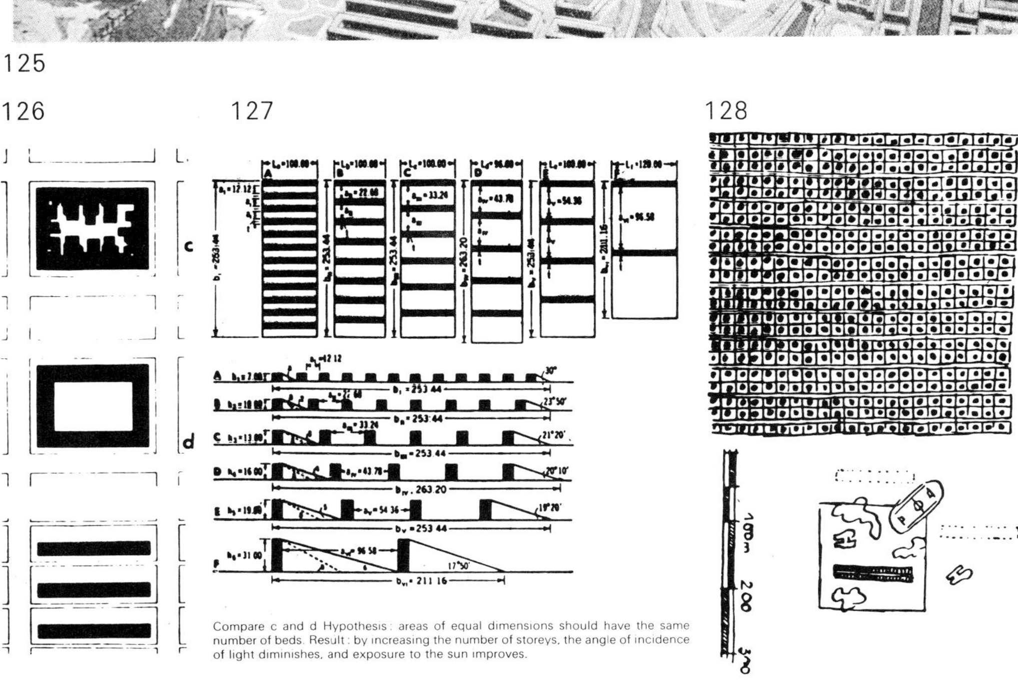

Compare c and d Hypothesis: areas of equal dimensions should have the same number of beds. Result: by increasing the number of storeys, the angle of incidence of light diminishes, and exposure to the sun improves.

factors do not allow this type of comparison, since the elements are too disparate. I have included Figs. 126–128 here to show how biased the arguments are which have been used as propaganda for the construction of terraced building and the detached 'machine for living'. 'The town was covered with a cancerous growth . . . and so had to be opened up by separating out its functions, introducing more open space into the town etc.'

'The need for expansion demanded vast built up areas, and so the town had to be concentrated, built upwards etc.' Fig. 124 shows an unplanned, small settlement: a type which has always existed and which can be seen all over the world. So this type of unstructured development is in no way a novelty in town planning. All that was new was that planners began, towards the end of the 19th century, to design such a type of unstructured development on the drawing board. The colossal pressure for expansion of cities led to over-rapid decision making. Solutions were necessarily simplified, house-plans reduced to a minimum, building technology was stifled for economic reasons. Functional, constructional and capital concerns were the order of the day. Architecture was a low priority.

Further stages of development which precipitated the erosion of urban space in the town planning of the 20th century:

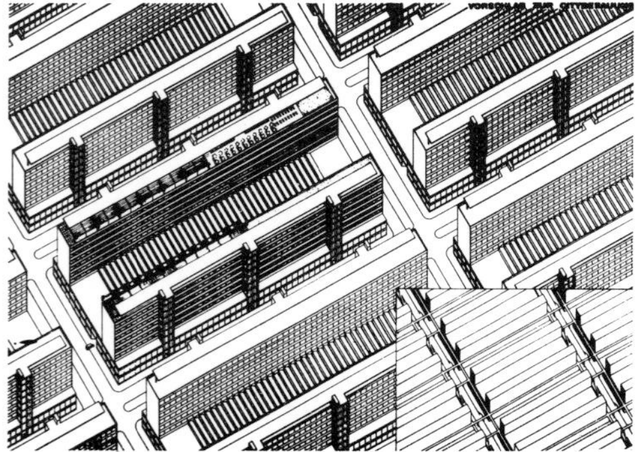

129

1919
129 and 130 Ludwig Hilberseimer: proposal for a city. Hilberseimer was one of the first to take his designs for urban development back to first principles: the house or row of houses and their services. In his later studies he uses a less rigid approach and yet the problem of urban space remains totally neglected.

1921
131
Kibbutz in Nagalal (Israel). Architect Richard Kauffmann. Looked at from the point of view of the superficial plan, this is a realisation of Ledoux's ideal city. The recognisable qualities of urban space are absent. A kibbutz is the very place where one would expect particular emphasis to be given to building types which promote community life.

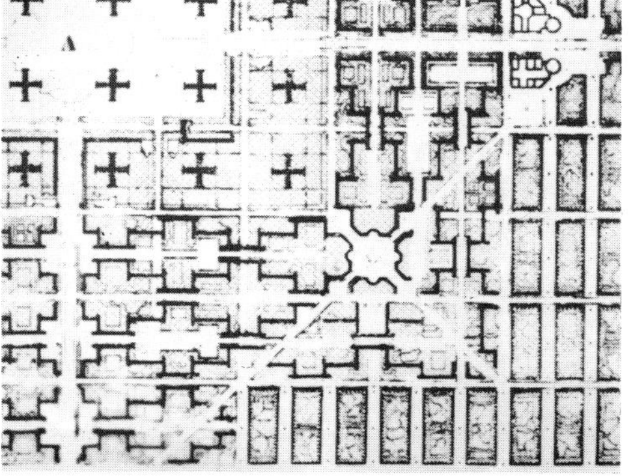

132

1922
132 Le Corbusier: scheme for a contemporary city of three million inhabitants. The quality of life projected here by Le Corbusier certainly conforms with Howard's ideas, but this does not apply to the proportions of the whole. What is interesting are the spatial concepts which underlie this plan. They are repeated in all Le Corbusier's proposed town plans, right into the sixties: the grid system, 'redents' terracing and the isolated tower block. The streets and squares produced by the grid system have been among the most basic elements of town planning since its beginnings. The urban spaces in Le Corbusier's scheme are designed as multi-storey circulation for vehicles and pedestrians in the traditional sense. They have proved unworkable in their form, although the green courtyards barred to traffic have not. The 'redents' terracing has evolved from the grid-system. The forms of the open spaces are numerous, embracing whole sections of residential streets and courtyards.

The schematic repetition of the grid-system and 'redents' terracing is equally questionable. In both cases orientation on the pedestrian level is made extraordinarily difficult. From this stage of development it is only a short step to isolated tower blocks with spaces in between designed only for traffic. The building as a perfect functional unit (as in the 'cité radieuse') is cut off from the spatial play and logic of the town plan. So naturally the individual requirements of this unit are easier to meet. Commerce was very quick to grasp this and is responsible for the questionable success of the idea.

It is hard to say what type of space we are dealing with in the case of isolated buildings of such a scale. It is not considered by Sitte, for whom only the closed system of urban space is a reality. Corb speaks of the 'Poésie de l'espace indicible' in relation to the internal space of a building. As far as I am aware he made no clear statements about external space. In his *Urbanisme*, he has this to say of the Place Vendome: 'the architectural style has more than a hint of the work of an interior designer . . . the buildings of the "Invalides" developed quite differently on their open site.' This offers an interesting comparison with Sitte, who makes endless suggestions as to how the new buildings on the Vienna Ring, some of which stand alone, may be integrated into a harmonious urban space by means of additional building. The fascination of the free-standing building mass has been extensively covered by Siegfried Giedion in his book *Space, Time and Architecture*, and I am certainly not exaggerating when I say that he has made this fascination the sine qua non of modern architecture and town planning. Mies van der Rohe speaks of the 'transparency of space', primarily in the sense of a flowing transition from internal to external space. However, transparency – applied to urban space – is a questionable aesthetic concept. A building supported on pilotis is without doubt transparent in one sense. Earth and sky can be perceived through buildings dotted around the landscape. Glazed facades can produce effects of unexpected charm, which may pass for transparency. However, this is not a concept basic to the control of either internal or external space. It is the stamp of a monument to detailing. Even Mies van der Rohe neglected urban space in his handful of town planning projects, devoting himself entirely to the individual structure and its specific problems.

1924–25
133 J. J. P. Oud completed the Kiefhoek workers' housing in Rotterdam, surely one of the greatest achievements in the fields of architecture and town planning of the twenties. Although Oud is largely working with

isolated rows of terraced housing, a recognisable unity in terms of the configuration of urban space is maintained. The solutions which he finds for dealing with the corners of the triangular open space are masterly. This aesthetically important achievement is missing from other parts of the development. The estate stands in direct line of descent from Berlage's ideas of town planning.

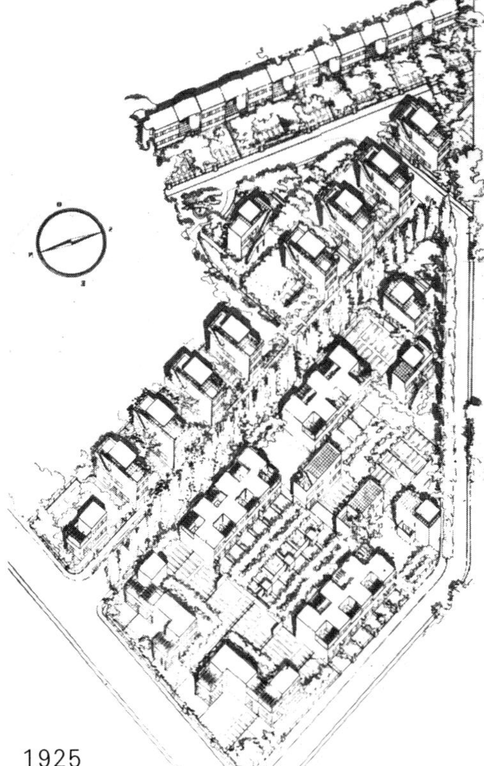

1925
134 Fruges estate in Pessac, near Bordeaux. Taking a contrasting approach to J. J. P. Oud, Le Corbusier constructs his Fruges estate predominantly using detached houses (cf Tony Garnier's 'Cité industrielle'). There is no recognisable overall spatial plan, although the relationship between individual buildings is carefully judged.

135 In the same year Le Corbusier and Pierre Jeanneret planned a new centre for Paris, known as the 'Plan Voisin', which derives from the 1922 scheme for a city of three million inhabitants. The scale of the project corresponds to the size and importance of Paris as Le Corbusier understood it ('Paris prend de l'époque . . .'). For us, with the hindsight granted by fifty years of planning experience, this plan bears almost tragic significance. The concept of a high-density city centre revealed its negative side after the Second World War. Paris was not spared. The strikingly abstract design underlying this scheme, realised under the direction of a major architect, unfortunately generated an unforgivable epidemic of 'urban blight'. Even putting spatial concerns on one side, a mass of purely functional considerations militate against such excessive urban centralisation.

1926
136 Ernst May, Römerstadt development, Frankfurt am Main. From 1925 to 30, Ernst May was chief planner for the city of Frankfurt. Within the framework of the development plan which

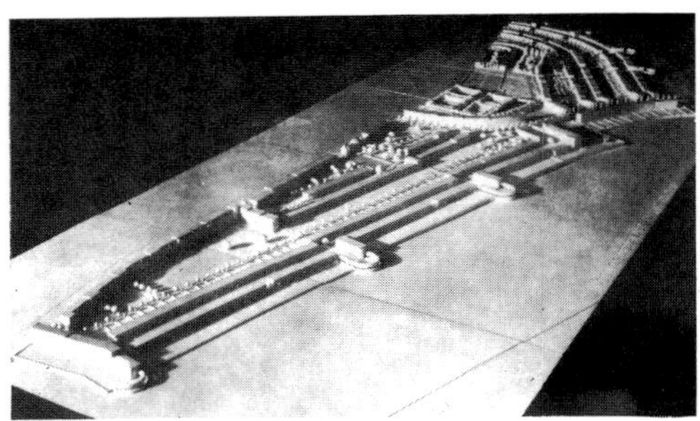

he himself had initiated, he built the housing developments in Frankfurt suburbs which established his reputation as a planner and had a strong influence on future trends in residential planning, both in Germany and abroad. The quality of these developments (Praunheim, Bornweiler Hang, Bruchfeldstrasse, Römerstadt) is in every way comparable with J. J. P. Oud's Kiefhoek housing. In detailed planning, he too lost spatial continuity, and one can already sense the impulse towards the exclusive use of row housing which May was to develop further in his work in Russia in 1930–34.

1925–26
137 Bruno Taut, Britz development, Berlin. The interesting feature of this is the horseshoe-shaped square which, although visibly intended as the focal point of the estate, is in a different spatial register from the streets which lead to it. The architecture and space on the perimeter of the complex are not clearly delineated.

138 Rundling estate in Leipzig, architect Hubert Ritter. Although one can detect the use of noteworthy spatial markers here, the overall concept is not without its limitations. The same criticism may be levelled as against the exclusive use of terraces: the reduplication of identical elements destroys all sense of direction and acts as an obstacle to the inhabitant's ability to identify with his environment. These factors are all the more worrying in the case of a concentric plan than with an orthogonal structure.

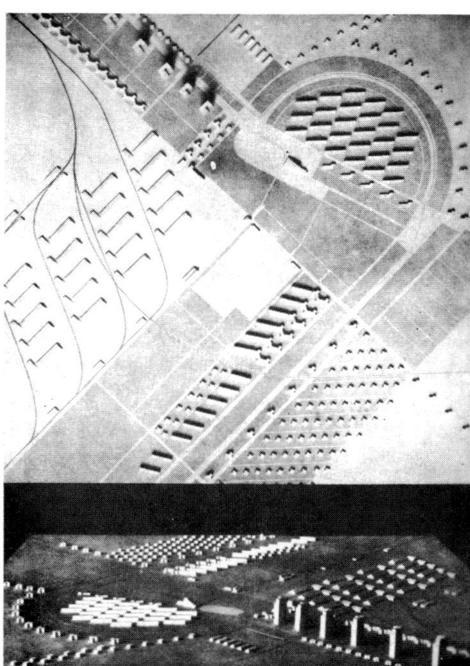

1927
139 Kostino estate, Moscow. Architect Nikolay Landowski. A very aesthetic layout . . . As a piece of graphic art this scheme has a similar appeal to El Lissitzky's sketches and was certainly of comparable quality. The designs of those German planners who worked in Russia between 1930 and 1934 are essentially more sterile. Landowski's design however takes no account of urban space.

1927
140 and 141 Weissenhofsiedlung, Stuttgart, produced in collaboration by the following architects: Mies van der Rohe, Le Corbusier, J. J. P. Oud, Gropius, Peter Behrens, Josef Frank, Mart Stam, Richard Doecker, Ludwig Hilberseimer, Hans Poelzig, Hans Scharoun, Adolf Schneck, Bruno and Max Taut, Victor Bourgeois.

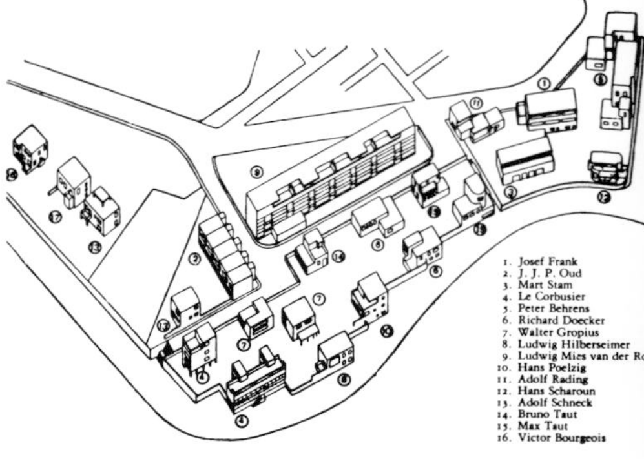

141 The architectural signature which the estate bears is remarkably uniform. But in planning terms the individual buildings remain distinct. The estate was built as a showpiece in the context of an exhibition by the Deutsche Werkbund. In competition, the Würt-

temberg Werkbund, which felt excluded from the enterprise, built its own estate at the same time, adjacent to the exhibition site. They wished to show that Stuttgart was a match for the International Movement in architecture. The result was respectable German architecture striking a heroic posture. Conceptually, it was planned on the grid system. At the time this enterprise was laughed out of court by the 'modernists', who in turn were subject to the type of insults which became the order of the day in Nazi Germany. Today we can judge this professional infighting with a certain detachment. The so-called 'reactionary' development of the Württemberg Werkbund had planning qualities which were lacking in the Weissenhofsiedlung: in architectural terms the reverse was true.

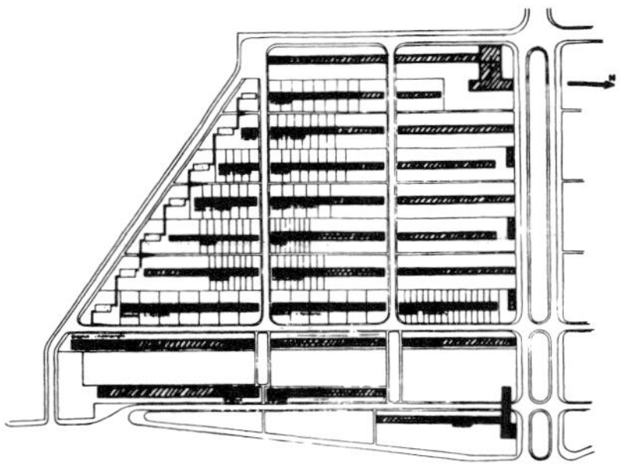

1927–28
142 Dammerstock development, Karlsruhe. The development plan was conceived by Walter Gropius and the architects Haesler, Riphan, Roeckle and others were involved. An important terrace complex which is undoubtedly well thought out. Spatial criticism: the city is reduced to a mathematical problem. Throughout the estate, the area between the terraced rows can be seen as a kind of street, with no distinction between space to the front and space to the rear. These spaces are reduplicated and break off sharply at the boundaries of the site. Such an abstract structure is incapable of being extended beyond its demarcations. No answer is given to inherited problems.

1928–30
143 Jarrestadt, Hamburg. Between 1923 and 1933 Fritz Schumacher was chief city planner of Hamburg. Under his directorship residential districts were built with exceptional spatial features, comparable with the famous courtyard housing of Vienna.

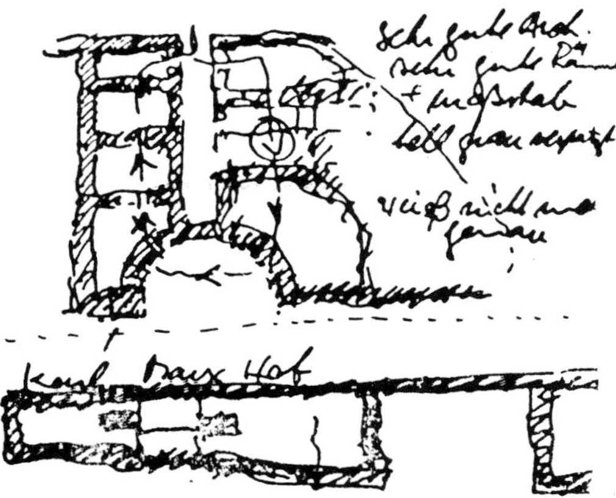

144 Karl-Kreis-Hof and Karl-Marx-Hof, Vienna, c. 1930. Schumacher conceived the overall plan of the Jarrestadt. He used an architectural competition to find the best Hamburg architects, who then carried out the detailed planning. Karl Schneider executed the central courtyard. A good example of the way in which different planners can collaborate successfully.

1929
145 'Mundaneum' project by Le Corbusier and Pierre Jeanneret. This project is not meant as a residential city, but as a utopian vision of a spiritual capital for the world. In any historical summary of the decline of the notion of urban space this piece of work occupies a position of crucial importance. Le Corbusier's conception of the way life should be lived in the modern

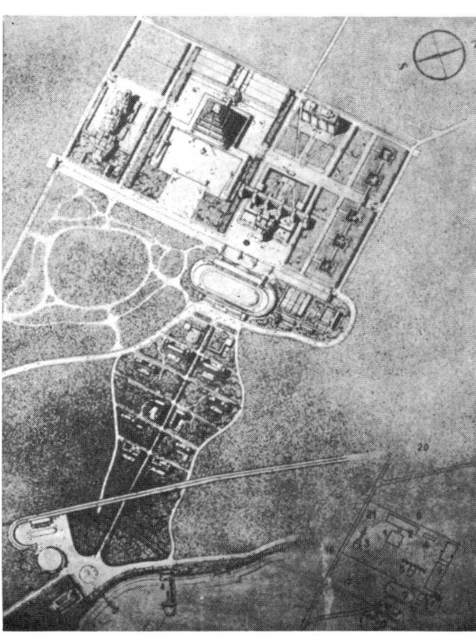

world finds its final expression in the detached 'unités d'habitation' situated in the residential zone below the stadium. The spatial idea behind the organisation of the centre is based on free-standing monumental buildings surrounded by lower structures. There are direct typological relationships with Roman baths and Palladian villas. The whole complex is quite perfectly thought out according to classical rules for architectural composition, and I know of no contemporary of Le Corbusier who could have achieved comparable artistic results. My critique of Le Corbusier's legacy to town-planning theory must therefore always be seen in the context of the respect which I have for him as a creative artist. In his town planning projects, he never allowed himself to be seduced into architectural banalities, as was the case with Hilberseimer for example.

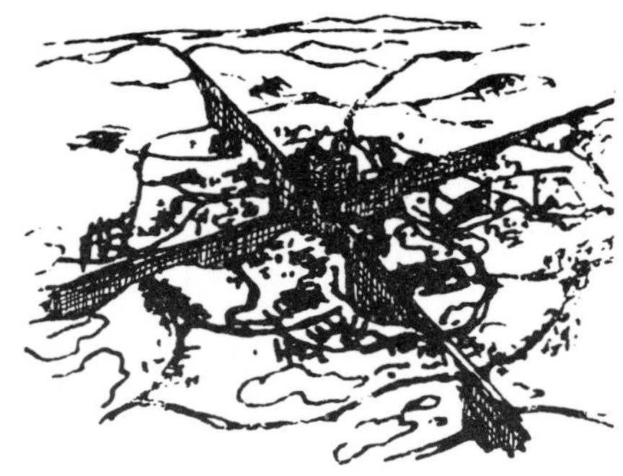

146 Urbanisation of Sao Paulo, Brazil.

147 Urbanisation of Algiers.
Both projects by Le Corbusier and Pierre Jeanneret.

Why have I taken so many of my examples from the work of Le Corbusier? Because it fully realises the most significant stages in the progress of modern town planning – invariably executed in the most arresting and uncompromising way. On his travels through South America he sketched plans for the potential development of Sao Paulo, Rio de Janeiro and Buenos Aires. In these, he attempts to harness the urban explosion by using gigantic rows of buildings which slice through the body of the city and carry roof-level motorways. So of course the buildings, stretching for miles, are forced to adopt the form of the street plan, which from a town planning point of view is not of great value. The development of the citadel above Algiers, on the other hand, is designed on the courtyard principle, but on such a vast scale that it can no longer be perceived as enclosed space.

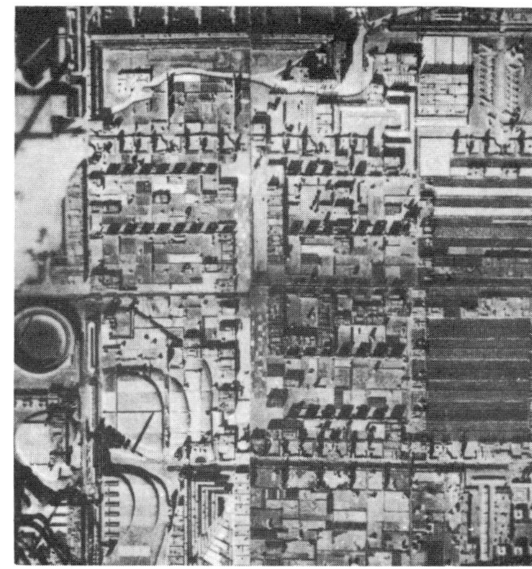

1932
148 Broadacre City by Frank Lloyd Wright. Wright's conception of the ideal, decentralised form of settlement, meant as a protest against the inhuman overcrowding in America's major cities. Here man's contact with nature is restored, but at the cost of sacrificing the spatial system of the town.

1933
149 and 150 Plan for expansion of Antwerp by Le Corbusier and Pierre Jeanneret. The main concept behind this project is that of the 'redents' terrace, already evident in the ideal city plan of 1922. The perspective sketch shows how imaginatively the space can be used within such a structure. However, if this spatial type is repeated on a large scale, each individual space loses its significance and the inhabitant finds orientation difficult.

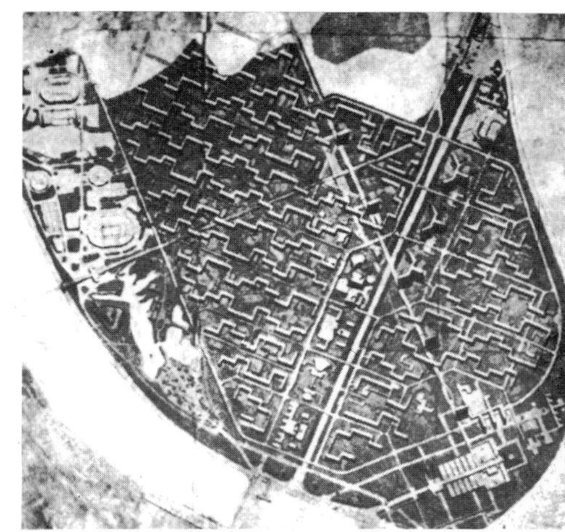

150

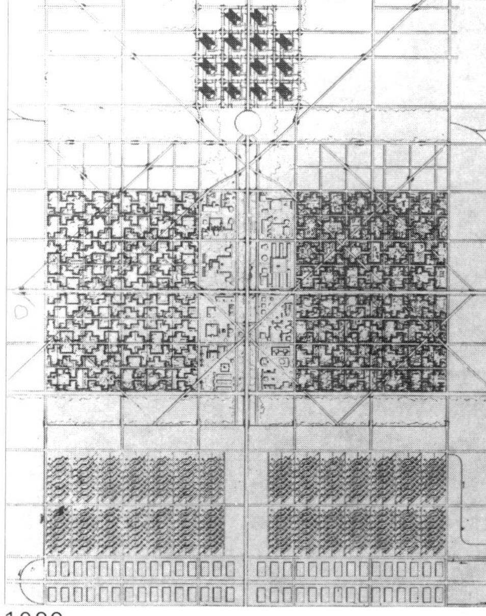

1933
151 Plan for an ideal city by Le Corbusier. This plan is a revised version of the 1922 city for three million inhabitants. The political and administrative centre is pushed to the head of the city. This motif will be repeated twenty years later in the planning of Chandigarh. Cultural and commercial activity takes place in the heart of the complex, flanked by residential areas, with the industrial zone at the foot. The 'anatomy' of the city is broken down into its functional components in this

plan. We have come to realise today that this theory of the compartmentalisation of function has had a negative influence on urban life. From the point of view of urban space, the connections between the various elements are only fragmentary, and do not add up to an integrated system. The siting together of the arts buildings in the centre is very reminiscent of the way in which Fischer von Erlach drew up his visionary town plans.

1934
152 Nemours (North Africa). Project by Le Corbusier and Pierre Jeanneret. As in the Mundaneum project, the free-standing 'Unité d'habitation' is positioned here as a living unit of appropriate size, 'Unité de grandeur conforme'. Urban space in the traditional sense is absent from this project.

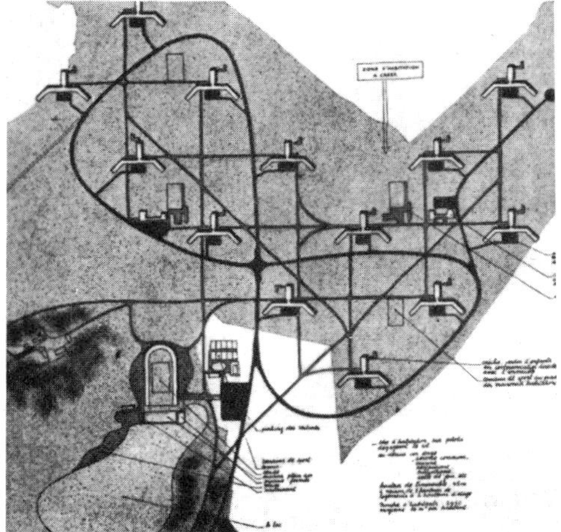

1935
153 Hellocourt, Alsace–Lorraine (France). Project by Le Corbusier and Pierre Jeanneret. The same comments apply to this as to the Nemours project. Only the house type has changed.

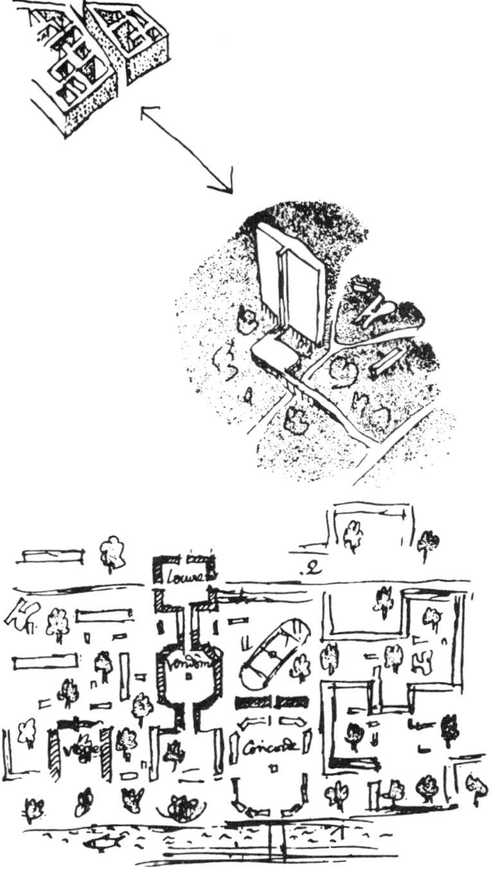

1937
154 and 155 Sketches by Le Corbusier for the reworking of his 1925 project for the centre of Paris. In this scheme, the cruciform tower-blocks have been replaced by Y-shaped and simple slab blocks. I only include these sketches to illustrate how superficial was Le Corbusier's concern with urban space.

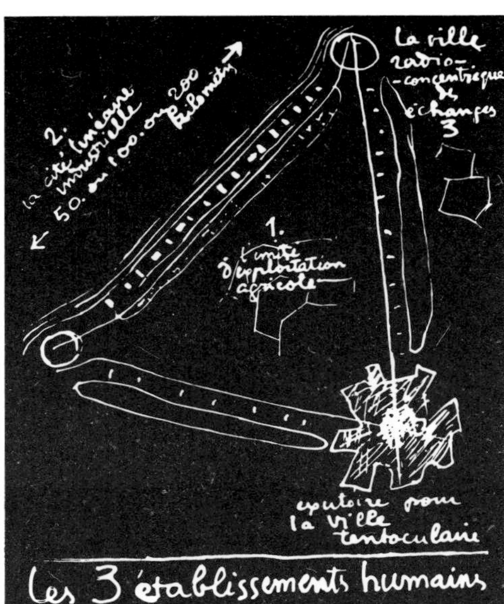

1942
156 Sketch by Le Corbusier from *Les trois établissements humains*. During the war years many theoreticians applied themselves to the question of how Europe should be reconstructed after the holocaust. Le Corbusier's proposal is based on the legacy of Soria y Mata. From the same period came a similar study by Hilberseimer for the expansion of London.

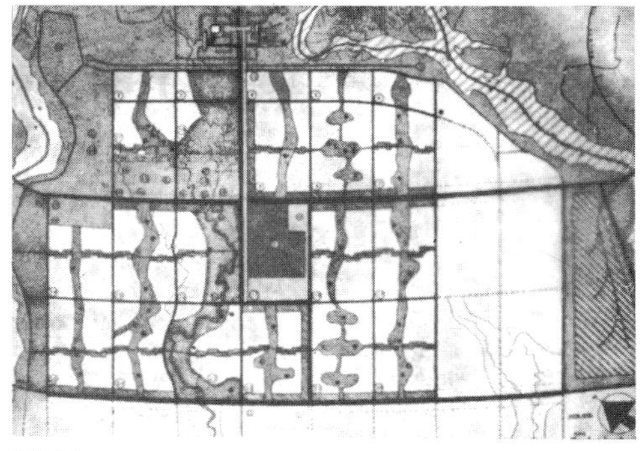

1946
157 New centre for St. Dié (France), project by Le Corbusier. From the purely architectural point of view, this composition gives a foretaste of the perfection of the Capitol at Chandigarh, built later, particularly in the central positioning of the arts buildings. The visual fascination of these projects derives from the buildings as isolated units and their aesthetic completeness, and not from a spatial composition with geometrically definable space expressed in streets and squares.

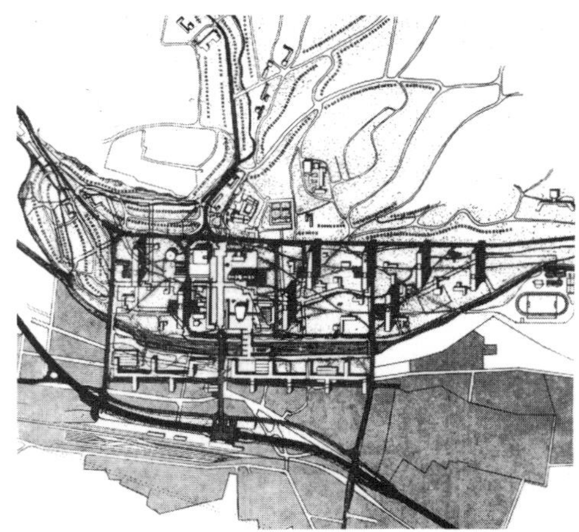

1952
158 Development plan of Chandigarh, Le Corbusier. Compare the plans for ideal cities, Figs 132 and 151.

1953
159 Lijnbaan, Rotterdam. Architects van den Broek and Bakema. This shopping street in Rotterdam connects the station area with the town centre. For the first time in post-war planning, an attempt is made to formulate unified street-space. It is unfortunate that this development functions exclusively as a shopping street with no integration of housing. This is located behind the Lijnbaan and consists of isolated high-rise slabs. They were designed by a different architect. The idea of the pedestrian street closed to traffic served as a model in the years which followed, though generally as an isolated development with no spatial relationship to the surrounding urban fabric.

1955
160 Gratiot development, Detroit. Architect Mies van der Rohe and Hilberseimer.

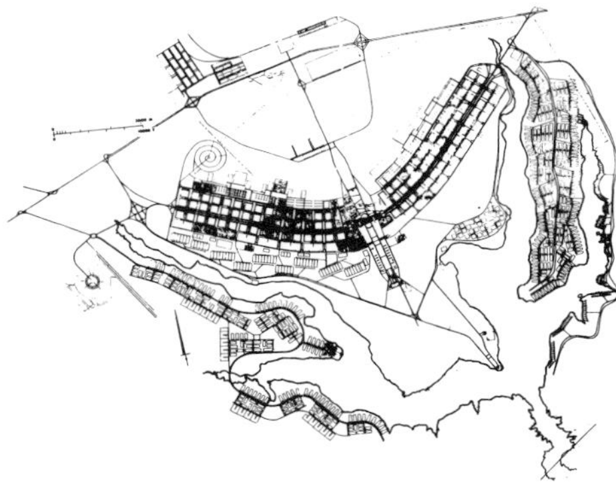

1957
161 Brasilia. Architects Lucio Costa (planning) and Oskar Niemeyer (architecture).

162 Residential buildings in Brasilia.

The spatial features of the last three examples are identical. The complete breakdown of traditional patterns of urban space appears to have reached its culmination. The abstract vision of the separation of various functions within the city has finally found its way into the holy writ of town planning departments. The dreams of the twenties appear to be realised . . . And yet! One or two intelligent planners are beginning to establish that this ideology of the 'new city' challenges the very validity of the city as an organism.

One of the earliest attempts to restore density and continuity to the built environment in the city was the 1962 scheme by Candilis, Josic and Woods for a city of 100,000 inhabitants at Toulouse le Mirail.

1962
163 Toulouse le Mirail. Architects Candilis, Josic, Woods. In this scheme, large parts of which have now been built, pedestrian zones were designed to be free of traffic, and some of the house fronts face on to these precincts. Therefore, there are no streets or squares in the accepted sense. They could however have been created with ease in this project, and one could have dispensed with the unnecessarily high tower blocks.

164 Centre of Berlin, 1960. Architects Peter and Alison Smithson. In this project the idea of the traffic-free

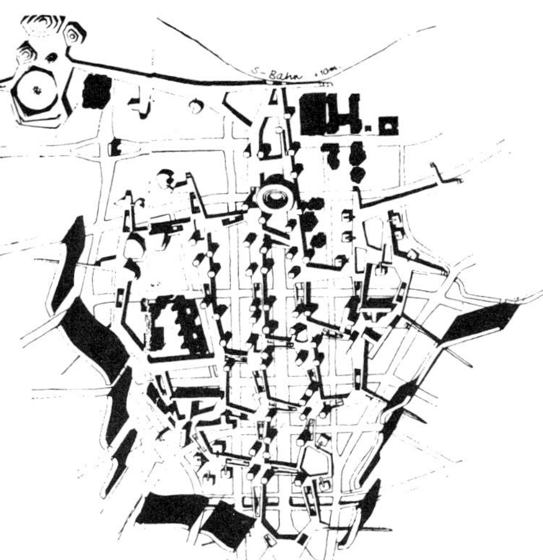

pedestrian street is executed with due regard to technical and functional demands. Economical use is made of tower blocks to flank the street, with the result that one cannot speak of a coherent impression of space along its full length. In this respect, the Toulouse le Mirail project goes a step further.

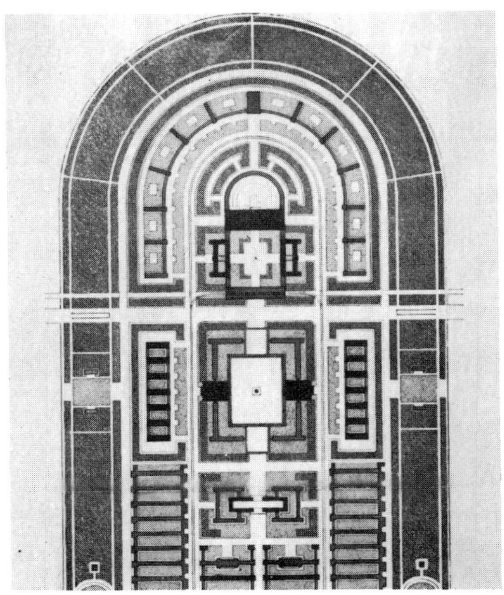

1964

165 Ideal town plan by C. Reinhardt (Vienna). There is something incongruous about this plan as a product of the sixties, coming in the middle of the urban experiments of Yona Friedmann, Schulze–Fielitz etc. It is more reminiscent of the schematic plans of Hilberseimer and other architects of the twenties and is still inspired by the idea of the city having a crowning feature, as outlined by members of the Frühlicht group. In Chandigarh and Brasilia too this idea was expressed on a monumental scale. The spatial qualities of this plan however were again devalued by the mechanical repetition of identical parts. There is a clear spatial demarcation between city centre and residential areas.

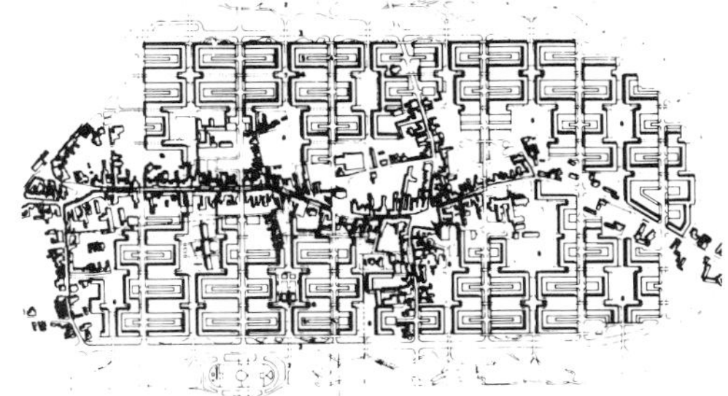

166 Aalter, Belgium. Author's scheme.

At this point I would like to draw my list of illustrations to a close, otherwise this chapter would turn into a history of modern town planning. Yet I hope that I have adduced sufficient material to support my thesis that as far as modern town planning is concerned the concept of urban space has by and large fallen into disuse. To be fair, I must emphasise that in defiance of this universal trend repeated efforts have been made to combat the erosion of our cities. It would be a worthwhile academic exercise to bring out the direct antithesis between these two tendencies. To be more precise, the post-war developments of the fifties and sixties have not progressed much beyond the terraced building of the twenties.

It could be argued that space is created just the same between two terraces. True, this fragmentary space can be classified in an aesthetic category, but it can only be understood as a part or adjunct. And the multiplication of such fragments results in a system of identical incomplete spaces, lacking both continuity and the qualitative differences so important to urban orientation.

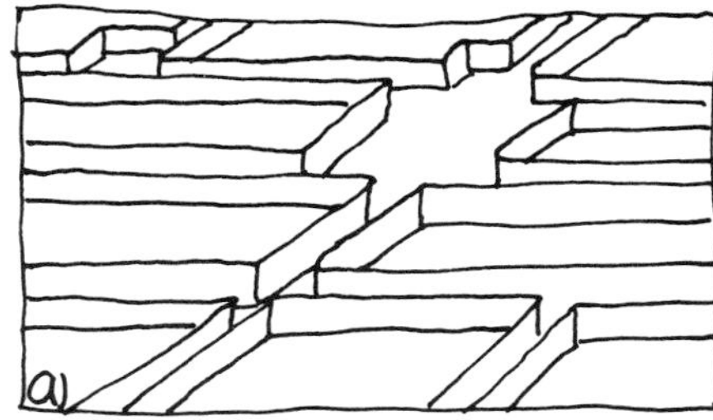

167 (a) Traditional spatial arrangement of cities. If we look at the spatial continuum of a cohesive urban structure from a distance and in somewhat simplified terms, it can be compared to the barriers which channel pedestrian movement. If there is a gap in the barrier, we will have to cope with shortcomings in the system of orientation.

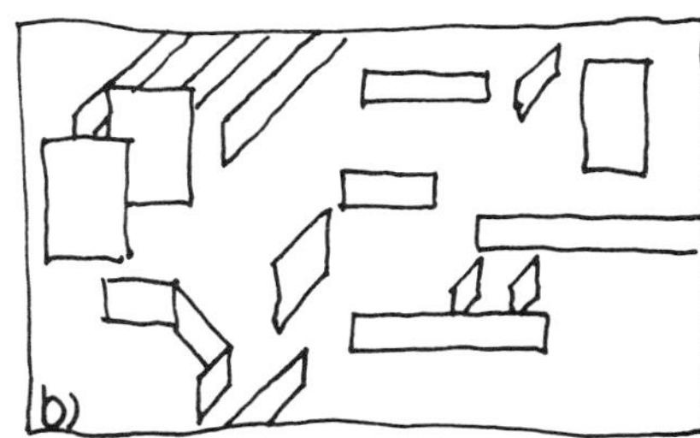

168 (b) The modern city.

Extending this metaphor to our present-day situation, it could be said that from a spatial point of view our towns are composed of forlorn and isolated sections of 'barrier', battered on all sides by every conceivable stream of activity and with no margin left for meaningful activity or orientation. This contradicts the urban architecture as defined by Sitte and is nothing more than a jumble of buildings.

The erosion of urban space is an ongoing process which has been with us for the last fifty years in the guise of technological progress serving a democratic society. Every measure which contributes towards this destructive process can appear justified, because of the power of the lobby which makes its profits out of the phenomenon. It is a war waged by technological and financial interests, unparalleled in history. The palaces of past dynasties and their grandiose cultural expression seem positively modest by comparison. Functions and methods have certainly changed. The only real difference is that our age will leave few buildings behind which will be seen as worthy of preservation by later generations. We have come to an adequate awareness of the problems of refuse disposal created by consumer goods with built-in obsolescence. The consequences of transferring this fetish for disposables to the world of building do not bear thinking about. The irresponsibility with which even qualified planners advocate disposable architecture to compensate for the absence of long-term planning is disturbing. This phenomenon is essentially more than a passing fashion. It has all the characteristics of an ideology which aims not only at buildings acknowledged as temporary, but also at the majority of contemporary structures which are designed to last. We feel quite properly ashamed of the mediocrity of our built environment, and seem to be quite prepared to foot the bill for demolition and subsequent rebuilding. But we must recognise that the life-span of a concrete structure is scarcely comparable with that of a timber-framed building. I am convinced that post-war German architecture will suffer from these shortcomings for the foreseeable future.

The car has created wastes in our cities, and this process has been accelerated by another, equally effective factor: the separation of the various urban functions. In the nineteenth century the urban structure grew intolerable in its complexity. The disentangling of urban functions in the twentieth century was an understandable response on the part of planners to a problem without historical precedent. The whole was parcelled out into functional units: living, recreation, work etc., solutions appropriate to each type were evolved and spatial relationships imposed. The abstract prototype for such an approach to town planning was Le Corbusier's 'Ville radieuse' of 1930. The Athens Charter, published three years later, became its theoretical rule-book. This model was used almost intact for the construction of Chandigarh in the fifties.

URBAN SPACE WAS NOT DEFINED IN THE ATHENS CHARTER

In the sixties there was a surge of reaction against the clinical separation of urban functions. The balance between the public and the private realm was unsettled (H. P. Bahrdt). City centres, which by this time had turned into areas containing nothing but shops and offices, were virtually deserted outside working hours. New residential zones on the outskirts of the city turned into dreary dormitory suburbs. A fresh demand arose for the reintegration of urban functions, and the catchword 'urbanism' was used to conjure up visions of a lost atmosphere. There has been no shortage in recent years of proposals and visions intended as antidotes to the effects of the Athens Charter.

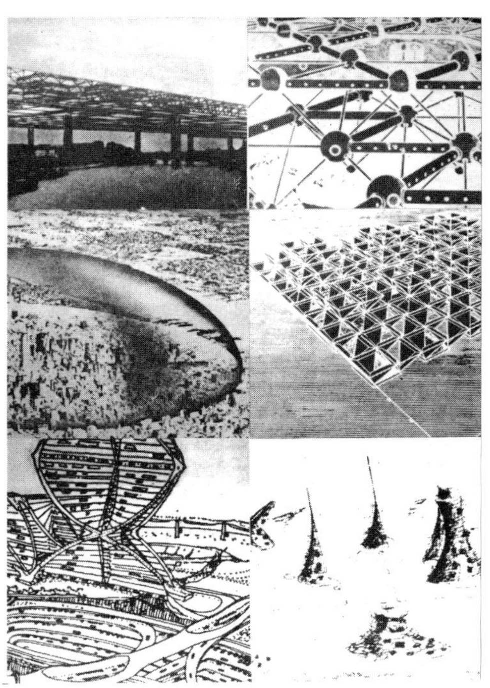

169 Designs for utopian cities by Yona Friedmann, Buckminster Fuller, Kurokawa, Xenakis and others.

These contain little which is of practical use on the technical side. Friedmann's proposals for building on top of old towns are absurd. Friedmann, Fuller, Soleri and the Metabolists all sought a solution to the problem in monstrous, whimsical building types. These extravagances are a symbolic illustration of the dead-end in which town planning finds itself today. They are solutions which only consider one facet of the problem and must fall down on grounds other than their fantastic waste of technological resources. Not that the utopian dream can be evaluated by the yardstick of expense of course. One or two of these proposals lead one to suspect that the idea may be an end in itself, without possessing the aesthetic quality of the utopias of the Renaissance for example. They offer no real alternative to the blind alleys which the Athens Charter has led to.

Urbanism on the other hand is no panacea either. It is interpreted today as an active process, something to be imposed. Urbanism is embodied in every facet of city life and experience, and not only where this is at its most concentrated.

So we should be concerned not with activity alone, but at the same time with the framework in which it takes place. This framework is urban space.

The more full, chaotic and dramatic this framework, the more 'urbanism' seems guaranteed in the eyes of many planners.

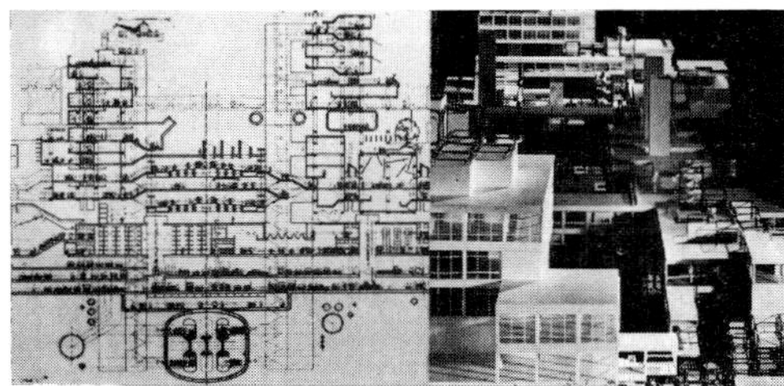

170 Utopian city by Jos Weber.
171 Utopian city, called the 'Metastadt' by Richard Dietrich.

However, it is not the planners who shape and control urban living. It is located according to the dictates of market research men. The planner on the job then has no alternative but to submit to the demands of his client. And if the client believes that a suburban shopping centre with motorway access is more efficient and yields greater profits, the planner's opinion on the suitability of the project is not sought. 'Urbanism' cannot be achieved by the mere creation of high building density, and certainly not by such enormous expenditure.

CRITIQUE OF PRESENT-DAY PATTERNS OF URBAN DEVELOPMENT

By 'urban development' I understand the outward expansion of a town, and the internal renewal and adaptation of its fabric. My observations relate primarily to large cities, where development problems are particularly pressing. The growth of such cities is constantly controlled by land-use plans. If one looks at these plans over a period of 10–15 years, it is noticeable that at each new stage the area given over to building development increases under the pressure of expansion, until the administrative boundaries of the town are reached. The internal restructuring proceeds at the same tempo. Slum housing gives way to commercial and office buildings. Planning authorities have no better alternatives to these two trends in urban development, and even if they did have would lack the powers needed to put them into practice.

The growth of a major city today is not only the concern of its own inhabitants. A large proportion of its work-force commutes long distances from places outside the city limits and an increasing number of residents are moving out, away from the pollution of the inner-city. The city has become a regional planning problem. We lack the ideas and facilities for planning which would enable us to evolve a coordinated programme to meet the needs of the region. Part of such a programme would of course be the establishment of appropriate bodies at a national level which would balance the demands of every region – a department of planning perhaps, which would be responsible for keeping records of all regional development and taking corrective action when this was necessary for the sake of national development.

This does not involve any 'Napoleonic' master plan. I am simply trying to start people thinking about planning on the scale which seems appropriate to today's problems. Transport planners have been working on this scale for some time. Their plans are not confined to strict regional boundaries. The world-wide railway network has already caught town planners unawares; highway and motorway building has done the same; and I fear that new and faster transport systems will be put into operation in the near future, with a similar lack of consultation with the town planners.

The highway has always been the moving force behind urban development. But seen in its proper perspective, transportation is subordinate to the needs of the human community. The effectiveness of any utopian city must be measured against the technological potential of existing modes of transport. The technology of house building is of secondary importance. The most primitive building methods still produce the best results in housing today. This is not true of the stagecoach. So we must develop urban models which among other things will be able to accommodate the private vehicle, whichever form this may take. At the moment, we cannot work on the assumption that this mode of transport will be dispensed with. We can only hope that the state will bring pressure to ensure that the car conforms as soon as possible to the requirements of public health. Today's urban sprawl must be promptly stopped and all new towns must be planned as part of an integrated super-regional development plan.

It is the aim of this study to provide this utopia, whose demands are so modest, with a realistic and workable set of tools, which have nothing in common with the spectacular planning fantasies which I have used as examples in the preceding text. Not least, this work is intended as a corrective to the Athens Charter and its consequences.

WHAT MODELS FOR DEVELOPMENT WILL MEET THE FUTURE DEMANDS OF URBAN GROWTH?

Any prediction must be reasonably realistic and technically and administratively feasible by today's standards. It will have to avoid visualising the town according to narrow ideological prejudice, whether this is of a socio-political or technical nature. Social utopias of the last 200 years have shown the limitations of such visions, as have the technological utopias of recent years. No precise planning solutions exist for a given social order. Man's demands on his environment remain constant, whatever the system. In totalitarian states people's needs are artificially manipulated, but this changes nothing of their essential nature. In more liberal societies fulfilment of these needs meets numerous administrative obstacles which have built-in restrictions comparable to those of authoritarian governments. In the case of powerful regimes, the position of planning bodies is very strong. By virtue of their authority, they can instigate and carry out very far-reaching schemes. In comparison, the position of planners in a constitutional democracy is disproportionately weak, since it is their role to mediate in conflicts of interest between one group of citizens and another. In reality we can see that there are only minor differences between the planning efforts of the two types of social order, which in many cases produce the same results and if anything can only be distinguished in their intentions. Let us compare the Stalinallee in East Berlin, laid out under a totalitarian regime, and the 'Quartier de la Défense' in Paris. The former is conceived as a ceremonial avenue on the familiar French pattern, decorated with some ornaments in doubtful taste. The latter sacrifices rigid distribution of space in order to appear open, unstructured and generously proportioned. The individual architectural features in Paris were created at incomparably greater expense than those of the Stalinallee 20 years before, yet the result is an embarrassing lack of taste. The ornamentation of the Stalinallee, like that of the Moscow metro stations, was intended to beautify the property of the people within the limitations of the means available. The parallel aim was to use these buildings to gloss over the actual brutality of the regime. (The same observation could be made of Italy and Germany during the thirties.) In the capitalist countries, the brutality of monopoly capital is flaunted with the same brazen self-assurance. I have no wish here to debate the legitimacy of either system.

An objective comparison undoubtedly establishes that the Stalinallee creates a sense of coherent street-space, while the 'Quartier de la Défense' lacks any recognisable spatial coherence. It also indicates that the Stalinallee is not a monument which is indissolubly linked with the system of government in power at the time. It derives from the bourgeois boulevard, and seen as such must logically stand in contradiction to the system which produced it. From the point of view of urban planning, the only difference between these two diametrically opposed societies lies in minor details of standards and technique.

What is the current position with regard to the aesthetic demands made by town planning? There has been a frightening move towards uniformity, brought about by the machine age. The religious faith in the wonders of technology has markedly declined in recent years. Environmental pollution has contributed towards this decline. Can regions be helped to identify with their urban culture through the art of architecture as Sitte envisaged it? It is correct to say that art in general – music, cinema, theatre, literature, painting etc. – is subject to the same standardisation as is 'town planning for Planet Earth'. The style of the Pointillistes was imitated everywhere, just like Action Painting, Pop Art etc. Every period in art has its fashions. However, they were never so short-lived as they are today. Modern aesthetic movements are so limited in their scope and so lacking in substance that they lose all credibility after a very short time.

German town planning over the last 25 years has come up with a variety of fashions with serious implications – fashions which were either home-grown or imported from abroad. Imported fashions were in the majority and like all imitative acts they falsified and coarsened the originals.

As I see it, one of the vital tasks of this study is to follow my criticial comments on the current situation and my analysis of urban space with a concrete concluding statement. This conclusion should synthesise what we have learned in the preceding pages and attempt a prediction of the type of urban structure which I feel has some future potential. I have maintained that the town is a regional problem. Similarly, the growth of several towns of different size in the same region has become a problem of national concern. As numerous examples from previous chapters have shown, Soria y Mata, Le Corbusier, Hilberseimer and others considered the planning of urban growth as a facet of larger scale regional planning.

Before I become more specific about my own proposals, I believe it worthwhile to outline the methods and administrative structure which would facilitate regional planning. A centralised information bank must assemble all the facts pertaining to urban and community development: industrial growth, introduction of new industries, population growth and movement, commuting patterns, nature reserves, farmland, traffic routes etc. In every region of Germany this data is already being collated on a continuous basis and could therefore be evaluated immediately by such an organisation. Since the job of this body would be to coordinate the growth of cities in the regions, the implications of the data would have to be tested against planning requirements.

The development models which I consider appropriate for the future are the linear or chain systems as conceived by Soria y Mata towards the end of the 19th century. The stunning vision expressed by Soria y Mata in his book encompasses an urban plan which is laid out according to the transportational demands of urban growth and so avoids the highly complex structural network necessitated by concentric development. Soria y Mata also placed his ideal city in a super-regional context. Le Corbusier took up this idea in *Les trois établissements humains*. The Pampus Plan of J. B. Bakema is also part of a super-regional plan for the area between Rotterdam and the Ruhr. My proposal for the expansion of Stuttgart draws upon the same intellectual tradition. Of course a presupposition is that our cities are capable of further expansion. Given the economic situation in the seventies, it does look as if the height of the construction boom is past. The population explosion in Europe has also flattened off. This is yet another reason why planners in our continent should occupy themselves to a greater extent in coming years with the renewal and adaptation of existing structures. I also believe that we must look for ways of carrying out corrective work on our inhuman new towns, short of pulling them down completely. In spring 1974 I worked on an exercise with students in London to investigate what alterations could be made to Cumbernauld new town in Scotland to create a cohesive urban structure, with due regard to pre-existing reality. Similar studies should be instigated in almost all cities: this would be a worthwhile task for the planning departments of our universities.

CHAPTER 3

RECONSTRUCTING DEVASTATED URBAN SPACE

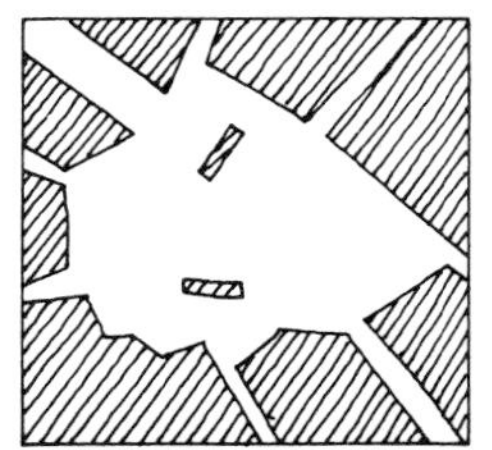
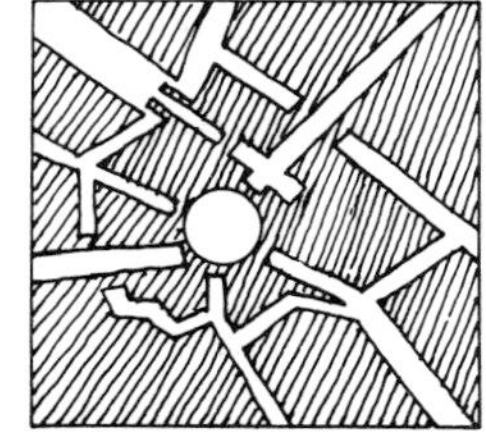

WITH EXAMPLES FROM THE CITY CENTRE OF STUTTGART

CHAPTER 3

RECONSTRUCTING DEVASTATED URBAN SPACE WITH EXAMPLES FROM THE CITY CENTRE OF STUTTGART

INTRODUCTION

MOTIVATION AND OBJECTIVES WHICH GAVE RISE TO THIS STUDY

As a result of the devastation of the Second World War, the constraints imposed during the reconstruction period and the subsequent 'car-orientated' programme of costly civil engineering projects in the centre of Stuttgart, the former coherent urban structure which had been responsive to local conditions was destroyed to a catastrophic extent. The heart of the old city, a bare thousand metres across, was broken up into a large number of small islands battered by waves of heavy traffic.

The *raison d'être* of these studies was to fill the gaps separating these isolated fragments of town as effectively as possible. This problem must involve anyone concerned with the fate of the town in which he lives, even if it is not his birthplace.

As an architect I have tried to describe the spatial bricks and mortar with which these voids, existing as they do in so many cities, can be filled. At the same time workers in other disciplines must lay the necessary foundations for these bricks and mortar, tailoring their plans to suit the requirements of different localities. It would be impossible for the architect alone to find a successful solution to this problem. So this work should be seen as the stimulus for a whole variety of long term scientific research.

The spatial concepts which I am proposing here are therefore necessarily idealistic. They have been worked out without the mandate of the town in question and are not intended to be realised without qualification. In no sense have I taken the considerations of real estate into account. However, all my suggestions are thoroughly 'practical': that is, technically, legally and financially realistic. The recently completed motorways will scarcely be affected by the new proposals. Generally speaking, the existing building fabric has also been respected. The only innovation in terms of local politics is that rather more far-sighted forward planning is needed for future urban restoration and reconstruction on this scale. The very programmes outlined here should theoretically be realisable in a city like Stuttgart within the next fifty years, if there is no significant deterioration in present conditions. I make the attempt in my schemes to win back downtown Stuttgart for the pedestrian, without ousting the car in the process. In practical terms this means using redevelopment to weld together seamlessly the isolated areas at those critical points, whose significance for the pedestrian's spatial awareness was eroded in the post-war years because of costly civil engineering programmes. Particular attention is paid in these studies to restoring the continuity of spatial experience within an urban context.

I have designed streets and squares for the pedestrian, harmonised as closely as possible with the existing structure and showing the utmost consideration for the legacy of the past.

ANY PLANNING INNOVATION IN A CITY MUST BE GOVERNED BY THE LOGIC OF THE WHOLE AND IN DESIGN TERMS MUST OFFER A FORMAL RESPONSE TO PRE-EXISTING SPATIAL CONDITIONS.

This principle has effectively disappeared from modern town planning. No-one would dispute the fact that, with the birth of modern architecture, town planning as Camillo Sitte understood it, and the urban space as an external reality decipherable in aesthetic terms, were sacrificed to a chaotic pseudo-democratic and pseudo-humane urban ideology. Our cities bear living and visible testimony to this – the evidence can be unequivocally understood even by the layman.

The brutal power of capital controls this urban planning for its own dubious purposes. This condemnation may appear a gross generalisation, but in view of the colossal blunders of contemporary town planning it can scarcely be described as an exaggeration.

The town planning legacy of the last thirty years – of questionable value – will be a headache for many future generations, and it requires a certain optimisim on my part to believe that the human instinct for survival will be up to coping with the problem in time to carry out the necessary corrective measures. I hope my optimisim is not misplaced.

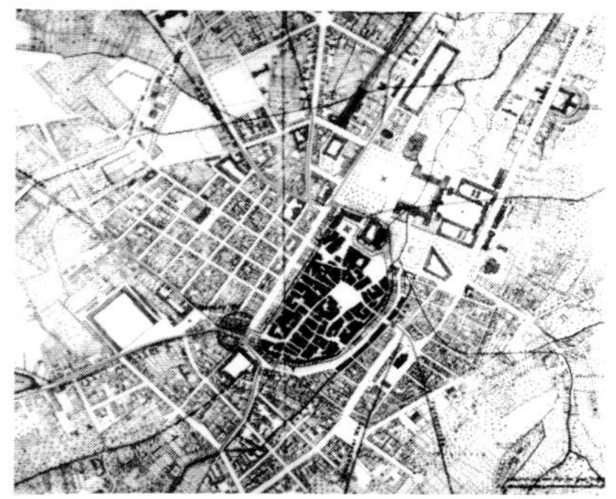

172 City as it was in 1304.

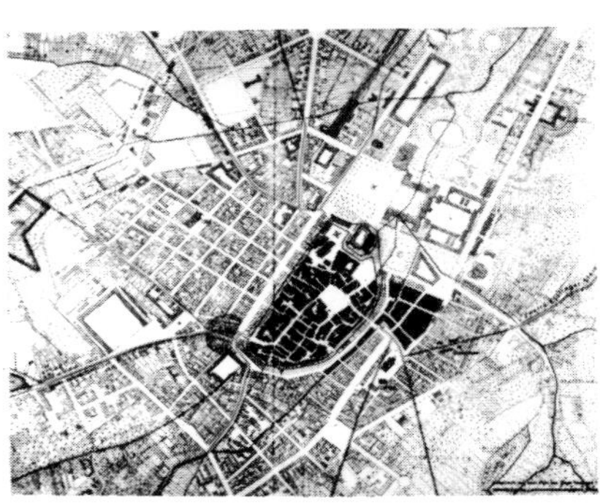

173 1350.

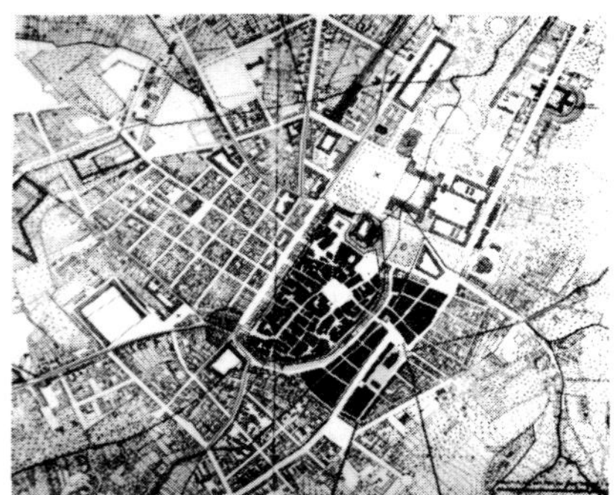

174 1393–1450.

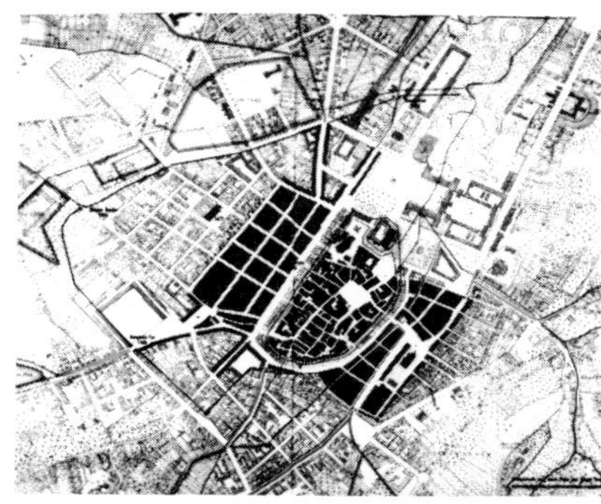

175 1465.

176 1490–1520.

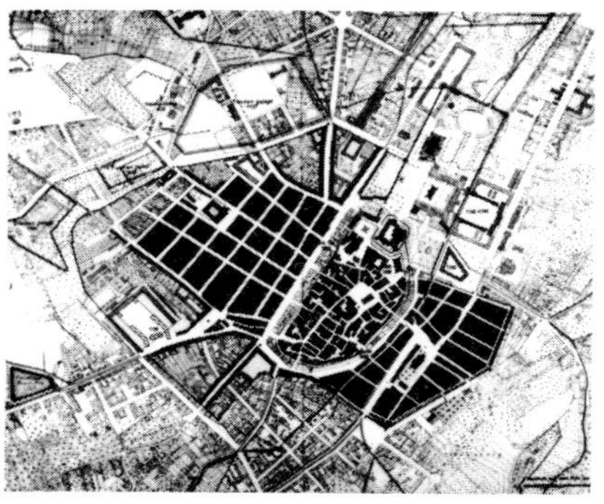

177 Late 16th to mid-18th century.

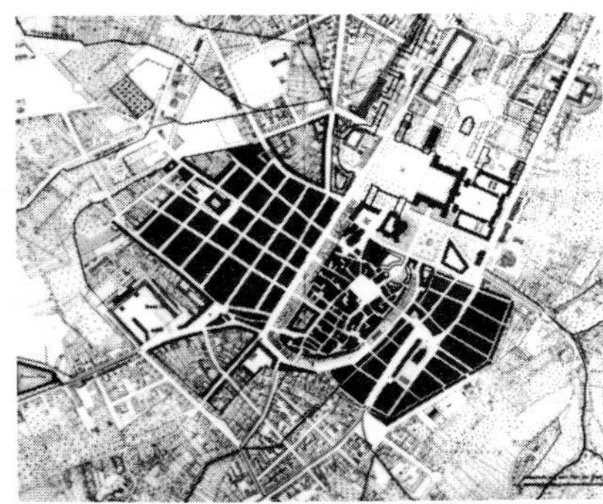

178 Plan for the Residenz by R. F. H. Fischer 1782.

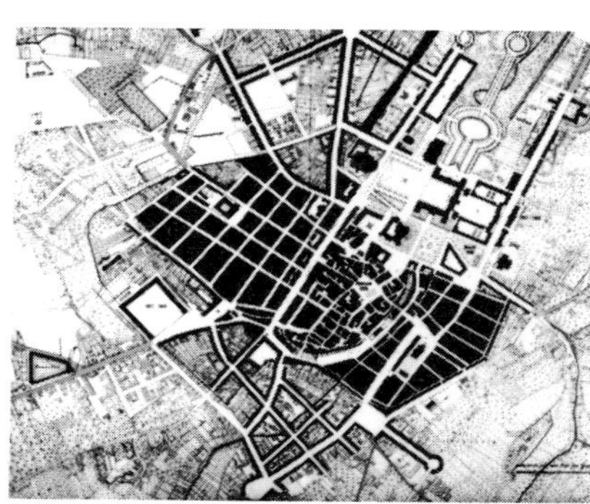

179 Plan for the Residenz by N. F. von Thouret after 1800.

172–179 Stages in the urban development of Stuttgart between the 14th and 19th centuries. Taken from Karl Weidle *Der Grundriss von Alt Stuttgart* Atlas E. Klett Verlag, Stuttgart 1961. Scale 1 :25 000.
The basis is an 1855 plan, on which the various stages of growth are shown in black.

THE DEVELOPMENT OF THE TOWN

The homogeneous and generously proportioned developments for the northern and southern parts of Stuttgart emanate from the second half of the 15th century. For more than 300 years these plans shaped the growth of the town. It was only at the beginning of the 19th century with the plans of Thouret among other things that the development was first pushed beyond these boundaries.

The major stepping stones for further urban growth were the definitive plans for the Königstrasse as part of the Marstall, the creation of the Friedrichsplatz as a result of the layout of the six streets which intersect at that point, the building of the new Katharinenhospital, the Polytechnic and the Alleenplatz (now the Stadtgarten), the Rotebühlkaserne, the Österreichische Platz, the Wilhelmsplatz, the expansion of the Hohe Carlsschule, the Neue Schloss and the monumental buildings surrounding the Schlossplatz, the construction of the Neckarstrasse and the erection of the cultural buildings bordering it, such as the Wilhelmspalais, the Staatsarchiv, Landesbibliothek, Staatstheater and Staatsgalerie. The link-up between Stuttgart and the older settlement of Bad Cannstatt was achieved through the architect Thouret's ambitious plans for the Schlossgarten.

Sound knowledge of the historical development of Stuttgart is of critical importance for any new plan, as each period builds as a continuation of what has gone before. Thus it is that ideas which became bogged down at the planning stage, or plans once executed but effaced over the years, may be valid for our contemporary redevelopment schemes.

So for example I have tried, when thinking of ways to rebuild the Schlossplatz, to take my direction from the ideas of the architects responsible for its original conception and construction. It would be out of place to launch into an in-depth analysis of the history of Stuttgart at this point. I will confine myself to illustrating this development visually, with reference to plans. Careful comparison of separate stages of development can give more information at a glance than can be conveyed briefly with words.

SHORT HISTORY OF STUTTGART

From *Bollmann Bildkartenverlag* (author unknown).

Until well into the middle ages Stuttgart was overshadowed by the much older town of Cannstatt, which was of much greater importance at the time. The Romans had built a castle here at the end of the 1st century A.D. to protect their roads from the Rhine to the Danube through the Neckar and Rems valleys, and around this a civilian settlement grew up. This settlement not only served as a military stronghold and administrative centre for the Romans, but also retained its importance during the Alemannic period. The assembly place and judicial centre of the surrounding tribe of the Alemanni was nearby. It was here, in the year 746, that the Frank Karlmann carried out a mass execution of the Alemanni in the area. Only later did Stuttgart step on to the stage of history.

According to tradition, Duke Liutolf of Swabia founded a stud-farm (Stuotgarten) around 950 in a broad section of the Nesenbach valley, and this gave its name to the settlement and subsequent town which grew up around it. The name first appears in records around 1160 with a nobleman called Hugo de Stutkarten. The settlement of 'Stukarten' in its own right is mentioned for the first time in a document of 1229. The earliest known seal of the town on a document of the year 1312 shows a shield with two horses one above the other. The heraldic device was later simplified to show a single horse. The settlement came into the possession of the Lords (who in 1130 became the Counts) of Württemberg, who had built themselves a fortress on the Wirtenberg (above Stuttgart–Untertürkheim) and took their name from it.

Around the middle of the 13th century Stuttgart received its town charter from Count Ulrich I (1241–65). Count Eberhard I (1279–1325) defended himself there in 1286 and 1287 against the German King Rudolf of Habsburg. In a document of 1286 a mayor and twelve judges are named for the first time; and the title of 'citizen' (cives) is first used. In the imperial war waged by Kaiser Heinrich VII on the Counts of Württemberg, Stuttgart fell to the imperial city of Esslingen between 1311 and 1315. After the end of these hostilities Count Eberhard transferred his family seat and the remains of his ancestors from Beutelsbach to Stuttgart. Stuttgart thereby became the most important place in the county. The town covered more or less the area which today is bounded by the Königsstrasse, Eberhardstrasse, Karlsstrasse and Planie. In the 14th century the Leonhards or Esslinger quarter grew up on the south eastern fringes of this area around a chapel dedicated to Leonhard, and the 15th century saw the growth in the north west of the Liebfrauen or Turnieracher quarter (named after a chapel dedicated to the Virgin Mary). The latter gradually took on the character of a 'wealthy' quarter during the 16th and 17th centuries. Stuttgart really blossomed for the first time under Count Ulrich V (1433–80). In 1450 the counts' palace was built on the market place, and the town hall was erected next to it between 1456 and 1458. The collegiate church was built as an enlargement of a late gothic hall church, and until 1806 remained under the exclusive jurisdiction of the parish of Stuttgart. The Leonhardskapelle was replaced by a church with a triple nave. In the upper quarter of the town a Dominican monastery was founded in 1473, and the Church attached to it has been known since the time of the Reformation as the Hospitalkirche. Hänslin or Aberlin Jörg was the principal architect of all three churches. In 1482, Stuttgart was officially granted the status of capital city; in 1495 Württemberg was elevated to the position of a duchy. By this time Cannstatt – granted its city charter by King Ludwig of the Bavarians as early as 1330 – had been far outstripped by the much newer city of Stuttgart.

During the troubled reign of Duke Ulrich (1503–19 and 1534–50) the country was shaken by a number of wars. The repercussions of the uprising of 'Poor Konrad' (1514) and the Peasants' War (1525) were even felt in the provincial capital. Furthermore, from 1520 to 1534 Stuttgart was under Austrian rule. 1534–5 saw the beginnings of the Reformation, and peace was gradually restored in the country. A new peak of activity was reached by the builders of the second half of the 16th century. During the reign of Duke Christoph (1550–68) the old Wasserburg of Aberlin Tretsch was completely rebuilt and expanded. Its lovely arcaded courtyard is one of the most highly regarded achievements among German renaissance castles. To the north east of the castle, a pleasure garden was built during the reign of Duke Ludwig (1568–93), embellished by the architectural masterpiece of Georg Beer's Neue Lusthaus. To the south of the old castle, Heinrich Schickardt added a further magnificent renaissance palace between 1599 and 1609: the Neue Bau. The increase in population also mirrored the overall prosperity of the town. Approximately 4,000 people lived in Stuttgart in 1400; by 1589 the

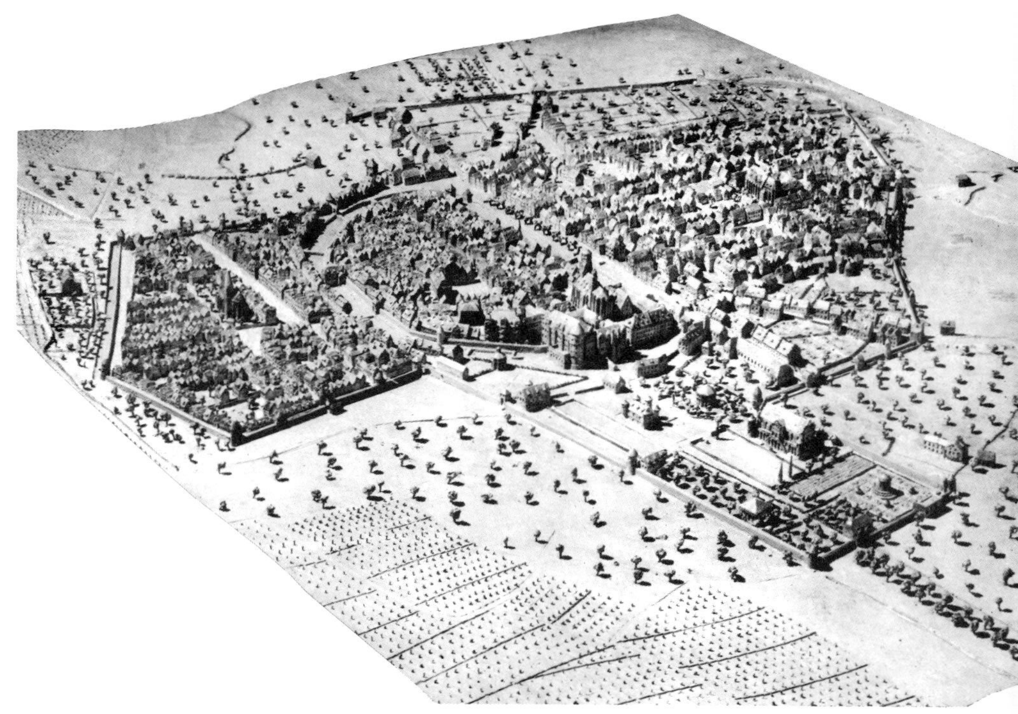

180 Model of the city in 1600, by Karl Berrer, 1914. Photo: City Surveyor's office.

181 View of the City of Stuttgart. Grabado de Merian, 1634.

Ansicht der Stadt Stuttgart

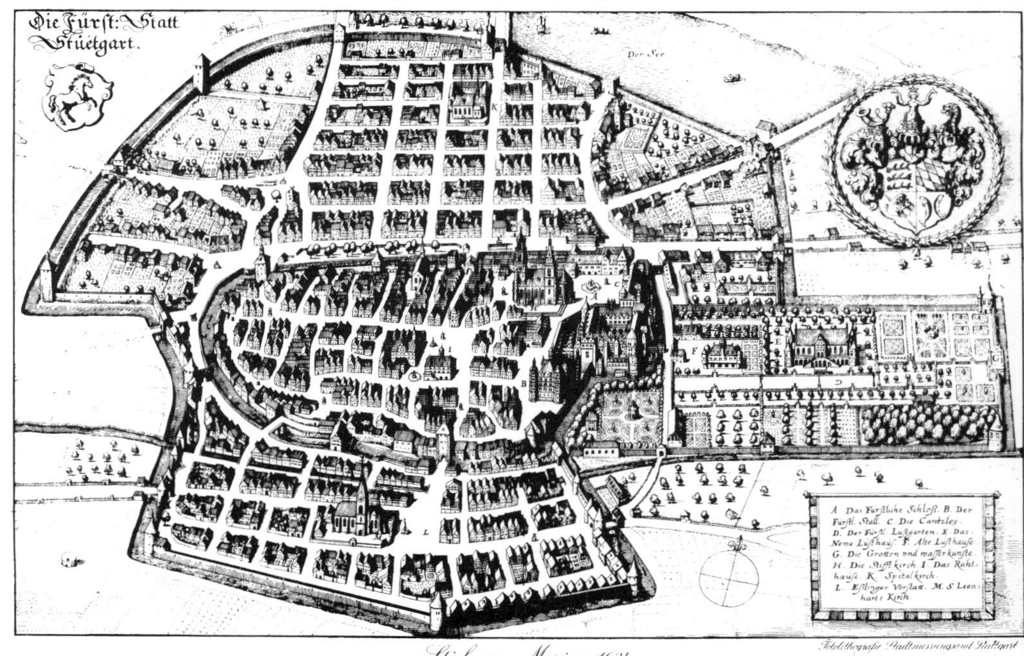

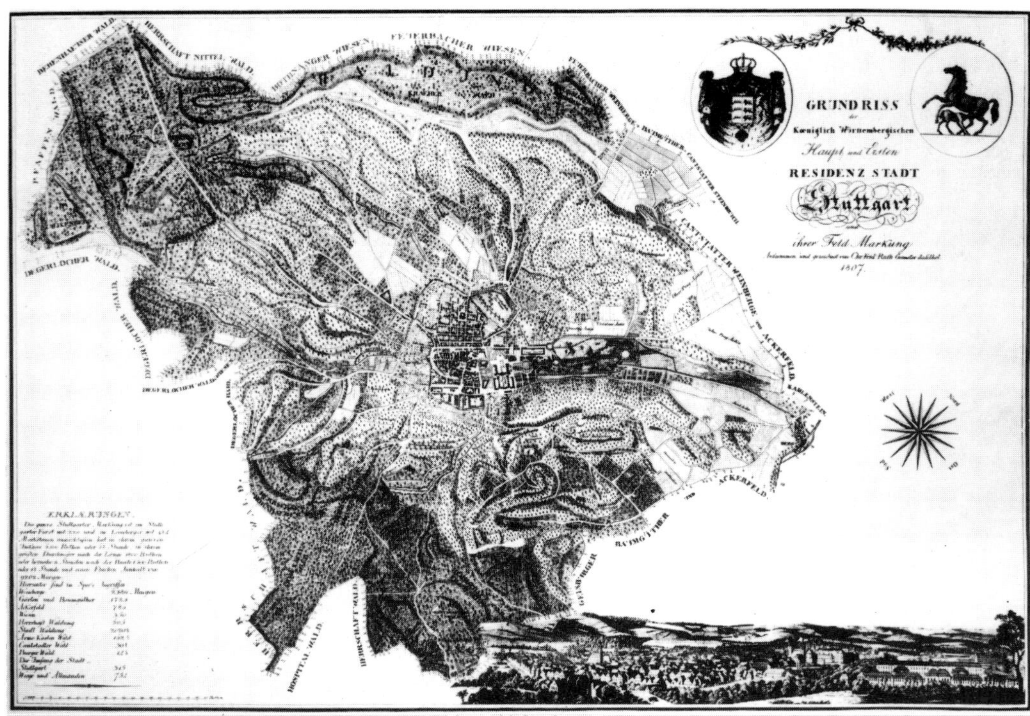

182

183 Bird's-eye view looking up the valley. Stadtarchiv Stuttgart.

figure had risen to 9,000. The principal economic basis for this prosperity was wine-growing. Vineyards were planted around the valley, while the narrow valley floor supported little in the way of agriculture. Trade at this time was largely centred around the court. Stuttgart, like everywhere else, found its prosperity curtailed by the 30 Years' War, and in 1648 its population amounted to a mere 4,500. It took a long time for the countryside and the Court to recover from the effects of the war. In 1686 the Gymnasium Illustre was inaugurated. With the foundation of Ludwigsburg by Eberhard Ludwig (1693–1733), Stuttgart's position as seat of the Court was seriously threatened. It was only under Karl Eugen (1744–1793) that Stuttgart regained its former status as capital. He commissioned the building of the Neue Schloss by Retti, de la Guèpière and R. F. H. Fischer in the late baroque and rococo style. In 1775 the library of Ludwigsburg was transferred to Stuttgart. The 'military academy', planned and laid out on a grand scale by Karl Eugen, was moved from Schloss Solitude to Stuttgart in the same year. As the 'Hohe Karlsschule', it went down in German educational history and brought its founder the reputation of an enlightened and wise monarch. It was here that Friedrich Schiller received his education as a military surgeon between 1773 and 1780, and here that he wrote his first work 'Die Räuber'. Vital to the cultural life of the Court was the Duke's patronage of art, music and theatre, which ran parallel to his interest in education and learning. With the building of good roads Stuttgart also came to play a more active part in the network of communications; from about 1705 a permanent coaching station was established there. At the end of the 18th century Stuttgart's population numbered around 20,000.

In the year 1803 Duke Friedrich II (1797–1816) was installed as elector;

on the 1st of January he was crowned king. At this point Stuttgart became the seat of the royal court in a state greatly increased in area by the cession of numerous territories. This initiated a new wave of building. The old city walls and gates were demolished. The 'Grosse Graben' was transformed into a ceremonial avenue and became the Königsstrasse (1811). Entire new districts of the town were planned and started by the King's master-builder Thouret. Between 1805 and 1818 the royal parks were laid out in the English style. The same passion for building also inspired Friedrich's successor, Wilhelm I (1816–64). He commissioned Salucci to build a burial chapel on the former site of the Stammburg Wirtemberg (1820–1824). The same architect was responsible for the royal country house 'Rosenstein' (1825–29) overlooking the Neckar near Cannstatt, and for the Wilhelmspalais in the town itself (1834–39). Thouret built the Cannstatt Kursaal between 1825 and 1827 in an extremely restrained classical style. Ludwig Zanth was the creator of the Moorish-influenced Wilhelma (1842–46), while Christian Leins designed the Villa Berg (1845–53) and the Königsbau (1856–59), facing the Neue Schloss. Other public buildings were the State Archive, the Fine Arts Museum, the State Library and the Mint. Stuttgart at this time was the undisputed cultural centre of its state. Gustav Schwab, Wilhelm Hauff, Ludwig Uhland, Eduard Mörike, Nikolas von Lenau, Georg Herwegh, Ferdinand Freiligrath and Wilhelm Raabe lived for a time in Stuttgart. Some found their last resting place there.

The advance of industry in the second half of the 19th century radically changed the economic and social structure of the city. King Friedrich had already taken the first steps to promote economic development in his capital. However, a perceptible rise in the volume of trade and industrial activity

184 Aerial photograph from the south- east.
Photo: Strähle, Schorndorf c. 1920 from Karl Weidle *Der Grundriss von Alt Stuttgart*.

185 Overall plan 1913. Scale 1 : 35 000.

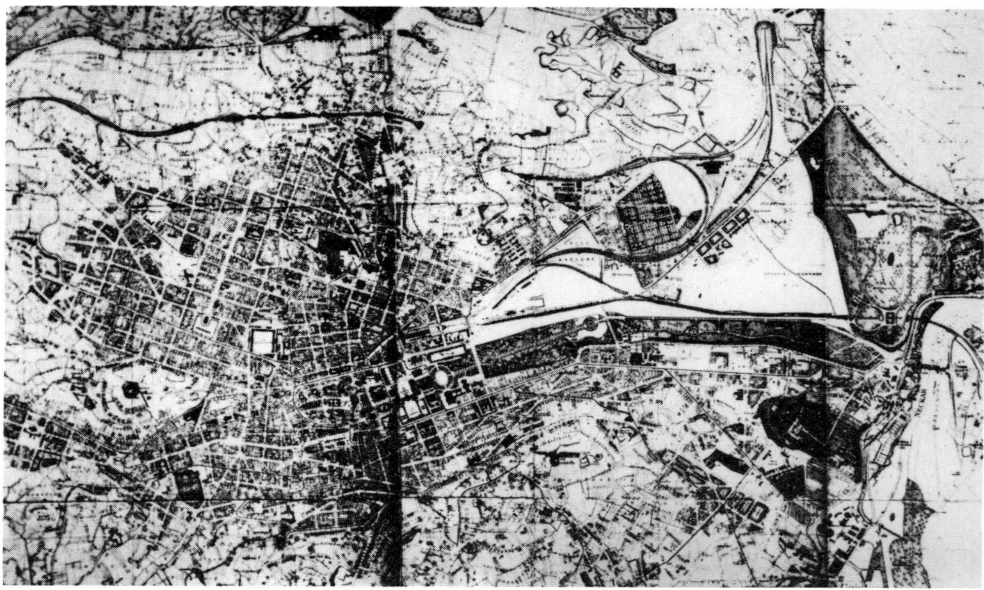

186 Aerial photograph from the north-east.
Photo: A. Brugger, from *Stuttgart und seine Nachbarn.* Franckhsche Verlagshandlung, Stuttgart 1965.

187 Overall plan 1971. Scale 1 : 30 000.

only took place after the establishment of the Customs Union in 1834.

A factor of decisive significance here was the completion of the railway network which served Stuttgart. The stretch between Cannstatt and Esslingen went into operation in 1845. By 1846 the line already connected Ludwigsburg, Stuttgart and Plochingen. The service was extended to Heilbronn in 1848, and to Ulm and Friedrichshafen in 1850. During these years thriving industries grew up in Stuttgart in chemicals and pharmaceuticals, dyeing and machinery. In 1810, J. F. Cotta transferred his publishing house from Tubingen to Stuttgart which, as the home of this and the publishers Hallberger and Kröner, became the principal centre in south west Germany for printing and the book-trade. The production of musical instruments (piano making) also developed and attained a considerable reputation. The significance of this industrial development becomes clear if one considers the population statistics. In 1830 Stuttgart had approximately 25,000 inhabitants; in 1852 the figure had doubled. The number of factories grew from 17 to 173 between 1832 and 1861, and the number of workers employed in them from 600 to 4,000. This prosperity continued to grow vigorously. In the 1880's the foundations were laid for the Bosch factory in Stuttgart and the Daimler plant in Cannstatt. Since then both companies have spread the name of their city of origin throughout the world.

At the end of the century Stuttgart, with its population of around 175,000, had become a major city. In 1905 other localities were incorporated into the city for the first time on a large scale: Cannstatt, which had achieved almost international fame during the 19th century as a spa on the strength of its rich mineral springs, Untertürkheim and Wangen. This agglomeration took

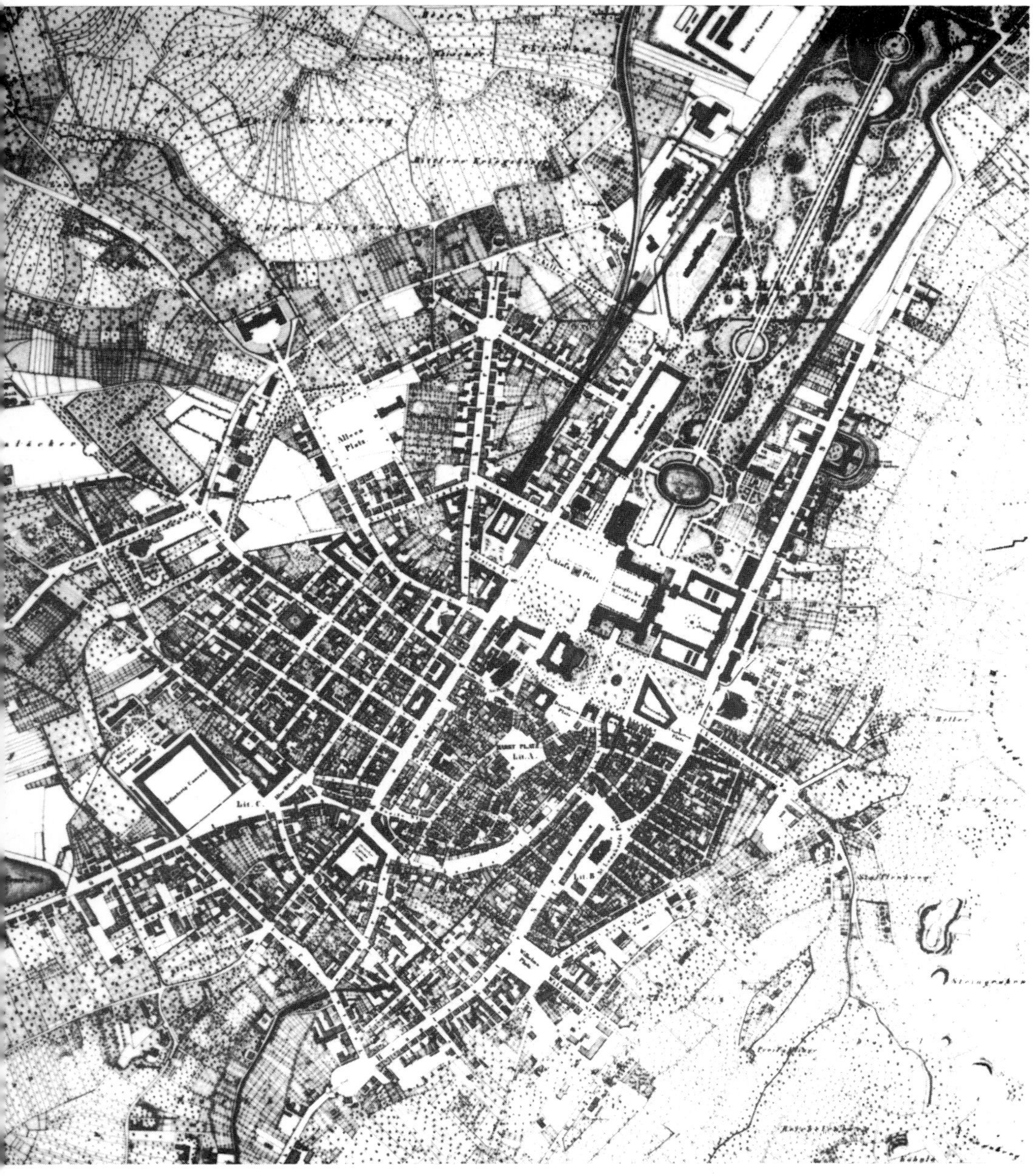

the city boundaries as far as the Neckar. In 1908 Degerloch was incorporated and a first step was taken in the direction of the Filder. The First World War, the 1918 Revolution – followed by the abdication of the universally popular King Wilhelm II – and the inflationary period only briefly checked the development of greater Stuttgart as an industrial entity. In the first decades of the 20th century, the buildings were produced which brought world-wide renown to the Stuttgart school of architecture and its design principles: the Kunstverein building (Fischer), large and small auditoriums of the Württemberg State Theatre (Littmann), the new station (Bonatz), the Tagblatt tower (Osswald) and the Schocken department store (Mendelsohn), as well as the Weissenhofsiedlung. Then the war came. The first air-raids took place in 1940, followed in 1943 by the first large-scale offensive and in 1944 by the almost total destruction of the city centre. At the end of the war, after 53 air-raids, some 60% of Stuttgart was destroyed. It was occupied by French troops on the 21st April 1945 and was included in the American occupation sector on the 8th July

188 Stuttgart 1855, cf. as it was in 1970.

1945. The clearance of bomb-sites, the supply of food and energy, and coping with housing problems dominated the life of the city for the next few years. In 1950 the German Horticultural Show was held here as the first high point in Stuttgart's recovery. In 1953 Stuttgart became the capital of the Land of Baden-Württemberg. In 1956 an extension to the new town hall was built on the Marktplatz and a new concert hall for Stuttgart (the Liederhalle) was opened. Since 1956, Stuttgart's new landmark – the television tower of the Süddeutsche Rundfunk, more than 200 metres high – can be seen from miles around. In 1958 Stuttgart's port on the Neckar was opened, and this brought the city and the surrounding industrial area into the network of European waterways and connected it with the great seaports.

At present some 632,000 people live in Stuttgart. Every effort is absorbed in trying to overcome traffic problems. New buildings and streets are springing up all around. And yet Stuttgart still manages to maintain its reputation as 'the city between forest and vine'.

189 Stuttgart 1970, cf. as it was in 1855.

190–195 Typical Stuttgart bourgeois houses of the 19th century.

196–201 Plinths and entrances.

202–207 Entrances.

208 Wilhelma.

209 Königsbau.

210 Villa Berg.

211–213 Balconies.

PROPOSALS FOR THE RECONSTRUCTION OF DEVASTATED URBAN AREAS

I have restricted myself to describing the individual projects illustrated in the adjoining overall plan. I have begun in the station area, and made a round tour, as it were, of the new planning proposals for the university campus, the Rotebühlplatz, the Johannesstrasse, the Feuersee and from there across to the Österreichische Platz, Wilhelmsplatz, the Leonhardskirche, Charlottenplatz, the Staatsgalerie and back to the station. For each location, by means of plans and models, I have provided a direct comparison between its historical development since the mid-19th century, its present condition, my new planning proposals and how they fit in with the existing building fabric.

214 Scale 1 : 33 000.
Overall plan of all new planning proposals.
1 Station.
2 University.
3 Rotebühlplatz.
4 Johannesstrasse, Feuerstrasse.
5 Österreichische Platz.
6 Wilhelmsplatz.
7 Leonhardskirche.
8 Charlotten–Schlossplatz.
9 Königstrasse.
10 Staatsgalerie.
11 Schlossgarten.

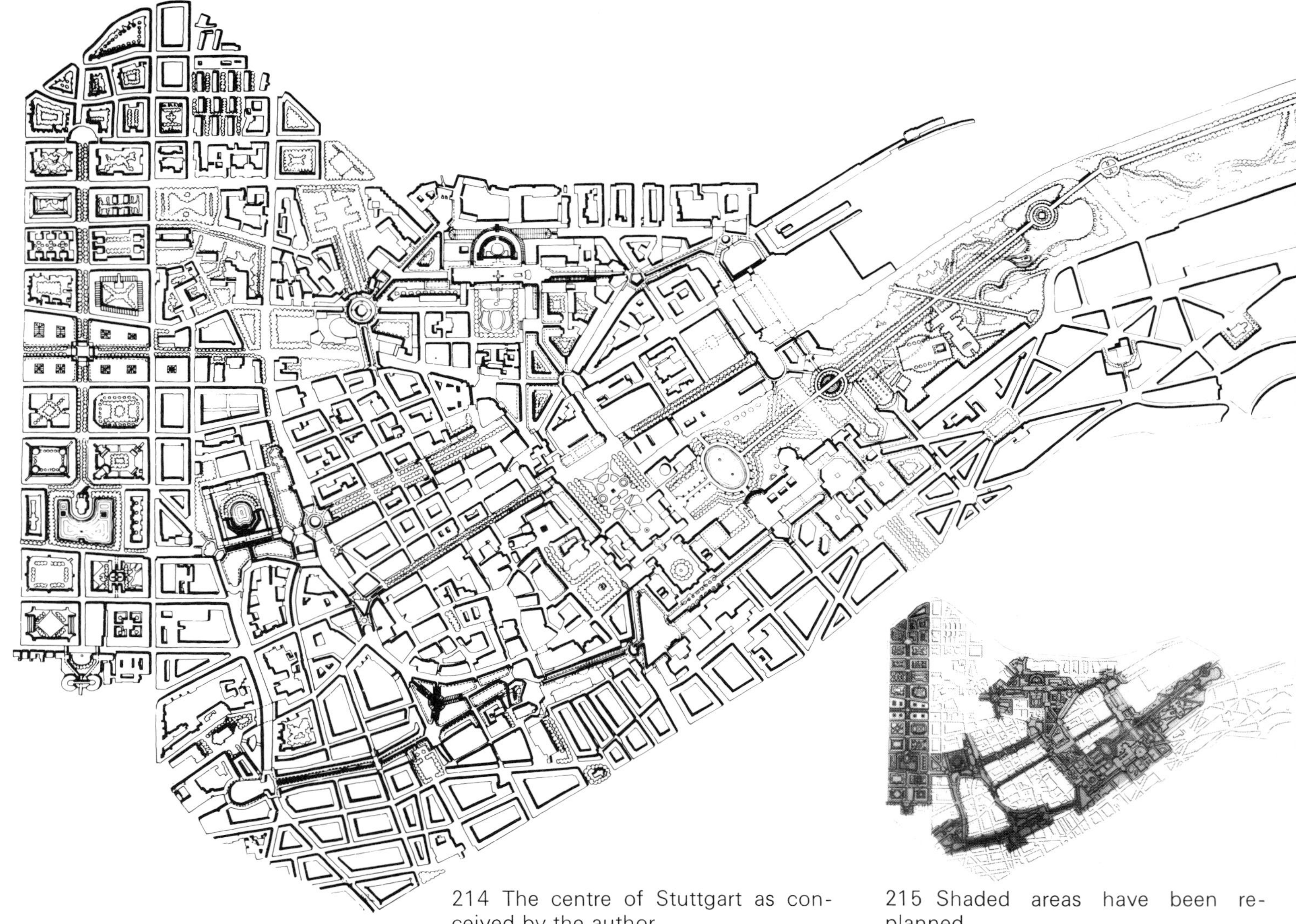

214 The centre of Stuttgart as conceived by the author.

215 Shaded areas have been replanned.

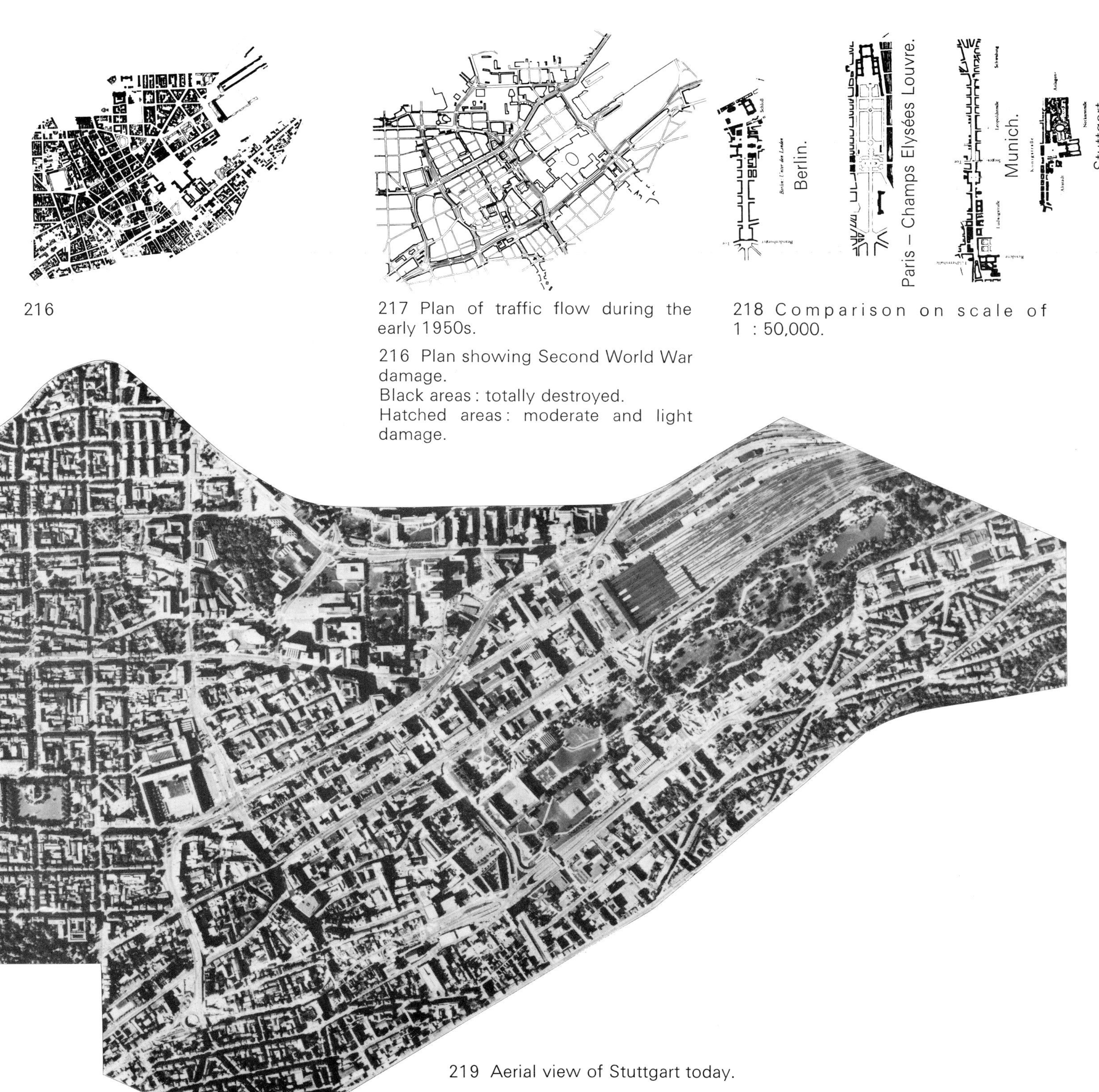

216

217 Plan of traffic flow during the early 1950s.

218 Comparison on scale of 1 : 50,000.

216 Plan showing Second World War damage.
Black areas: totally destroyed.
Hatched areas: moderate and light damage.

219 Aerial view of Stuttgart today.

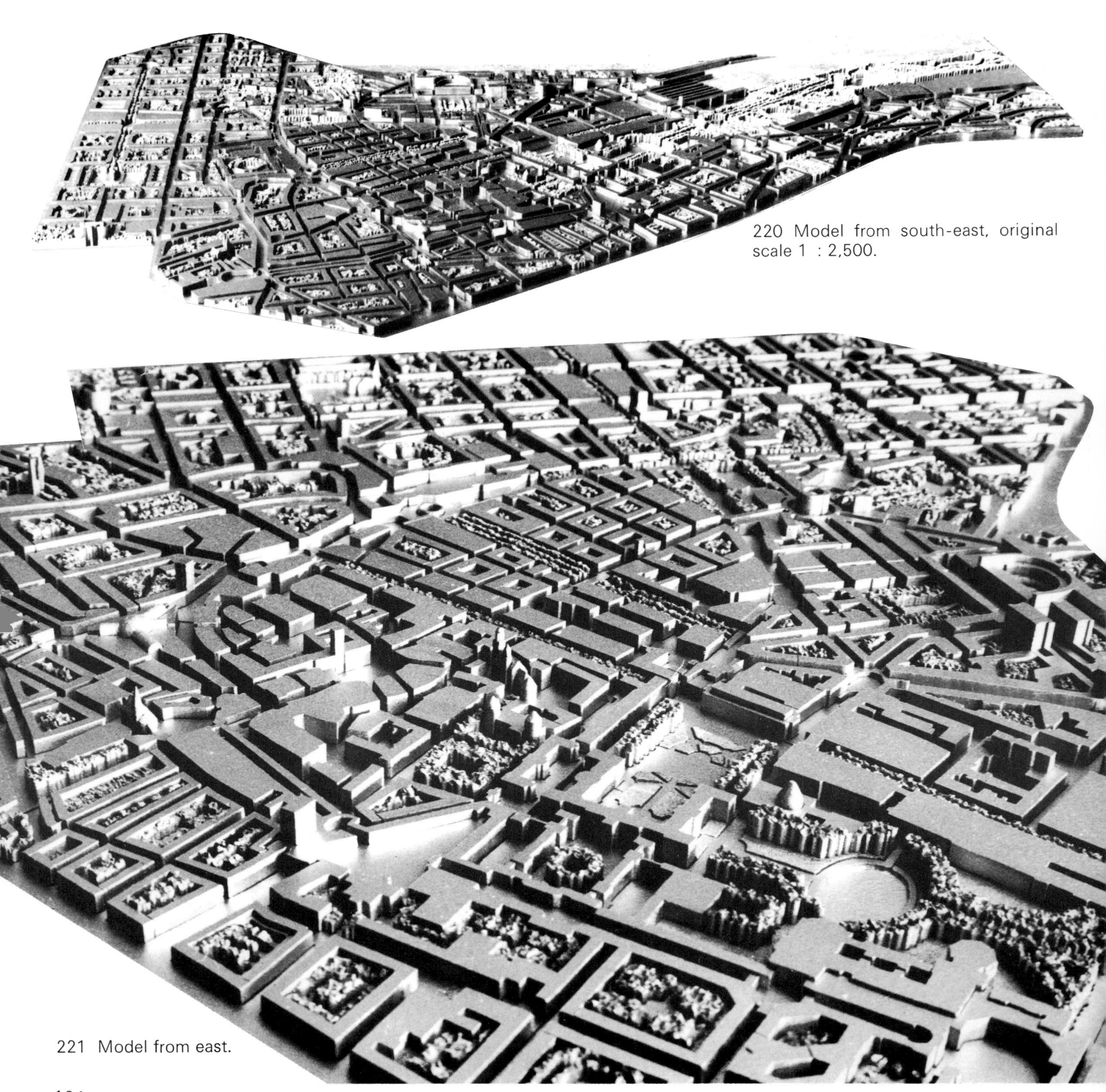

220 Model from south-east, original scale 1 : 2,500.

221 Model from east.

222 1855.

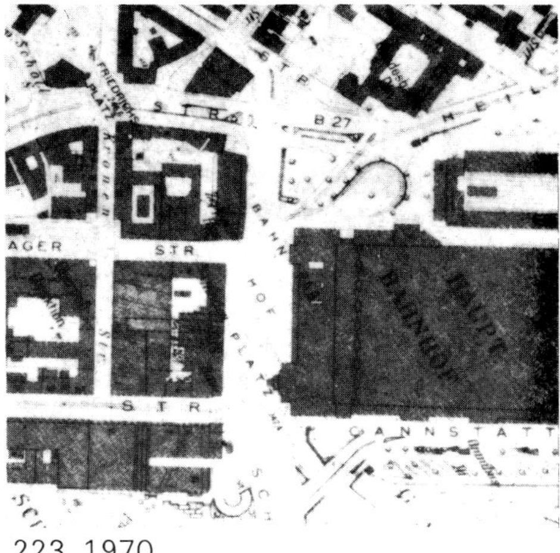

223 1970.

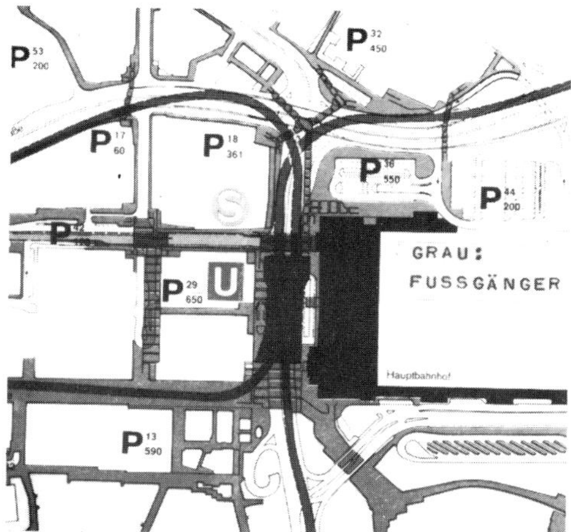

224 Traffic plan showing overhead and underground railways.

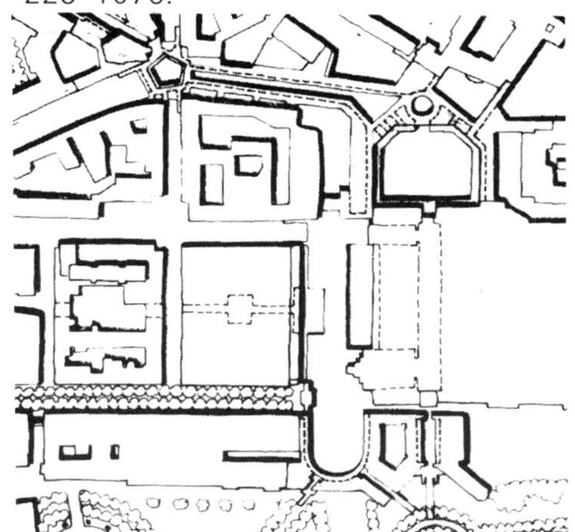

225 New planning proposals.

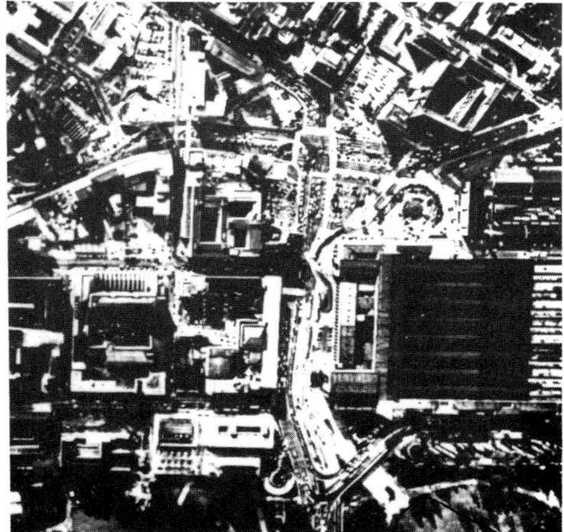

226 Aerial view of station area today.

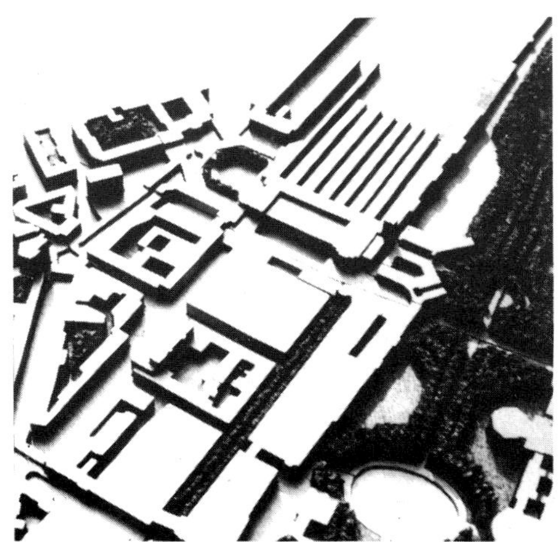

227 Model of new plans.

STATION AREA

The traffic plan of the city of Stuttgart restricts the use of the squares to the north and west of the station to motorised traffic, while pedestrians can only gain access to the station by subway. In some respects this may be a practical arrangement – for example when one has to reach the tube or local main-line stop – but it cannot seriously be considered as a final and satisfactory solution. If they are unavoidable, I am prepared to accept the below-ground areas as regulators of traffic flow. However, they are an inadequate substitute for urban space in the open. Since work beneath the station squares has recently been completed, there is no point in attempting further alteration here (see traffic plan). I suggest therefore that a new level be constructed above the roadway, which will lead away from the station across the flow of traffic, at the same level as the raised station concourse. The temporary bridge put up in front of the station while building works were in progress could serve as a model for this proposal (see photo Fig. 232). The objection could be made that such a move might considerably influence and distort the visual effect of the buildings on the square. At the planning stage I went into this problem thoroughly, and came to the conclusion that the gain in terms of how people experience their environment justifies the alteration to the existing fabric and its impact.

Certainly the architects Bonatz and Scholer would have designed the station differently had they been forced to accommodate this kind of raised platform. As the proposer of such a solution I had to find some means of expressing the impact of the building in a new but equally valid way, without impairing its significance. In old cities there are countless examples of new and aesthetically pleasing urban types being generated as the result of the redefinition of spatial limits. On the other hand, there are cases of the original appearance of an area being altered, without any compensating spatial balance being created. An example of this was the way in which so many buildings were built around Mainz cathedral over the years, to the marked detriment of its architectural impact. One result of this is that a stranger to the town has to make a laborious search before finding the entrance. The expectations raised by the building's silhouette in a picture of the town are rudely disappointed.

The thesis outlined above would materially affect the planning of the station in the following ways: on no account must any further building obscure the unique proportions of the arcades. The raised platform must be given sufficient clearance at this point. In the very high-level entrance area, however, the platform can be built right into the station concourse. This then means a change in the proportions of the projecting entrance. The new proportions must be carefully studied. This is true of the 'Hindenburgbau' opposite the station, a building of a quite outstanding architectural interest in a significant central position. The form of the platform must obey the rules of existing structures in such a way as to harmonise with their character.

In addition, I suggest that the Königstrasse should not enter the Bahnhofsplatz directly but through a kind of spatial caesura of the type formed by Thouret's Königstor (King's Gate) before its demolition in 1924. At this new 'gateway' steps and ramps would link the Königstrasse with the surface of the new level.

At this point I would like to include a few short comments on so-called 'functionless' city architecture. This and other types of monument or 'urban decoration' have with a few exceptions fallen into oblivion. It was thought possible to replace them with the instruments of technology and traffic signals. Sculptors today try to emulate the architectural scale with over-sized works while failing to fit them to the basic elements of surrounding buildings. One-off shock effects, obsessed with structural complexity, are highly rated. In most cases their impact wears off after a short time. And yet I welcome these statements, even if I consider much of this contemporary street furniture tasteless and ephemeral. They do at least prove that the need for something over and above pure functionalism has not been completely crushed. As part of the thought process defining the typological characteristics of urban architecture and space artists will have to create a new vocabulary with a contemporary meaning. Society will have to provide the means for this, even if not in the financial sense. If this argument were not valid, museums, opera houses, concert halls and churches would change their function and become shops and factories. History offers enough examples of iconoclasm or the demolition or recycling of historic buildings. Part of the reason for this was the injustice of social abuses. When eliminating potentates, the op-

229 The Königstrasse, between the station and the Schlossplatz.

228 Arcade on the west side of the station.

230 Northern exit of the station.

231 Central station, southern entrance. Architects Bonatz and Scholer 1910–27.

pressed classes have also tried to get rid of the symbols of their power. This seems legitimate at the time, but time stills the waves of anger and teaches men to value the buildings of the past for their architectural quality, even when their original functions have ceased to apply. The beauty of a building alone can justify its existence. ('. . . et c'est utile, puisque c'est joli' – Antoine de Saint-Exupéry.)

Architecture without explicit function, which I am discussing here, is a very modest phenomenon. It should be meaningful within its historical context, appropriate to its location and of

232 Temporary bridge put up during building works on the Bahnhofsplatz.

the correct typological register for the surrounding space. And in my opinion this holds good for the 'gateway' between the Königstrasse and the Bahnhofsplatz.

233 View of the Friedrichstrasse (left) and Kriegsbergstrasse (right).

The Königstrasse should also be planted with a double row of plane trees. This device allows one to dispense with the costly street furniture which has been proposed. It should then become an exclusively pedestrian street. Only an avenue of trees can make the architectural chaos of this street halfway bearable by screening it off with its leaves and branches. I consider this proposal one of the cornerstones of the renovation of Stuttgart. Such a measure seems to be too easy, and it has never been considered up until now. The oppressive climate during the summer months of the valley in which Stuttgart lies provides sufficient justification in itself, even disregarding the unique atmosphere which an avenue of trees creates. I further propose to continue the line of buildings on the south side of the Königstrasse across the Schillerstrasse and up to the south side of the station. They would create a semicircular spatial stop for the elongated Bahnhofsplatz. This form is derived from the roundel placed in this location by N. F. Thouret behind the Königstor. The station tower should be pierced to give direct access from the main hall to the Schlossgarten.

Describing town planning proposals is a tedious business, and it is asking a lot to expect strangers to read them. They only become clear when the definitive plans are available for consultation, as these can provide a wealth of further information which is impossible to describe in words. The new level continues round to the northern part of the station area and as an extension of the booking hall forms an open space which could be particularly valuable as a meeting place. At all times of day and in every season the station is an extremely popular meeting point for migrant workers. These people could use this spot as a further source of information to help them on arrival, offer them cheap places to sleep and facilitate contact with their compatriots.

From this space, a traffice-free shopping-street or bazaar would lead on to the Friedrichsplatz and from there to the university. The pedestrian street is conceived of as a light 'flyover' running along the centre of the street, with the greatest available clearance between it and the houses. I see the open pedestrian area as being very narrow, not more than 3.5 metres. In addition, there would be an arcade on both sides of some 2 metres. The shops on the 'bridge' could be double-storeyed. The junction on the Friedrichsplatz would be bridged by the same structure, thus creating a new space which in its geometric configuration would remain faithful to Thouret's ideas. In reality, no original building survives from the square as he designed it. It was completely destroyed in the last war. The present traffic flow would not be altered by the new proposals.

THE UNIVERSITY AREA

Since the majority of the university buildings will be moved over the next few years to a permanent site in open countryside outside the town, the first question is of course whether it makes any sense to carry out improvements to the remaining institutes on their present site. I am working on the assumption that the arts faculties at least must be integrated into the town. Unfortunately what has happened is that a large number of ancillary buildings necessary to an established university town have not been provided here, and it would be difficult to build them at this point. It is also worth considering whether one should attempt some integration on the campus of other urban functions, so that activities other than those of the university could be guaranteed. Student halls of residence, as well as rented and owner-occupied flats should be provided on the campus.

The new plans cover the area between the Friedrichsplatz and the Liederhalle, Königsbau and Katharinenhospital. Since the potential uses of this area have not yet been established by an analysis of its needs, my new planning proposals should be seen purely as a hypothetical solution or an abstract exercise. They should help to illuminate practical difficulties encountered in replanning this part of the city and a model based on my proposals should resolve such problems. The central theme of the structure I have proposed was the linking together of the crucial elements of the

235 1855.

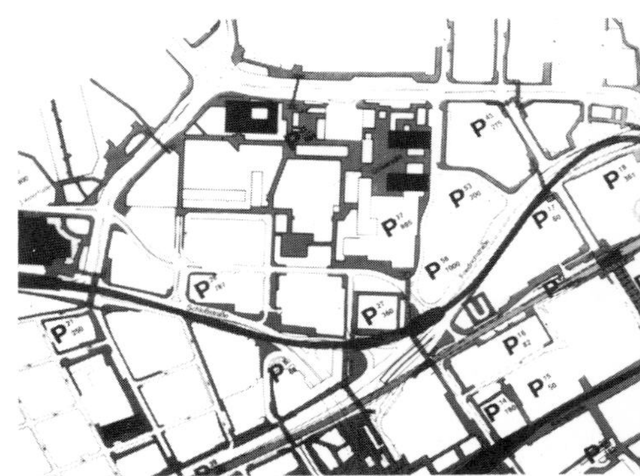

237 Traffic plan with local main-line and underground railway network currently under construction. Shaded area: pedestrian zones.

234 Aerial photo.

239 Aerial photo from south-west.

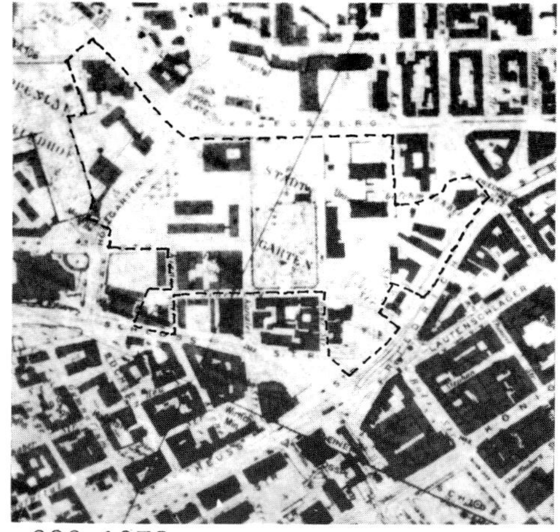

236 1972.

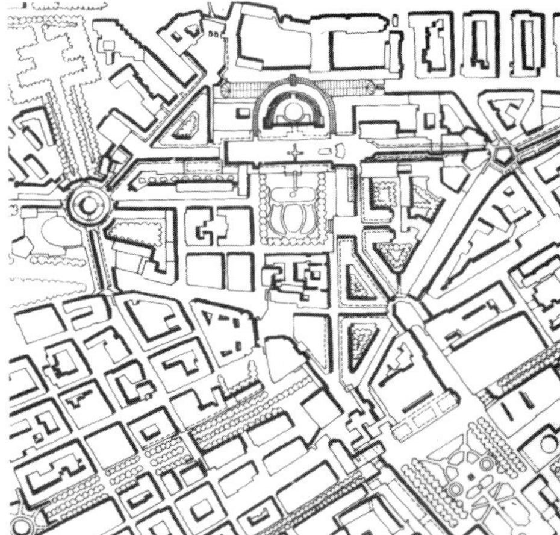

238 New planning proposals.

240 Integration of the old and the new.

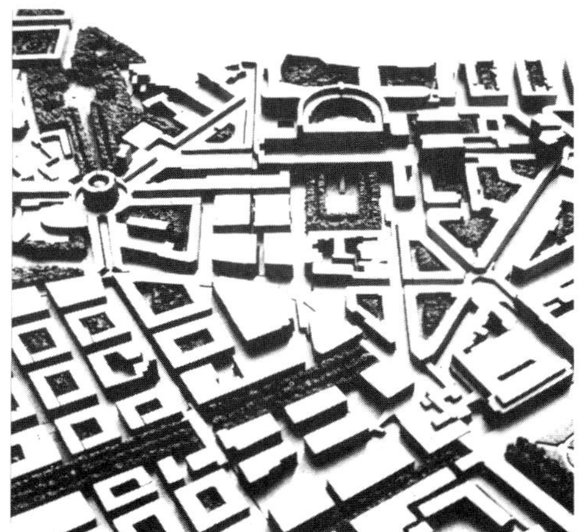

university area and their relationship to the existing urban fabric. So I have designed a traffic-free precinct connecting the Hahn tower, college buildings, library, refectory, Liederhalle and Linden museum. I have planned for a sightline to run from the centre of this east-west axis to the Bolzstrasse and the Kleine Schlossplatz. These designs, in terms of the height of the buildings, harmonise with the scale of the town as it is. This is true of both its old and its new buildings. The isolated tower blocks on the Keplerstrasse are integrated as fully as is the rest of the former polytechnic on the Huberstrasse. It can be mathematically proved that low-rise, high-density building can render the use of high-rise building redundant.

Unfortunately there is no possibility now of the Katharinenhospital being moved from its present site on the busy Kriegsbergstrasse, so we must think in terms of improving it by radical structural alterations. This could be done by building a multi-storey extension over the adjacent street, thus creating two inner courtyards and bringing complete quiet to the hospital. This dual purpose addition above street level would serve as an extension both to the hospital and the university.

The approach to the refectory today does not even have the elementary safety measures of traffic lights or pedestrian crossings. Anyone who sees the way in which hundreds of students risk their lives every lunch time to cross the four-lane street between the university area and the refectory will be shocked by this scandalous state of affairs. I never cease to be amazed at how little fuss people make, how little they take issue with such blatant and irresponsible negligence on the part of city planning departments. I would further suggest that the Liederhalle and the Linden museum be connected with the 'campus' in the same way as the refectory. The curved rear elevation of the Liederhalle gave me the idea of creating a circus at the junction of the Breitscheidstrasse and the Holzgartenstrasse. This is the meeting point of the routes of pedestrian access from the Herdweg

241 Model of the university area.

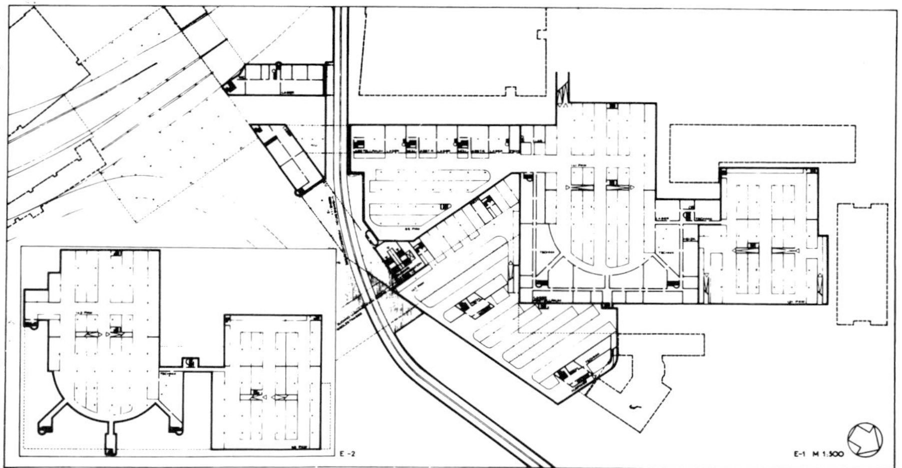

242 Plans of 1st and 2nd floor levels.

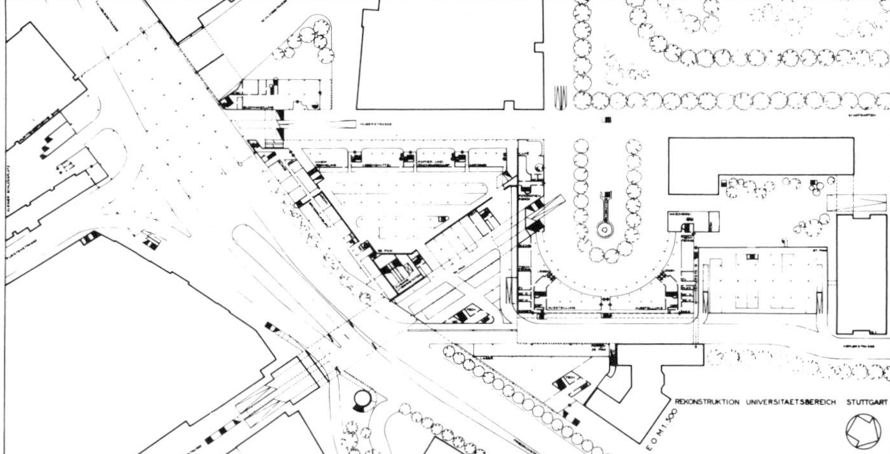

243 Plan of ground level.

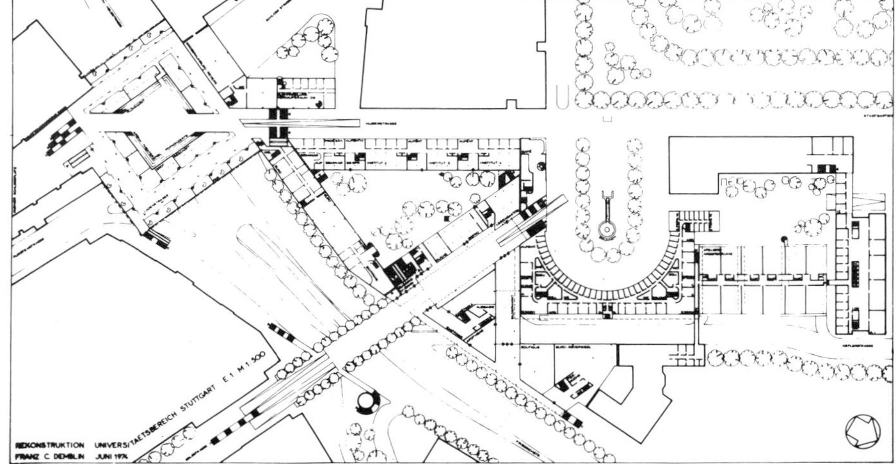

244 Plan of 1st floor level.

and the Hoppenlau cemetery, which then continue across the Büchsenstrasse directly to the old Marktplatz.

I would like to add a question at this point which is always posed with this type of project: 'What is the justification for such a massive and expensive redevelopment of our streets, and can we be optimistic that this kind of action will represent a sound investment?' Answer: Given the horrifying extent to which the spatial logic of the city centre of Stuttgart has been destroyed, some of the measures proposed here are the only way in which the lost scale of the city can possibly be restored. It is certainly true that these corrective measures are more expensive today than sensible and far-sighted plans would have been. But since we cannot undo the results of the last thirty years, we must plan for the future and decide whether – and to what extent – these corrective measures must be undertaken.

STUDY OF THE UNIVERSITY AREA: SCHEME BY FRANZ C. DEMBLIN

For some areas in this chapter, as an alternative to my own planning proposals, I have included work produced between 1973 and 1974 by architectural students under my direction at the University of Stuttgart. There is a clear intention in all their designs to revive areas whose spatial qualities had been destroyed, using an architectural vocabulary which on one hand respects the existing fabric and on the other hand opens up fresh possibilities for the pedestrian in parts of the town which because of their lack of charm had previously held little attraction.

245

246

247

248

245–248 Sketches of pedestrian areas.

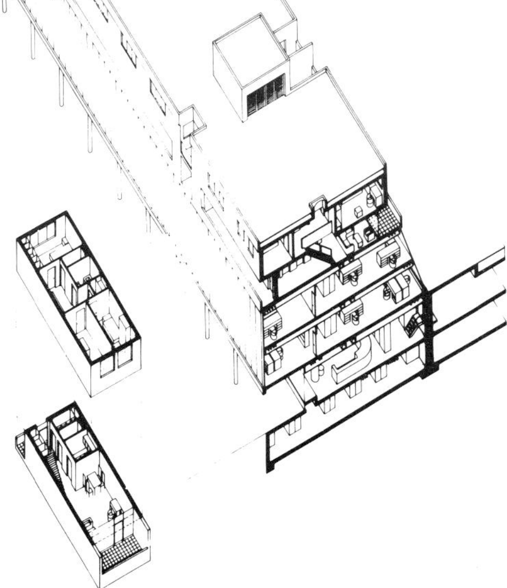

249 Scheme for the Huberstrasse in the university quarter.

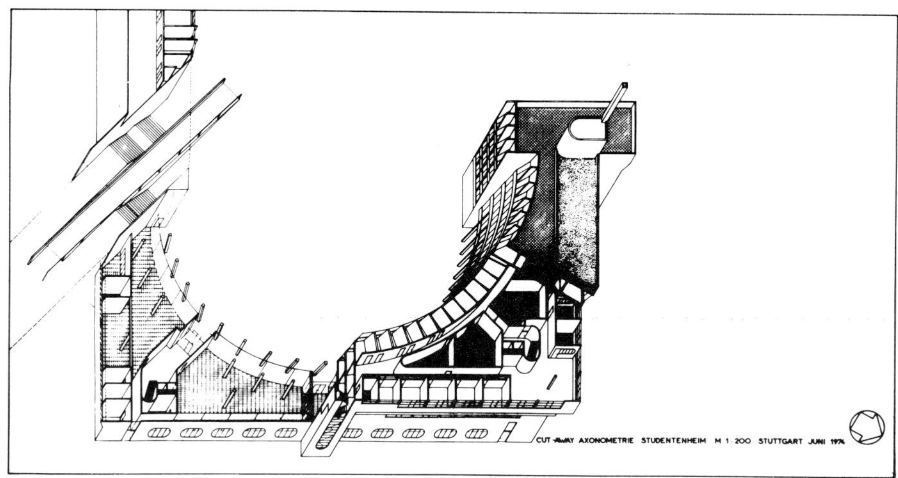

250 Isometric section of student hall of residence.

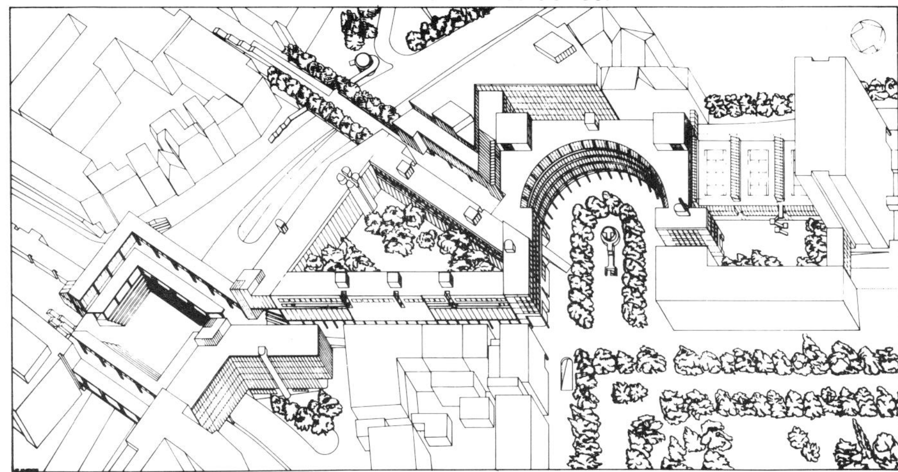

251 Isometric view of new plan.

252 Model of new plans.

THE ROTEBÜHLPLATZ

The old U-shaped Rotebühl barracks were built in the years 1827 to 1843. Today it stands in danger of demolition. Architecturally it is modest and discreet. It cannot be said that it is immediately attractive to the conservationist. Moreover, after its partial wartime destruction, the building suffered considerable alteration during rebuilding. For example, the open arcade running round the courtyard was walled up. The central section of the main wing has been replaced by a tasteless modern concrete facing. On the other hand, the height of the central wing was increased by three floors, and the architectural results here were pleasing. The clarity of the overall form of the building still remains impressive, and with its location on the boundary between the old part of the city and 'Stuttgarter Westen' it has an important articulating function.

The scheme:
I suggest the retention of the original structure of the Rotebühl barracks, the reopening of the original arcade around the courtyard and the enclosure of the courtyard (now built around on three sides) by an architectural device which will serve a double purpose. On the far end of the Rotebühlstrasse a glazed gallery should be built leading to an elongated square containing the entrances to the tube and railway stations. The complexity of this scheme derives from the failings of past architecture, which never found a positive way of carrying on the tradition embodied in the development plans of the 15th century. It seemed to me a matter of priority to design a structure for this site which might reconstitute its lost spatial coherence.

At this juncture one must certainly raise the question of why the space here was laid out in such an enclosed way. The answer, I believe, is that since the overall street plan of Stuttgart is 'open', any urban spaces which have a particular functional or architectural

253 View of the Rotebühl building courtyard.

254 View of the Fritz-Elsas-Strasse from the Rotebühlplatz, with the Rotebühl building on the left.

255 View of the Rotebühlstrasse from the Rotebühlplatz, with the Rotebühl building on the right.

256

257

258

259

256–259 Details of the former Rotebühl barracks (now the city finance office) after rebuilding.

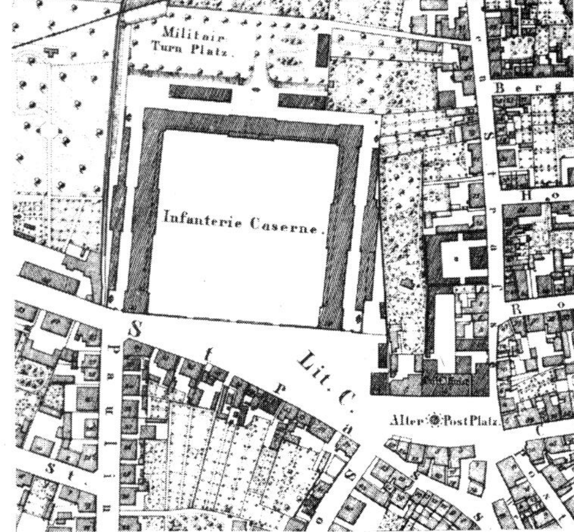

260 1855.

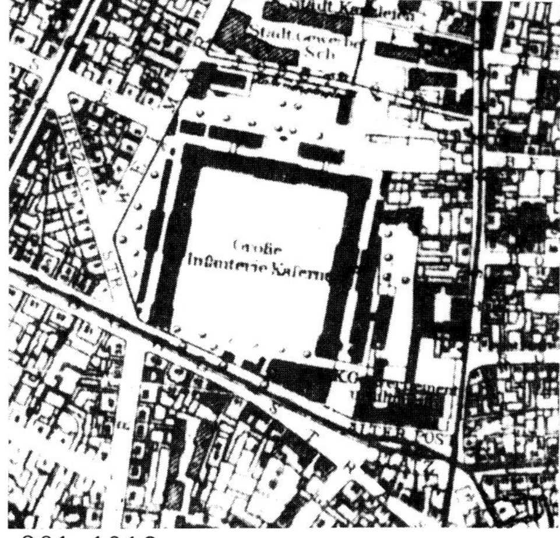
261 1913.

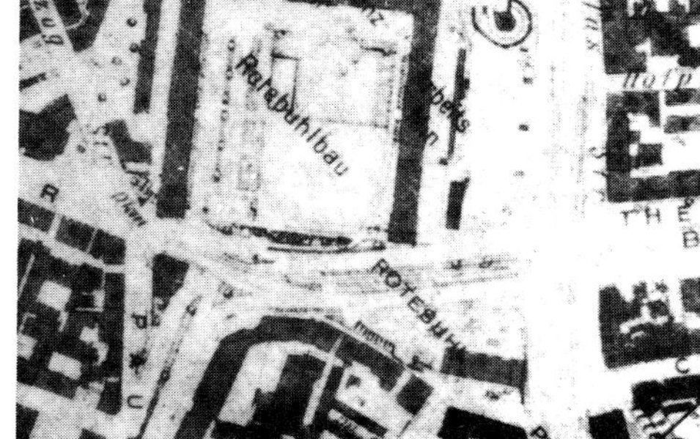

262 1972.

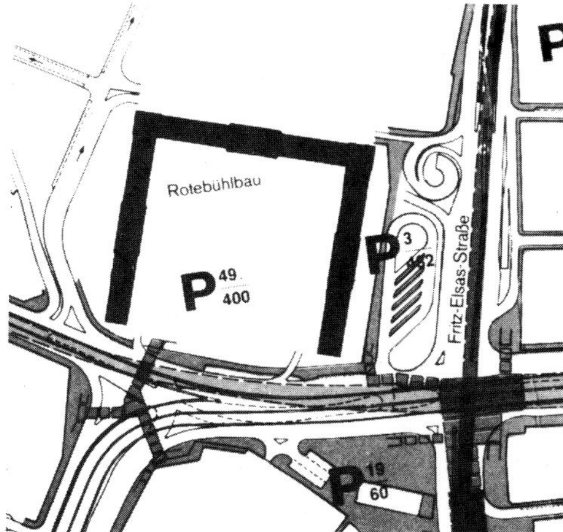

263 Traffic plan.

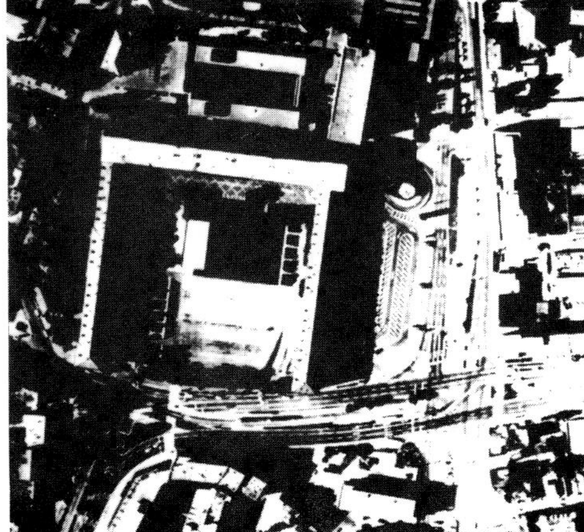
264 Aerial photo of the Rotebühl area as it is today.

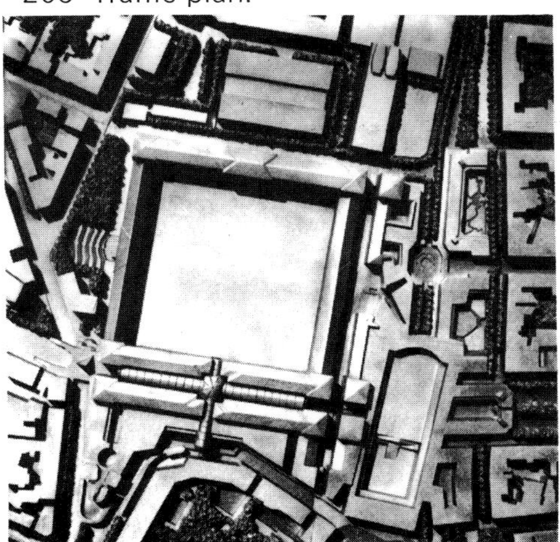
265 Model of new plans.

significance should obey a certain rhythm of their own. The Rotebühlplatz is certainly the kind of site to which this argument applies, as are the other squares which I shall deal with later.

I have deliberately drawn on historical examples in formulating these plans, in order to show that these spatial types can retain their validity today, irrespective of their period and style. Although Bramante created the market-place of Vigevano, he did not invent the spatial type on which it was based. All that happened was that Bramante intelligently applied the spatial type in the right place, with due regard for the historical conditions which he found there. The same square can be built using today's architecture, without any accusation of eclecticism or historicism. A building type is by definition a highly rational and fully thought out solution to a given architectural problem, and one which has been tried and tested over the course of generations. It would be naive of our technological age if we underestimated the value of this historical lesson.

The buildings which I am examining here look as if they are meant to be the work of a single architect. True, the plans are no-one's work but my own, and it is hard for me to empathise with other people who might work on them. However, each element is conceived in such a way that even a large number of planners could work on them independently without seeing their own personal understanding of architecture violated. Broad spatial and building types are all that I have defined. I have of course produced this final version as the culmination to a whole series of plans.

The quality of the overall spatial schema disciplines and determines the interplay of the individual architectural elements. None of them should play more than a background role, or they would risk seriously damaging the spatial harmony of the whole.

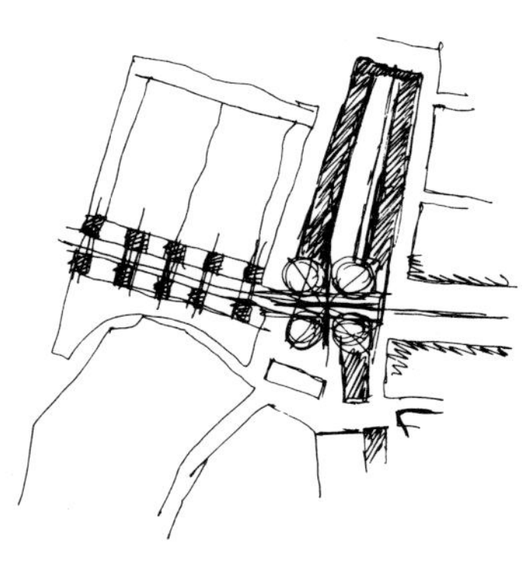

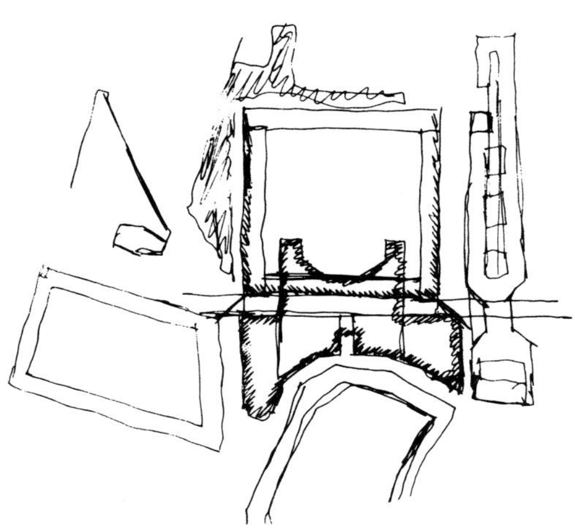

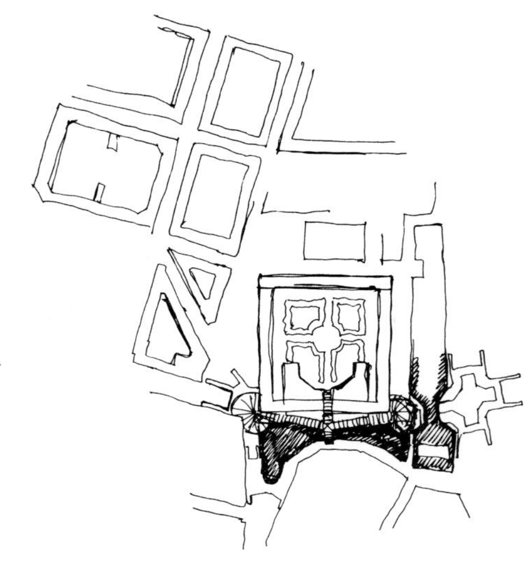

266 Sketches of the Rotebühlplatz.

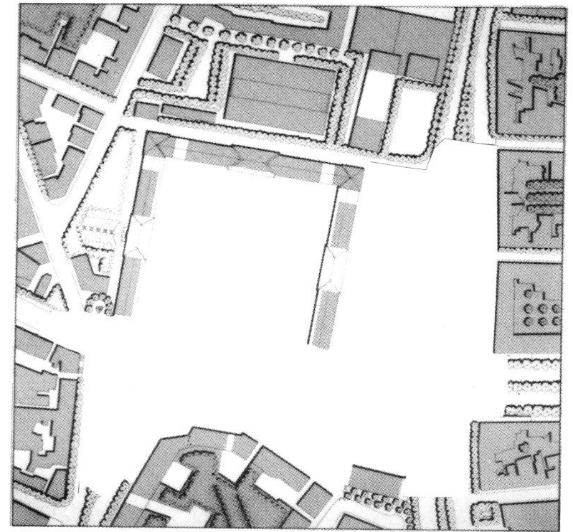

267 As it is today.

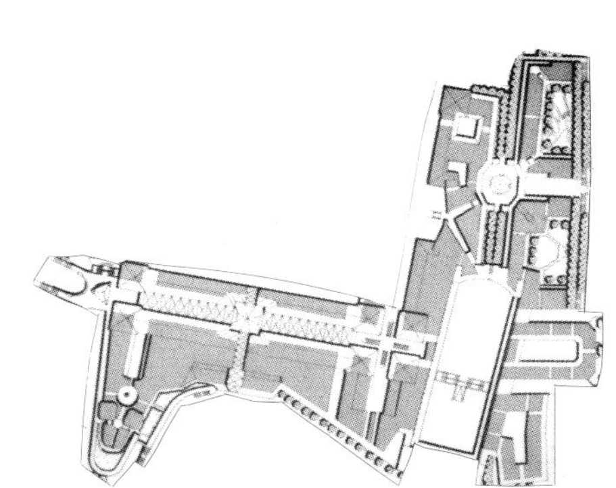

268 New plans.

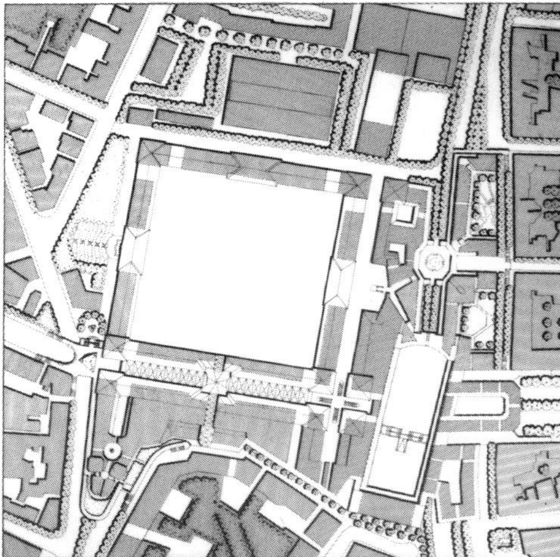

269 New plans superimposed on present layout.

270 Sketches of the Rotebühlplatz.

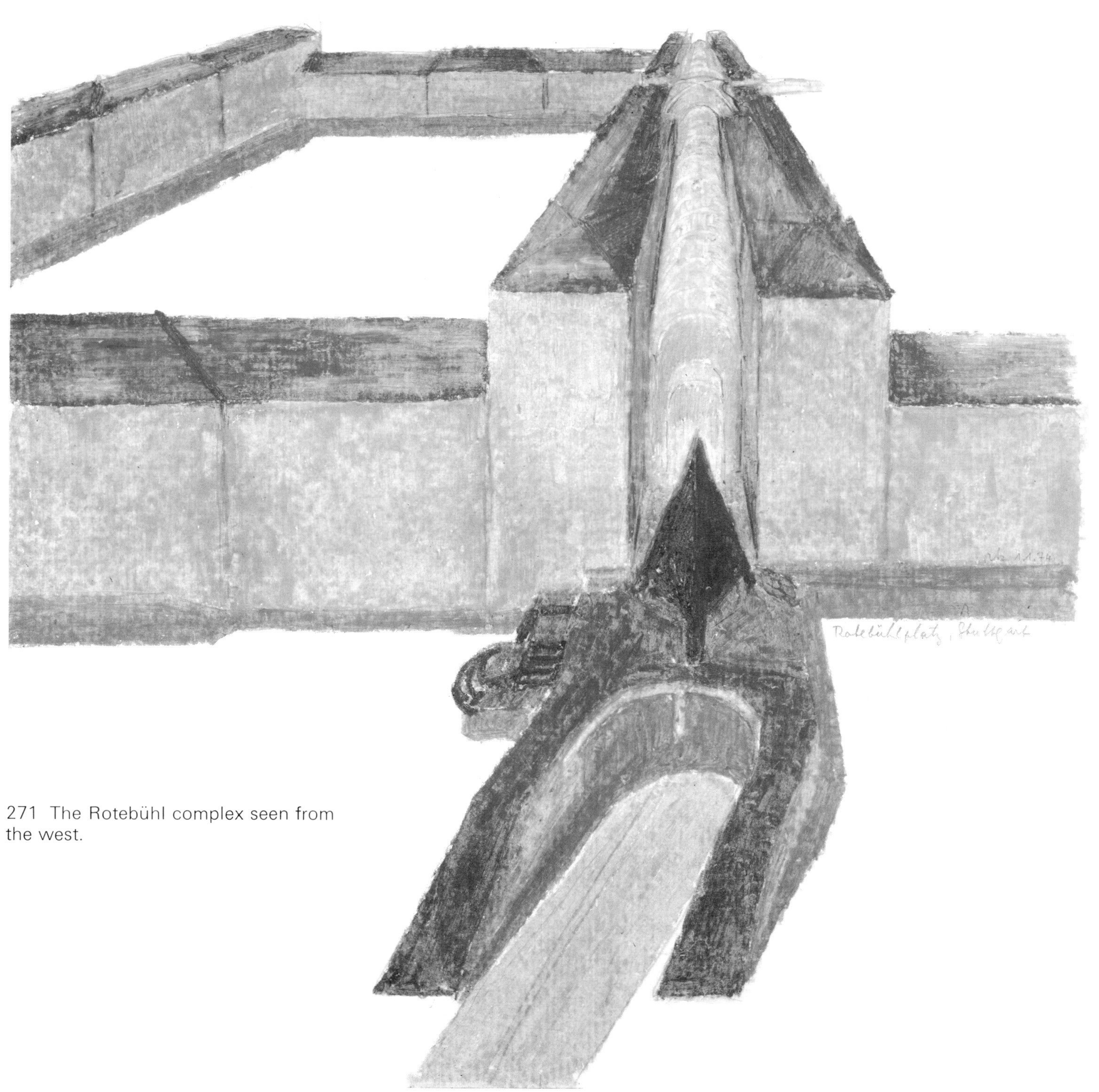

271 The Rotebühl complex seen from the west.

272 Site plan, scale 1 : 1,850, showing plans for redevelopment of the Rotebühl building.

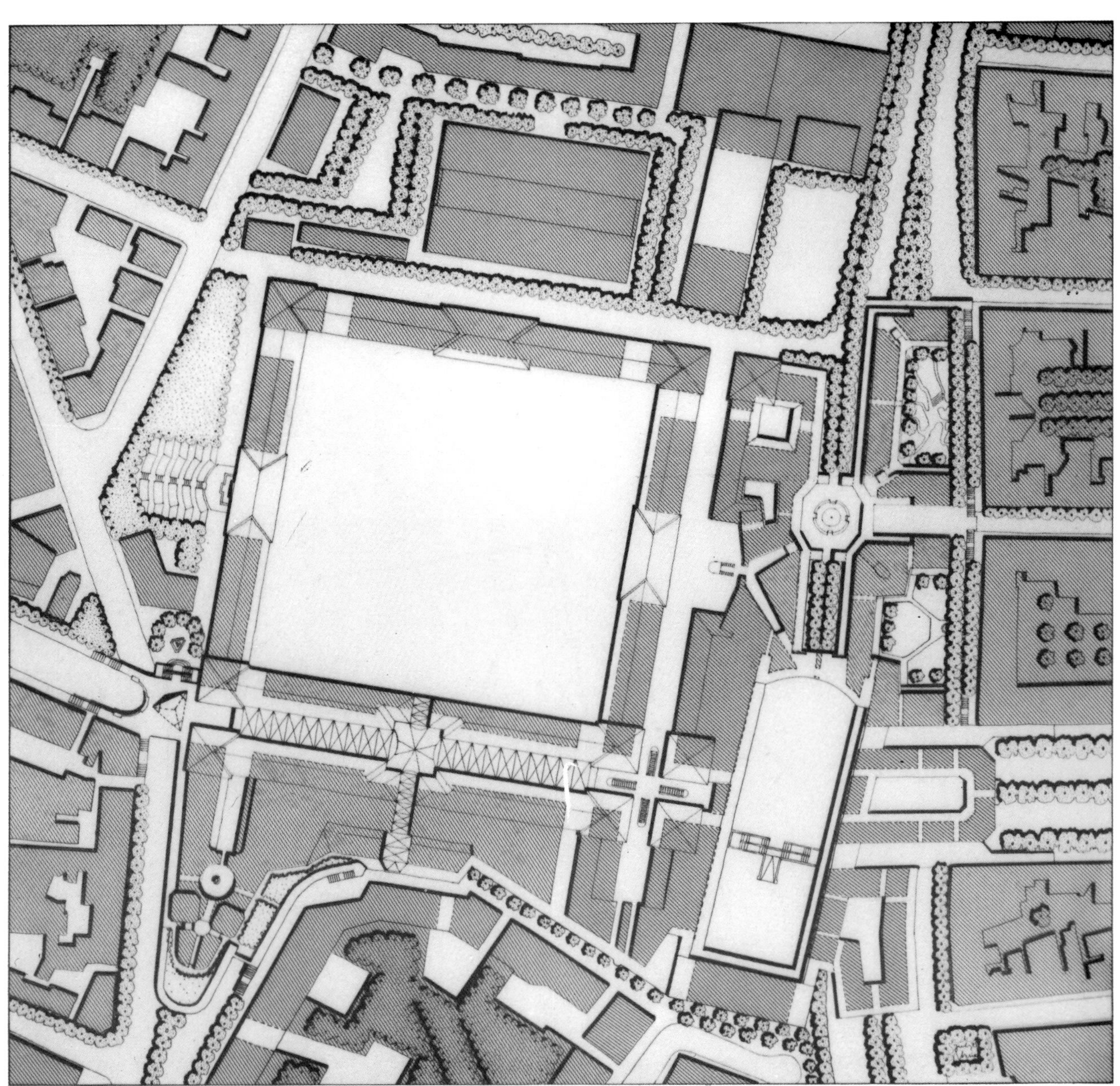

273 Model, scale 1 : 1,850, showing plans for redevelopment of the Rotebühl building.

274–277 Partial views of new proposed scheme (model).

274 Th. Heuss Strasse/Rotebühlstrasse axis.

275 Fritz-Elsas-Strasse.

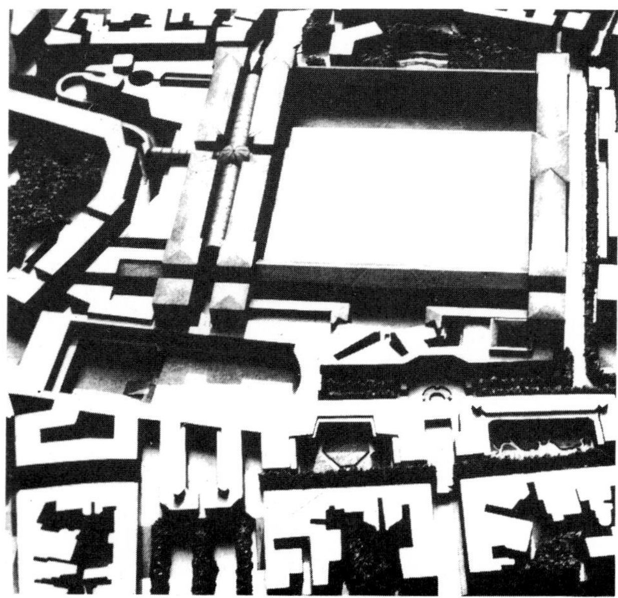

276 On the Rotebühlplatz today.

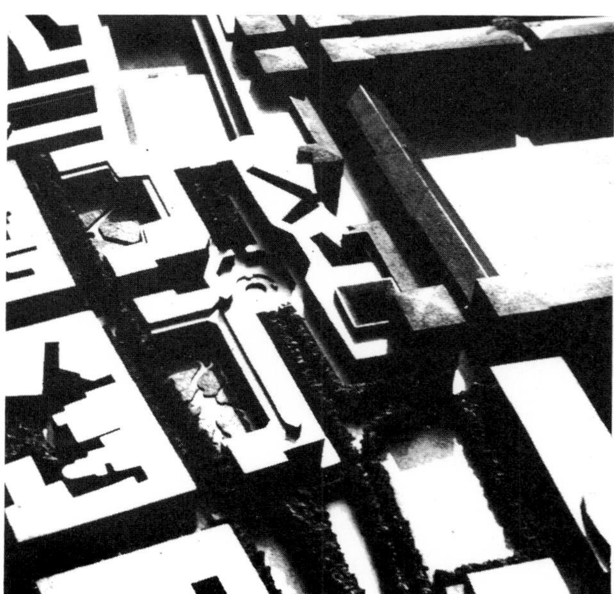

277 Entrance to gallery, Rotebühlstrasse.

278–281 Partial views of new proposed scheme (pastel).

278 Gallery on Rotebühlstrasse with railway station.

279 Entrance to gallery, seen from the Rotebühlstrasse. The Calwer Tor stood on this spot until the early 19th century.

280 Square with entrances to railway and tube stations on the present-day Rotebühlplatz, formerly known as the 'Alter-Post-Platz'.

281 Street showing the comparison between old and new. On the left is the Rotebühl building; on the right new buildings.

SCHEME BY WILFRIED WALLBRECHT

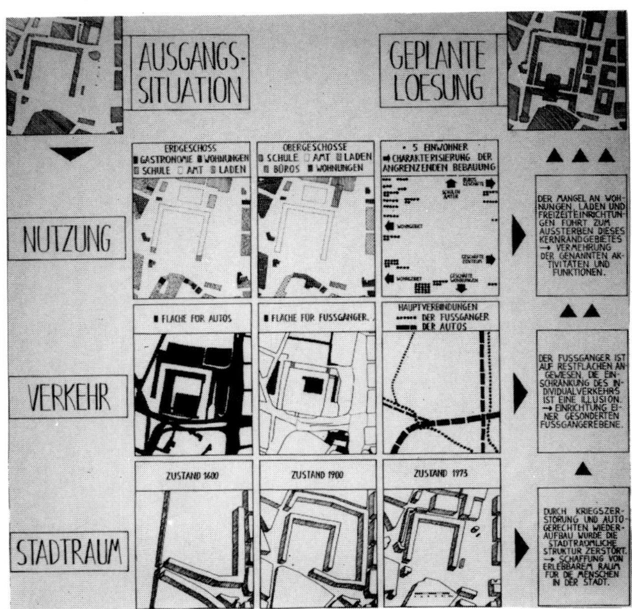

282 Analysis of the problem.

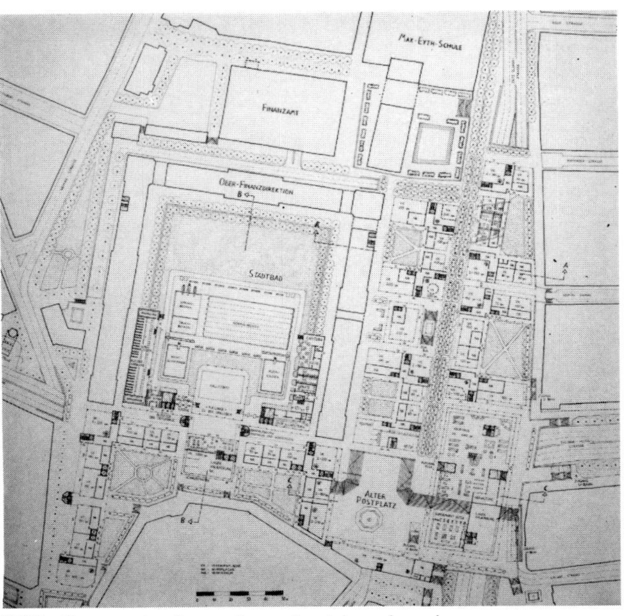

283 Ground plan of pedestrian level.

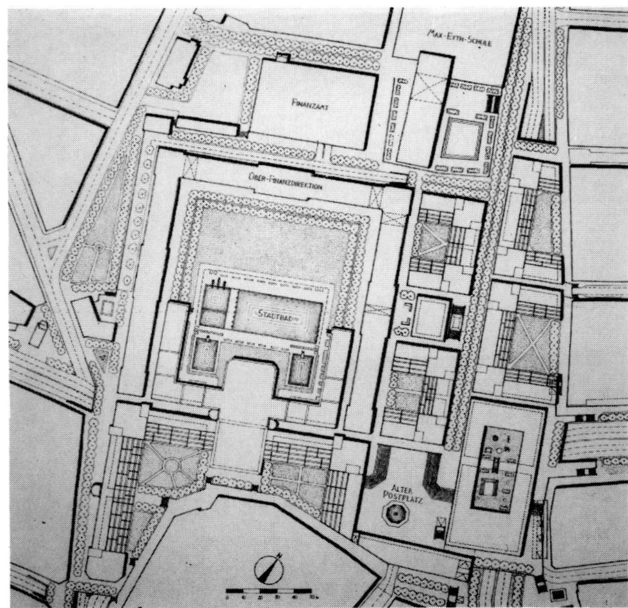

284 Roof plan.

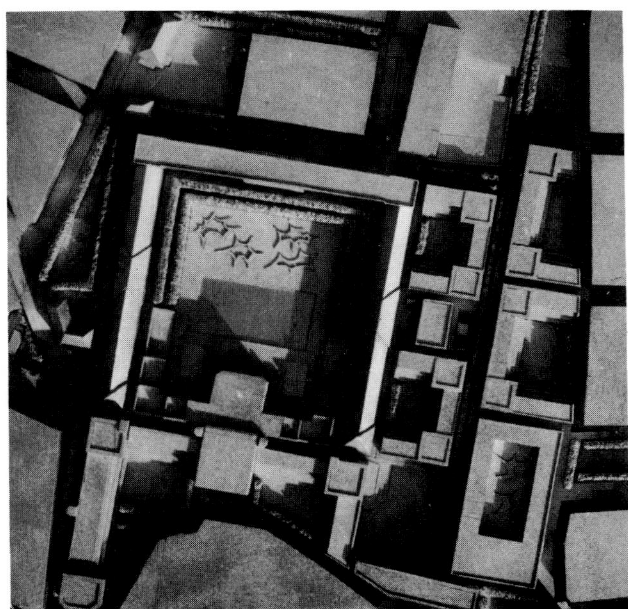

285 Model of redevelopment plan.

STUDY OF THE ROTEBÜHLPLATZ

SCHEME BY PUTZ AND WEBER

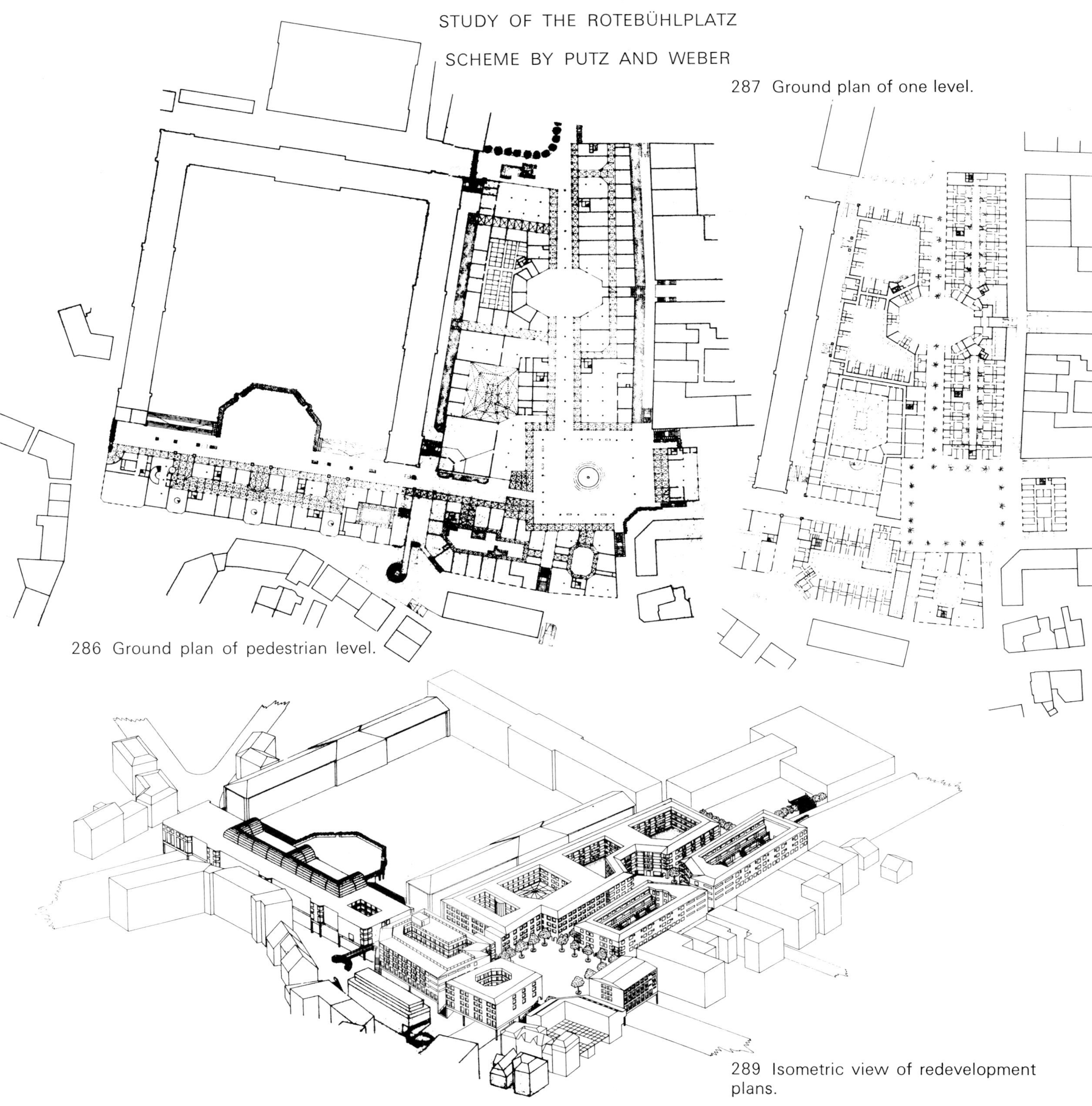

287 Ground plan of one level.

286 Ground plan of pedestrian level.

289 Isometric view of redevelopment plans.

JOHANNESSTRASSE – FEUERSEE

This is a sector of the district known as 'Stuttgarter Westen'. Most of it was built during the second half of the 19th century. The theme of these proposals for its renewal is to preserve the grid layout and carry out structural modifications in keeping with contemporary needs. When they were built, all the houses were set three metres apart at the insistence of the Fire Department. The result of this today is that street noise penetrates unremittingly to the inner courtyards. Blocking up these gaps could decisively improve living conditions. To complicate matters, the inner courtyards contain workshops and commercial premises built as annexes. We must come up with solutions to make the coexistence of housing and business tolerable. For example, a large part of the roof area above the workshops could be planted or used as a recreation area for residents. Children's playgrounds with extensive play areas could also be provided at roof-level. In the course of time, underground garages would have to be built beneath the courtyards.

It would make no sense to attempt a sudden and enforced separation of activities in an area whose hybrid quality has grown up gradually. The standard of craftsmanship and architecture in some of the buildings is so high that for this reason alone, extreme care must be taken with any alterations to the building fabric. I would also suggest that in this kind of district, particular attention should be paid to the conservation of streets and squares which play a vital part in town-planning terms. So any new building must conform with the structure and scale of the area. Greenery and ornamental lakes etc. should also be kept in harmony with the original plan and thereafter properly maintained. This does not mean that alterations and additions are impossible in the event of a changed set of circumstances for the town-planner; simply that wilful and reckless acts of planning vandalism should be prevented.

290 Scale 1 : 20,000 1913.

291 1972.

292 Model of renovation plan.

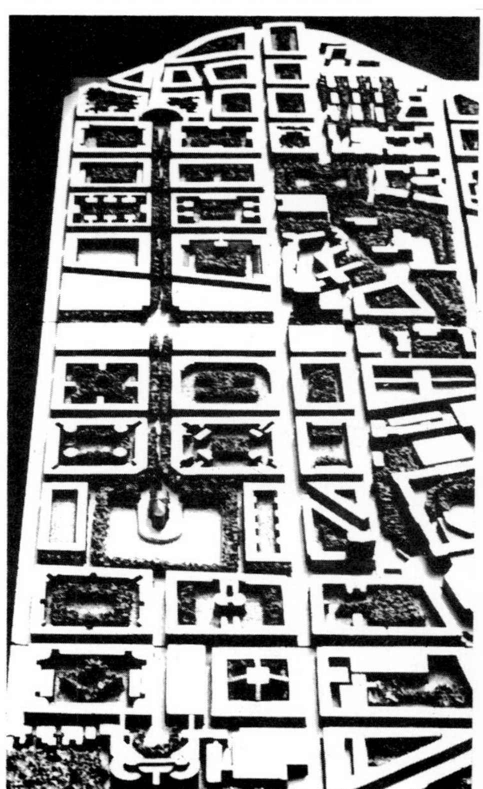

THE ÖSTERREICHISCHE PLATZ

Again I have taken Thouret's plans as a basis for alterations to this square. This decision may at first seem strange, given that not a single original building is left standing on it. All I am trying to do is to justify the thesis which I have outlined in the previous chapter.

No period in cultural history holds a patent on spatial types.

Thouret conceived of this square as a spatial extension to the area behind the city gate. This gate was purely decorative, having ceased to function as part of the fortifications. It is interesting, however, that a spatial extension was still planned beyond the gate. It was only this second, smaller square which formed a junction to the street. Unfortunately, later building on the outskirts of the town meant that this square – a work of genius – did not develop in accordance with the original plans.

I have adopted Thouret's theme of spatial gradation and a gradually intensifying build-up. But I have had to adapt this sequential approach to the reality of the new buildings which surround the square. The horseshoe-shaped open space with terraced buildings at its edge stretches right across the Hauptstätterstrasse, which is Stuttgart's most heavily used arterial road. So there was no reason to subordinate the spatial qualities of the square to those of the freeway. On the contrary, the freeway had to be disregarded. Opening up an access road towards the city centre would have been just as much of a problem.

The small lozenge-shaped square acts as a kind of distributor: from it, the Bazarstrasse leads to the Wilhelmsplatz; it creates a link between the Tübinger Strasse and the Marienkirche, as well as restoring the former link with the southern part of the town. I conclude from this that there is no reason why the new communication channels required should be blighted by traffic noise. The whole town is equally badly stressed by this problem. It is a curse to all city-dwellers, each of whom resorts to his own futile protest by blocking his windows or his ears. Impotent in the face of street noise, everyone takes out their unbearable neuroses on family and neighbours. There is only one way in which some measure of tranquillity can be guaranteed, and that is to provide a total shield between people and traffic.

The Österreichische Platz, Wilhelmsplatz and Charlottenplatz acted as the principal focus for streets connecting the old town with the southern parts of the city. Their purpose is very clearly visible from an examination of the street-plan. The layout is plainly orientated around these focal points. The function of such sites could have remained intact to this day had it not been destroyed by traffic. The squares mentioned above could even have been linked to each other by a commercially profitable shopping street which could partially or completely span the main road.

293 The Marienkirche, seen from the Paulinen bridge.

294 The Österreichische Platz and Paulinen bridge.

295 The pedestrian's view.

296 The Marienkirche, seen from the Österreichische Platz.

297 Spatial reality of the pedestrian.

298 The Hauptstätterstrasse, seen from the Österreichische Platz.

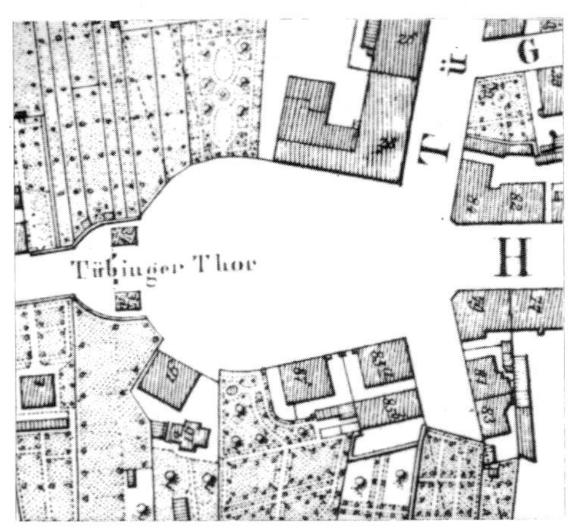

299 1855 (Thouret).

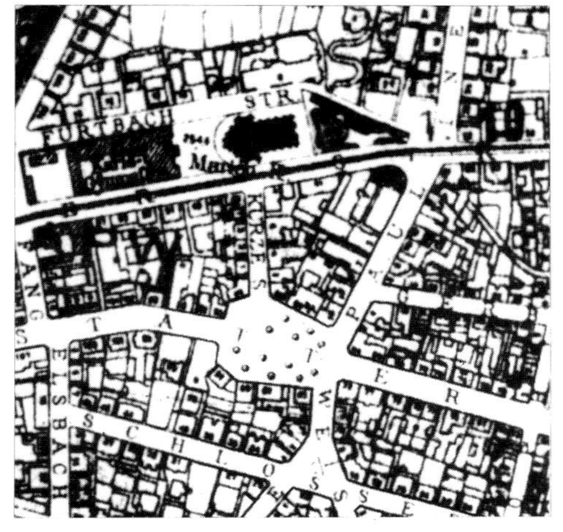

300 1913.

301 1972.

302 Traffic plan.

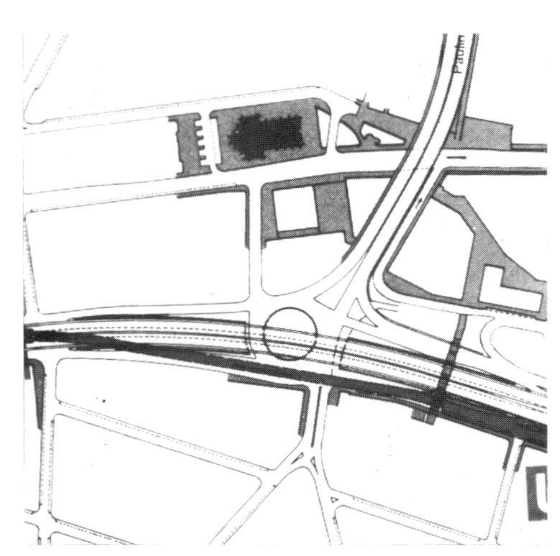

303 Aerial photo 1969.

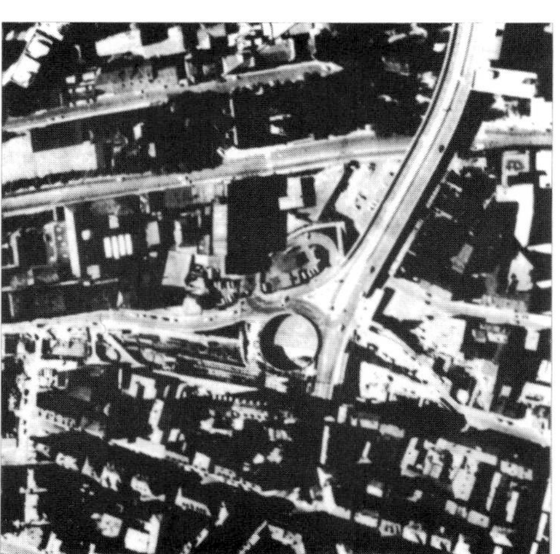

304 Model of new planning proposals.

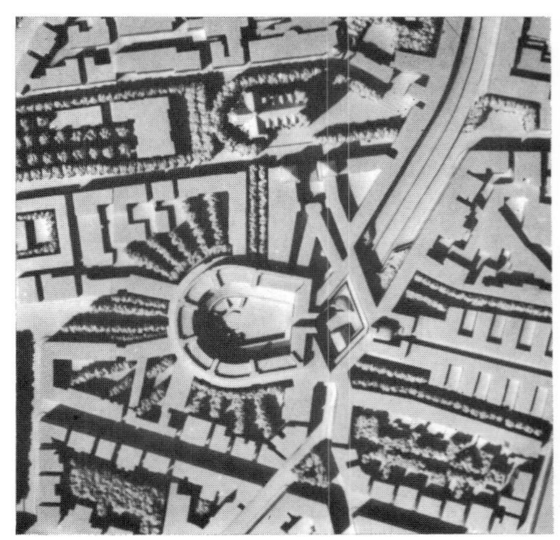

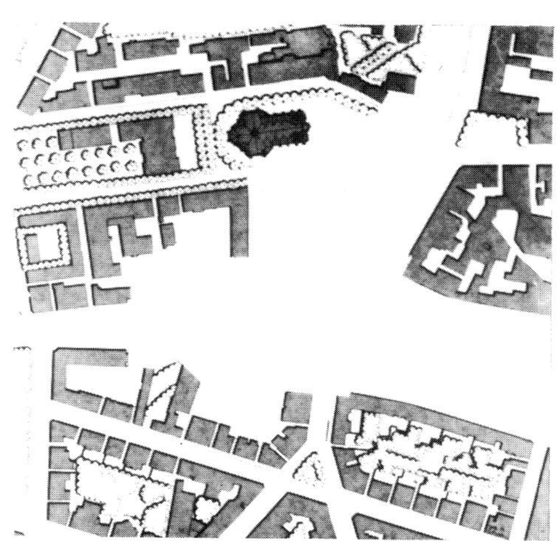

305 The Österreichische Platz as it is today.

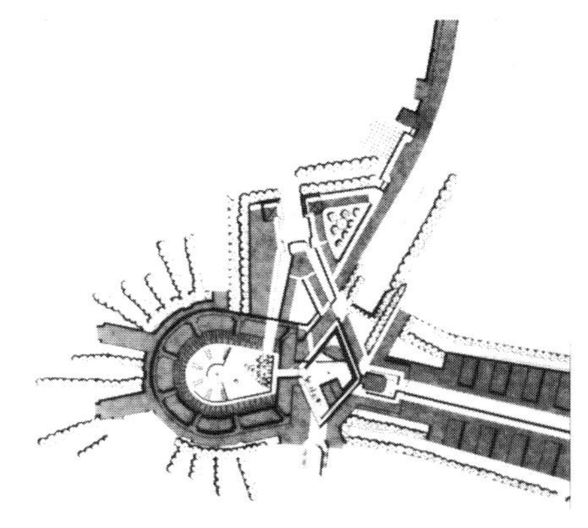

306 New plans.

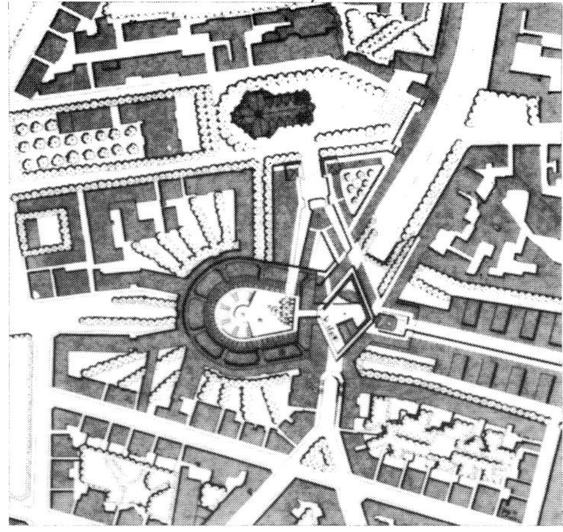

307 New plans superimposed on present layout.

308 Development of the Hauptstätterstrasse.

309 Detail of model.

310 View of model from the south.

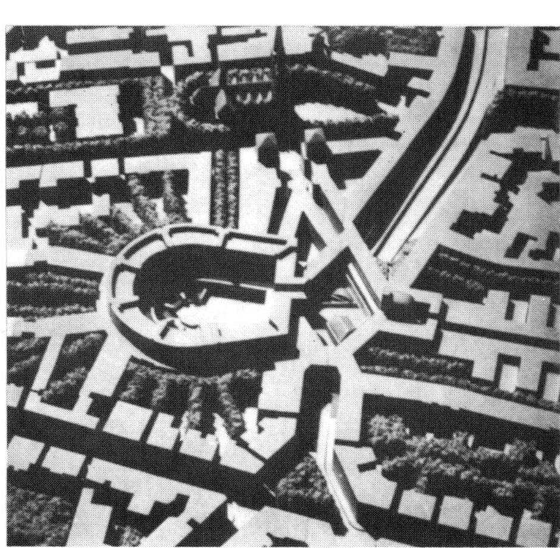

311 Site plan, showing redevelopment of the Österreichische Platz, scale 1 : 1,850 approx.

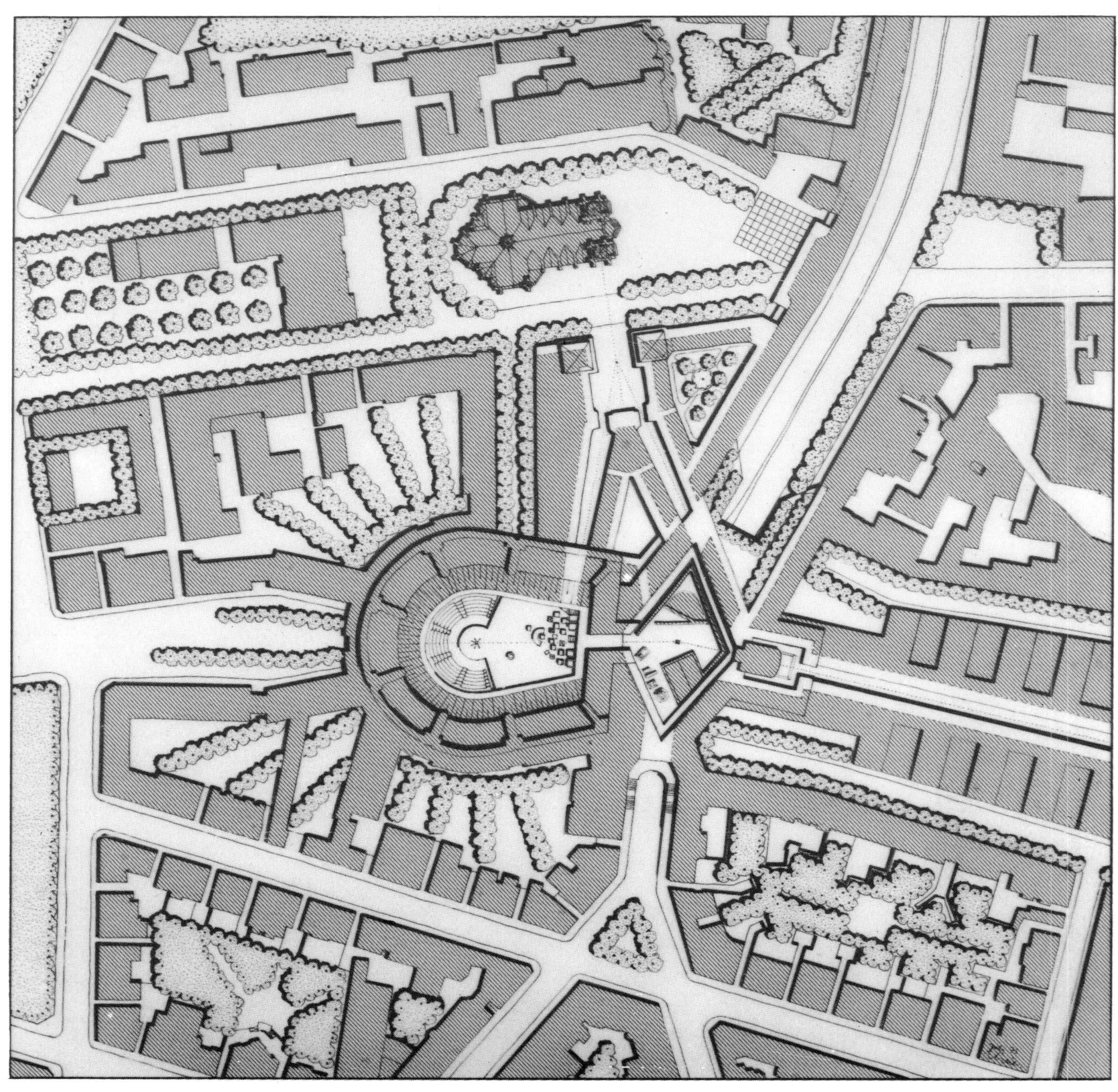

312 Model of redevelopment of the Österreichische Platz, scale 1 : 1,850 approx.

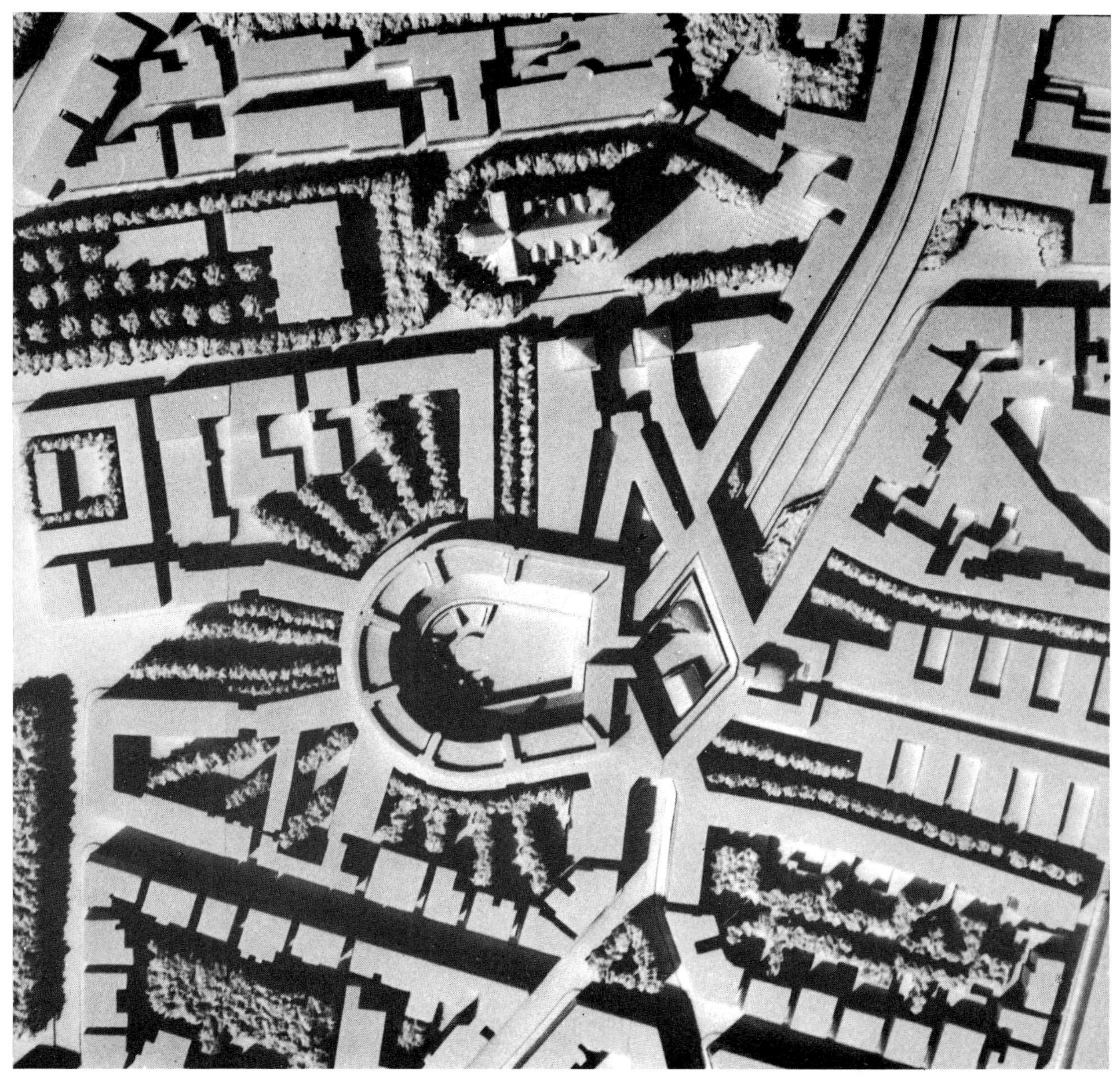

313 The Österreichische Platz itself: original size pastel.

314 Small square giving access to the Österreichische Platz: original size pastel.

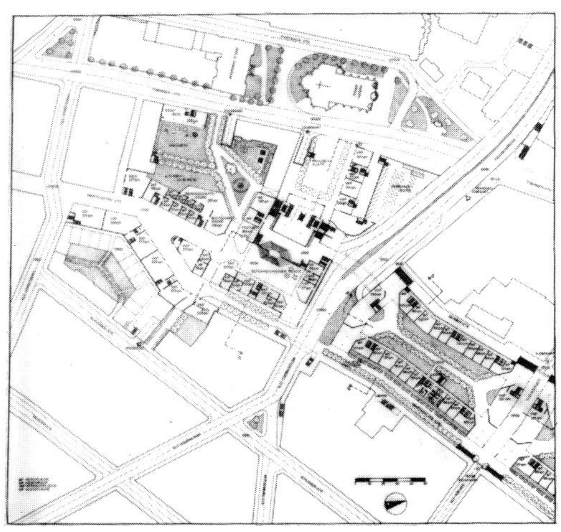

315 Ground plan of pedestrian level.

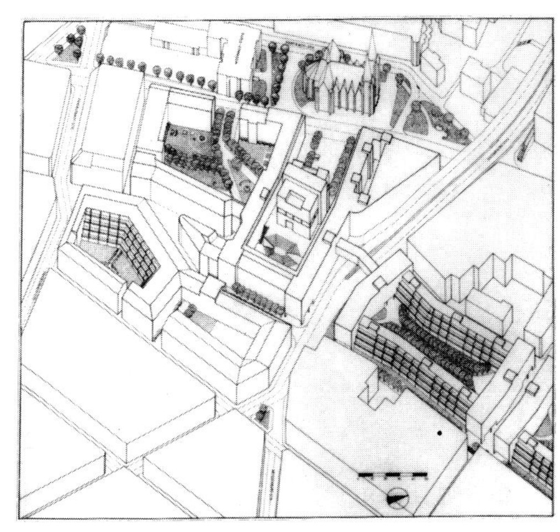

316 Isometric view of scheme.

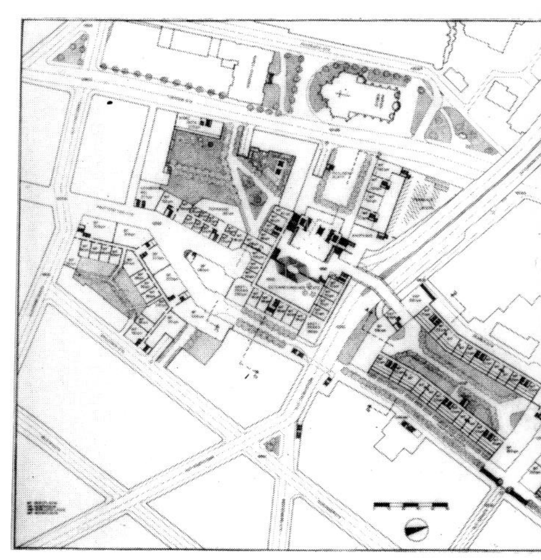

317 Ground plan of one level.

STUDY OF THE ÖSTERREICHISCHE PLATZ

SCHEME BY RENATE HUMMERICH

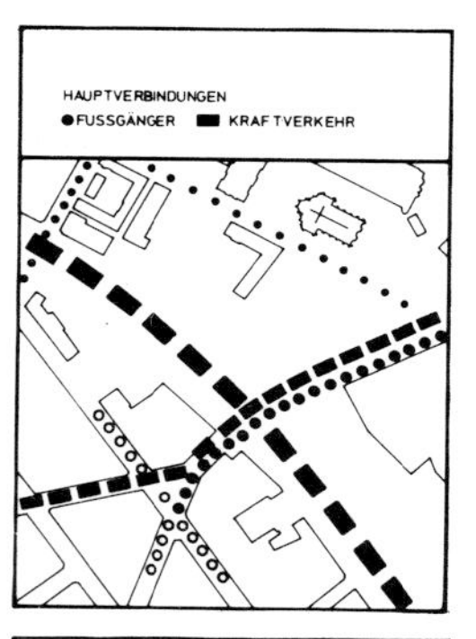

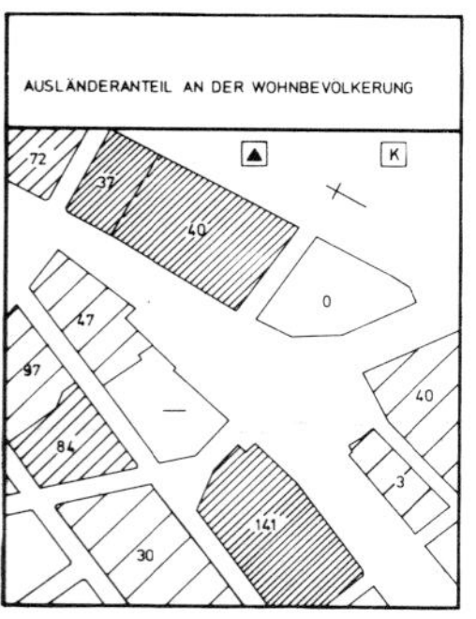

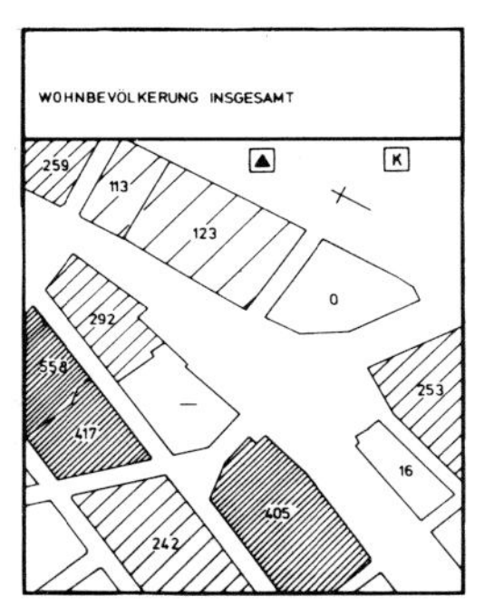

VORSCHLAG ZUR NUTZUNGSERGÄNZUNG:
KIGA/KITA LÄDEN POST
ALTENHEIM BUROS WO WOHNUNGEN

P G K WO WO WO WO WOHNGEBIET ZENTRUM WO WO

AUSGANGSSITUATION

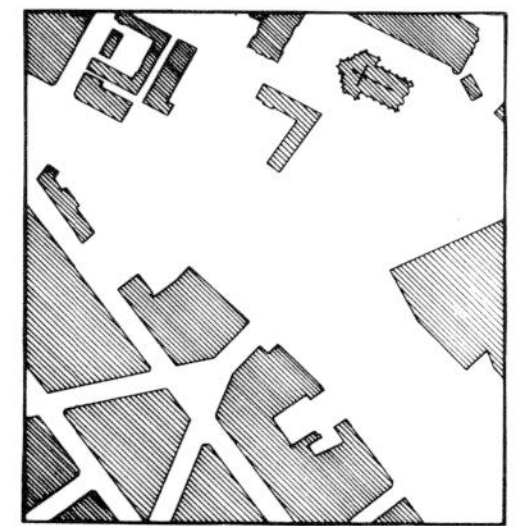

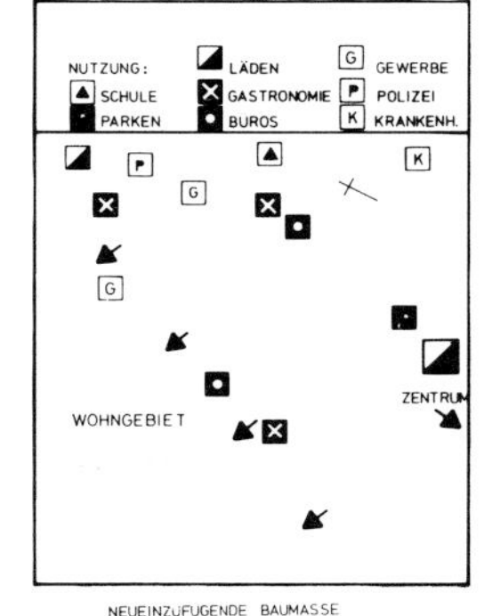

NEUEINZUFÜGENDE BAUMASSE

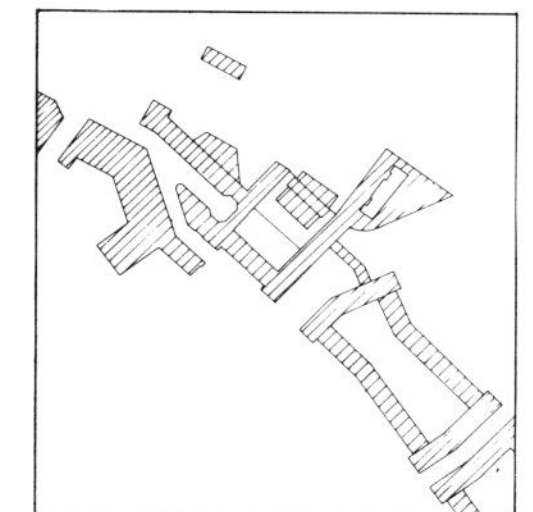

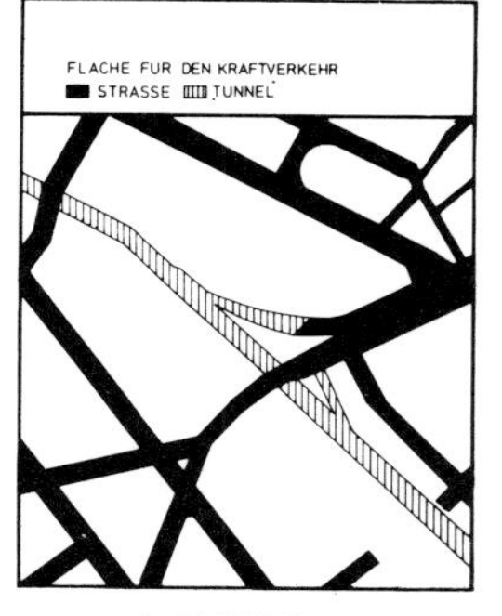

LÖSUNGSVORSCHLAG

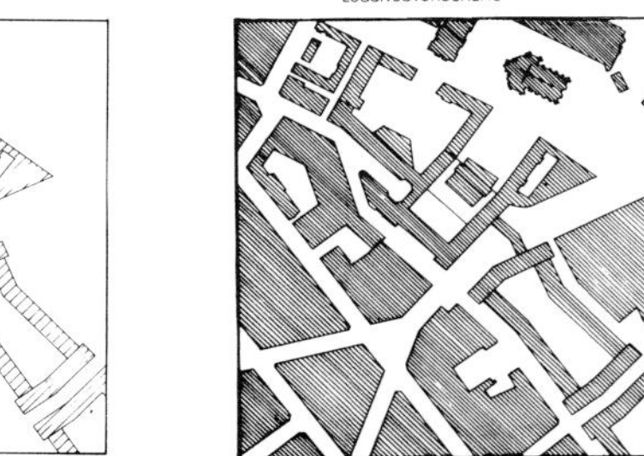

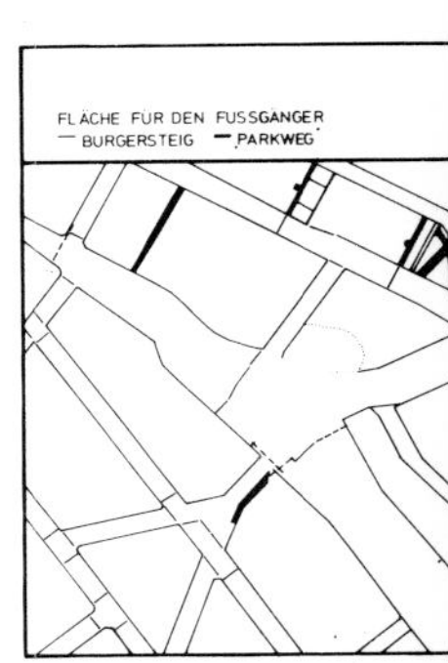

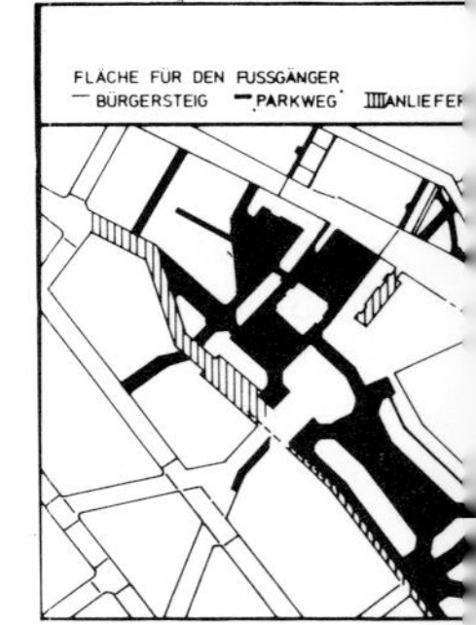

319 Hauptstätterstrasse 1880.

320 The Leonhardsplatz before the Second World War.
Photo: Metz Brothers, Bild-Verlag, Tübingen.

THE WILHELMSPLATZ

THE LEONHARDSPLATZ

The key themes of this project are:
1 To enclose the Wilhelmsplatz.
2 To build around the Leonhardskirche a square forming a unit of appropriate scale.
3 To restore the traditional profile of the Eberhardstrasse, along which the old 13th century citadel walls ran.
4 To assimilate existing road junctions into the street plan by means of new buildings. It is vitally important to establish this complex site as an effective point of visual orientation.
5 Since Stuttgart's nightlife takes place in the quarter around the Leonhardskirche, any new plans would have to offer amenities of a not entirely monastic character. These amenities should neither isolate nor drive out the nightlife.
6 It is obvious that all these new development plans should provide for a certain percentage of rented and privately owned accommodation, and the local authorities are duty bound to ensure that such accommodation can be rented at reasonable prices.

321 1855.

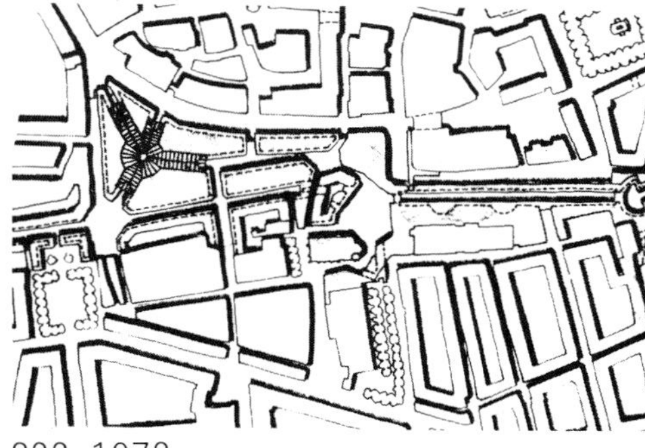

322 1972.

323 New plans.

324 View of model.

325 Aerial photo of the old town of Stuttgart from the south-west, c. 1930. In the foreground is Erich Mendelssohn's Schocken building.
Photo: Stähle, Schorndorf.

326 The extent of devastation of the old town in the Second World War. Photo: Brugger, Stuttgart.

327 The Wilhelmsplatz today.

328 The Hauptstätterstrasse today.

329 The Leonhardsplatz.

330 View of the Wilhelmsplatz and old town.

331 The Hauptstätterstrasse today.

332 Siegle-Haus by Theodor Fischer.

333 The Wilhelmsplatz.

334 The Hauptstätterstrasse today.

335 The Leonhardsplatz and Leonhardskirche.

STUDY OF THE WILHELMSPLATZ – LEONHARDSPLATZ – HAUPTSTÄTTERSTRASSE AREA

SCHEME BY STEFAN BÖHM

The main concern of this scheme is to reintegrate two parts of the town which are now completely cut off from each other by the broad slash of the Hauptstätterstrasse, and in so doing to create a meaningful configuration of urban space for the pedestrian. This means robbing traffic of its absolute pre-eminence and establishing an important centre in this part of the town by building new residential accommodation, shops, offices, restaurants and cultural and social amenities. Important features of the scheme are a glazed covered arcade, an open-air theatre and the replanning of the Leonhardsplatz.

Plan of ground level.

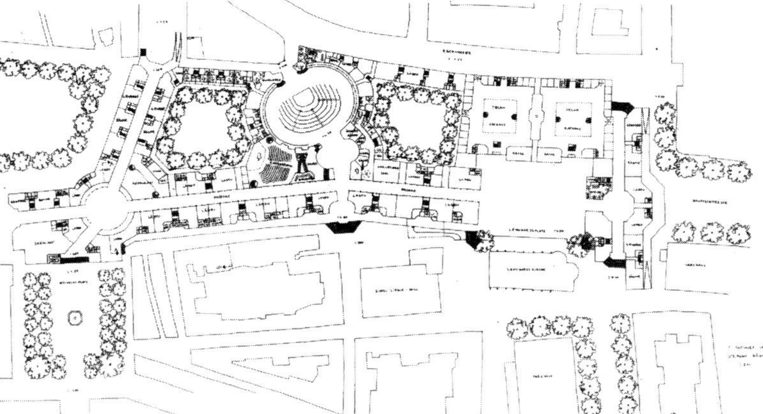

3 Ground plan of pedestrian level.

9 Model of new plans.

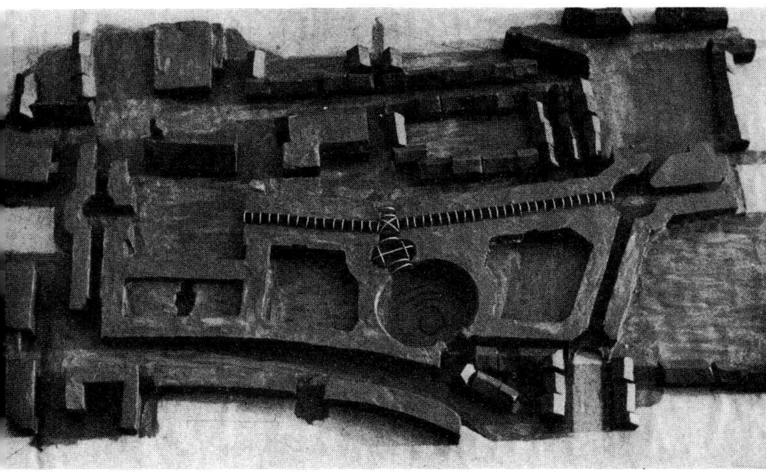

340/1–6 Preliminary design alternatives and models.

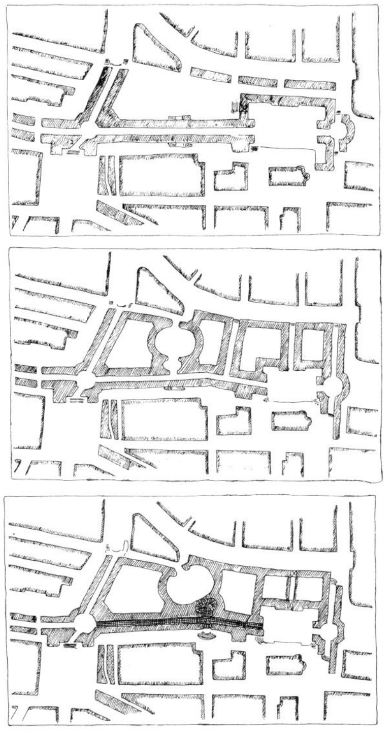

STUDY OF THE WILHELMSPLATZ – LEONHARDSPLATZ – HAUPTSTÄTTERSTRASSE AREA

SCHEME BY CHRISTA DIEHL

341/1–10 Preliminary design alternatives.

RESULT	EVALUATION	Independent character of the urban space in relationship to spatial qualities of adjacent areas	Coherence of the newly-formed area by virtue of creating a central focal point	Preservation of historical features of fundamental importance to development of urban structure (e.g. city walls, Eberhardstrasse and Wilhelmsplatz)	Move towards the completion through new building of urban areas where the existing building fabric has been inadequately developed	Relationship of new building forms in adjacent areas to existing state of development	Continuation of pattern of squares in use in town centre into surrounding residential areas	Efficient pedestrian communications between centre and residential suburbs	Clearly defined network of pedestrian communications and good possibilities for pedestrian orientation		PLANNING ALTERNATIVES
	12.5% UNUSABLE	Fulfilled	Not fulfilled	Fulfilled	Fulfilled	Fulfilled	Fulfilled	Fulfilled	Fulfilled		A. 1 HISTORICAL SOLUTION
	62.5% UNUSABLE	Not fulfilled	Not fulfilled	Fulfilled	Fulfilled	Fulfilled	Not fulfilled	Not fulfilled	Not fulfilled		A. 2 BUILDING COMPLEX
	25% UNUSABLE	Fulfilled	Fulfilled	Fulfilled	Fulfilled	Fulfilled	Fulfilled	Not fulfilled	Not fulfilled		A. 3 ORGANIC BUILDING COMPLEX
	100% UNUSABLE	Not fulfilled	Not fulfilled	Not fulfilled	Not fulfilled	Not fulfilled	Not fulfilled	Not fulfilled	Not fulfilled		A. 4 LIBERATION OF THE TOWN
	62.5% UNUSABLE	Fulfilled	Not fulfilled	Fulfilled	Not fulfilled	Not fulfilled	Not fulfilled	Not fulfilled	Fulfilled		A. I 2 MAIN LONGITUDINAL AXES
	37.5% UNUSABLE	Fulfilled	Not fulfilled	Fulfilled	Fulfilled	Fulfilled	Not fulfilled	Not fulfilled	Fulfilled		A. I 2 MAIN LONGITUDINAL AXES
	100% USABLE	Fulfilled	Fulfilled	Fulfilled	Fulfilled	Fulfilled	Fulfilled	Fulfilled	Fulfilled		A. I 2 MAIN LONGITUDINAL AXES
	62.5% UNUSABLE	Fulfilled	Not fulfilled	Fulfilled	Not fulfilled	Not fulfilled	Not fulfilled	Fulfilled	Not fulfilled		A. I 2 MAIN LONGITUDINAL AXES
	37.5% UNUSABLE	Not fulfilled	Not fulfilled	Fulfilled	Fulfilled	Not fulfilled	Fulfilled	Fulfilled	Fulfilled		A. II 3 MAIN LONGITUDINAL AXES
	37.5% UNUSABLE	Fulfilled	Not fulfilled	Fulfilled	Not fulfilled	Not fulfilled	Fulfilled	Fulfilled	Fulfilled		A. II 3 MAIN LONGITUDINAL AXES
	87.5% UNUSABLE	Not fulfilled	Not fulfilled	Not fulfilled	Not fulfilled	Not fulfilled	Not fulfilled	Fulfilled	Not fulfilled		A. II 3 MAIN LONGITUDINAL AXES
	100% USABLE	Fulfilled	Fulfilled	Fulfilled	Fulfilled	Fulfilled	Fulfilled	Fulfilled	Fulfilled		A. III DIAGONALS
	12.5% UNUSABLE	Fulfilled	Not fulfilled	Fulfilled	Fulfilled	Fulfilled	Fulfilled	Fulfilled	Fulfilled		A. III DIAGONALS
	50% UNUSABLE	Fulfilled	Not fulfilled	Fulfilled	Fulfilled	Not fulfilled	Not fulfilled	Fulfilled	Not fulfilled		A. IV 4 MAIN LONGITUDINAL AXES
	50% UNUSABLE	Fulfilled	Not fulfilled	Fulfilled	Fulfilled	Not fulfilled	Not fulfilled	Fulfilled	Not fulfilled		A. IV 4 MAIN LONGITUDINAL AXES

342 Criteria for selection of preliminary design alternatives.

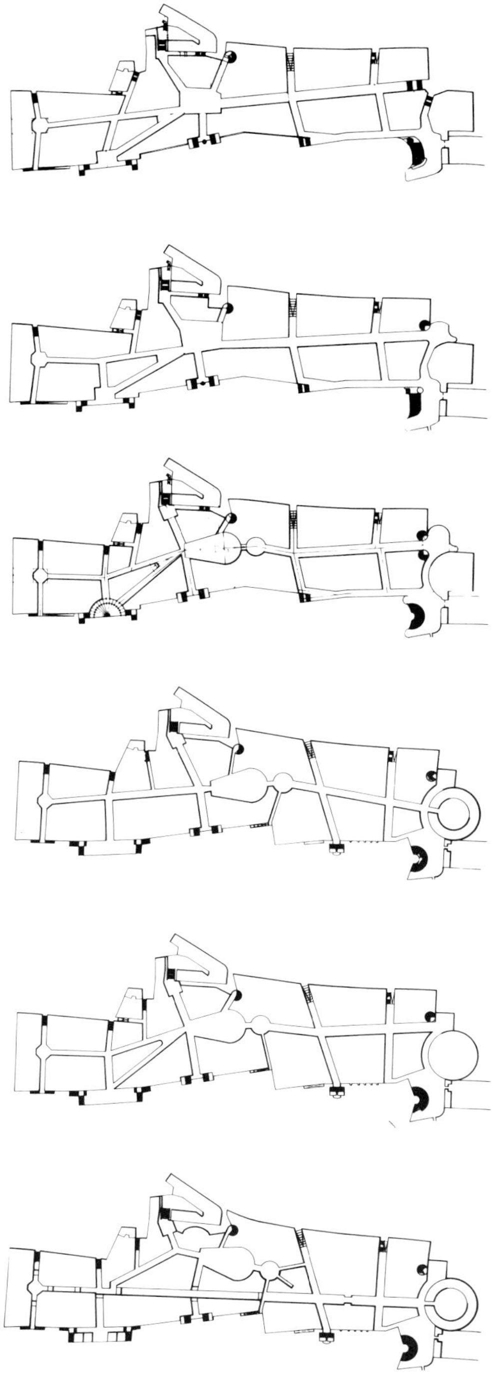

343/1–6 Design alternatives for the Wilhelmsplatz – Hauptstätterstrasse area.

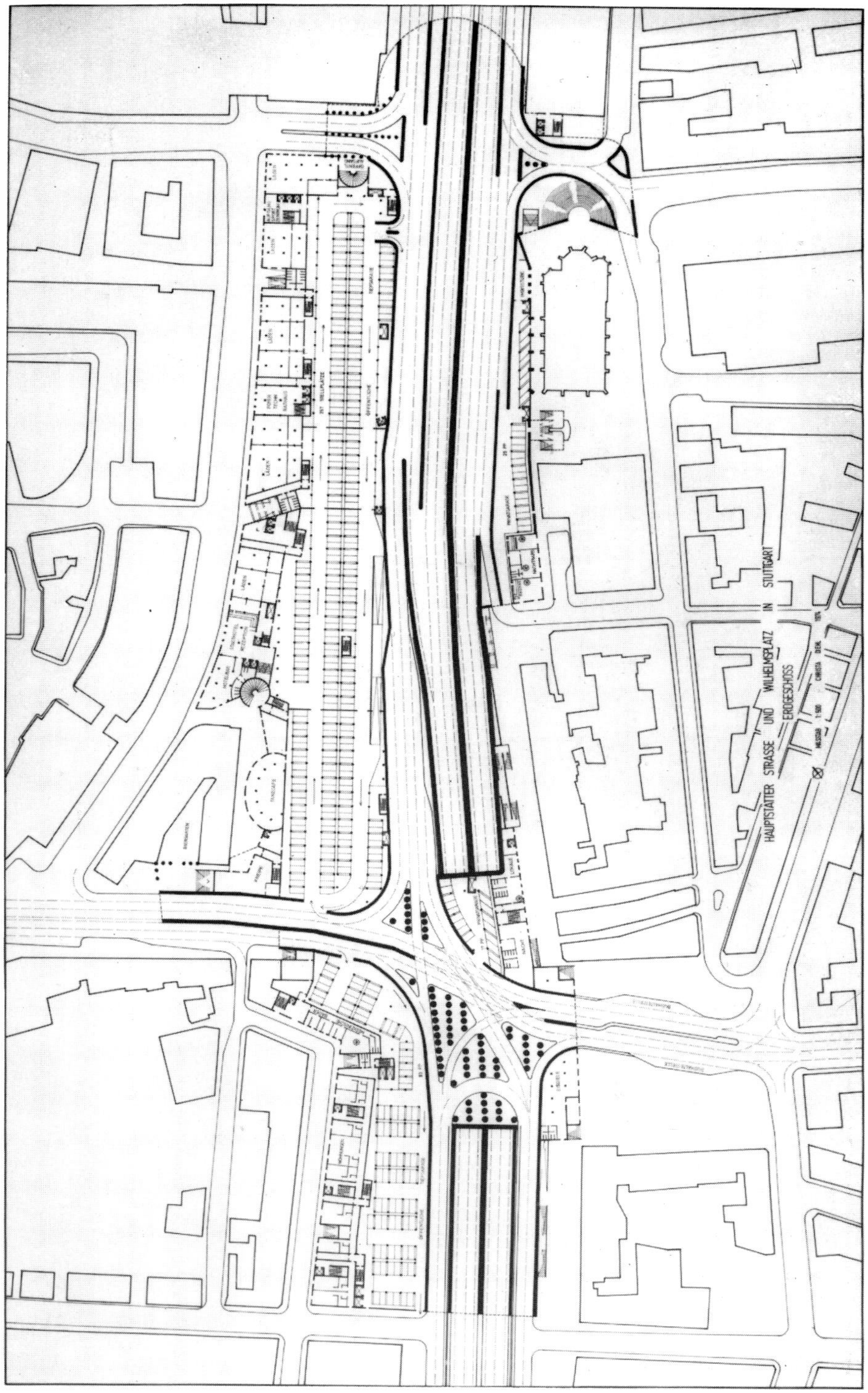

344 Plan at ground level.

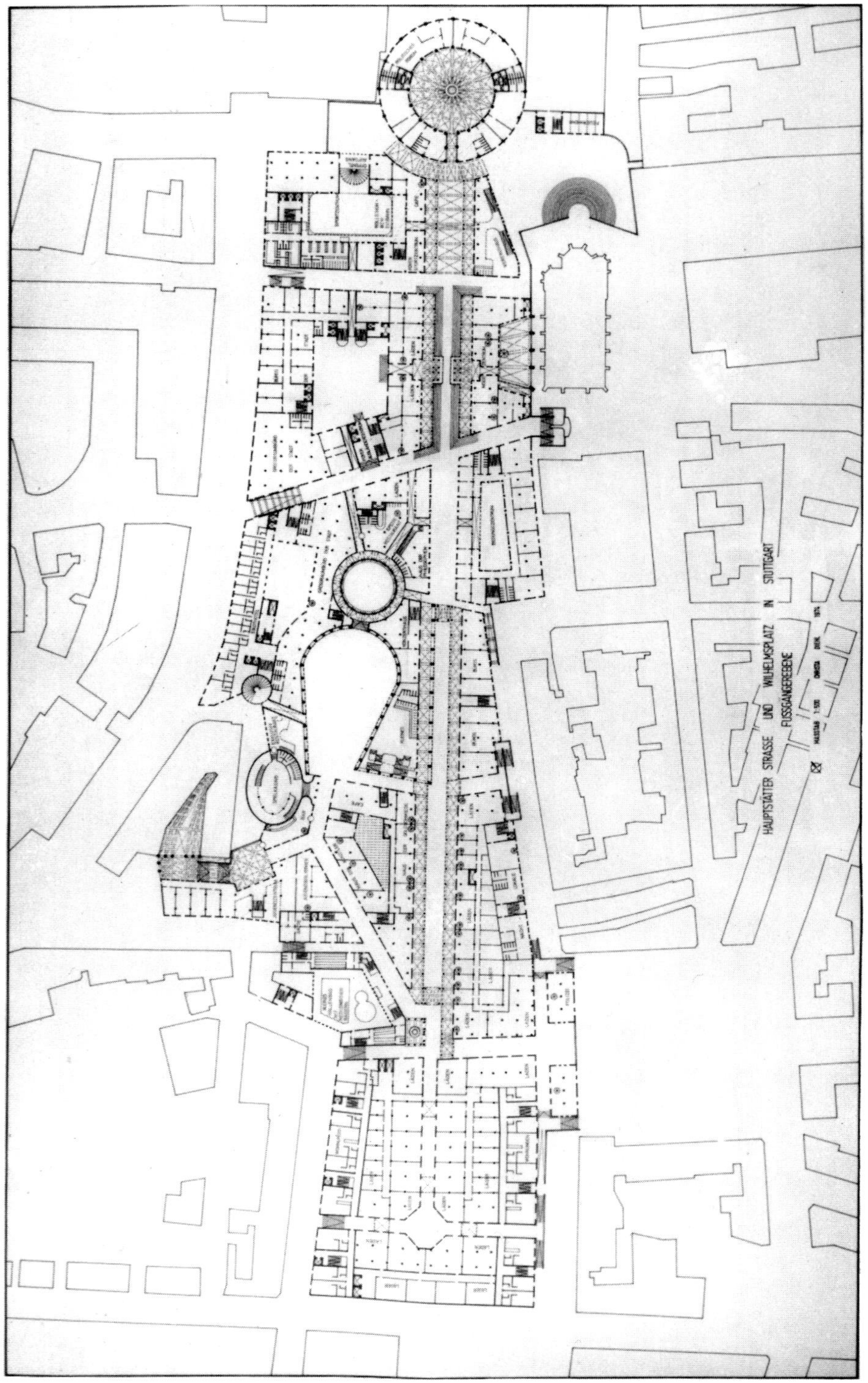

345 Ground plan of pedestrian level.

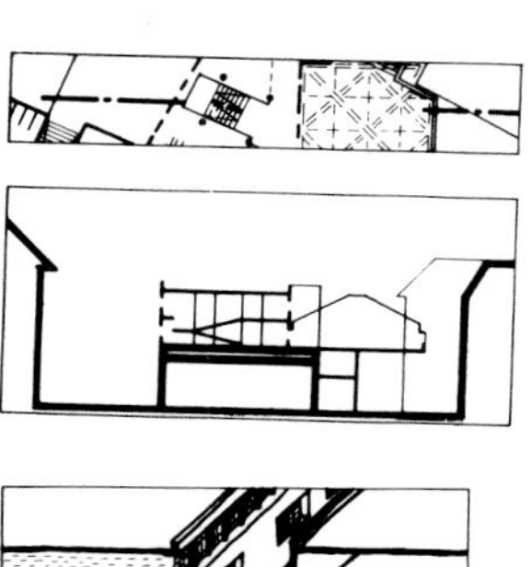

346 Youth centre, section and view.

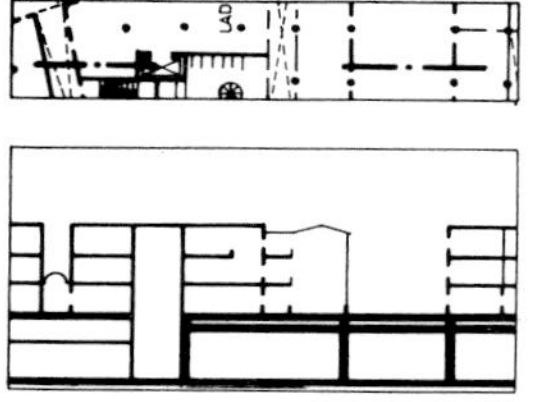

347 House of the Philosophers, section and view.

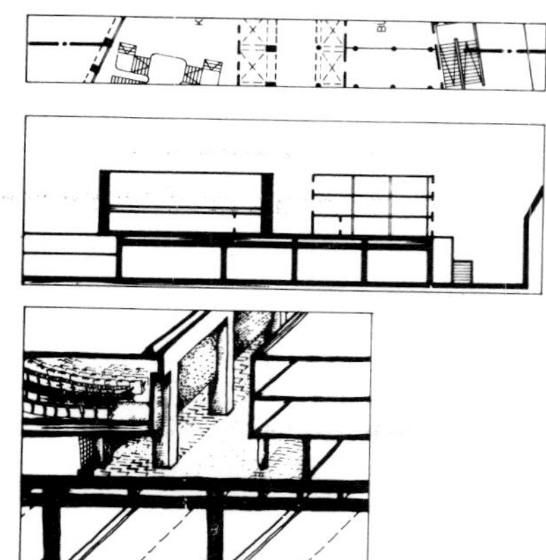

348 Small concert hall, section and view.

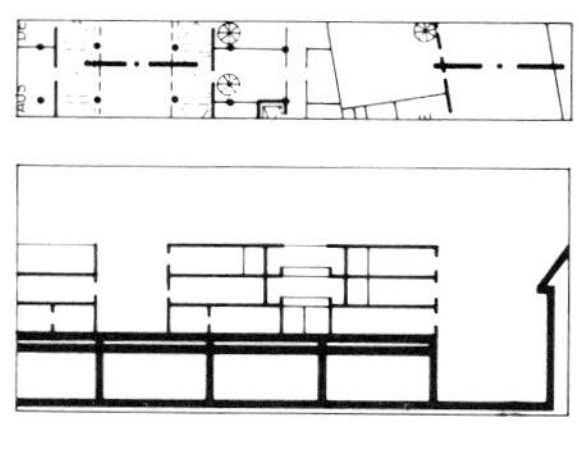
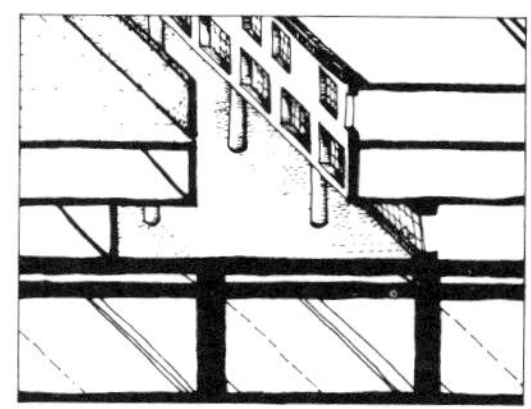

349 Office building, section and view.

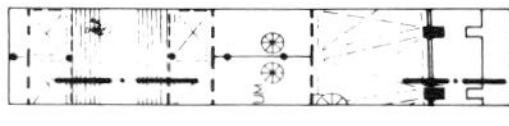
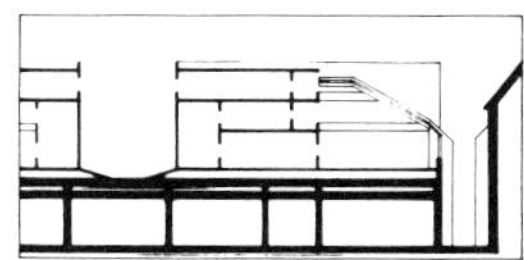

350 Office building, section and view.

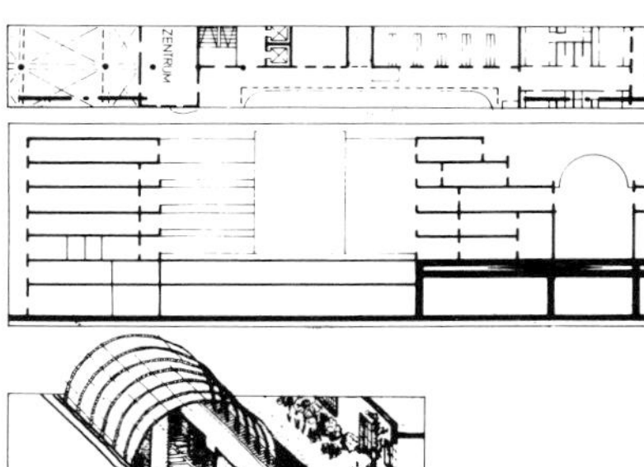

351 Sports centre, section and view.

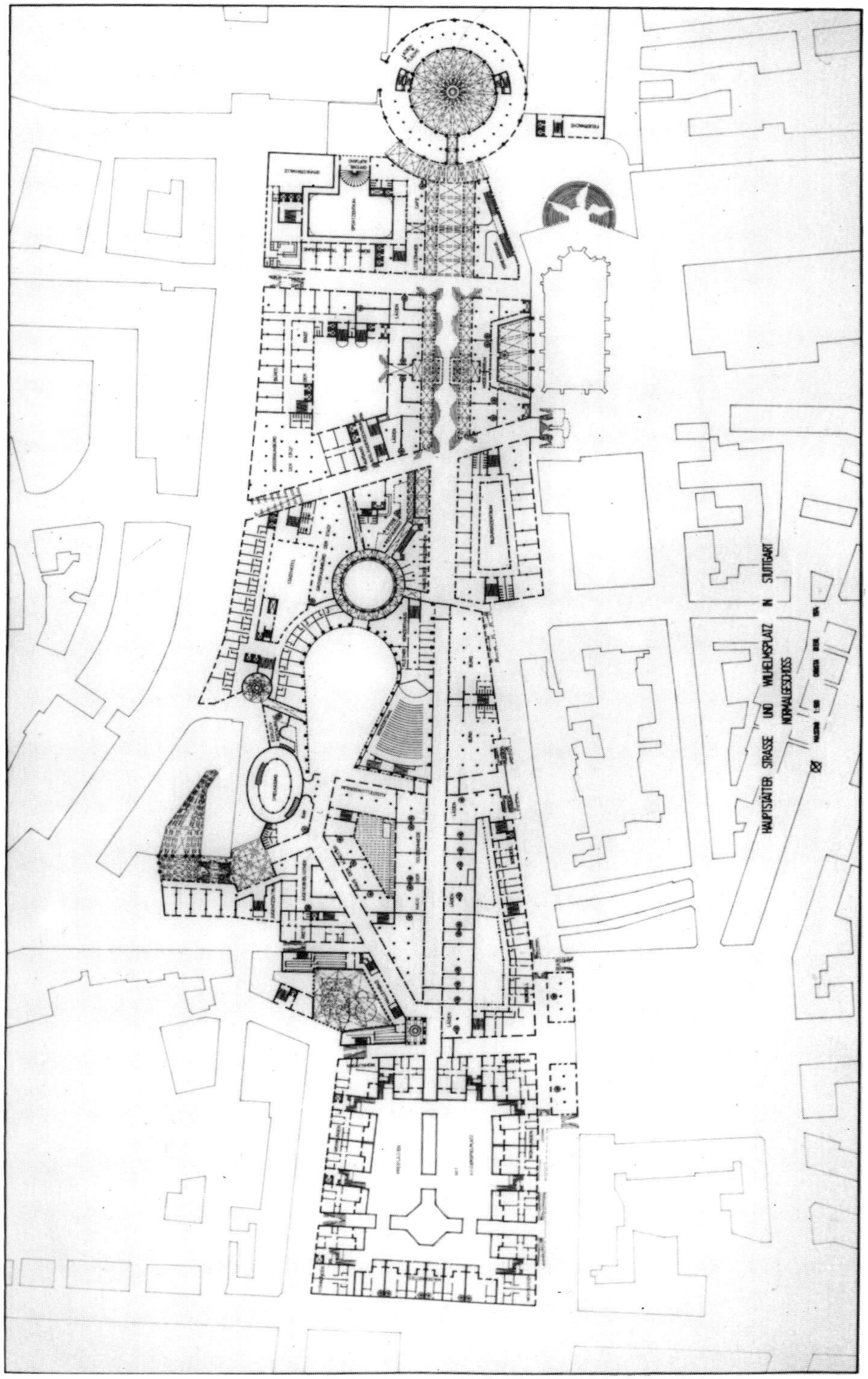

352 Ground plan of one level.

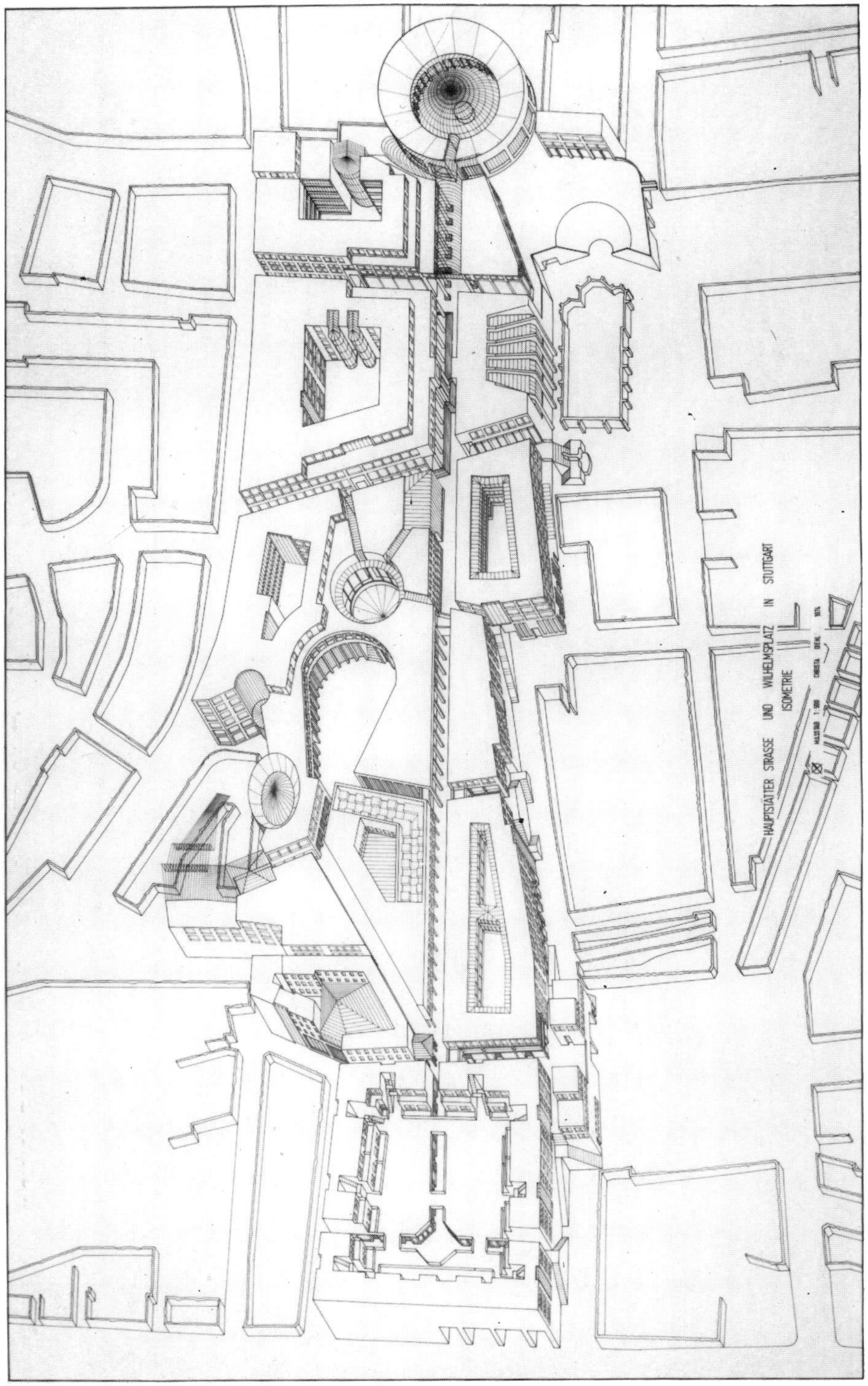

353 Isometric view of new planning proposals.

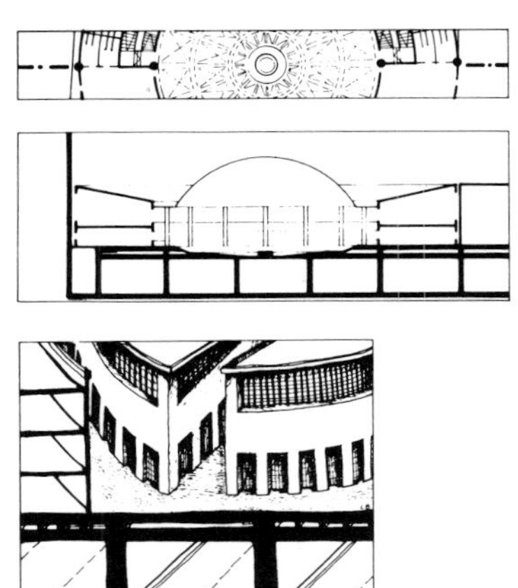

354 Political Forum, section and view.

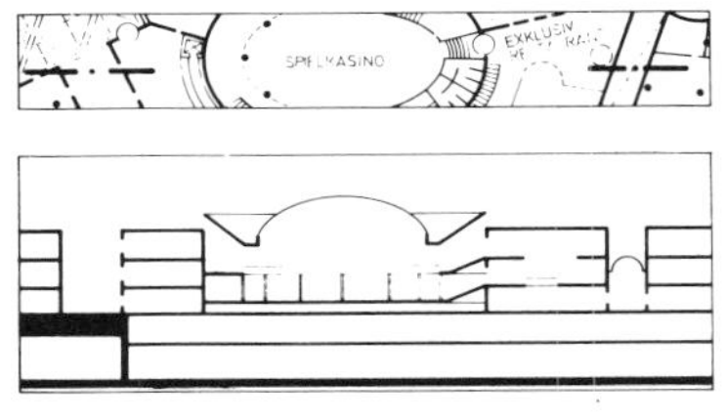

355 Casino, section and view.

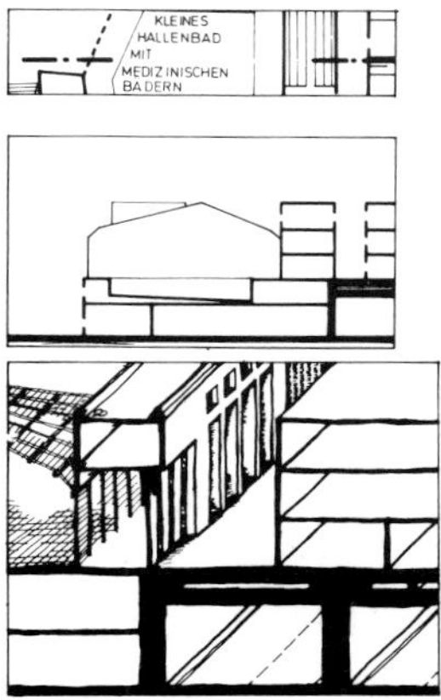

356 Small swimming baths, section and view.

357 Detail of model.

358 Detail of model.

359 Detail of model.

360 Model of new planning proposals.

361 Schlossplatz and surrounding area 1954. Photo Brugger.

362 Schlossplatz and surrounding area 1961. Photo Brugger.

CHARLOTTENPLATZ – SCHLOSSPLATZ

In view of the development of this area today, it is hardly appropriate to go on using the term 'square'. I will try to describe the fundamental elements which would turn the site back into a meaningful square for the pedestrian. I propose to restore the Hohe Carlsschule to its original state as built by Leger and Fischer between 1740 and 1748. This building, which had been only partially destroyed in the war, was completely demolished in the 50s to make way for two additional traffic lanes. Its architectural qualities were an essential complement to those of the Neue Schloss, whose rear elevation has lost its spatial meaning since the demolition of its counterpart. In response to the two principal wings of the 'Carlsakademie', which were only connected to the central courtyard by bridges, Retti, the planner of the Neue Schloss, hit on the idea of a pair of recessed sections at this point in the facade. Since the prinicpal wings are no longer standing, this 'architectural dialogue' has become meaningless.

At this point I would like to recall that in 1927 Paul Schmitthenner to a large extent rebuilt the former Orphanage of 1705, directly opposite the Hohe Carlsschule, according to its original plan. At the time, this work was violently criticised by the 'modern architects' as a reactionary piece of conservationism. But if Schmitthenner had not dealt so reverently with the building, the town would have felt the loss of an outstanding building type.

I have chosen this proposal for the reconstruction of the Hohe Carlsschule as a point of principle, since I find it incomprehensible – in terms of cultural history – that this building complex should have been demolished simply to make way for a road-widening operation. It is true that architecturally it may have lacked the splendour and rich ornamentation of the Neue Schloss. The central wing was designed as a barracks. Yet its spatial qualities were conceived on a grand scale and they played an important role in the development of Stuttgart in the 18th century.

I have made use of the exceptional spatial character of the area between the Akademie, the Orphanage and the Stadbibliothek to create a clearly defined triangular square. The Bazarstrasse, leading from the Leonhardskirche, does not meet the square directly, but shortly before doing so broadens out into a little circus. The smaller buildings on this circus block off the direct view from the Bazarstrasse to the Charlottenplatz. The transition from one to the other lies between two round towers, from which the axes of the Bazarstrasse and the Konrad-Adenauer-Strasse lead. The Charlottenplatz is surrounded by an arcade. The Stadtbibliothek (or Wilhelms-Palais), built by Salucci between 1834 and 1840, harmonises with the rest of the buildings around the square, and nowadays its main front entrance is once again accessible as originally planned.

The west side of the Neue Schloss is an open U-shape with slightly projecting lateral extensions which scarcely contribute anything to the spatial qualities of the site. A modest central projection accentuates the strength of the main facade. The busy street completely cuts the building off from the Karlsplatz opposite.

I propose to round out this spatial fragment by introducing a building which will be a mirror-image of the facade of the Neue Schloss described above. The east wing of the castle, whose facade faces on to the park, is similarly given spatial coherence by avenues of trees (as planned by Thouret). This site, with the facade of

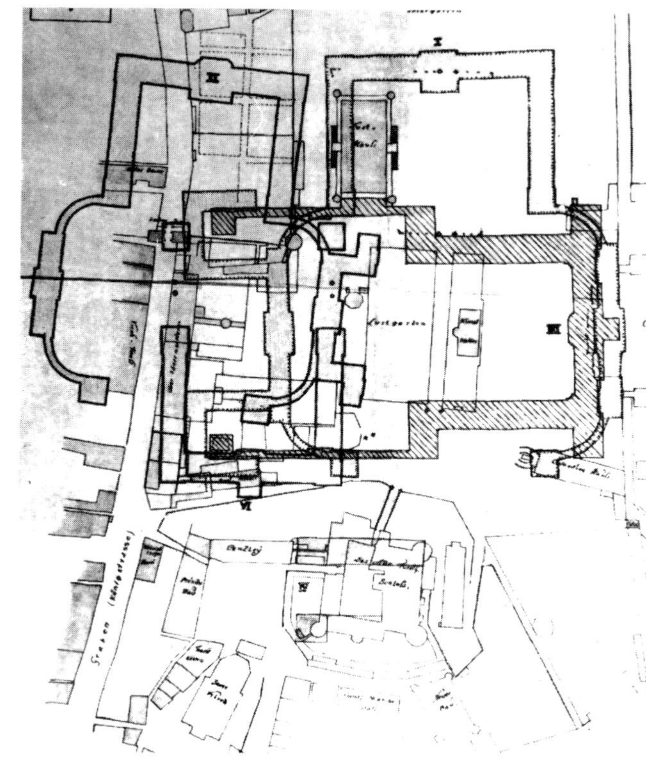

363 Various alternative schemes for the Neue Schloss site by Retti, c. 1750.
After Scholl, *Leopold Retti*, Verlag Bürgel, Ansbach (from K. Weidle).

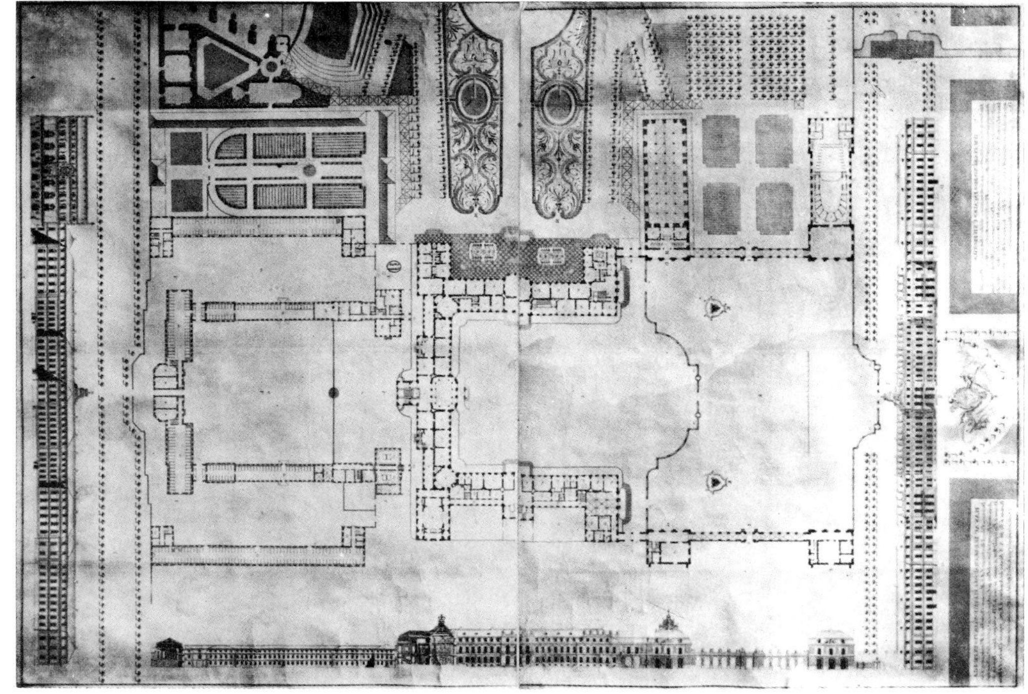

364 Retti's plan for the Neue Schloss.
After Scholl, from K. Weidle.
Engraving by Claude Lucas, Paris 1750.

365 The Charlottenplatz, with the Staatstheater in the background and the Wilhelmspalais on the right.

366 Salucci's Wilhelmspalais 1834–39.

367 The Charlottenplatz, with the Orphanage (1705) restored by Schmitthenner on the left and the Neue Schloss on the right.

368 View of the Planie, with the Alte Schloss in the background.

369 Facade of the Neue Schloss facing the Hohe Carlsschule.

370 The Charlottenplatz, with the Leonhardskirche in the background and the Orphanage on the right.

the castle in the background, would make an admirable spot for an open-air theatre. The steps where spectators would be seated happily forms a quite natural transition between the higher plane of the street and the level of the square. The primary function of new buildings on this square and on the Charlottenplatz should be a cultural one.

Between the Neue Schlossplatz, the Alte Schloss and the Kanzlei (Chancellery) I have planned for a further new building, to give spatial coherence to the Schlossplatz in the same way as the Kunstverein building. This had always been Retti's intention, as we can see from his original plans. Fischer took the same idea almost to its logical conclusion and linked his building plans directly with the Alte Schloss and the Kanzlei. His plan for the northern end of the Schlossplatz is worthy of note. The architects Leins and Knapp built the imposing Königsbau on this site between 1855 and 1859, a building which looks like a relic of the famous Roman colonnaded streets of Palmyra and Timgad.

The Schlossplatz could also be enclosed by a pair of gateways, which would provide a spatial boundary between the square and the entrance to the Königstrasse. As I have already said, I believe that the Königstrasse should be planted with trees, except towards the Schlossplatz end. There is still a mass of detail to be gleaned from the overall plan, especially as regards those points where old and new buildings meet, but it is impossible for me to go into them all.

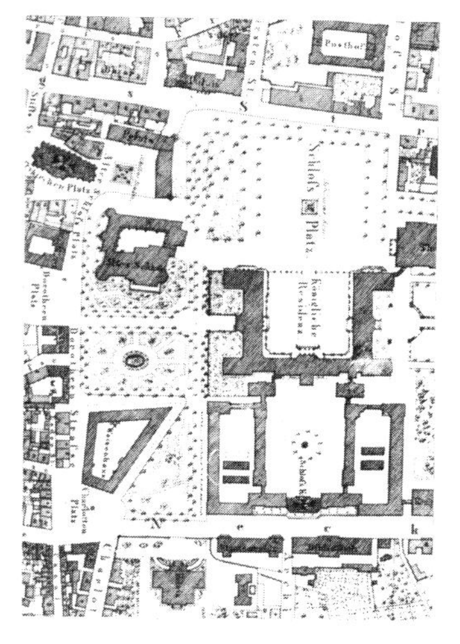

371

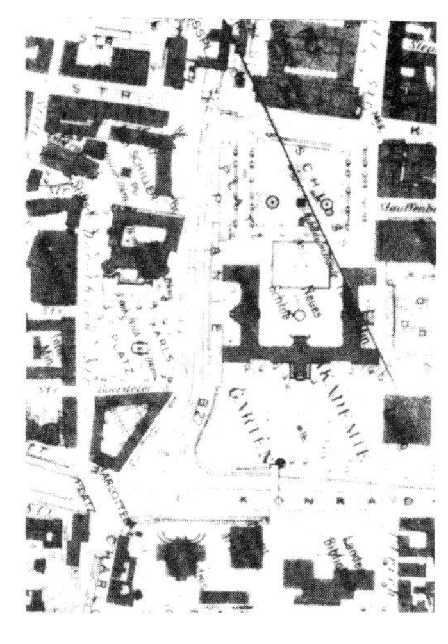

372

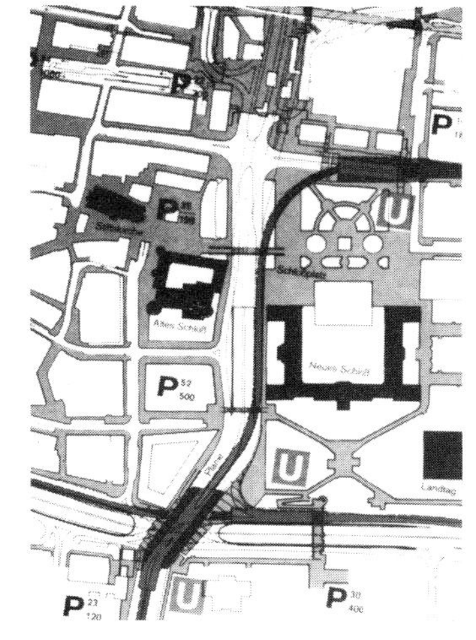

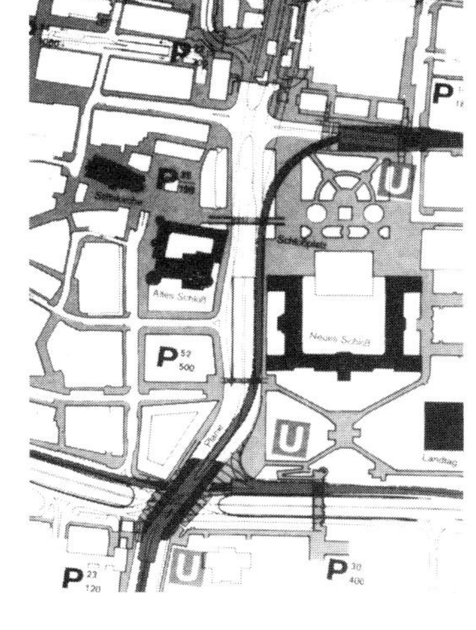

373

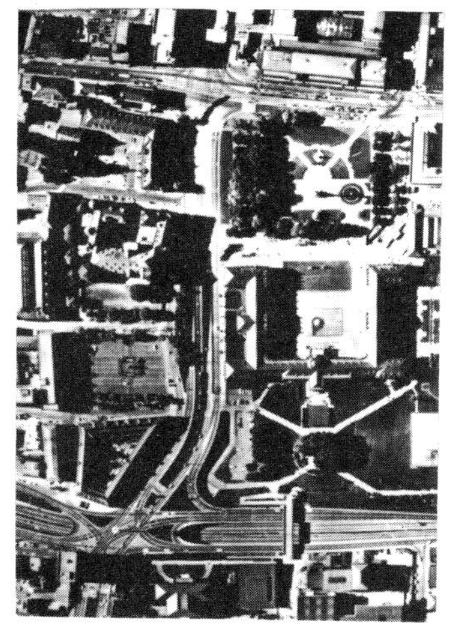

374

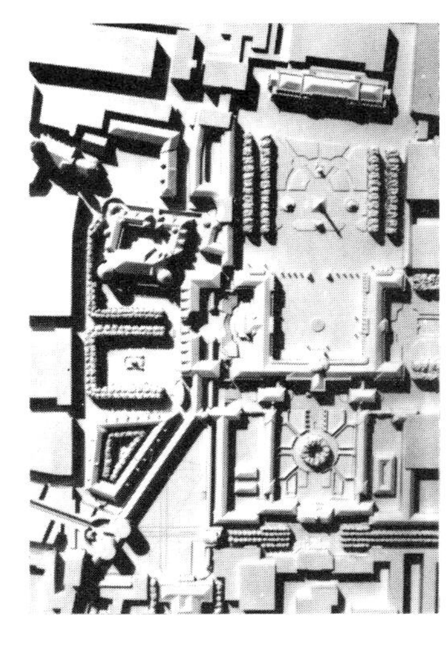

375

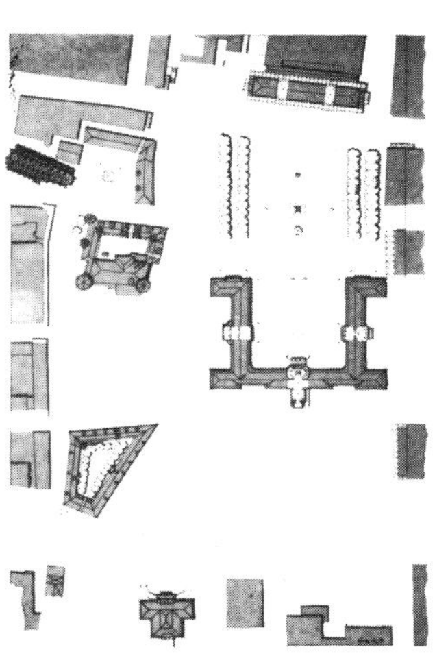

376

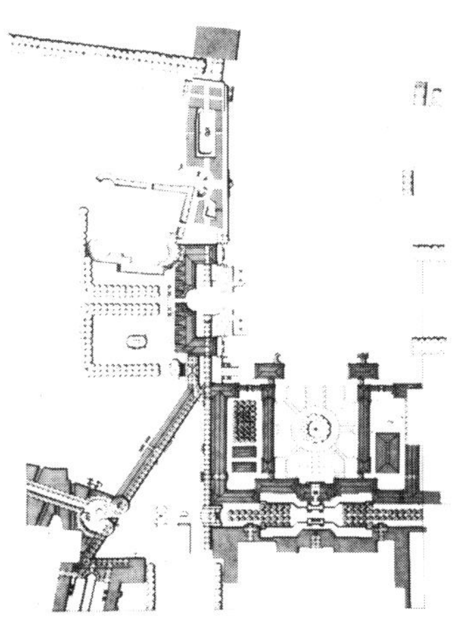

377

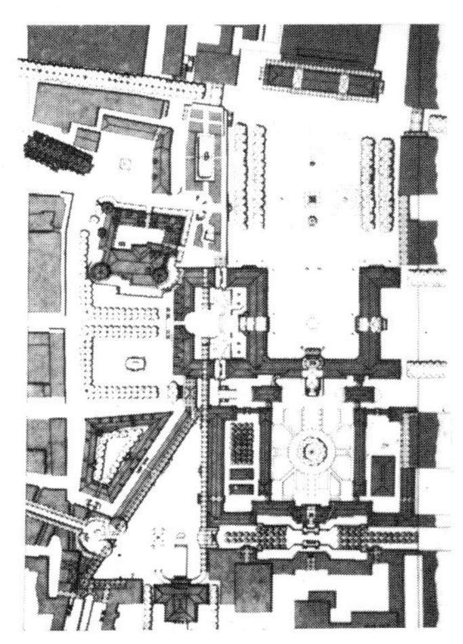

378

371 1855.
372 1972.
373 Traffic plan.
374 Aerial photo 1969.
375 Model of new planning proposals.
376, 377, 378 The area as it is today, showing new plans and their superimposition on existing layout.

379 Charlottenplatz – Schlossplatz,
scale 1 : 2,000 approx.

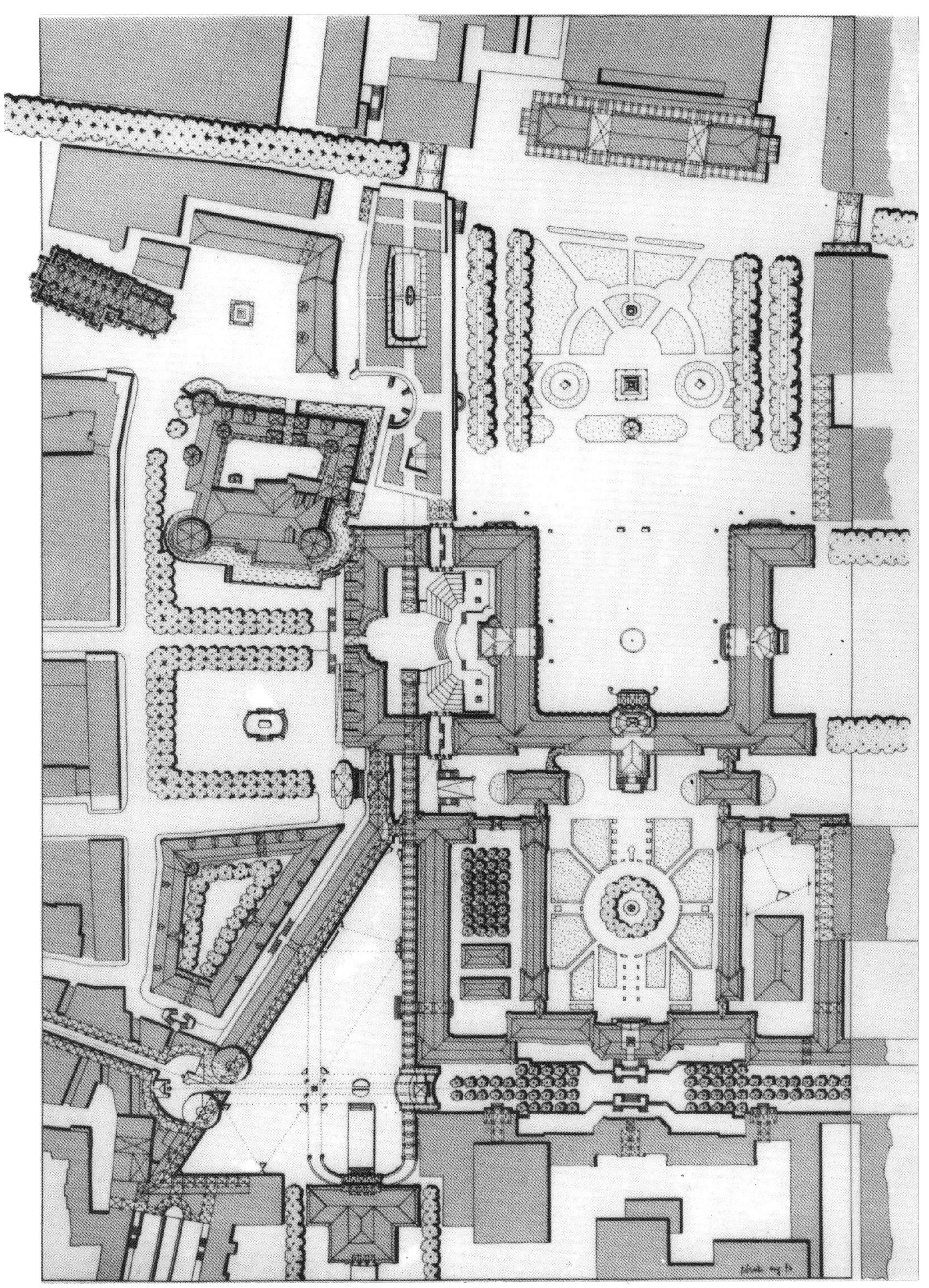

380 Charlottenplatz – Schlossplatz,
scale 1 : 2,000 approx.

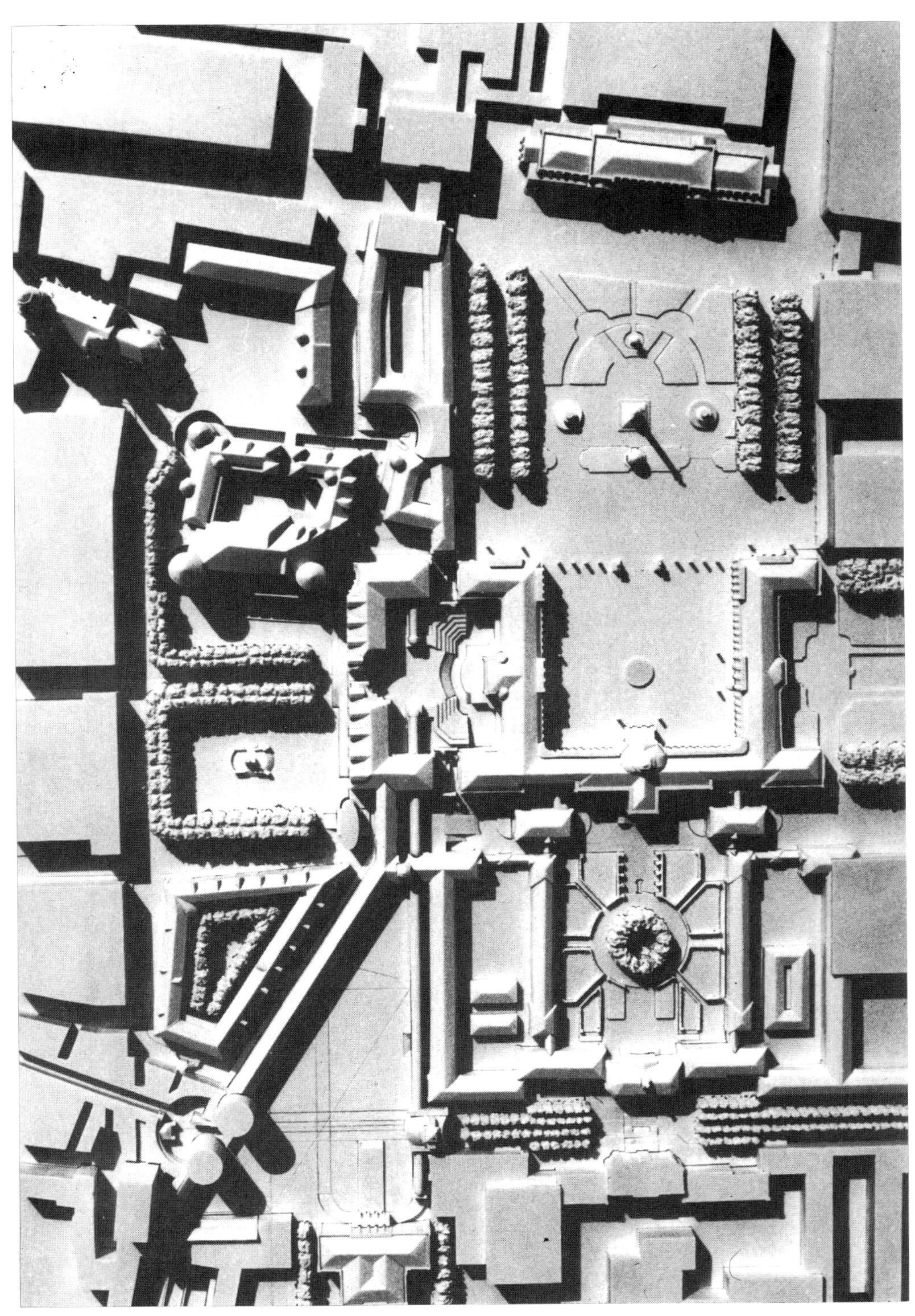

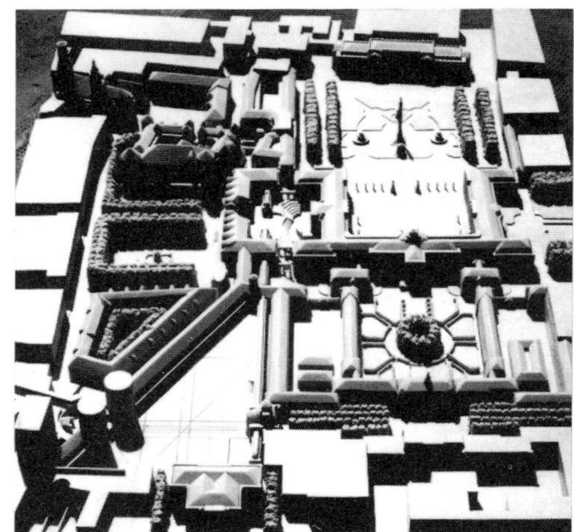

381

382

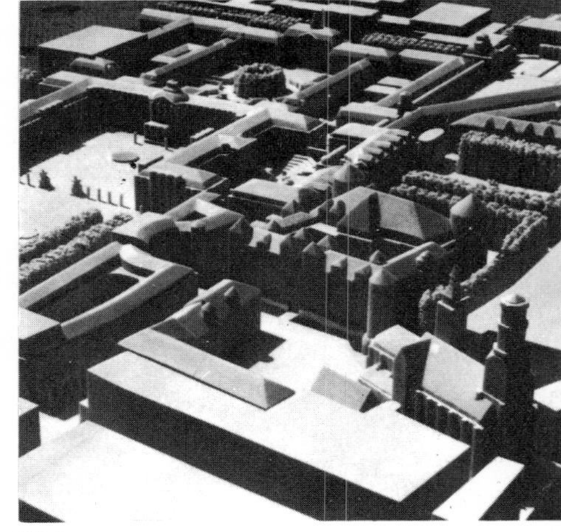

383

384

MODELS OF PLANS FOR THE CHARLOTTENPLATZ AND SCHLOSSPLATZ (PARTIAL VIEWS)

381 Overall view from the south-east.
382 Planie axis: on the left the Schlossplatz, Neue Schloss, Hohe Carlsschule; on the right (foreground) the Alte Kanzlei (Old Chancellery), Alte Schloss, Karlsplatz, Orphanage; (background) the new Charlottenplatz with the Wilhelmspalais.
383 View from the north-west. In the foreground the Collegiate Church (13th–15th centuries) and the Schillerplatz.

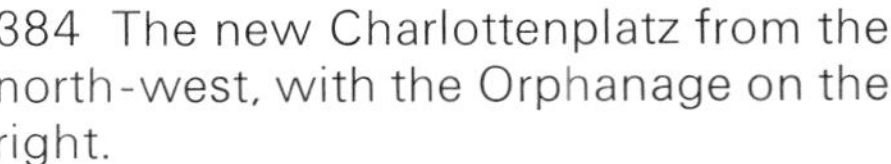

384 The new Charlottenplatz from the north-west, with the Orphanage on the right.
385 The same square from the south-east.
386 The Bazarstrasse looking across the Holzstrasse, and the entrance to the Charlottenplatz.
387 Looking along the Konrad-Adenauer-Strasse towards its junction with the Charlottenplatz, with the Landesbibliothek and Hauptstaatsarchiv on the left.

385

386

387

388

389

390

388 The 'pendant' to the west facade of the Neue Schloss and the open-air theatre.
389 The Königstrasse and the gateways separating it from the Schlossplatz.
390 The Schillerplatz (bottom left); Alte Schloss (right); boundary separating the mediaeval town from the new Schlossplatz (top).
391–394 Other details of model.

391

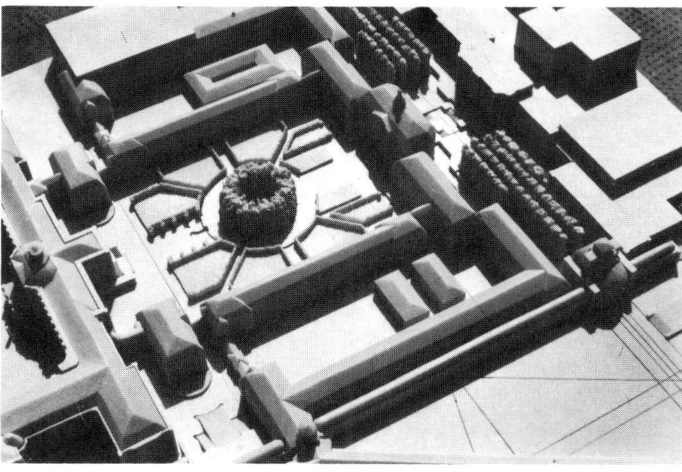
392

393

395/1–11 Sketches of the Charlottenplatz – Schlossplatz scheme.

395/1 Composition of the Charlottenplatz.
395/2 Small circus adjoining the Charlottenplatz.
395/3 The Charlottenplatz, seen from its narrowest corner.

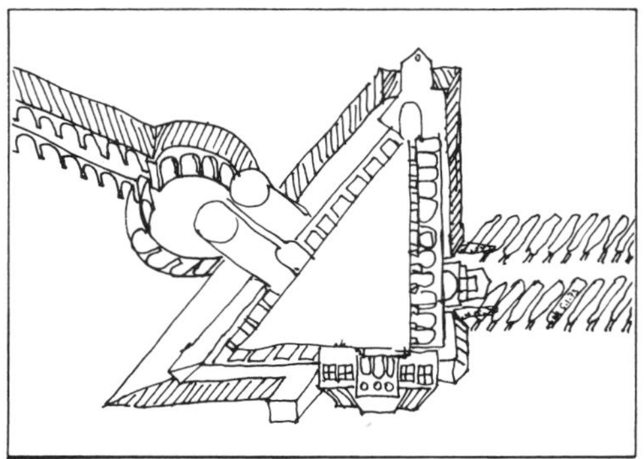

395/7 Monument in front of the Orphanage.
395/8 Open-air theatre on the west side of the Neue Schloss.

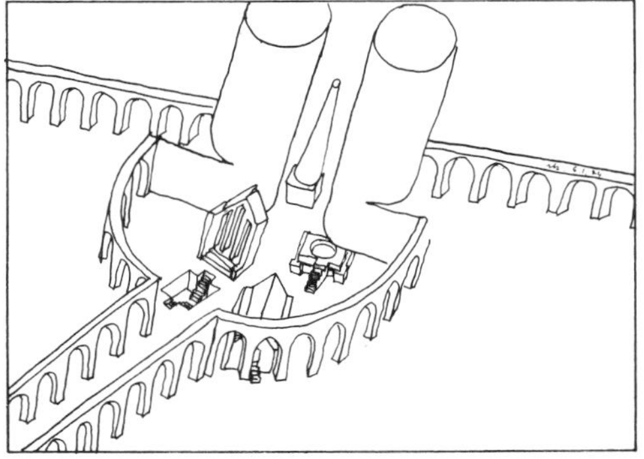

395/4 Small circus looking towards the Bazarstrasse.
395/5 The Bazarstrasse.
395/6 Section of the Charlottenplatz.

395/9 The Charlottenplatz, seen from the entrance to the Stadtbibliothek.
395/10 Mock arcade on the west side of the Neue Schloss.
395/11 Theme: small circus with objects.

396 Design for the seat of the Stuttgart court as executed c. 1830.
Pen and wash drawing by Thouret, from the Stadtarchiv collection (from Paul Faerber: *Fr. von Thouret, ein Baumeister des Klassizismus*, Kohlhammer–Verlag Stuttgart 1949).

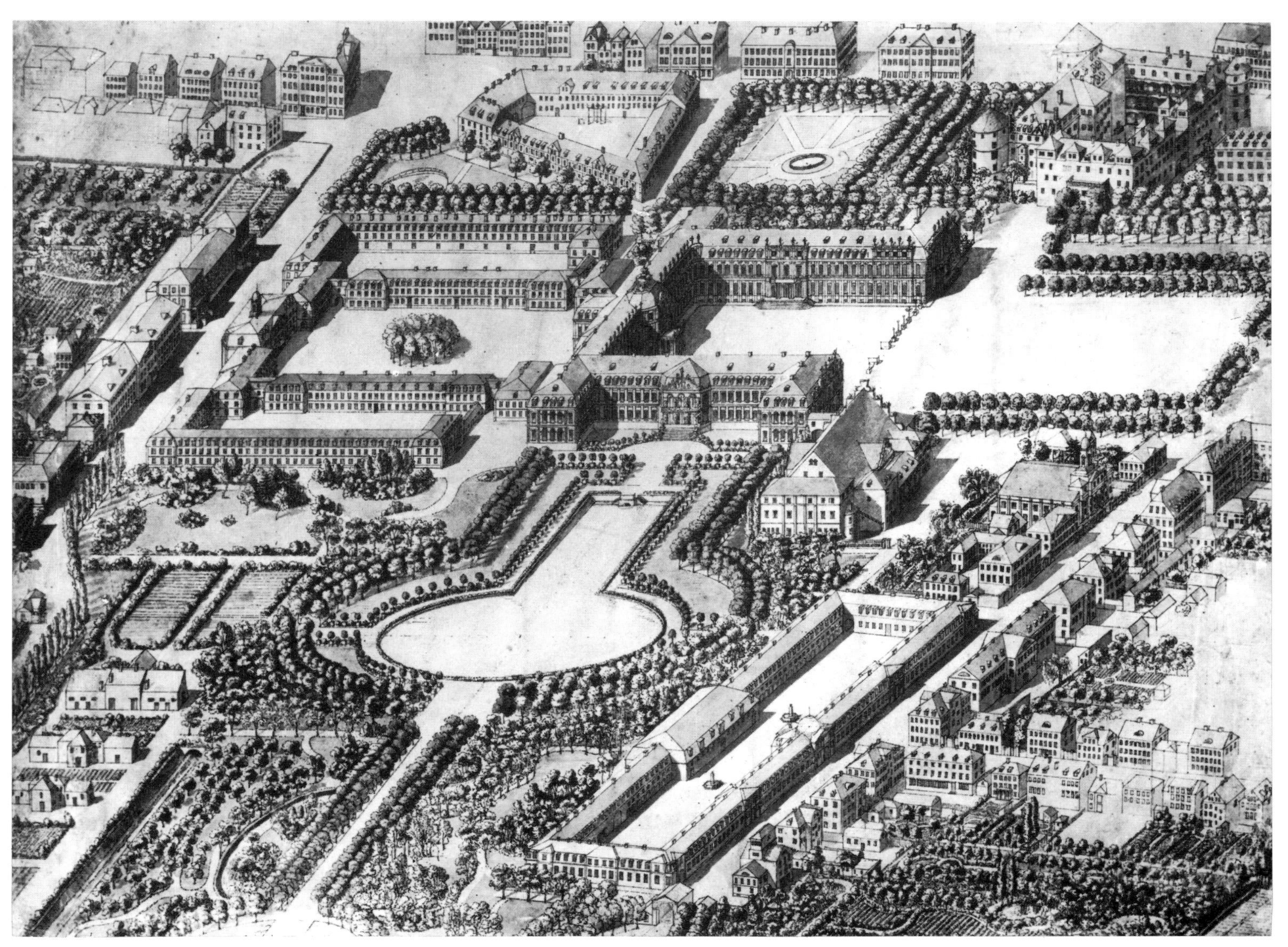

STUDY OF THE CHARLOTTENPLATZ AREA

SCHEME BY OTTO HIPPIN

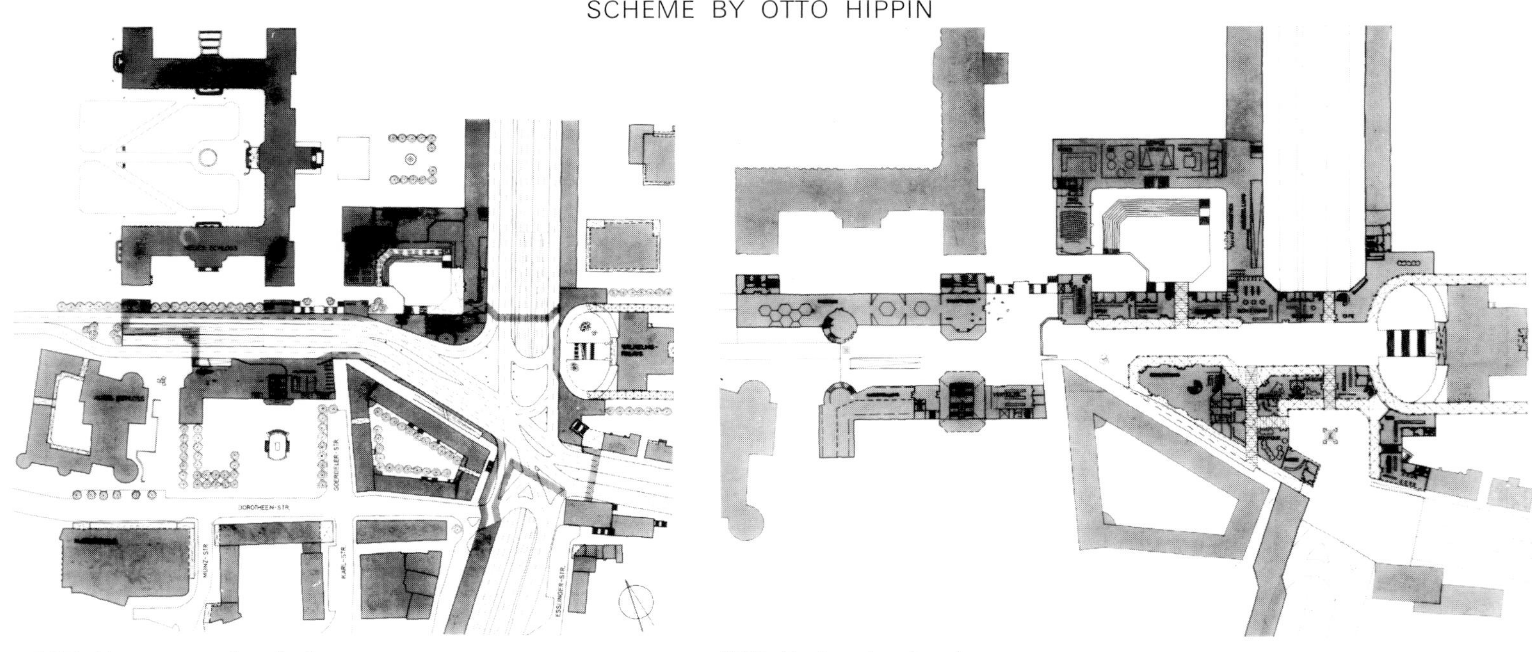

397 New street-level plan.

398 Pedestrian level.

399 View of roof level.

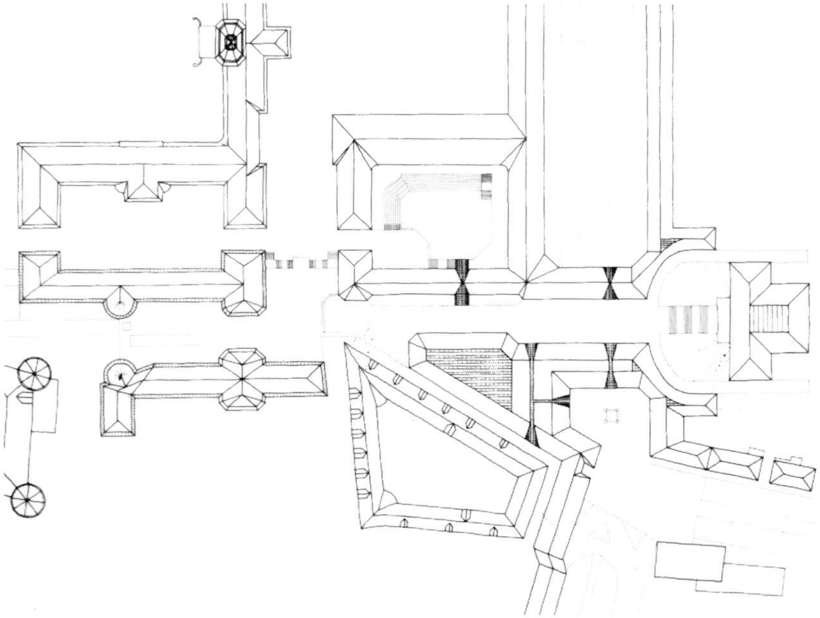

400 Isometric.

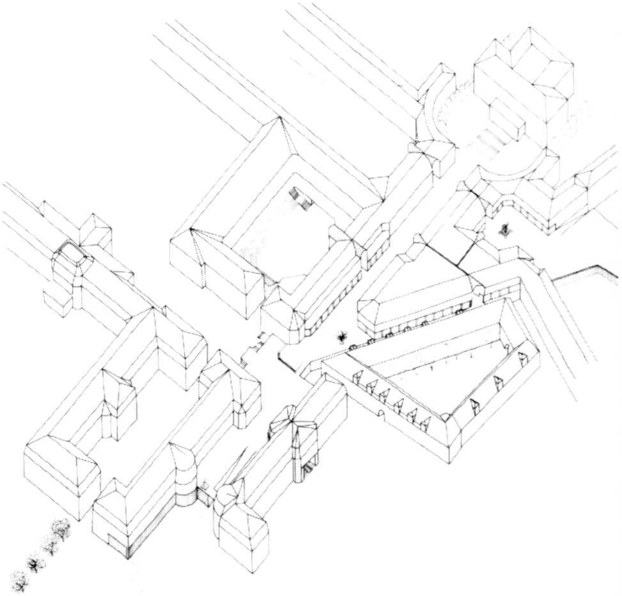

THE STAATSGALERIE

In my new plans for this section I have tried to integrate the existing arts buildings on the Konrad-Adenauer-Strasse into a coherent spatial pattern and to plot an axis which will link them overall. The former Neckarstrasse was conceived by Thouret as a kind of 'cultural street' on the model of the Unter den Linden in Berlin. Since the site remains as prestigious as ever – located as it is parallel to the Königstrasse and the Schlossgarten – there is every reason for it to be further improved. Among other things the famous old natural history collection could be restored to its original location, instead of being uprooted and given a new home outside the city area, as is currently planned. The elegantly proportioned Staatsgalerie building, designed by Gottlob Barth between 1838 and 1842, is now effectively cut off from its immediate surroundings by a new underpass which has been built on its doorstep.

401

402

403

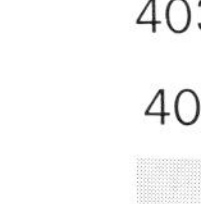

404

405

401 Engraving by Willmann (1871) from the Stadtarchiv collection. In the foreground is the Museum der Bildenden Künste (Staatsgalerie), with the Mint opposite.
402 Barth's Staatsgalerie (1838–43).
403 The Konrad-Adenauer-Strasse, formerly known as the Neckarstrasse. On the left, the Landtag (State Parliament) on the site of the Hohe Carlsschule, the Staatstheater; in the background the Staatsgalerie; on the right the Alte Landesbibliothek and the Staatsarchiv.
404 The Staatsgalerie seen from the station.
405 View of the Neckarstrasse.

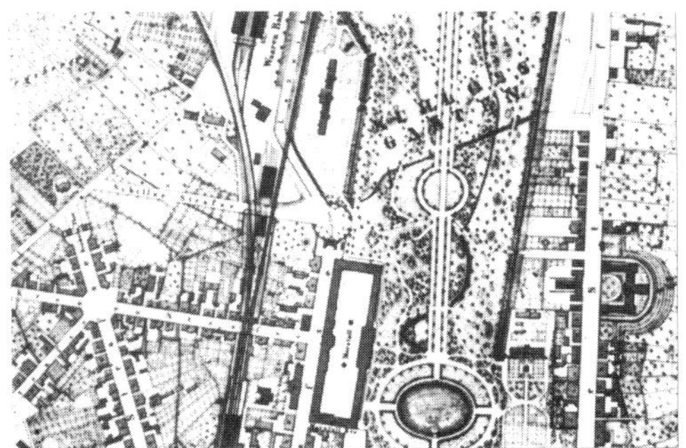
406 1855.

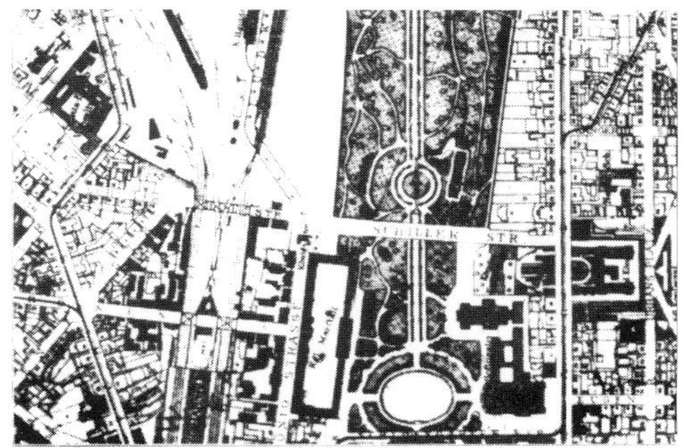
407 1910.

The new road-bed was laid so close to the building that no room remained for a sidewalk. The incredible idea for solving this problem was to construct a pedestrian subway through the cellar of the two wings of the gallery. Since the completion of work on the new traffic system, the museum has recorded a marked decrease in the number of visitors.

408 1972.

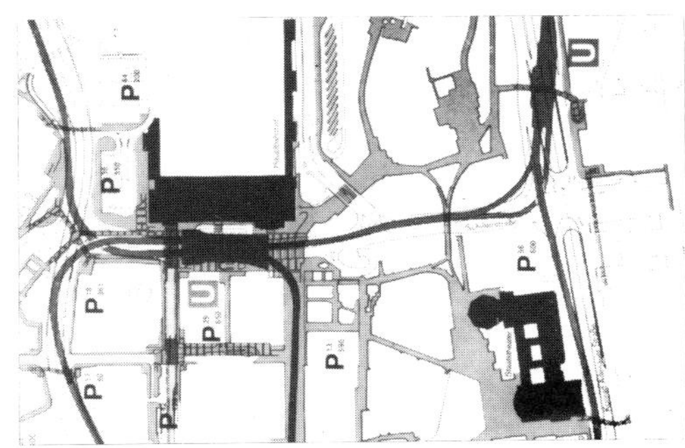
409 Traffic plan.

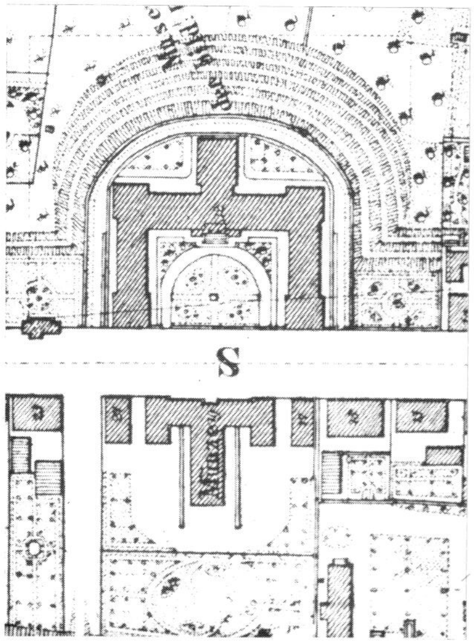

410 New plans.

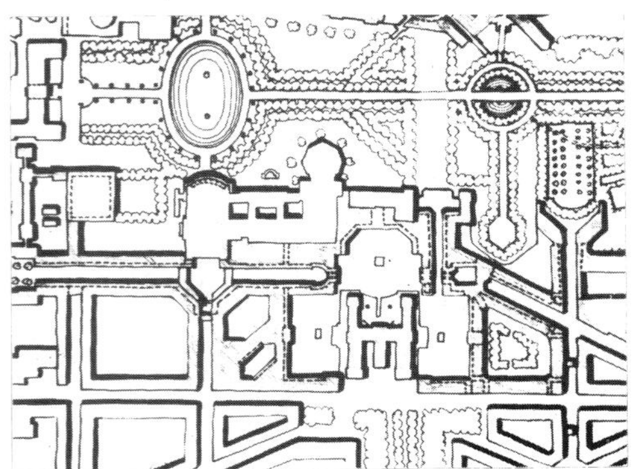

411 Model of new plans.

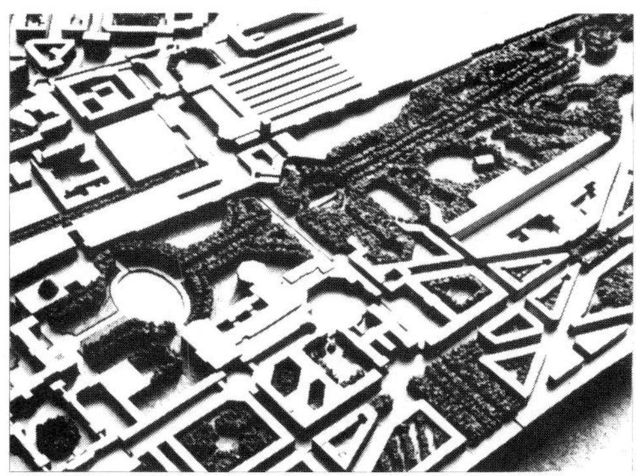

412 Museum der Bildenden Künste and Mint, both on the Neckarstrasse, as they were in 1855.

THE SCHLOSSGARTEN

The park, as originally laid out according to Thouret's plans in 1812, was deformed to a frightening degree in preparation for the 1961 National Horticultural Show. A so-called 'up-dating' took place. It was a deficient understanding of how to deal with an existing historic site which led to this absurd act of wanton deforestation. I am sure no-one ever dreamt up the idea of forest clearances on this scale in the park at Versailles or Schwetzingen.

There was another comparable act of destruction in the incomprehensible deforestation of Ludwigsburg castle near Stuttgart in 1968.

There are plans for the next National Horticultural Show to be held in the lower grounds of the Schlossgarten in 1976. I trust that history will not repeat itself then.

My proposal is to restore the Schlossgarten according to Thouret's design. The photo on the next page shows the avenue of plane trees in the lower grounds. It is now 162 years since they were planted. The impression produced by this green space, now that the trees have grown to their present size, surely bears comparison with the spatial glories of an architectural masterpiece. The man-made and the natural must reciprocally support, complement and enrich each other.

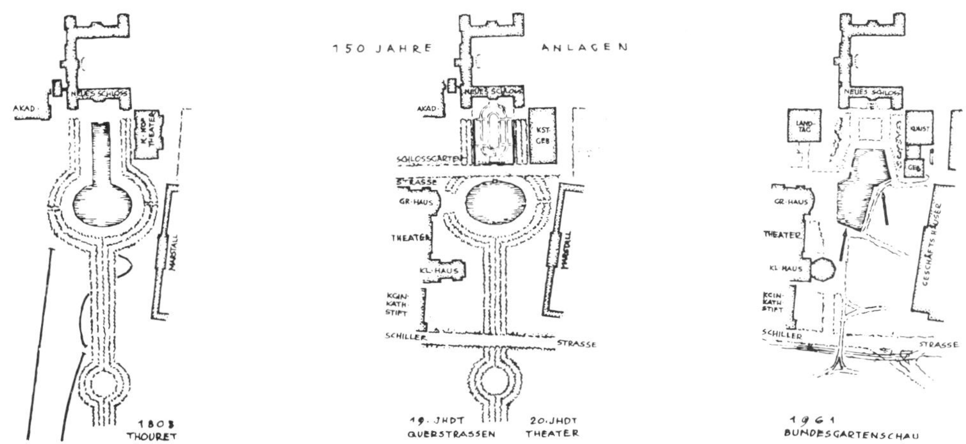

413–415 Changes in the layout of the Schlossgarten since 1808.

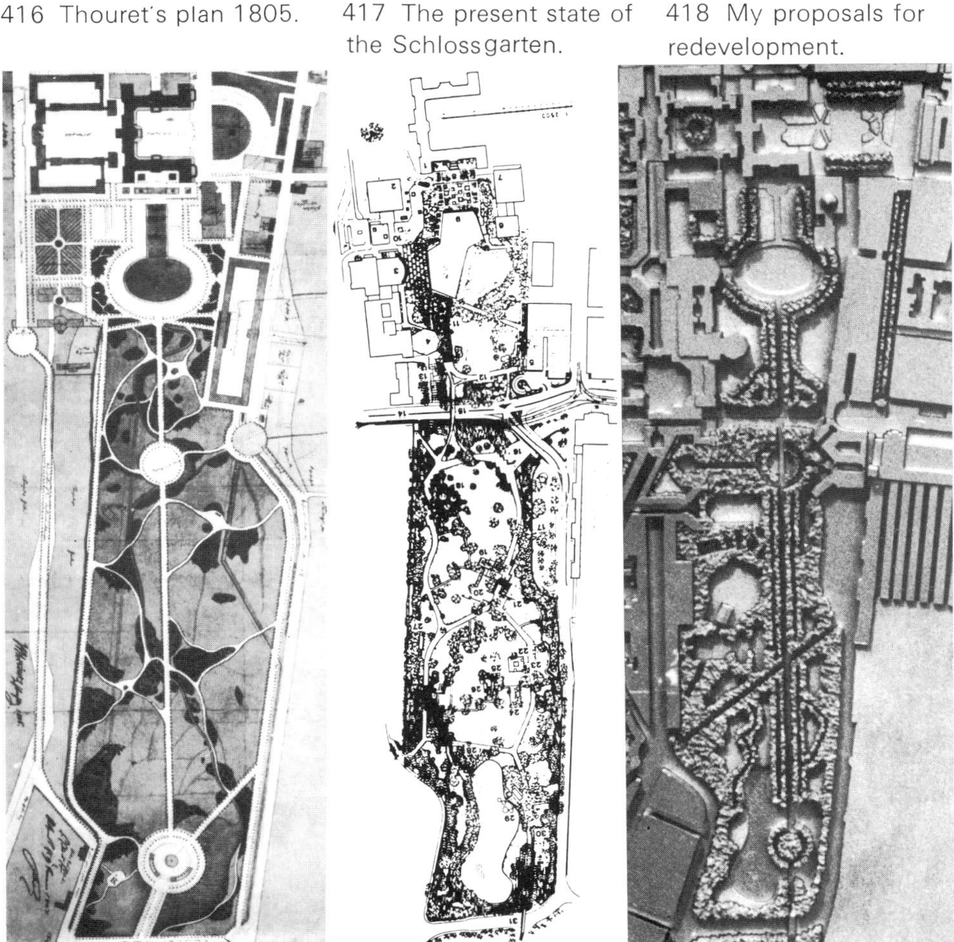

416 Thouret's plan 1805.

417 The present state of the Schlossgarten.

418 My proposals for redevelopment.

419 Avenue of plane trees in the lower castle grounds, planted in 1812.

EPILOGUE TO THE CHAPTER

RECONSTRUCTING DEVASTATED URBAN SPACE

In the course of our stroll through various parts of Stuttgart for which I have suggested possible approaches to reconstruction, I have deliberately skirted around the development of the town in the post-war years of rebuilding, and have restricted myself to documenting its present state with plans, aerial shots and photos. I hope that this material, together with my new planning proposals, has spelt out my views unequivocally, and that I can omit any critical comment on the gradual process of destruction which Stuttgart has undergone. People will reproach me for having energetically – almost desperately – attempted to create patterns of urban space requiring such enormous investment that no local authority will risk bankruptcy by putting them into practice. Without a doubt, contemporary town-planning, with its total disregard for spatial problems, is a more attractive proposition in the current socio-political climate. It is no coincidence that priority is given to traffic and the other trappings of technology, rather than to people's need for a tolerable urban environment. Of course, not everyone in a town will assign the same importance to the poetic or musical elements of urban space. Experience also indicates that the inhabitants of old towns whose original state has been preserved do not take the same interest in their quality as outsiders. It is quite superfluous that they should, since the spectacle forms the backdrop to their daily lives. They are entirely at one with their environment and the history which is so intimately bound up with it. The source of this feeling of identification is the architecture of the town and its complex scenario. As in other German cities, Stuttgart's inhabitants and physical environment were thrown into

420 Vignette from J. Sauter's etching. 'Warhaffte Conterfactur der Fürstlichen Hauptstatt Stutgarten', 1592.

Text of vignette Fig. 420

Stuttgart in Württemberg,
Famous capital of that state,
Lies also in a fair valley,
Graced by vineyards all around.
May God preserve
The beauty of its form at noon.

. . . may God PRESERVE the beauty of . . . FORM . . .

chaos by the Second World War. The awareness of historical values was extinguished by the enormity of the devastation and remained impotent in the face of the pressing need to reorganise the essential elements of the town. These have now been restored, but I am clearly not alone in asking whether some elements may not have been overlooked in the rush to rebuild. Yet previously, through a mixture of people's unwitting laziness and the familiarity of its appearance, the town had been taken for granted. Only one or two theorists had devoted themselves to the full range of the town's interests, and so nobody was prepared for 'zero hour' when it came. Developments over the last thirty years have made it abundantly clear how short-sighted was the idea of the supposedly perfect 'functional commercial city'.

The material included in this chapter was assembled as part of a course I was teaching at the Institut für Zeichnen und Modellieren of the University of Stuttgart, under the direction of Professor J. Uhl. It forms an introduction to the thematic presentation of a programme written up in the Institut during summer 1973 and worked at over four semesters, in such a way as to suggest the maximum possible range of alternative schemes to students.

The projects presented here were exhibited at the 1973 Triennale in Milan, in 1974 in San Sebastian, in 1975 at the Art Net Gallery in London and the Stuttgart Kunstverein. They have also been published in a number of architectural periodicals.

CHAPTER 4
APPENDIX

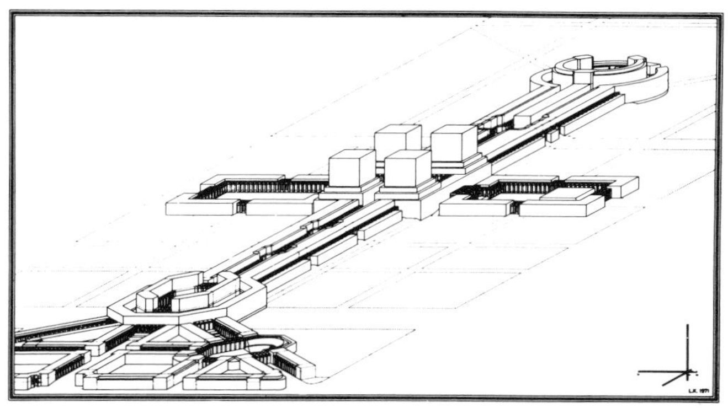

CHAPTER 4

APPENDIX

STUTTGART AND THE AXES OF ITS DEVELOPMENT

After my exhaustive description of the planning problems of Stuttgart's town centre, I would like to add a chapter dealing with possible ways in which outlying areas of Stuttgart might be developed. This research, like the rest, has not been sponsored by the city authorities. It was undertaken of my own accord and so – like the preceding chapter – should be regarded as an idealistic set of solutions. The basic assumption underlying a plan of this kind is of course that circumstances will dictate further urban growth. Since the turn of the century, the population of Stuttgart has grown from 175,000 to its present size of more than 700,000, and that of the central Neckar valley area (the Greater Stuttgart region) from 1.5 million in 1950 to 2.2 million inhabitants in 1966. This growth resulted mainly from the migration of population caused by the industrial expansion of the region. If this industrial growth stagnates as it has in the last two years, the effect is to put an immediate brake on the population explosion. I am not competent to offer a forecast about this, but I do feel inclined to believe that there will be a lot more changes in Europe before the next two hundred years are out. And why should we not envisage 'realistic' plans for the future on this kind of time-scale? For I live in hope that the human race will not have been altogether wiped out by then.

So let us consider the development plans for Stuttgart as a blueprint for a more or less distant future.

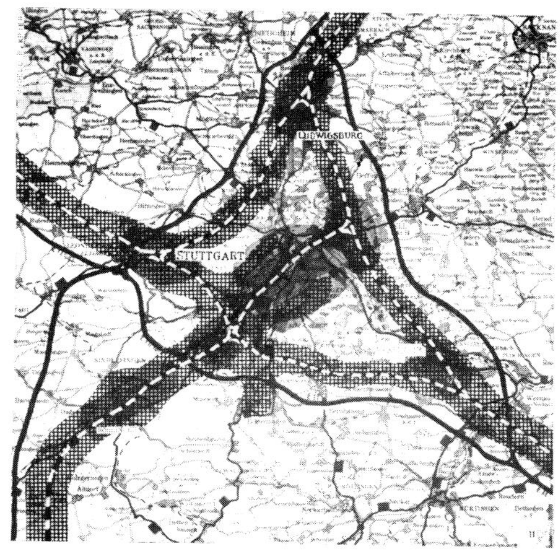

Key:
Development Areas – the shaded areas are the suggested concentration zones on the edges of the city. These zones are closely connected by A, B and C roads.

A, B & C roads

Motorway

421 Axes of development in the Greater Stuttgart region (see key).

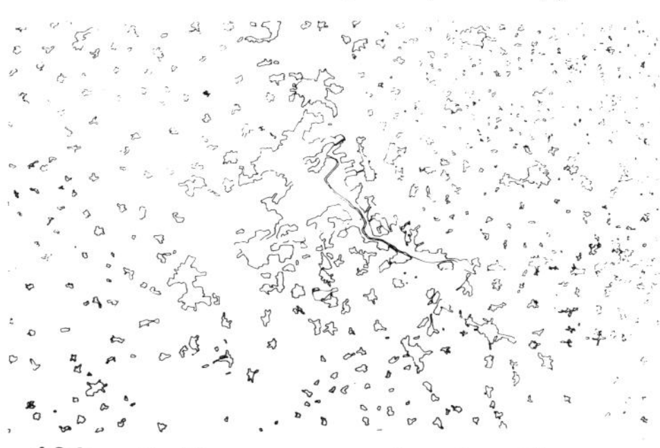

422 Built-up areas in the Greater Stuttgart region.

423 Linear city development system on the Soria y Mata model.

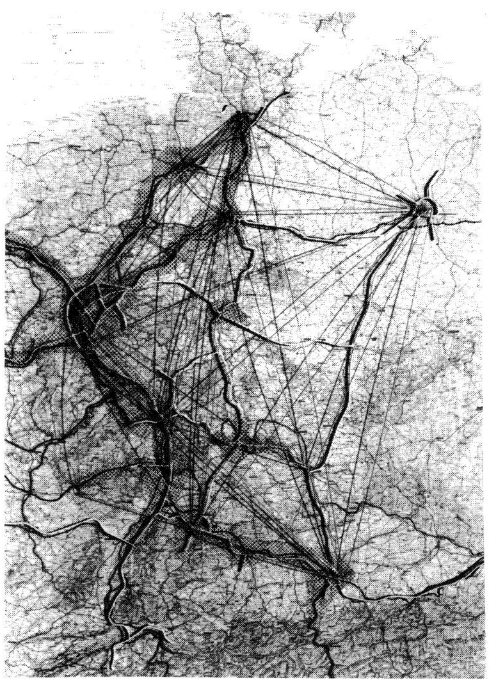

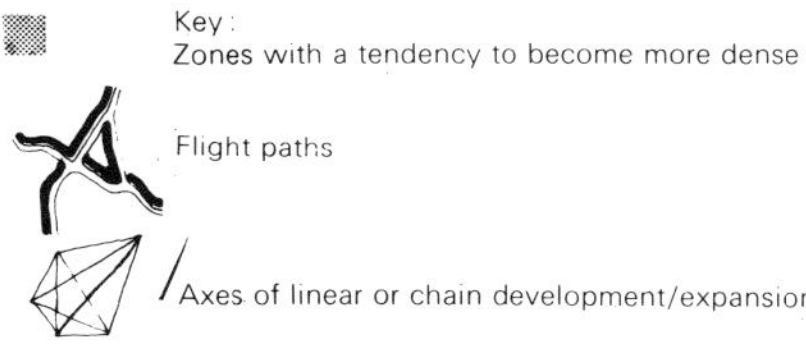

424 Model for urban development in the Central European context.

This complex structural intensification of public and private communications will have a far-reaching influence on future town and city development policies. Like transportation, urban planning – both in the cities and smaller communities – must be harmonised and coordinated with the larger regional plan.

However far-fetched this model may seem, I feel it to be of the greatest importance if we are to avoid the formation of further chaotic, unplanned complexes such as the Ruhr valley. The plain of the Rhine between Karlsruhe and Frankfurt is already well on the way to becoming a similar kind of development.

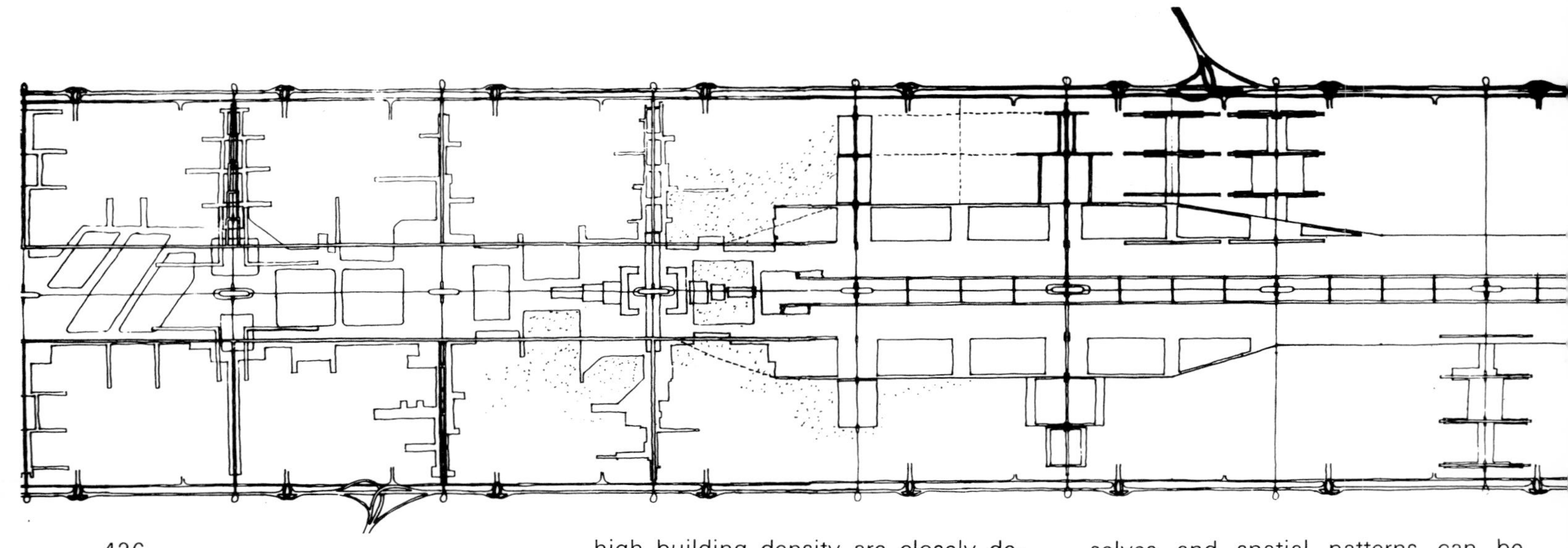

426

It was also important to simulate a democratic planning process. Areas of high building density are closely defined within a fixed framework. On the other hand, the buildings themselves and spatial patterns can be freely articulated. Each neighbourhood unit contains approximately 12,000

425 Photomontage showing section of development to the west of Stuttgart city centre.

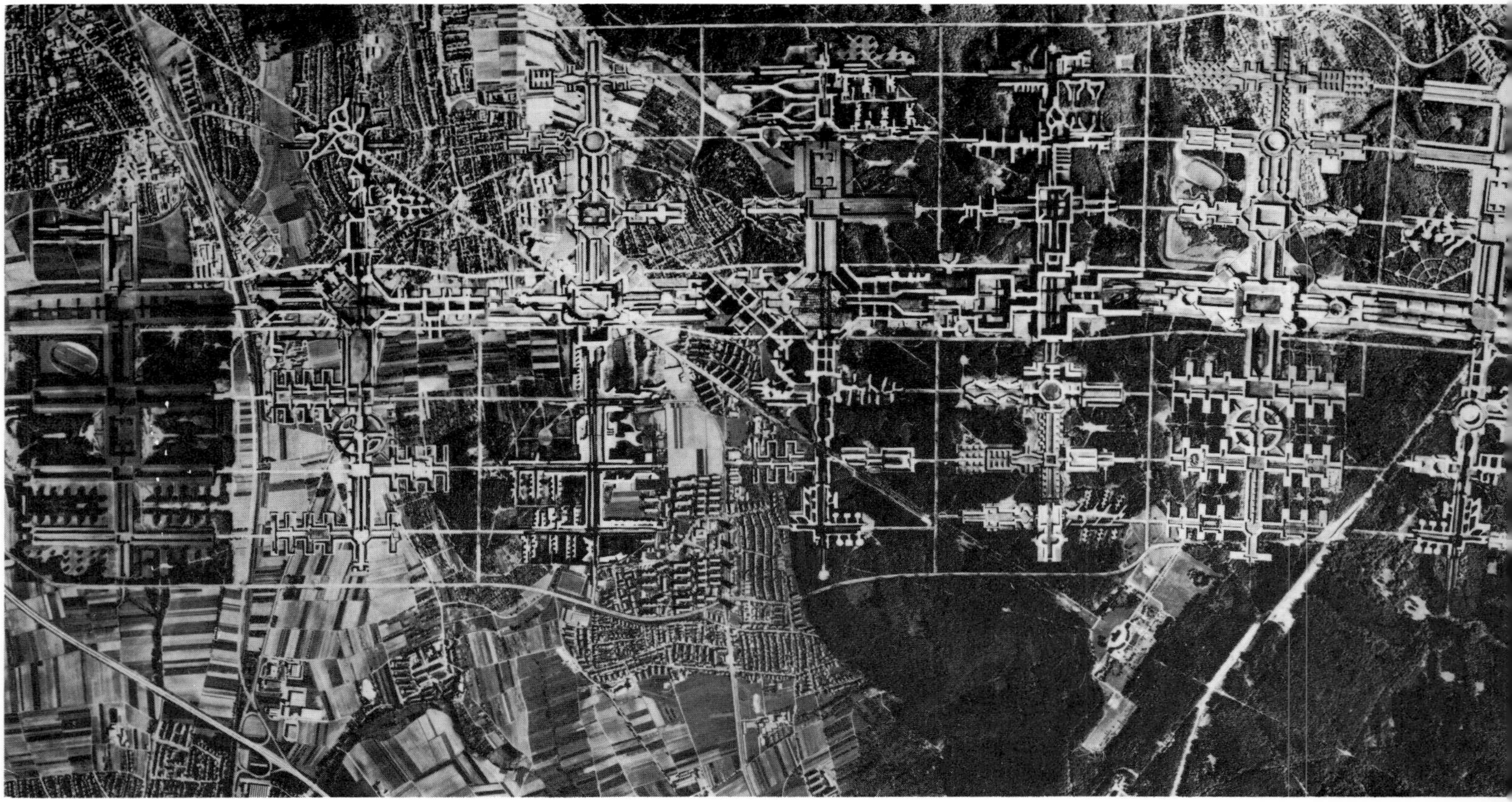

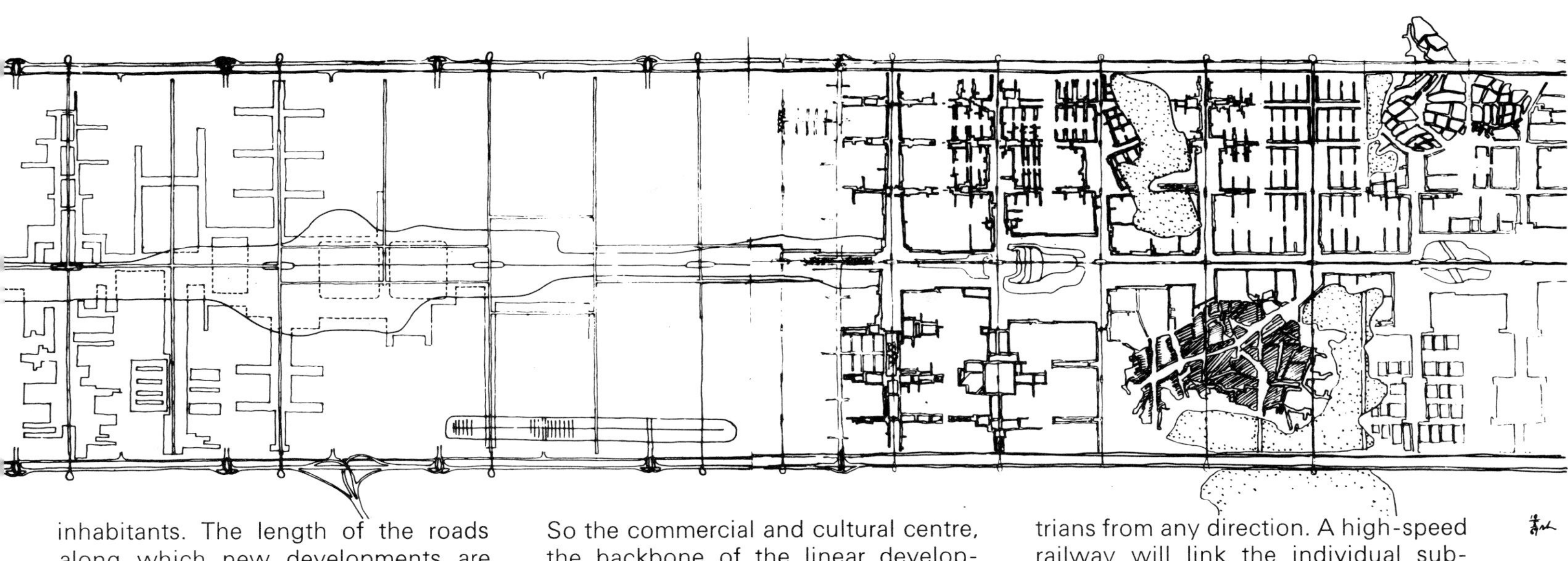

inhabitants. The length of the roads along which new developments are located varies between 1 and 1.5 km. So the commercial and cultural centre, the backbone of the linear development, is easily accessible to pedestrians from any direction. A high-speed railway will link the individual subcentres.

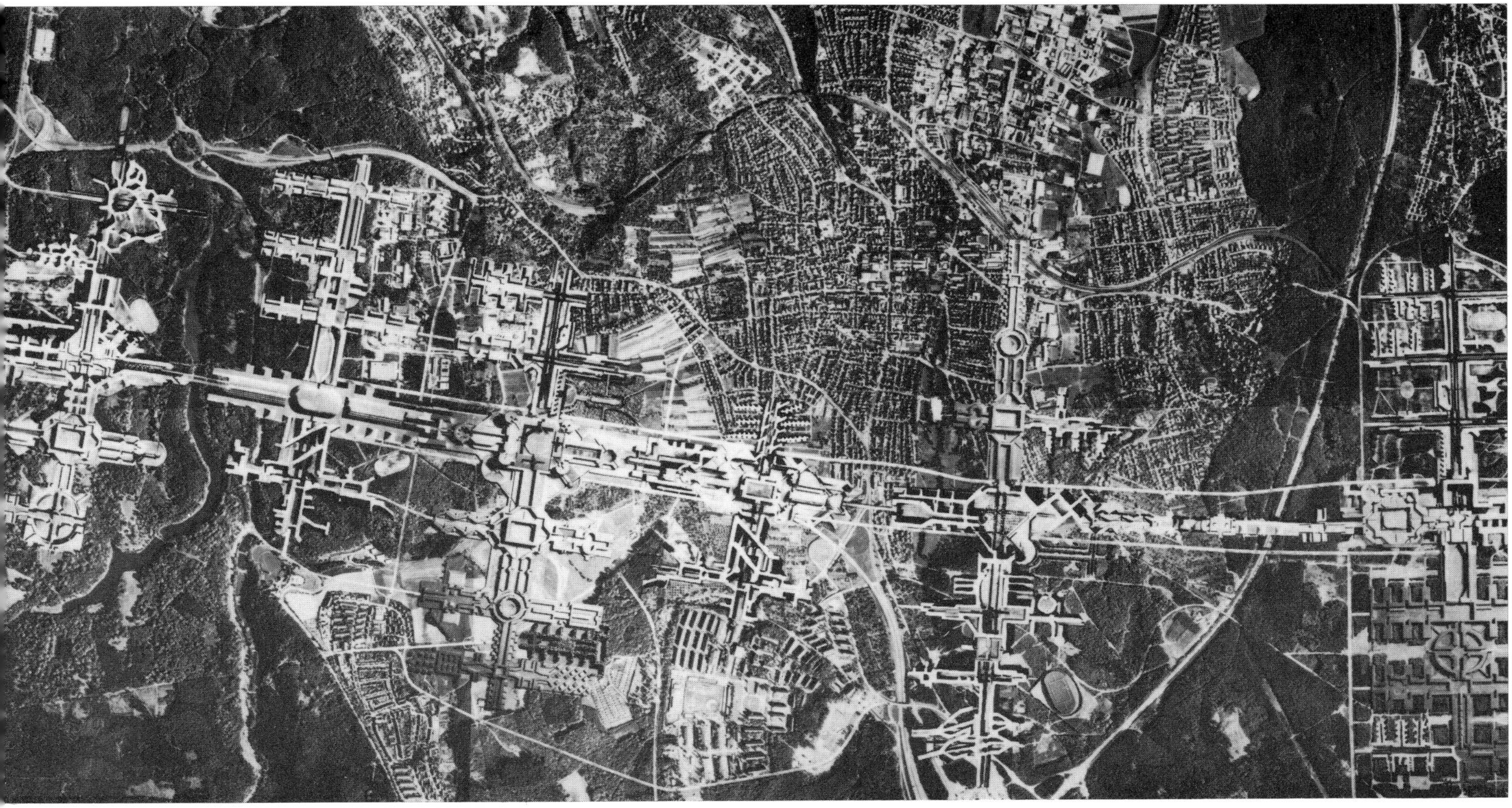

427 Town centre, Stuttgart/Leinfelden, 1971. Scheme by author and

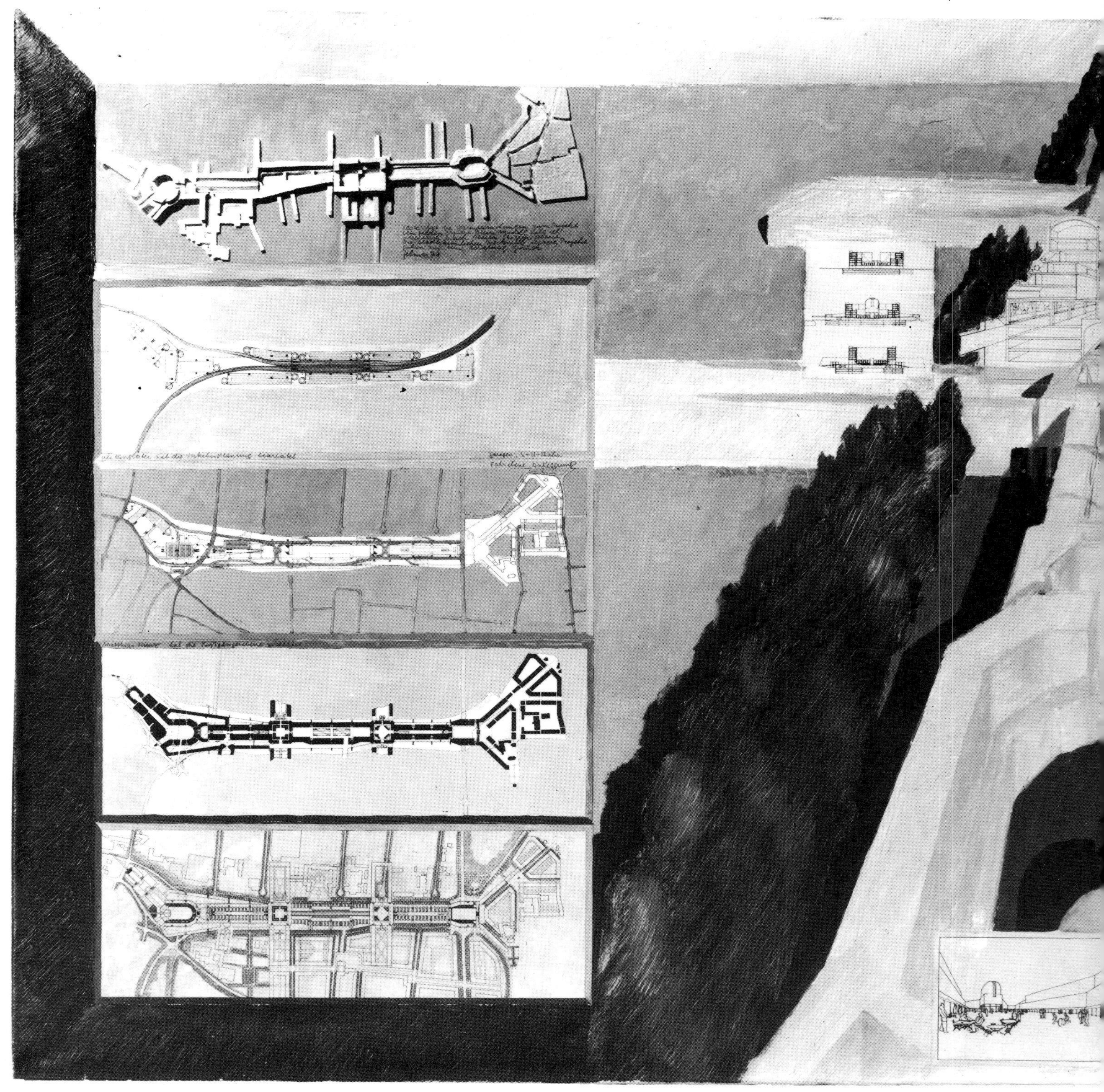

AIC (Architektur und Ingenieur Co-operativ, Stuttgart).

PROJECTS FOR A NEW TOWN CENTRE FOR STUTTGART/ LEINFELDEN BUILT OVER UNDERGROUND AND MAINLINE RAILWAY

This structure is designed as an alternative to the shapeless sprawl of our cities. It ensures that urban concentration will be feasible in the vicinity of efficient roads and railways, as well as future high-speed modes of transport. Without the presence of these channels of communication the whole idea is absurd. The structure lays particular emphasis on the creation of continuous and integrated pedestrian areas. My model, which envisages the entire completed structure from the outset, contains a variety of spatial situations of this type, each realised with very distinct architectural means.

427

Both schemes were submitted as entries in a competition for a new town centre. The jury found them excessively monumental and they were eliminated in the first round of selection.

The main criteria for both pieces of work were:

1 The creation of a coherent but varied system of urban space.

2 The preservation of the human scale in the height of the buildings and the spatial continuum.

3 Individual elements of particular significance have been allowed to interrupt this scale.

4 Traffic and pedestrian areas have been laid out on different levels.

5 These projects should be regarded as blueprints embodying certain architectural principles. They contain elements corresponding to specific building types, which coordinate the building and development process. It is wrong, therefore, to assume that these plans can only be meaningful if seen as the work of a single architect.

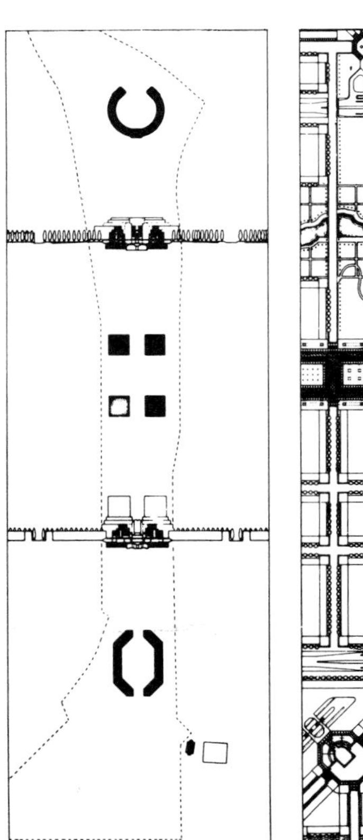

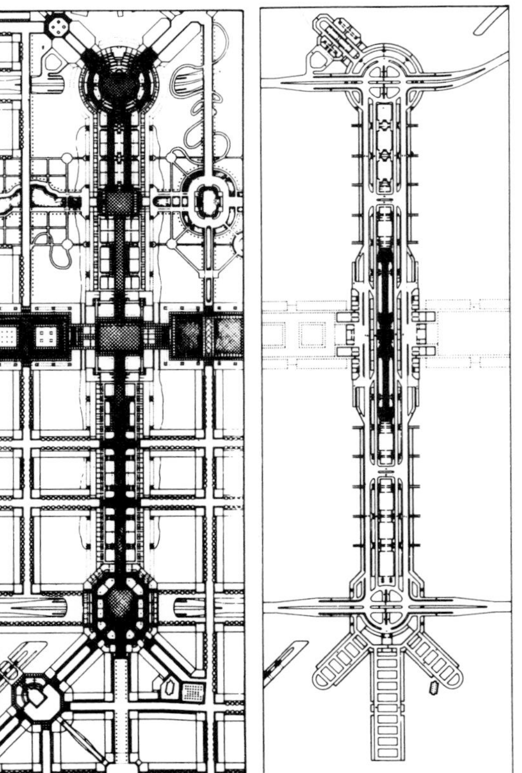

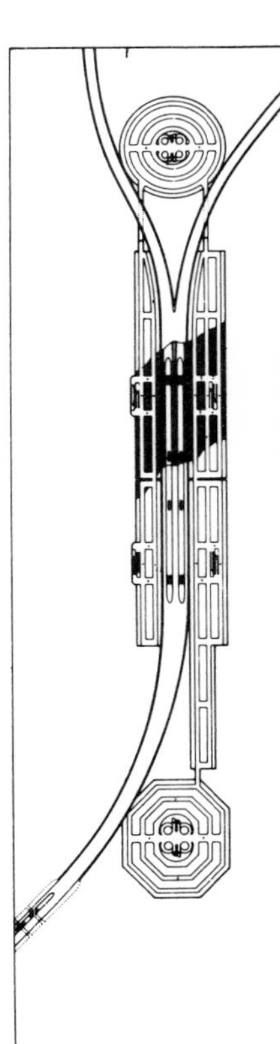

428 Scheme by Leon Krier.

POSTSCRIPT FOR ARCHITECTS

'LET'S PUT ARCHITECTURE BACK IN ITS PROPER PLACE'

This was how a dozen or so of Germany's most eminent architects concluded a New Year's manifesto on architecture in 1974, published in a number of architectural periodicals. At the same time a year later, when architects were not alone in having lapsed into melancholy, I was prompted to draft a reply to their rallying-cry. I hope it will be clear by now to everyone who has read my book just what I mean by the city and its architecture. I have made extensive use of illustrations to bring out my full meaning. I believe that many of my arguments can be strengthened by a postscript in the form of a manifesto. What has disfigured our cities to such a degree is not only the loss of urban space discussed here but also the mediocrity of the architecture. My brother Leon, who teaches architecture in London, has made a great contribution through his application of fundamental theoretical tendencies. The worth of these tendencies will be demonstrated by the debate on a professional level which I hope will be stimulated by this book. My architectural work has acquainted me with the likely opponents of such a theory of urban space. They will not be found in the ranks of those who use or live in our cities, but will spring from the mass of 'specialists'. For it will be they who will see their irresponsible treatment of architecture challenged.

(1) ARCHITECTS . . .

Every building is designed by an architect. They alone are responsible for their creations, and in my opinion only they can be held accountable when gross errors occur.

The architectural manifesto to which I have referred reads too much like a feeble attempt on the part of its authors to absolve themselves of a cultural culpability whose magnitude and threat to their position they fully recognise. And because it is bad form socially and professionally to point the finger at one's colleagues, only one of the demands of their manifesto was aimed directly at architects, and then only to exhort them to remember the superiority of their mission. This is asking both too much and too little!

I don't want to let the writers of this 'mea culpa' off the hook yet. I must stress that I am not only attacking eminent, award-winning, successful architects, but also the generation which has not yet made its mark on the German building scene. It is irrelevant for the architect to bemoan the fact that his client has no understanding of design problems, and that the architecture produced on commission must necessarily reflect the taste and preconceptions of his client. Most clients can be talked round, where there is sufficient professional conviction and commitment on the part of the architect, although of course this will eat into his fees. And let's be honest, fewer and fewer of us are prepared to take this first step. How terribly revealing it is that no-one can be expected to comply with this outrageous demand – except poets and dreamers perhaps.

How many of our colleagues have the strength of character to turn down a commission when the client refuses to accept the quality which the designer would like? I am arguing then that we, as architects, should face up to the responsibility which is ours from the moment that we put our name to a feasible design, and that we should stop laying the blame for our own inadequacy on the wicked client's doorstep. Let us put ourselves in the position of someone who wants to buy a lamp. Our hypothetical customer has no professional expertise in the production or sale of lamps. He is therefore quite passive, simply looking forward to having his tastes met by a specialist, and a specialist alone, who has devoted his whole life to the lamp problem, and as a result may reasonably be expected to know something about it. Let's leave out the question of the utility and functional adequacy of the said lamp. Our customer is offered such a wide range that after visiting three or four shops, he masters his indecision and in desperation makes a choice which suits his wallet. For even the untutored customer soon realises that well-designed lamps are always expensive and that the protracted search for a good, reasonably priced article often comes to nothing. Whether he is buying shoes, hats or furniture, the same problem is all too familiar to him.

We have all had experience of the lamp buying syndrome, and have all asked ourselves which criteria govern this kaleidoscope of kitsch.

Basically, the problem of the quality of the lamp is closely related to the problem of the quality of a building. Who is responsible for the mediocrity of the merchandise: the manufacturer, the designer or the consumer? The manufacturer and the designer set up a cliche-ridden customer profile based on their questionable market research. They deliberately use seductive designs, almost totally divorced from the function of the object, to increase sales. And who can criticise the consumer for making a wrong choice when he is confronted with such a proliferation of trash?

The architectural client finds himself in the same position!

I am constantly aware that laymen expose the negative qualities of our built environment with unerring certainty, simply as a result of their comparison of old and new. The response of the professional to this criticism

hedges the central question with remarks like:
'We are constrained by economic viability, technology, traffic, politics . . .' But none of these constraints justifies the superficial treatment administered to our patient 'architecture'. We have always known the patient in this ailing condition and have difficulty in imagining him healthy.

The call for 'more design' in our manifesto indirectly raises the question of what the nature of that design should be. Just as in our example of buying the lamp, in architecture design is open to many interpretations. Above all we must establish what role it plays in an overall architectonic system. The three most important determining factors which characterise architecture are function, construction and form. None of these factors takes precedence over the others and none can be neglected in favour of another. In the design process each aspect must be developed in parallel and neither organisation, construction nor form can be considered separately. Thus architecture, as a result of this coordinated process, must always provide a meaningful expression of inner structure, without necessarily exposing the 'innards'. The form of the human body has always been the prototype for structural principles in architecture. In addition, nature provides us with countless other models whose visible aesthetic qualities are perfectly in accord with their biological system.

Quite simply, the concern for form is the fundamental problem of architecture, and one which cannot be solved in purely verbal terms. The architecture we are talking about must be illustrated, if only through drawings. So any polemic on the subject in the form of a manifesto must remain a piece of empty and esoteric trivia, and the notes I am writing now should also be seen in that light. However, this in no way diminishes the value of a discussion of form.

Whatever form architecture may adopt, it must always create the same aesthetically controlled impression as the example from nature mentioned above. I have yet to see a tree which looked aesthetically wrong or defective. The same is true of landscape.

Architecture should engage interest not only because it is fashionable or novel. It should also remain sensitive to changing functional requirements, and be characterised by features whose intrinsic strength is such that the overall effect is not harmed by signs of use and wear and tear. Only a handful of masterpieces which have survived from the past show us what the true qualities of architecture should be. Our age has an extraordinary dearth of such examples.

Let us emphasise yet again the principal conclusion of this section: that the architect, and the architect alone, is responsible for the form of his work.

The remarks which follow deal with the origins of 'second-rate architecture' and the audience to which my remarks are addressed consists of its authors: the architectural profession.

(2) PLANNING TIME . . .
is clearly something which most of my colleagues cannot manage to fit in. The fee scale which architects have set up in fact only covers the cost of the most perfunctory work. If we look at the problem from this point of view, no-one can be reproached for showing too little concern for architecture. It is essential that the reform of the fee scale, which has been under discussion in parliament for years, be settled once and for all. This is not to say that we could necessarily look forward to better architecture as a result. Time is of the essence in the planning process, and the architecture of the thirty years since the war has suffered from being built prematurely before the underlying ideas had been fully worked out on paper. From time immemorial architecture has been realised through the medium of drawing. These drawings have always been produced manually, which is convenient but slow. This laborious method is similar to the creative process of the painter, musician or author. Science has yet to prove that the design process can be effected with the help of electronic aids.

Question: 'Why should the architect not attempt to meet his schedules in the shortest possible time with minimum expense and maximum profit?'

Answer: 'He defines objectives which by their very nature are to do with meeting man's most central needs as an individual and member of a social group. These needs are not purely functional in character, but also have ethical, social and cultural implications. This means something more than the normal run of consumer goods. Architecture supposedly has an unlimited life, and so will stand for an unknown length of time in a landscape which will be affected by it either positively or negatively. Every building, no matter how private it is intended to be, has a role to play in public space whether it likes it or not, and God knows it is liable to become a permanent cultural irritant.'

In the field of architecture then, the most basic laws of commerce and management cannot be applied literally. The time factor is normally restricted by these laws, but in this case must be relaxed to allow the complex interplay of function, construction and form to be adequately developed. As a rule, those designers generally regarded as outstanding need as much time as possible before handing their designs over to the builder.

(3) BUILDING TIME . . .
is another important factor in the creation of architecture. It is almost entirely dictated by the financial plans

of the client and so often exerts disastrous and inescapable pressure on the design team. One of the favourite selling lines of the speculative builder is an emphasis on rapid building time. Apart from increasing the likelihood of repairs, this consideration will cease to be relevant in the future.

(4) THE MONOPOLY OF PLANNERS . . .
Not only is architecture usually planned and built too hurriedly; also, too few architects try and design too much in the time available. Here again, the profession has fallen into the trap of succumbing to the temptations of the free market economy. Work commissioned has become gigantic in its scale. The public sector, in an attempt to keep on top of the work, looks to the design team to solve the problem rationally, completely and unanimously, by working flat out and drawing on the full range of its professional expertise.

I have no wish to question the capability of the well-organised team. By and large, post-war architecture in Germany has been carried out in a perfectly organised way. The virtue of organisation has not been in short supply in this country. But the uniform dreariness of recent large projects produced by these teams has driven even the layman to the barricades. This is a good indication of the healthy commonsense of those who use buildings and gives rise to the hope that the reform of architecture is possible as a result of outside initiatives. I have said that architecture cannot be marketed like any other consumer product. We must learn from history that large-scale projects are not automatically better handled by correspondingly large teams. The laws of the production line cannot be applied to the design and production of architecture. Large-scale projects cannot be dealt with rapidly – even by large practices – unless the problems are simplified. Technical optimisation will all too easily lead to an overstepping of the limits which man, as a fixed point of reference, can tolerate, both physically and psychologically. Here we come up against the problem of scale, which will be more closely examined in its own right at a later point.

The fascination of our historic cities derives from the almost infinite variety of their spatial forms and the buildings which shape them. Every age rationalises available technology in its own way, and this applies equally well to timber-framed buildings as to large brick or sandstone structures. Architecture has never suffered as a result of this: quite the opposite! The wealth of expression results above all from the fact that the scale of projects came within the compass of the individual architect, that enough time was available for detailing the often endlessly complicated building elements, and that the client also understood and promoted architecture as an art-form. People still knew how to build in ways appropriate to both the town and the country. In the towns, buildings were expected to participate in a dialogue with the substance of the past and not to stand disconnected from the basic structural elements of the town as they do today, sustaining their own peculiar existence in permanent isolation. Every new urban building must obey the overall structural logic and provide a formal answer in its design to pre-existing spatial conditions!

I would go as far as to say that this is a key formula which, if correctly interpreted, may radically cure our unbalanced ideas.

I have suggested that the complexity of our historic towns is somehow tied up with their scale. This involves private housing as well as palaces of more generous proportions. The compulsive addiction to unarticulated and brutal gigantism is a phenomenon of our time. Never before in the history of building has there been an age in which identical elements have been repeated horizontally and vertically with so little variation as they are today. Without a doubt, this is the product of purely mathematical calculation. From a purely pragmatic point of view I would have some faith in it if large projects were structured to enable many small architectural teams to work on them. These groups of super-individualists would have to be able to work together in such a way that their product (for example, an estate of 500 units), when completed, would seem to come from a single mould, with the gain of greater variety and without ruining the client financially.

Much has been said recently about participation. In this book, I am arguing in favour of the participation of our many unemployed architects in the important building schemes of our day. My only fear is that the profession is not susceptible to change from within. I feel that our education has not equipped us for this. The legislators could do something towards helping this crippled profession to its feet by encouraging participation through the establishment of appropriate competitions.

(5) PLANNING AND DESIGN IS A CRAFT . . .
which is exercised at the drawing-board. Any architect in charge of an office who spends most of his time on management and getting jobs loses not only the habit but also the ability to draw. Many of our colleagues are actually proud of this and point to it as a tribute to their success. I know of no good architect who has drawn badly: and none who has failed to cultivate the art of drawing with the passion it deserves. The perfection of the spatial idea is directly linked with perfection in drawing. Skilled management and verbal adroitness are of no use here.

Anyone who opts out of the discipline of drawing has forfeited his professional status.

(6) ARCHITECTURE IS NOT A FASHION . . .

to be discarded like a worn-out shirt in exchange for a new one. But this is exactly what happens today. On the international scene, architectural 'styling' changes as fast as the cut of trousers. A style which hits England one year will reach Japan the next, apparently refined in some respects. We live in an era of unlimited technological and formal potential, and it is precisely this illusory progress which reveals itself as the Achilles' heel of the age, which bears all the marks of an experimental period of expansion. And yet we treat this freedom a bit too lightly What I optimistically refer to as a period of expansion is seen by others as a symptom of cultural decline.

Without wishing to pass judgment on these views, I would simply like to offer a word of warning against seeing everything in black and white. Neither technology nor anything else has fulfilled the hopes placed in absolutes. Adolf Loos' attack on ornament was in its way as immoderate and implausible as the blinkered interpretation of the slogan 'Form follows function'. The truth in architecture has much in common with the philosophical dimensions of existence: neither can be discussed superficially. Fashions cannot be pinned on to them. I believe that future generations will have little hesitation in getting rid of our architectural blunders. Our generation is bequeathing to its children a vast rubbish dump of non-recyclable building materials. I am repeating my request to architects to control their individual arrogance, not to allow themselves to be caught up in superficial fashions and to bear in mind the fundamental features of architecture which outlive all fashions.

(7) SCALE . . .

features prominently in all these remarks. I do not want to fulminate against large complexes and tower blocks, as people used to rage against the railway and the steam engine eighty years ago. I only want to suggest that tower blocks for example also take up a lot of space which has no further justification than to provide a setting for the tower block. The open space gained has never been put to appropriate use. Empty green spaces between tower blocks inhibit communication as much as the buildings themselves. Streets and squares on a small scale have for thousands of years proved that they work ideally as zones of communication. By 'small scale' I mean distances easily covered on foot, or (where height is concerned) the number of levels accessible by stair. This all sounds very old-fashioned, but must be seriously taken into account if due respect is to be paid to the fixed unit of 'man' which we alluded to earlier. This factor concerns me all the more since most of the tower blocks with which I am familiar were built that way for no very good reason. They are little more than billboards in an unusually favoured position, announcing on the skyline the power of a company, a city authority etc. We are sick of such idiocies; no-one cares about the way they flaunt their wealth. With their superior view over town and country side, many have become physically comfortable islands of loneliness.

We are still not well enough informed about the effect of this type of building on people's lives. I find man too valuable to be used as a guinea-pig. But others do not share my scruples on this score! Since I have had children of my own, my attitude to the problem has changed.

(8) OUR DEFECTIVE SENSE OF HISTORY . . .

is to blame for much false interpretation of the past and also characterises our relationship with the future. The wish to cut oneself off from the heritage of the past is extremely short-sighted. By doing so, one deprives oneself of thousands of years' worth of experience. At the beginning of the century, the pioneers of the modern movement frivolously flaunted this attitude. And yet all of them had enjoyed a sound education and were very knowledgeable about history. Their attitude can easily be dismissed as a defiant reaction, intended above all as a harangue against their position in society, and against their fellow students at the Akademie who remained stuck in their old ways. It was a different matter with the pupils of these pioneers, and with their students in turn. They felt able to do without the grounding which had fitted the pioneers for their transformation into 'moderns'. And we today, armed with our pitifully inadequate know-how, must make up for a great deal that has been neglected. I have a faint suspicion that a new pioneering situation will grow out of this.

We have learned how little is achieved by technological advance and how rapidly the glow of new inventions fades when they are backed by nothing more than technological novelty. This does not denigrate the usefulness of experimental technology: it simply puts it into perspective. Care must be taken that it does not attempt on its own to initiate new development while making unjustifiable claims for universality.

I would go so far as to maintain that nowadays it is more useful to imitate something 'old' but proven, rather than to turn out something new which risks causing people suffering. The logical and attractive building types and spatial structures left to us by anonymous architects have been improved upon by countless succeeding generations. They have matured into masterpieces even in the absence of a single creator of genius, because they were based on a perfectly refined awareness of building requirements using simple means; the result of an accurate understanding of tradition as the vehicle for passing on technical and artistic knowledge.

All my dire warnings inspire considerable gloom, and one fears that it will prove impossible to do justice to the demands I have outlined.

However, not all the blame should be laid on architects, whether they are involved in building or administration. To be fair, some of the rubbish should be dumped back in the universities, for it was there that the whole avalanche started rolling.

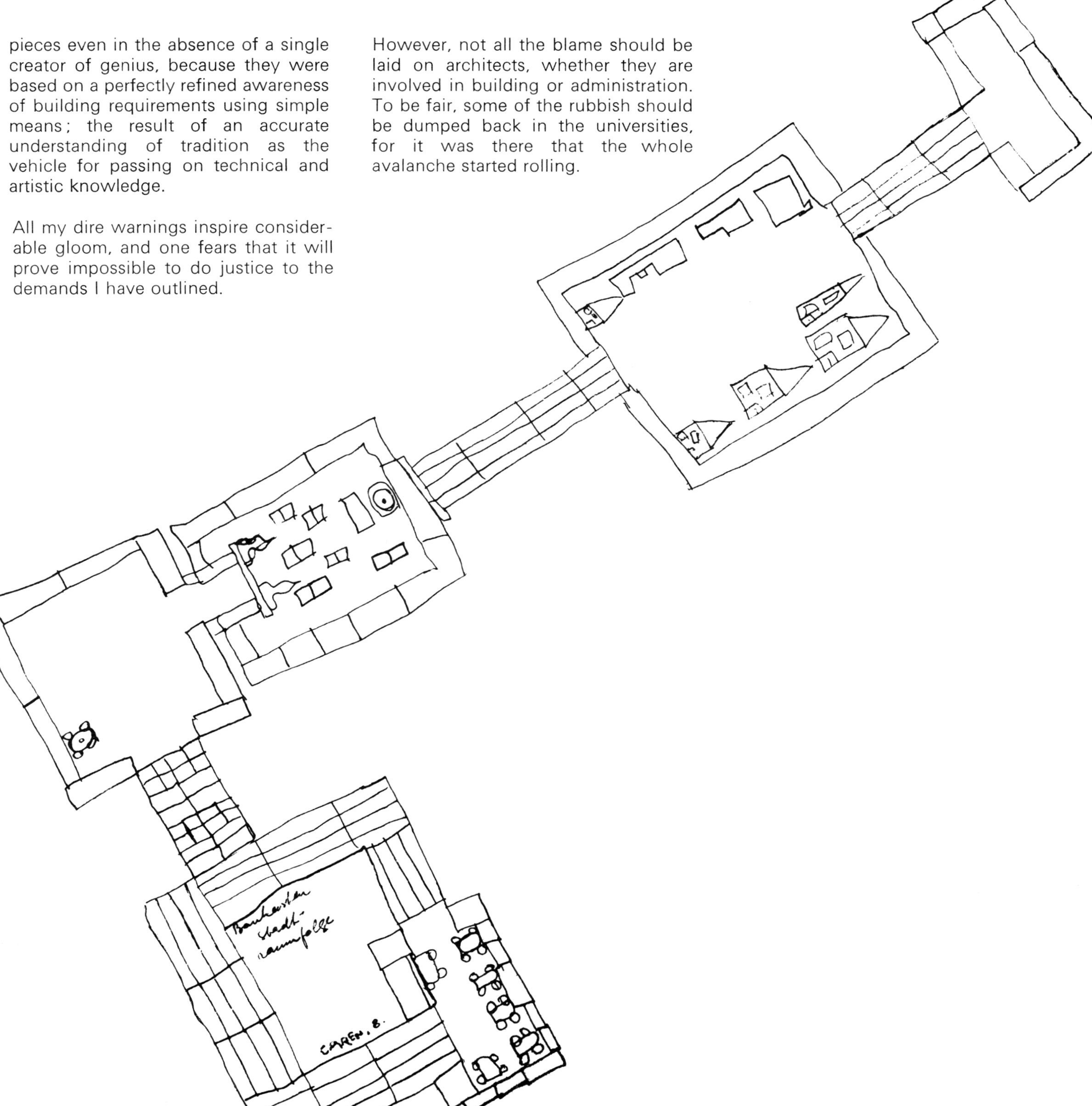

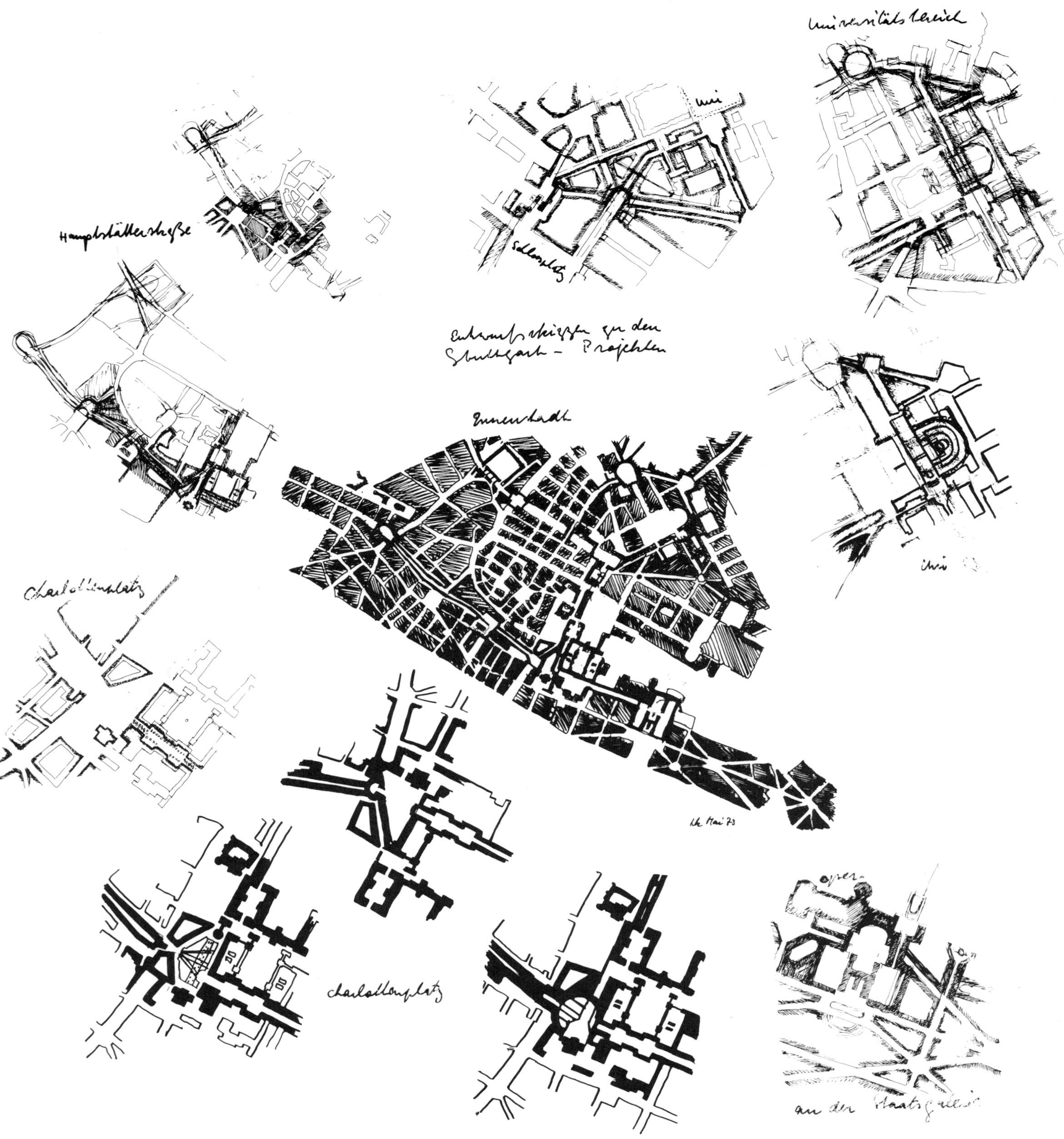

Universitätsbereich
uni
Hauptstätterstraße
Schlossplatz
Entwurfsskizzen zu den
Stuttgart-Projekten
Innenstadt
Charlottenplatz
LK Mai 73
Charlottenplatz
oper
an der Staatsgalerie

BIBLIOGRAPHY

CHAPTER 1

1. Egli, Ernst *Geschichte des Städtebaus*, volumes I, II, III, Eugen Rentsch Verlag, Erlenbach-Zürich u. Stuttgart 1959, 1962, 1967.

2. Lavedan, Pierre, *Histoire de l'urbanisme*, volumes I, II, III, Henri Laurens édition, Paris 1952, 1959, 1960.

3. Marini, Mario, *Atlante di storia dell'urbanistica*, Editore Ulrico Hoepli, Mailand, 1963.

CHAPTER 2

1. Albers, Gerd, *Entwicklungslinien im Städtebau. Ideen, Thesen, Aussagen 1875–1945*, Bertelsmann Fachverlag, Düsseldorf, 1975.

2. Albers, Gerd, *Was wird aus der Stadt?*, R. Piper & Co. Verlag, München, 1972.

3. Bahrdt, Hans Paul, *Die moderne Grosstadt*, Rowohlt Taschenbuch Verlag GmbH, Reinbek bei Hamburg, 1961.

4. Boullée, Ledoux, Lequeu, *Revolutionsarchitektur*, Staatliche Kunsthalle Baden-Baden, 1970.

5. Brinckmann, A. E., *Stadtbaukunst*, Berlin, 1920.

6. Buekschmitt, Justus, *Ernst May*, Verlagsanstalt Alexander Koch, Stuttgart, 1963.

7. Durand, J. N. L., *Précis des leçons d'architecture données á l'Ecole Polytechnique*, Paris, 1802.

8. Gantner, Joseph, *Grundformen der europäischen Stadt*, Anton Schroll Verlag & Co., Vienna, 1928.

9. Giedon, Sigfried, *Space, Time, Architecture*, Harvard University Press, 1941.

10. Gurlitt, Cornelius, *Handbuch des Städtebaues*, Berlin, 1920.

11. Hilberseimer, Ludwig, *Entfaltung einer Planungsidee*, Verlag Ullstein, Berlin, 1963.

12. Howard, Ebenezer, *Gartenstädte von morgen*, first German edition Eugen Diederichs Verlag, 1907, Verlag Ullstein GmbH, Berlin-Frankfurt/M.-Wien, 1968.

13. Joedicke, Jürgen, *Geschichte der modernen Architektur*, Gerd Hatje Verlag, Stuttgart, 1958. English translation *A History of Modern Architecture*, 1959.

14. Kallmorgen, Werner, *Schumacher und Hamburg*, Deutsche Akademie für Städtebau und Landerplanung, Landesgruppe Hamburg und Schleswig-Holstein, Verlag Hans Christians, Hamburg, 1969.

15. Kaufmann, Emil, *Architecture in the age of reason*, The President and Fellows of Harvard College, Dover Publications Inc., New York, 1955.

16. Le Corbusier, *Manière de penser l'urbanisme*, Editions de l'Architecture d'Aujourd'hui, Boulogne-sur-Seine, 1945.

17. Le Corbusier, *Les trois établissements humains*, Cahiers forces vives éditions de minuit, Paris, 1959.

18. Le Corbusier, *Vers une architecture*, Editions Vincent, Fréal & Cie, Paris, 1958. English translation *Towards a new architecture*, Architectural Press, 1946.

19. Le Corbusier, *Oeuvre complète*, Edition Girsberger, Verlag fur Architektur (Artemis), Zurich, 1910–1960.

20. Ledoux, Claude-Nicolas, *L'oeuvre et les rêves de Ledoux*, Editions du Chêne, 1971.

21. Pawlowski, Christophe, *Tony Garnier*, Centre de recherche d'urbanisme, Paris, 1967.

22. Rossi, Aldo, *Texte zur Architektur*, Verlag der Fachvereine, E.T.H., Zurich, 1974.

23. Rossi, Aldo, *L'Architettura della città'*, Padua, 1966.

24. Schumacher, Fritz, *Probleme der Grosstadt*, Leipzig, 1940.

25. Schumacher, Fritz, *Vom Städtebau zur Landerplanung* and *Fragen städtebaulicher Gestaltung*, Tübingen, 1951.

26. Sitte, Camillo, *City Planning according to Artistic Principles*, Phaidon, London n.d.

27. Soria y Mata, Arturo, 'La Ciudad Lineal', magazine from 1897, Madrid.

28. Stewart, Cecil, *A prospect of cities*, Longmans, Green and Co. Ltd., London and Harlow, 1952.

29. Stirling, James, *Buildings and Projects 1950–1974*, Thames and Hudson, 1975.

30. Stübben, Joseph, *Der Stadtbau*, Darmstadt 1890, second edition, Stuttgart 1907, third edition, Leipzig, 1924.

31. Ungers, Oswald Mathias, *Veröffentlichungen zur Architektur*, edited at the Technische Universität Berlin vom Lehrstuhl für Entwerfen VI, 1964–70.

32. Wagner Otto, *Die Grosstadt. Eine Studie über diese*, Wien, 1911.

33. Zevi, Bruno, *Spazi dell architettura moderna*, Giulio Einaudi Editore, Turin, 1973. English translation *Architecture*

and Space, Horizon, 1975.

34. Zucker, Paul, *Town and square*, Columbia University Press, New York, 1959, The MIT press, Cambridge Massachusetts and London, England, 1970 and 1973.

CHAPTER 3

1. *Geschichtsdaten und Merkwürdigkeiten von Stuttgart*, reprint of the original 1815 publication. Omnitypie-Gesellschaft, Stuttgart, 1969.

2. Borst, Otto, *Stuttgart, die Geschichte der Stadt*, K. Theiss Verlag, Stuttgart und Aalen, 1973.

3. Brugger, Albrecht, *Stuttgart und seine Nachbarn*, Franckhische Verlagshandlung, Stuttgart, 1965.

4. Faerber, Paul, *Nikolaus-Friedrich von Thouret, ein Baumeister des Klassizismus*, W. Kohlhammer Verlag, Stuttgart, 1949.

5. Hildebrandt, Hans, *Stuttgart wie es war und ist*, W. Kohlhammer Verlag, Stuttgart, 1952.

6. Speidel, Wilhelm, *Giovanni Salucci, der erste Hofbaumeister Konig Wilhelms I. von Württemberg*, W. Kohlhammer Verlag, Stuttgart, 1936.

7. Wais, Gustav, *Alt Stuttgart*, in two volumes, W. Kohlhammer Verlag, Stuttgart, 1954.

8. Wais, Gustav, *Stuttgarts Kunst- und Kulturdenkmale*, W. Kohlhammer Verlag, Stuttgart, 1954.

9. Wais, Gustav, *Die Schillerstadt Stuttgart*, W. Kohlhammer Verlag, Stuttgart, 1955.

10. Wais, Gustav, *Stuttgart im neunzehnten Jahrhundert*, Deutsche Verlagsanstalt, Stuttgart, 1955.

11. Weidle, Karl, *Der Grundriss von Alt Stuttgart*, E. Klett Verlag, Stuttgart, 1961.

12. Widmann, Oskar, *Reinhard Ferdinand Heinrich Fischer (1746—1812). Ein Beitrag zur Geschichte des Louis XVI. in Württemberg*, W. Kohlhammer Verlag, Stuttgart, 1928.

LIST OF ILLUSTRATIONS

All photos and drawings are by the author unless otherwise stated. Illustrations were taken from the following publications: (page and illustration numbers refer to the books in question)

BUEKSCHMITT *Ernst May* p. 44 fig. 29.

GIEDION, SIGFRIED *Space, Time, Architecture* (English edition 1952), p. 578 fig. 283, p. 579 fig. 285, p. 592 fig. 295.

HILBERSEIMER, LUDWIG *Entfaltung einer Planungsidee*, p. 17 fig. 6, p. 23 fig. 9, p. 135 fig. 121.

HOWARD, EBENEZER *Garden Cities of Tomorrow*, p. 36 fig. 21.

JOEDICKE, JÜRGEN *Geschichte der modernen Architectur*, p. 108 fig. 178, p. 179 fig. 318.

KALLMORGEN, WERNER *Schumacher und Hamburg*, p. 95 fig. 58.

LE CORBUSIER *Grundfragen des Städtebaus*, p. 63 fig. 16, p. 89 fig. 31. *Les trois établissements humains*, p. 125.
Oeuvre complète 1910–1960, p. 289 extract, p. 293 extract, p. 300 photo of model, p. 305, p. 306, p. 307 extract, p. 320 extract.

LEDOUX, CLAUDE-NICOLAS *L'Oeuvre et les rêves de Ledoux*, p. 51, p. 53.

MORINI, MARIO *Atlante di storia dell'urbanistica*, Madrid p. 360 figs. 1,387 and 1,390, Naples p. 345 fig. 1,323, Palmyra (Arcade) p. 93 fig. 404, St. Petersburg p. 306 fig. 1,295, p. 307 fig. 1,298, Pompeii p. 109 fig. 463, Rome (Forum of Caesar) p. 103 fig. 450, Spalato (Palace of Diocletian) p. 87 figs. 366 and 367, Tony Garnier p. 361 fig. 1,391.

ROSSI, ALDO *Texte zur Architectur* (ETH Zürich), p. 62.

STIRLING, JAMES *Buildings and projects 1950–1974*, p. 52 photo of model, p. 164 four drawings.

ZEVI, BRUNO *Spazi dell'architettura moderna*, fig. 55/4, fig. 55/6, fig. 226/1, fig. 261/1–3, fig. 286/1 and 2.

WEIDLE, KARL *Der Grundriss von Alt Stuttgart*. Text: fig. p. 73, fig. p. 87, fig. p. 89. Atlas: plan 16, 17, 19, 20, 21, 22, 24, 30, 31, plate III, V, VII, XII, XIII, XV, XVIII, XXIII, XXV.

BRUGGER, ALBRECHT *Stuttgart und seine Nachbarn*, pages 50, 59, 60, 62, 63, 64.

CITY PLANNING DEPARTMENT: plans of Stuttgart 1807 and 1855, aerial photos of centre of Stuttgart, vignette from etching by J. Sauter 1592.